$7.50

Readings in
Minority-
Group
Relations

Readings in
Minority-
Group
Relations

Edited by

David L. Ford, Jr.
University of Texas at Dallas

UNIVERSITY ASSOCIATES, INC.
7596 Eads Avenue
La Jolla, California 92037

Preface

Although there is an extensive body of literature on minority-group relations, it is difficult to find a single, cumulative source for significant developments and recent organizational practices and programs in the field. The purpose of this book is to satisfy a clear need for a collection of selected material that offers useful explanations of basic concepts, examples of practical research applications, and new trends and techniques in minority-group relations in organizational settings.

The book is designed for present and potential managers, human relations and organizational consultants, personnel administrators, students of organizational behavior and management, and others who are interested in managing the interface between "different" groups of people. In addition to serving as a supplement to any management or organizational behavior text, the book can be used in upper-division undergraduate and graduate courses in organizational behavior, management, personnel and industrial/organizational psychology, and organizational theory.

The primary objective of the book is twofold: (1) to provide the reader with a background on how minority-group members adapt and accommodate to various types of organizational circumstances, and (2) to help the reader understand the differences in behaviors and job-related outcomes for white and nonwhite organization members. In addition, the book aims to provide a basis for managers to analyze the modes of adaptation of minority-group members in organizational settings.

I selected a number of recent survey, laboratory, and field research studies along with a few studies that were completed and reported in the

1950s. These earlier articles provide a historical perspective on the current status of minority-group relations in this country. Articles were selected to (a) stimulate interest in and discussion of minority-group relations, (b) contribute to the reader's understanding of minority-group relations in organizational settings, and (c) relate to the conceptual and/or theoretical framework of minority-group relations. Although many other articles could have been included, those chosen meet the criteria for selection especially well.

I wish to express my thanks and appreciation for the interest and cooperation of the authors and publishers who granted permission to reprint their materials; they made this book a reality.

D. L. Ford, Jr.

July 1975
Dallas, Texas

Contents

Employment Programs for Minorities

Testing and Evaluation Procedures

Introduction

Minorities in Organizations

The industrial work culture and its effects on attitudes toward work and on the behavior of persons employed in business have been the topic of many contemporary research studies. The diverseness of these studies includes such areas as need deficiencies and/or satisfactions of blue collar and managerial employees (Schwab and Cummings, 1970), superior-subordinate relationships (Bowers and Seashore, 1966), union-management relations (Miller, 1966), and work-group processes (Likert, 1961, 1967). Not until very recently, however, has the variable of race been introduced to a significant degree in behavioral research studies.

The concern with race-related issues in the work or organizational environment is due, in part, to the attention being given to correcting a number of the nation's social ills. Researchers, practitioners, management consultants, and clergymen have devoted much of their energies to understanding and improving minority-group relations in organizational settings. Theories and findings generated through scholarly research are being used and applied by managers and practitioners as well as by organizational consultants in an effort to bring about improved organizational climates conducive to a satisfying and enjoyable work experience. Outside formal work organizations, consultants and clergymen are attempting to make civic and church organizations aware of the dysfunctional consequences of many of the institutional practices to which minority-group members are subjected.

According to Van den Berghe (1967), race in the United States is a special, identifiable, and extreme instance of invidious status differentiation, which makes it an especially tempting target for the analysis of social behavior. Recent findings from a number of race-related organizational studies offer support for Van den Berghe's contention about the importance of race in American society and the accompanying effects that it may have in a number of areas, particularly in organizations.

Both military and industrial organizations have been the settings for recent investigations into the differences between various racial and/or ethnic groups. The results of these studies suggest that differences, especially between black and white subgroups, can be attributed to a number of causes, among them: (a) the degree of discrimination based on race or national origin, (b) race-related cultural differences, (c) the racial composition of work groups, and (d) the prevailing organizational climate. The latter area is frequently a source of psychological stress suffered by many minority professionals in predominantly white organizations.

Although the lack of a congenial organizational climate can adversely affect the survival, growth, and advancement opportunities of *all* employees, it certainly seems to affect minority employees significantly: by reminding them of their past plight, by reinforcing the minorities' historically perceived lack of opportunity, and by severely reducing the genuine motivation of minority employees to overcome endless subtle hurdles in order to achieve self-fulfillment within the organization. Thus we are faced with the question of how the organizational life of minority-group members can be improved.

This book is intended to help people understand some of the theory, research, and applications in the behavioral sciences that provide a basis for the analysis of managing minority-group relations within organizations. It is planned to complement *Intergroup and Minority Relations: An Experiential Handbook,* edited by Howard L. Fromkin and John J. Sherwood.

The readings provide a theoretical and conceptual framework to guide the readers' behavior and actions as they attempt to work with groups of different people.

This collection of readings represents an attempt to provide the reader with a Gestalt perspective of recent developments in minority-group relations in organizations—including social interaction; leadership issues; worker values, expectations, and satisfactions; and organizational issues of integration, personnel selection, and evaluation.

Minority-Group Relations—A Definition

The term "minority-group relations," as used in this book, refers specifically to the patterns of interaction between black Americans and white

Americans. However, it is equally applicable to relations between white Americans and other racial minorities.[1] Since it is impossible to describe adequately the variety of minority experiences in this country, I have made some deliberate and conscious choices and have chosen to focus this collection of readings on the experiences of the largest racial or ethnic minority group in the United States. Thus, although it may be too presumptuous to assume that the experiences and goals of one group can be generalized to apply to other groups, this book emphasizes readings that explain the processes operating to keep black Americans in a subordinate position in American society.

Minority-Group Relations and Racism

It is no longer possible to view the "race problem" as a "Southern problem" rather than as a black problem (Epps, 1973). There is a race problem in America because there is racism in America. Racism can be defined as the practice of using considerations of race as a basis for decisions and policies that result in subordinating a racial group and maintaining control over that group. The emphasis is on *consequences* rather than on *intentions* (Epps, 1973). Racism is an adaptive system based on a set of norms, roles, and expectations assigned by or to individuals, groups, or organizations (Stafford & Ladner, 1973).

Both individual racism and institutional racism exist. Individual racism consists of overt acts of discrimination or violence by individuals. Institutional racism, on the other hand, is far more subtle, less overt, and less identifiable. It is, however, often difficult to separate individual and/or group attitudes from the institutions in which racism is incorporated. Institutional racism is a necessary condition for individual racism. An understanding of race or minority-group relations, therefore, requires an understanding of the institutional framework within which racial interaction takes place. The readings in this book intend to provide the reader with that understanding.

Promises, Promises—The Elusive Dream

Relatively few members of minority groups have been able to overcome the many obstacles on their road to managerial and professional careers. For those who do, there are often extreme personal costs; many do not enjoy the full benefits of their professional status within their organizations.

Several recent articles have emphasized the wide disparities between the career success and work experiences of black professionals and their white counterparts. Fields and Freeman (1972), for example, note that as late as 1972 there were still certain inequities that black professionals faced in terms of access to "equal opportunity" in industry, education, and government. They commented that blacks usually find themselves at the low end of the totem pole relative to career growth when compared with their white counterparts. They also noted that:

> Three major factors contribute to slow upward mobility for black professionals as compared with white professionals: (1) blacks enter jobs at lower salaries than whites; (2) promotion is slower for blacks; (3) as a group, black professionals eventually plateau in the corporate hierarchy. (p. 84)

Fields and Freeman also have noted a wide divergence in attitudes between black and white professionals regarding their companies' equal-opportunity programs: only 28 percent of the black professionals surveyed saw equal-opportunity programs as effective, whereas 76 percent of the white executives in these companies thought the programs were effective.[2] The authors thus concluded that business corporations have not convinced their black professionals that equal opportunity exists.

Bramwell (1973) concurs with the conclusions of Fields and Freeman by noting that "black professionals . . . have all the vaunted ingredients of success. They should be more successful than their equivalent white partners. But such is not the way of the world. The fact is that the black rarely reaches his goal of 'success' " (p. 24).

Perhaps one of the most damaging criticisms of the nature of organizational life and employment of black professionals is given by Taylor (1972b), who studied the effects of discrimination and organizational stress on the careers and aspirations of black executives in large corporations. The subjects of his study were black American executives (BAE's) in the *Fortune* 500 companies. The purpose of the study was to examine the climate experienced by black American executives and how they respond to the direct and indirect effects of the "executive suite." Some of the hypotheses of the study—which were, for the most part, verified by his results—included the following:

1. American corporations are not much different from American society and are committed more to technology than to people. The racial climate in the executive suite, as perceived by BAE's, is thus a reflection of current racial conditions in the American environment—bad.
2. Irrespective of a BAE's academic training, work experience, and job aspirations, white executives continue to see his primary corporate role as being in leadership positions directly related to minority affairs.
3. Because of specific on-the-job events or actions indicative of white racism, BAE's experience a variety of psychological defenses that serve as the starting point for several behavioral patterns for black and white executives.

4. The BAE will experience considerable conflict between being a member
   of a racial minority and a corporate representative of the management
   majority. (Taylor, 1972b, p. 91)

Black executives, according to Taylor, soon realized that the organizational structure imposes many injustices on them and that their jobs
and organizational relationships were not as fulfilling and rewarding as
one would expect. Rivalry, role ambiguity, self-doubt, increased responsibility, etc., are experienced by white as well as black executives, but the
latter are often at a disadvantage because usually they have reached the
executive suite by a path that did not necessarily provide the experience
and confidence that come from working one's way up in the system.

Taylor notes that psychological stress, strain, and frustration for
black executives in American corporations also arise from white racism
and the practice of programming blacks for failure. For example, he
relates the following experience of two black executives:

> In two organizations two BAE's had opportunities to attend an advanced
> management training program. Both men had supervisors who had never
> attended, and one of them thought such programs were a waste of time
> and money. The blacks were discouraged from attending the programs
> and were informed their work was good and that they would move along
> without the formal management training. One of the men discovered
> months later that he had missed a promotion because, in part, his super-
> visor included on his evaluation a note that the BAE was not interested in
> improving his management ability. The other executive experienced a sim-
> ilar disappointment and subsequently transferred to another division.
> (Taylor, 1972b, p. 96)

Very often black executives coped with such treatment by avoiding
contact with white managers or by trying to please whites in order to
compensate for any prejudice. A few of the black executives indicated
that they would try to conceal their identification with certain kinds of
black ideologies. Thus, these black executives found that it was in their
best professional and personal interests to abandon behavior that is
characteristically "black" and to embrace the behavior of their white
peers, i.e., the adoption of white roles (Taylor, 1972a). In another article
related to this study, Taylor (1973) comments that it is unrealistic and
psychologically unhealthy for some blacks to strive sincerely for and to
expect to receive promotions leading to top managerial positions.

While the results of the Taylor study may come as a surprise to some
people, other authors have reported evidence that validates these findings (e.g., Parker, 1974; Borus, Stanton, Fiman, & Dowd, 1972; Francis, 1973). A general trend or theme of these race-related studies in the
military, in business, and in industrial organizations seems to be that race

and the racial configuration of work groups make a difference in the kinds of experiences organizational members encounter and in the degree of satisfaction they associate with their work situation.

Recent Trends in Minority Relations

It is indeed unfortunate that in the seventies a growing sense of apathy to the continuing social, political, and economic inequities of minorities has developed in most (white) Americans. Although some gains have been made, funding in many domestic areas has been cut back or eliminated.

During most periods of American economic growth, minorities make modest progress, but during economic downturns and recessions, they usually lose many of these gains. They are the last to be admitted into the system and the first to be turned out. For example, minority unemployment statistics during World War II were very low, but they grew quite rapidly (at a rate twice that of nonminority unemployment) shortly after the end of the war (Doctors, 1974).

Today, the modest gains that have been achieved by many organizations through their affirmative-action and equal-employment-opportunity efforts may well be obliterated as a result of the economic recession and the companies' laying off of hundreds—even thousands— of employees. Since, in many cases, organizations are bound by the terms of union contracts in which the seniority rule is applied, the phrase "last hired, first fired" has become a cliché among many minorities caught in this situation. Although the strict application of the seniority rule to minority-group members recently hired under affirmative-action and equal-employment-opportunity guidelines is being contested in the courts, the result remains to be seen.

Professor Edward Banfield (1970) has argued that minorities have made substantial economic and employment gains in recent years. He further argues that our problems today are largely ones of perception— far too many unrealistic promises that have unfairly raised the expectations of minority-group members. Moreover, Banfield argues that the progress made by minorities in all social and economic areas can be expected to continue.

It is difficult for me to agree with Banfield's contention. I believe that if equal opportunity for all citizens were a reality, the expectations of minority-group members would be no different from those of the white majority. Minorities do not expect any more than what any individual would consider "an equitable piece of the pie."

Several trends are currently working against continued economic gains for minorities in the 1970s. The flight of industry to the suburbs has drastically increased, making it even more difficult for people in the inner city—minority-group members for the most part—to have access to jobs. As a result, many whites are fleeing the cities as well, resulting in an increase in housing segregation. The economic downturn of the mid-1970s has contributed dramatically to the unemployment rate among minority-group members, especially those in younger age groups. If another period of civil strife is to be avoided, people must work harder than ever before to minimize the dysfunctional consequences of the current economic situation. Now is a time for organizational and human relations consultants, personnel administrators, managers, students of the social and behavioral sciences, and others to be concerned with helping individuals deal effectively with different groups of people. As we have learned from behavioral and organizational research, the greatest amount of tension occurs at the interface between organizational subgroups.

Theory and Method in Minority-Group Relations

In recent years we have witnessed an accelerated trend toward research on minority-group relations. This can be seen, in part, in the call for a more formal statement of a theory of intergroup relations. Blalock (1967) stresses the need for more accurate measurement techniques in the study of minority-group relations, a more precise statement of the problems under investigation, attention to the system properties of discrimination, and more powerful quantitative tools for the study of that system.

Yinger (1973) notes that another trend in the study of minority and race relations is the formalization of a comparative approach (see, for example, Van den Berghe, 1967). As Yinger points out, however, the great bulk of scholarly work remains on a descriptive level, often guided by, but not vigorously derived from, a generally stated theoretical perspective. Yinger's discussion of recent developments in minority and race relations places the research conducted in recent years in four broad categories: (1) the social psychology of prejudice and discrimination; (2) pluralism; (3) minority and race relations in the major institutions, including economic, political, educational, and family; and (4) the civil rights movement, including studies of urban riots and black power.

The specific articles contained in this volume, however, apply a more detailed perspective to the study of minority-group relations. A majority of the articles represent recent attempts to meet the standards that Blalock (1967) calls for in his study of minority-group relations. That is, a number of the articles represent reports of laboratory and field-research studies in such diverse areas as racial attitudes and perceptions, work values and expectations, job satisfaction, minority leadership and competition, employment programs for minorities, and testing and evaluation procedures for minority-group members. All these areas reflect the attention that behavioral scientists have begun to give to these issues as they pertain to organizational behavior and the work environment.

The laboratory and field research methods are two of the more precise approaches to the study of organizational phenomena (Hellriegel & Slocum, 1974), with the former more demanding than the latter in terms of the degree of control that the researcher can exercise. Several of the studies in this book result from the use of survey research techniques. In most cases, regardless of research method, the researchers seek to investigate selected properties of organizational reality. Many of the reported findings demonstrate how certain situational factors in organizations account for differences in behaviors and work-related outcomes for black and white organizational members and also point toward the broad implications for effective management of minority personnel in organizations.

Plan of the Book

The book is divided into four major sections: minority-group social interaction, minority leadership and competition, the minority worker, and minorities in the organization. Many of the research areas previously discussed are covered under one of these four major divisions. In particular, the section on minority-group social interaction contains five articles covering the areas of racial attitudes and perceptions and the effects of social prejudice on behavior. The settings include both the laboratory and the field. The section on minority leadership and competition offers articles on minority leadership problems. The articles on the minority worker highlight research findings pertaining to work values, work expectations, and job satisfaction of minority-group members. Finally, the section on minorities in the organization contains articles dealing with the integration of blacks into white organizations, employment programs for minorities, and testing and evaluation procedures. Thus, the selections flow from an examination of social interaction in general to a study of leadership issues, to a consideration of the individual worker, and then to an examination of minorities vis-à-vis the organization.

This book may be more timely now than it would have been six or seven years ago because it can be used as a direct aid in helping consultants and practitioners to be *proactive* rather than *reactive* in their approach to minority-group relations. A proactive approach is necessary if we are to continue to make improvements in the area of minority-group relations.

Notes

[1]By "racial minorities" I mean those groups that are considered to be members of non-white racial and ethnic populations, including American Indians, Mexican Americans and Spanish-speaking Americans, Orientals, and members of other Third World racial and ethnic groups.

[2]Recruiting Management Consultants, *A Study of Black Male Professionals in Industry,* National Technical Information Service, Springfield, Virginia, 1973.

References

Banfield, E. *The unheavenly city.* Boston: Little, Brown & Co., 1970.

Blalock, H. M. *Toward a theory of minority-group relations.* New York: John Wiley, 1967.

Borus, J. F., Stanton, M. D., Fiman, B. G., & Dowd, A. F. *Work in America.* Cambridge, Mass.: M.I.T. Press, 1973.

Bowers, D. G., & Seashore, S. Predicting organization effectiveness with a four-factor theory of leadership. *Administrative Science Quarterly,* 1966, *11,* 238-263.

Bramwell, J. The black professional today: The multidimensional human. In R. Clark (Ed.), *Contact Magazine,* 1973, *3,* 22-24.

Doctors, S. I. *Whatever happened to minority economic development?* Hinsdale, Ill.: Dryden Press, 1974.

Epps, E. G. (Ed.). *Race relations: Current perspectives.* Cambridge, Mass.: Winthrop Publishers, 1973.

Fields, C. L., & Freeman, E. S. Black professionals: The gap is not closing. *MBA,* January 1972, pp. 73; 78; 82; 84.

Francis, H. M. Equal opportunity in national defense: There's room for improvement. *Contact Magazine,* Winter 1973, *5*(1), 39-42; 67.

Fromkin, H. L., & Sherwood, J. J. (Eds.). *Intergroup and minority relations: An experiential handbook.* La Jolla, Ca.: University Associates, 1975.

Hellriegel, D., & Slocum, J. Organizational climate: Measures, research and contingencies. *Academy of Management Journal,* 1974, *17,* 255-280.

Likert, R. *New patterns of management.* New York: McGraw-Hill, 1961.

Likert, R. *The human organization.* New York: McGraw-Hill, 1967.

Miller, E. Job satisfaction of national union officials. *Personnel Psychology,* 1966, *19,* 261-274.

Parker, W. S. Differences in organizational practices and preferences in the Navy by race. Unpublished technical report. Ann Arbor, Mich.: Institute for Social Research, 1974.

Recruiting Management Consultants. Black professionals: Progress and skepticism. *Manpower,* June 1973, pp. 9-13.

Schwab, D., & Cummings, L. L. Employee performance and satisfaction with work roles: A review and interpretation of theory. *Industrial Relations,* 1970, *9,* 408-431.

Stafford, W. W., & Ladner, J. Comprehensive planning and racism. In E. G. Epps (Ed.), *Race relations: Current perspectives.* Cambridge, Mass.: Winthrop Publishers, 1973, 354-368.

Taylor, S. A. Action-oriented research: An application of organization behavior methodology to black American executives in major corporations. *Proceeding of the Thirty-Second Annual Meeting of the Academy of Management.* Minneapolis, Minn., 1972, pp. 13-16. (a)

Taylor, S. A. The black executive and the corporation—A difficult fit. *MBA,* January 1972, pp. 8; 91-92; 96; 98; 100; 102. (b)

Taylor, S. A. A funny thing happened on the way up. In R. Clark (Ed.), *Contact Magazine,* 1973, *3,* 14-16.

Van den Berghe, P. L. *Race and racism.* New York: John Wiley, 1967.

Yinger, J. M. Recent developments in minority and race relations. In E. G. Epps (Ed.), *Race relations: Current perspectives.* Cambridge, Mass.: Winthrop Publishers, 1973, 4-22.

Minority-Group Social Interaction 1

Awareness is necessary for intergroup cooperation and improvement of communication between different groups of people. Ideally, persons who assist others to work effectively at the interface between different groups of people attempt to do so by increasing the level of awareness of the members of the client system. They show how a group's or an individual's own ideas and behavior affect other people and how these ideas and behaviors can facilitate or block the achievement of personal or group objectives.

White persons' cognitive, emotional predispositions toward non-white minorities have probably been studied more often than any other race topic. The great bulk of this research has dealt with racial prejudice and attitudes of whites toward nonwhite minorities. The two major sections of Part One are concerned with an examination of racial attitudes and perceptions and the effect of racial prejudice on behavior.

Racial Attitudes and Perceptions

The first section contains three articles that are concerned with racial attitudes and perceptions of black and white organizational members. In the first reading, "Effect of Race on Peer Ratings in an Industrial Situation," the authors examine the notion that a racial bias effect inevitably results in research involving peer ratings among minority- and majority-group members. The authors, Frank Schmidt and Raymond Johnson, conducted their study in a human relations training context. They suggest that peer ratings are a highly valid predictive device that is quite appropriate and useful in many integrated settings.

In the second selection, Harding and Hogrefe report the results of a study conducted in the early 1950s, which corroborates similar studies showing that interpersonal contacts between blacks and whites may result in greater cooperation in task-oriented behavior and favorable but limited change in attitudes among whites, although they may not affect attitudes and behaviors that were not task prescribed.

The article by Hill and Fox involves a study of attitudes and behavior of white and black supervisors toward their black, Puerto Rican, and white subordinates on dimensions that are not task prescribed. The results are interesting because they suggest that supervisors of both races may "go out of their way" to make their relations with subordinates of a different race appear nondiscriminatory.

Effect of Racial Prejudice on Behavior

The second section of Part One contains two articles that deal with racial prejudice and its effects on productivity and outcomes in a task situation. Both articles concern the manipulation of success expectancies by blacks in a task situation with whites. The Lefcourt and Ladwig article demonstrates that blacks are more likely to persist in task situations in which their behavior can determine the occurrence of reinforcements that are of high value to them. The article by Katz, Goldston, and Benjamin examines the effects of race, reward, and prestige on productivity and communications within biracial work groups. Black-white differences in some types of behavior were found to be attributable to the nature of the reward and prestige of the group.

Racial Attitudes and Perceptions

Effect of Race on Peer Ratings in an Industrial Situation[1]

FRANK L. SCHMIDT[2]
RAYMOND H. JOHNSON

The effect of race on peer ratings was examined in an industrial sample which was approximately 50% black and which had recently been exposed to training in human relations. Contrary to results in previous studies, no race effect was found. In addition, almost all the requirements for convergent and discriminate validity between the races were met. Possible explanations for these results and implications for the use of peer ratings in integrated settings were discussed.

A number of studies have aimed at clarifying the effects of certain characteristics of raters, ratees, and situations on peer ratings and nominations. For example, it has been found that, while friends appear to be favored with higher peer nominations, the validity of such nominations is not adversely affected (Hollander, 1956; Waters & Waters, 1970; Wherry & Fryer, 1949), and partialing the effect of friendship out of the nominations seems to leave validities virtually unchanged. Lewin, Dubno, and Akula (1971) found face-to-face interaction was apparently not critical in peer ratings; ratings made after watching ratees on videotape were almost identical to those made after fairly extensive face-to-face interaction. Length of acquaintance in face-to-face situations does not appear to affect reliability of peer ratings; reliabilities of ratings made after 3–4 days acquaintance were similar in size (.80s and .90s) to those of ratings made after longer acquaintance (Hollander, 1957); and peer ratings made of individuals by the same group of peers seem to be

Reprinted from *Journal of Applied Psychology*, 1973, 57(3), 237-241. Copyright © 1973 by the American Psychological Association. Reprinted by permission of the publisher and the authors.

stable over periods of up to 2 years (Wodder, 1962). It has even been found that peer ratings given to an individual are stable when the individual is moved from group to group within an organization (Gordon & Medland, 1965; Medland & Olans, 1964). Each of these studies underlines the relative lack of effect of acquaintanceship factors on the reliability and validity of peer ratings.

With the increasing incidence of racially integrated industrial work groups, it becomes important to know if such findings extend to the variable of race. Only two previous studies examining the effect of race on peer ratings were found. Both Cox and Krumboltz (1958) and DeJung and Kaplan (1962) found that raters gave significantly higher ratings to ratees of their own race than to those of the other race and that this effect was more marked for the black than white raters.[3] Nevertheless, black and white raters showed fairly high intercorrelations. In the Cox and Krumboltz study, the correlations between ratings produced by the two races for ratings of leadership ability given blacks, whites, and the total group were .75, .77, and .75 respectively; DeJung and Kaplan (1962) found between-race interrater correlations for ratings of combat potential to be .42 and .47 for two black groups and .52 for each of the two white groups.

These two studies share a number of characteristics. Both were carried out in military settings, the earlier study in the Air Force and the more recent one in the Army. In both studies, blacks constituted only a relatively small percentage of the peer groups studied, possibly resulting in a situation in which a black rating other blacks was usually rating his closest friends. The white, on the other hand, in rating members of his own racial group was rating nearly all of his peers, diluting the effect that would result if higher ratings were given to close friends. If such a friendship effect were operating, and if friendships tended to be race bounded, the greater race effect shown by black raters could have been traceable to the numerical imbalance between the races in the peer groups. Finally, both studies included peer ratings on only one trait, and thus did not allow assessment of discriminant validities.

The present study was an attempt to ascertain whether the race effect would be found in an industrial training setting in which blacks constituted roughly 50% of the peer groups and in which raters had recently been exposed to training emphasizing interracial fairness and understanding. The inclusion of two traits allowed the assessment of both convergent and discriminant validity of peer ratings from raters of different races via the multitrait-multimethod matrix of Campbell and Fiske (1959). This method has proven useful in prior studies in assessing the general construct validity of ratings produced by different categories of raters (Gunderson & Nelson, 1966; Lawler, 1967; Thompson, 1970).

Method

Subjects were 43 black and 50 white trainees in an experimental foreman-training program in a large midwestern manufacturing concern. Selection for the program was exclusively from the ranks of present hourly employees and was based on self-nomination, ability test scores, superiors' recommendations, and past work record. Average educational level was slightly above 12 years for both races. Mean age was 29.06 for whites and 31.09 for blacks. Subjects underwent training in six groups ranging in size from 11 to 24. In addition to a week of traditional lecture-oriented training, the men received 40 hours of intensive human relations training. The techniques of sensitivity training were combined with role playing exercises, immediate video feedback, and eclectic discussions of human relations principles. Racial differences and conflicts were aired and discussed whenever they arose.

As part of a larger study to evaluate this program, the men in each training group were asked to rate their fellow trainees on two traits, using a five-category forced-distribution rating scale. After crossing his own name off the list of group members, each trainee distributed his peers into the top 10%, next 20%, middle 40%, next 20%, and lowest 10% on each of two traits: (a) predicted future success as a foreman and (b) general drive and assertiveness. Descriptions of these traits are given in the following excerpts from the instructions read to the subjects.

> *Drive and assertiveness.* One trait we would like you, as a trainee, to rate your fellow trainees on is general assertiveness, pushing of self, or drive. A person high on this trait appears to be energetic, motivated, and self-confident. He takes the lead in discussions and in organizing tasks. People low in this trait, on the other hand, are somewhat shy and lacking in self confidence. They tend to be less aggressive and to speak up less often in group discussions.

> *Future success.* We would like you to estimate how successful your fellow trainees will be later on as foremen, when they actually have to deal with the day-to-day problems of a first-line supervisor. Do not base evaluations on how well the person has done in training but instead on how well you think he will actually do as a foreman later when he is on the job.

Trainees in each group were instructed as to the number of names that had to be placed in each of the five categories of the scale and were assured that their ratings were to be used for research purposes only and would not in any respect affect their futures with the company or the futures of their peers.

Analysis

By treating each rater as an "item," reliabilities[4] were computed separately in each of the six training groups for each trait. These ratings were of (a) the whole group by blacks, (b) the whole group by whites, (c) blacks by blacks, (d) blacks by whites, (e) whites by blacks, and (f) whites by whites.

Ratings given by blacks and by whites were based on an average across groups of 6.64 and 8.36 raters, respectively. In order to allow comparison of reliabilities between the races, the average of these two figures (7.50) was used in the Spearman-Brown formula to adjust each of the 12 coefficients in each of the six groups. Reliabilities were then averaged across groups to obtain final estimates.

For each trait a two-factor analysis of variance was employed to assess the effect of race. There were two levels of each factor: black versus white raters and black versus white ratees, with repeated measures on the ratee factor. Three blacks and 10 whites were discarded randomly for this analysis to provide equal Ns of 40 blacks and 40 whites. F_{MAX} tests indicated that the assumption of homogeneity of variance was met.

Three separate multitrait-multimethod matrices were constructed. The first contained ratings given to the combined group; the second, ratings given to blacks; and the third, ratings given to whites. This breakdown allowed for examination of differences in convergent and discriminant validity as a function of the ratee sample. It was expected that the two traits rated would show a moderately high positive correlation under all conditions and that, for this reason, the requirements of discriminant validity would be somewhat more difficult to meet than is usually the case (Campbell & Fiske, 1959, p. 103).

Results and Discussion

Table 1 presents the means and standard deviations of ratings on both traits assigned by each race to both races. The kind of race effect found by Cox and Krumboltz (1958) and DeJung and Kaplan (1962) would require that raters rate members of their own race higher than members of the other race (i.e., that there be a significant ratee by rater interaction) and that this effect be more marked for black than white raters (which would result in a significant ratee effect). In Table 1, it can be seen that there is a tendency for raters to rate same-race ratees higher in predicted future process than different-race ratees, but this effect is greater for white than black raters. Both white and black raters gave

Table 1

Mean Ratings and Standard Deviations of Ratings Assigned
by Raters of Both Races to Ratees of Both Races

Trait	White rater	Black rater
Predicted future success		
Black		
M	2.98	3.03
SD	.55	.65
White		
M	3.10	2.97
SD	.58	.54
Drive and assertiveness		
Black		
M	3.09	3.10
SD	.61	.64
White		
M	3.00	2.94
SD	.56	.66

slightly higher mean ratings on drive and assertiveness to blacks; however, neither the interaction nor the ratee main effect reached significance in either of the analyses of variance.

Of the three factors in this study which differed from those in past studies, it seems unlikely that the fact of a civilian rather than military setting would produce a strong effect in the direction of eliminating the race effect. If DeJung and Kaplan's (1962) hypothesis concerning race-bound friendships has validity, the critical variable accounting for the absence of a race effect may be the relatively large proportion (46.2%) of blacks in these peer groups, which created approximately equal probabilities that black and white raters rating same-race ratees are rating their close friends. The design of the study does not allow for separation of the effect of the friendship variable from the effect, if any, of the human relations training.

Tables 2, 3, and 4 present the multitrait-multimethod matrices for the ratee group as a whole, for black ratees, and for white ratees, respectively. The monotrait-heteromethod correlations are significant and large in all three matrices, thus meeting the requirement for convergent validity. The discriminant validity requirement that each convergent

Table 2
Multitrait-Multimethod Matrix for Black and White Raters
when Rating Combined Sample

Trait	1	2	3	4
Method 1 (black raters)				
Predicted future success (1)	(.70)			
Drive and assertiveness (2)	.61	(.85)		
Method 2 (white raters)				
Predicted future success (3)	*.70*	.64	(.83)	
Drive and assertiveness (4)	.52	.77	.71	(.82)

Note. The monotrait-heteromethod correlations are in italics.

validity be higher than the values lying in its column and row in the heterotrait-heteromethod matrix is met by all convergent validities in the three matrices. A second requirement for discriminant validity is that the convergent validity coefficient for each variable should be larger than the correlation between this variable and other variables in the heterotrait-monomethod triangles. Because of the pervasiveness of method variance, this requirement is seldom met by behavioral data (Gunderson & Nelson, 1966; Lawler, 1967; Thompson, 1970) even though it is usually interpreted to mean only that the *average* of the heterotrait-monomethod correlations must be smaller than the average of the convergent validity coefficients. In this data, the relatively high heterotrait-monomethod correlation produced by the white raters in each of the three matrices precludes satisfying the more stringent of the two conditions although, in each case, even this requirement is almost met. In all three matrices the average of the convergent validity coefficients exceeds the average of the heterotrait-monomethod correlation (.74 vs. .66 in Table 2; .72 vs. .58 in Table 3; and .76 vs. .75 in Table 4), but this less stringent requirement is only marginally met in the ratings given to whites. In view of the fact that predicted future success and drive and assertiveness were considered to be related concepts and were expected to show a relatively high intercorrelation and the fact that no studies with behavioral data could be found in which even this relaxed criterion was satisfied, the extent to which the present data meet this requirement appears quite adequate.

Table 3
Multitrait-Multimethod Matrix for Black and White Raters
when Rating Blacks Only

Trait	1	2	3	4
Method 1 (black raters)				
Predicted future success (1)	(.83)			
Drive and assertiveness (2)	.48	(.72)		
Method 2 (white raters)				
Predicted future success (3)	.65	.55	(.80)	
Drive and assertiveness (4)	.44	.78	.67	(.82)

Note. The monotrait-heteromethod correlations are in italics.

A third condition for discriminant validity is that the same pattern of correlations appears in all of the heterotrait triangles of both the monomethod and the heteromethod blocks. Since a minimum of three traits is necessary to assess these patterns, this requirement cannot be applied to these data. A final condition, that the reliability of each variable be higher than its heterotrait-monomethod correlations, is, with one exception, met for both traits in all three matrices.

In Table 4 it can be seen that the ratings by blacks of whites on predicted future success show a reliability smaller than the intertrait correlation in that monomethod block. This indicates perhaps that the black raters did not perceive predicted future success and drive and assertiveness as two separate traits in the white ratees. In black ratees, on the other hand, black raters seemed to see these traits as less related than did white raters (see Table 3).

Extent of method variance is indicated by the difference in level of correlation between the parallel values of the monomethod block and the heteromethod block (Campbell & Fiske, 1959). According to this yardstick, very little method variance due to race is evident in these data.

In general, these data meet the requirements for convergent and discriminant validity quite well. The peer ratings made by the two races in this study can quite safely be considered comparable methods of assessing these two traits.

In summary, these findings indicate that the racial bias effect in peers ratings does not inevitably occur and that an approximately equal

Table 4
Multitrait-Multimethod Matrix for Black and White Raters
when Rating Whites Only

Trait	1	2	3	4
Method 1 (black raters)				
Predicted future success (1)	(.66)			
Drive and assertiveness (2)	.73	(.74)		
Method 2 (white raters)				
Predicted future success (3)	.76	.73	(.86)	
Drive and assertiveness (4)	.60	.76	.77	(.81)

Note. The monotrait-heteromethod correlations are in italics.

proportion of minority and majority group members in peer groups and/or human relations training may be associated with its nonoccurrence. In addition, black and white raters were found to show relatively high levels of discriminant and convergent validity in assessing black ratees, white ratees, and combined groups. The implication is that the highly valid prediction device of peer ratings may be quite appropriate and useful in many integrated situations. Future research might well focus on the relative potency of training in human relations, the proportion in the peer group that is minority, and other factors in contributing to the elimination of the racial bias effect in peer ratings.

Notes

[1]This study was supported by the Chrysler Institute, Chrysler Corporation, Detroit, Michigan. The researchers are especially grateful to Dennis J. Deshaies for his support and assistance. They would also like to acknowledge the contributions of D. L. Maxwell, W. R. DeBusk, C. V. Roman, D. J. Lewsley, J. G. Hafner, A. M. Gray, and J. M. Hall.

[2]Frank L. Schmidt and Raymond H. Johnson were affiliated with Michigan State University at the time of publication of this article. Requests for reprints should be sent to Frank L. Schmidt, Department of Psychology, Michigan State University, East Lansing, Michigan 48823.

[3]Flaugher, Campbell, and Pike (1969) have found a similar race effect in ratings made by supervisors, but the psychological processes involved may be quite different from those involved in the race effect in peer ratings.

[4]Internal consistency reliabilities—since "item" responses were continuous, coefficient alpha rather than Kuder-Richardson formula 20 was the appropriate form.

References

Campbell, D. T., & Fiske, D. W. Convergent and discriminant validation by the multitrait-multimethod matrix. *Psychological Bulletin*, 1959, *56*, 81-105.

Cox, J. A., & Krumboltz, J. D. Racial bias in peer ratings of basic airman. *Sociometry*, 1958, *21*, 292-299.

DeJung, J. E., & Kaplan, H. Some differential effects of race of rater and ratee on early peer ratings of combat aptitude. *Journal of Applied Psychology*, 1962, *46*, 370-374.

Flaugher, R. L., Campbell, J. T., & Pike, L. W. Prediction of job performance for Negro and white medical technicians: Ethnic group memberships as a moderator of supervisors ratings. (ETS Service Report PR-69-5) Princeton: Educational Testing Service, 1969.

Gordon, L. V., & Medland, F. I. The cross-group stability of peer ratings of leadership potential. *Personnel Psychology*, 1965, *18*, 173-177.

Gunderson, E. K. E., & Nelson, P. D. Criterion measures for extremely isolated groups. *Personnel Psychology*, 1966, *19*, 67-80.

Hollander, E. P. The friendship factor in peer nominations. *Personnel Psychology*, 1956, *9*, 435-447.

Hollander, E. P. The reliability of peer nominations under various conditions of administration. *Journal of Applied Psychology*, 1957, *41*, 85-90.

Lawler, E. Multitrait-multirater approach to measurement of job performance. *Journal of Applied Psychology*, 1967, *51*, 369-381.

Lewin, A. Y., Dubno, P., & Akula, W. G. Face-to-face interaction in the peer-nomination process. *Journal of Applied Psychology*, 1971, *55*, 495-497.

Medland, F. F., & Olans, J. L. Peer rating stability in changing groups. (USA PRO Tech. Res. Note No. 142) Washington, D.C.: U.S. Army Personnel Research Office, 1964.

Thompson, H. A. Comparison of predictor and criterion judgments of managerial performance using the multitrait-multimethod approach. *Journal of Applied Psychology*, 1970, *54*, 496-502.

Waters, L. K., & Waters, C. W. Peer nominations as predictors of short-term roles performance. *Journal of Applied Psychology*, 1970, *54*, 42-44.

Wherry, R. J., & Fryer, D. H. Buddy ratings: Popularity contest or leadership criterion? *Personnel Psychology*, 1949, *2*, 147-159.

Wodder, N. C., & Hall, W. E. An analysis of peer ratings. *Personnel Guidance Journal*, 1962, *40*, 606-609.

Attitudes of White Department Store Employees Toward Negro Co-Workers

JOHN HARDING
RUSSELL HOGREFE

Since World War II a great many business firms have begun to employ Negroes as clerical workers and a few as sales people. This represents a radical departure from pre-war practice, and it is quite possible that a majority of white employees would have opposed the introduction of Negroes into such jobs if they had been consulted in the matter. However they were *not* consulted, in the vast majority of cases, but were simply confronted with a *fait accompli*. In this situation the behavior of white employees, even the most prejudiced, has been quite uniform. There have been almost no recorded instances of white collar employees leaving their jobs because Negro co-workers were brought in, and very few cases in which even so much as a protest was made. The behavior of white employees toward the Negro workers has been for all practical purposes the same as their behavior toward other white workers.

Since this is the case, why should we be concerned with the attitudes or feelings of these white employees? The answer seems to be twofold. In the first place, prejudice is usually regarded as a part of personality structure; and we are interested from a theoretical standpoint in knowing to what extent this structure is modifiable by various kinds of experience, even though the modification (or lack of it) may not be reflected in any ordinarily observable behavior.

In the second place, there are many situations in which the behavior of whites toward Negroes is far more a matter of individual choice than

Reprinted from *Journal of Social Issues*, 1952, *8*(1), 18-28, by permission of the publisher.

it is in the work situation, where employees must conform to the standards of behavior set by management if they wish to keep their jobs. Behavior of whites toward Negroes in such circumstances is likely to be far more dependent on varying degrees of prejudice than is behavior in more rigidly controlled situations. It is possible that the experience of working with Negroes may lead to changes in attitude which will make the white individual more ready to accept other relationships with Negroes *which are for him a matter of choice*. In this case changes in attitude as a result of the work experience would be of practical, as well as theoretical importance.

For the present investigation we were able to get the cooperation of two leading department stores in a large Eastern city. One of these stores had been employing Negroes in white collar jobs for about four years, and at the time our study was made (1951) had several score of them on its staff. The other store had been hiring Negro white collar workers only during the past year and had a much smaller number on its staff at the time of our study. There is no union organization among white collar employees in either store. Fair employment legislation has been in force in this area for several years, and has been largely responsible for the change in employers' attitudes toward Negroes in white collar jobs.

Survey Procedure

Respondents to be interviewed were selected by the personnel office of each store from departments in which Negro white collar workers had been employed for at least three months and from departments in which Negroes had never worked in white collar jobs. An effort was made to sample as many different departments as possible within each store. Within each department the employees chosen for interviewing were those with the *longest* service in that department. This meant that our respondents from mixed departments would be those with the longest period of work contact with Negroes, and reduced the possibility that respondents from all-white departments would have had previous experience with Negro white collar workers.

The great majority of our respondents who were working with Negroes had been in their present departments before the Negroes were brought in. In both stores it was the policy of management to assign Negro applicants to positions for which they were qualified without any regard to the attitudes of the white employees with whom they would be working. Transfers from one department to another were difficult to secure in any event, and were impossible if management suspected that the primary motive was a desire to avoid working with Negroes. Even if such transfers could have been obtained by subterfuge, they would have offered little security for the prejudiced employee, because the all-white department of today was likely to become the mixed department of tomorrow. For these reasons we could be fairly certain in advance of our study that there was no tendency for the more prejudiced employees in these stores to migrate out of the mixed departments. If there had been any such tendency it would have shown up in our data in the form of a shorter average length of service among respondents from mixed departments, as a consequence of a more rapid turnover of personnel. Actually we found no significant differences in this respect.

We were afraid we would not get honest answers from respondents if they realized we were primarily interested in work relationships within the stores, or that the survey was being carried out with the knowledge of the store executives. For this reason the interview was disguised as a general employment survey. Interviewers introduced themselves by saying: "I'm an interviewer from the Research Center for Human Relations. We're making a survey of a typical group of working people in _____ to see how many are employed at present and how many might be available for different kinds of jobs if the national emergency continues." The first three questions in the interview were: "What kinds of work have you done since leaving school?" "What would you like to be doing two years from now?" and "What is your present job?" The last two questions were: "Have you ever lived in the South?" and "Are there any circumstances under which you would be willing to take a government job outside the United States?" The remainder of the interview consisted of questions about respondents' present work situation, attitudes toward Negroes, and the usual background information. All interviewing was done at the repondents' homes.

Types of Work Contact

Four questions in the interview provided a basis for classifying respondents according to the nature of their work contacts with Negroes. These were: "What is your present job?"; "Are there any Negroes working in this department (or office)?"; "What kinds of work do they do?"; and "Have you ever worked on a job in which there were Negroes doing the same kind of work you were doing?" On the basis of these questions we divided our respondents into the following four contact groups: Group I: those working in departments in which there was at least one Negro whose status was equal to or higher than their own ($N=62$); Group II: those who had previously worked with Negroes on an equal status basis, but were not presently working in such a situation ($N=20$); Group III: those working in departments in which all the Negroes were of lower status than themselves, and who had never worked with Negroes on an equal status basis ($N=49$); Group IV: those working in all white departments who had never worked with Negroes on an equal status basis ($N=79$). Most of the people in Group IV had never worked with Negroes at all.

On the basis of a preliminary analysis we decided to combine Groups I and II into a single equal status contact group. There are no significant differences between Groups I and II in background characteristics, except that Group II has a higher proportion of people in supervisory jobs. Group II members have somewhat more favorable attitudes toward Negroes, but the difference is not statistically reliable. The effect of merging Groups I and II is to create a combined group which is more similar in most background characteristics to Groups III and IV than is either Group I or Group II taken alone.

This leaves us with three contact groups—equal status contact, unequal status contact, and no contact. There are no significant differences among these groups in age, sex, religion, education, residence in the South, length of service in their departments, or job satisfaction. Approximately one fifth of our respondents were under 30, two fifths between 30 and 50, and two fifths over 50 in age. Ninety-two per cent were women. Forty-three per cent were Protestant in religion, 35 per cent Catholic, and 18 per cent Jewish. Eleven per cent had attended college, 70 per cent had attended high school but not college, and the remainder had only a grade school education. One tenth of our respondents had lived in the South for at least one year. The median length of service in respondent's present department was seven and one half years.

Nearly two thirds of the respondents were satisfied with their present jobs, in the sense that they reported more things about their jobs that they liked than things they disliked. One third reported an equal number of likes and dislikes; and a very small minority—six per cent in the equal status contact group and two per cent in the other two groups —reported more negative features than positive. Approximately two thirds of the respondents in each group reported that they were making more money at the time of the interview than they had been a year previously.

There are no significant differences among the three groups in type of work done, except for supervisory jobs. Approximately half the respondents in each group are office workers and half are sales people. However, thirty-one per cent of the unequal status contact group hold supervisory jobs, while only six per cent of the equal status contact group and four per cent of the no contact group have such positions. (All of the supervisors in the equal status contact group come from our previous Group II—i.e. they have worked with Negroes on an equal status basis in the past, but are no longer doing so.)

12585

There were also significant differences in income among our three contact groups. Sixty-four per cent of the equal status contact respondents were making less than $40 a week at the time they were interviewed, while only 37 per cent of the unequal status contact group and 41 per cent of the no contact group had incomes as low as this. These differences in income must be borne in mind in our analysis of differences in attitude among the three contact groups.

Attitudes Toward Negroes

Six of our attitude questions were of the "social distance" type. One dealt with the general issue of discrimination in employment. Table 1 shows the wording of each of these questions and the percentage of answers favorable to Negroes in each contact group. On each social distance question an answer was considered favorable to Negroes if the respondent indicated a general willingness to accept that form of association with Negroes, even though she might have some reservations about it. Examples of such answers are: "No objection"; "That would be all right"; "Don't mind particularly"; "All right, I guess I wouldn't mind it"; and "I've become accustomed to it." On the discrimination question the only answer considered favorable to Negroes was a statement that they should have the same chance as white people to get any job.

The seven questions shown in Table 1 came in the latter part of the interview. They were not asked consecutively, but were interspersed with other questions, such as: "What do you like most about your present job?" "If you were offered a clerical job with the federal government in Washington at 20 dollars a week more than you are now making, would you take it?," and "Have you ever lived in the same neighborhood with Negro families?"

There are no significant differences among the three contact groups on any of the questions in Table 1 except Question 3, but on this question the differences are significant at the 99 per cent level of confidence. It seemed possible that there might be a trend toward more favorable answers on the part of the equal status contact group on questions other than number 3, even though this trend did not show up to a significant extent on any single question. To test this possibility a "social distance score" was constructed in which each respondent was given one point for each answer on Questions 1, 2, 4, 5 and 6 which was not favorable to Negroes. The mean social distance scores of the three contact groups are almost identical—3.13 for equal status contact, 3.08 for unequal status contact, and 3.09 for no contact.

The intercorrelations of these seven attitude questions are very high. The first six questions form a Guttman-type scale for each of the

Table 1

Percentage of Answers Favorable to Negroes
Among Different Contact Groups

Question	Equal Status Contact	Unequal Status Contact	No Contact
1. How do you feel about sitting next to Negroes in buses or trains?	73%	71%	70%
2. How would you feel about sitting down at the same table with a Negro in a lunchroom or cafeteria?	51	53	51
3. How would you feel about taking a new job in which there were both Negroes and white people doing the same kind of work as you?	73	61	48
4. How would you feel about working under a Negro supervisor?	37	29	33
5. How would you feel about living in a new apartment building or housing project which contained both white and Negro families?	13	22	18
6. How would you feel about having a Negro for a personal friend?	12	16	20
7. Do you think Negroes should have the same chance as white people to get any kind of job, or do you think white people should have the first chance at any kind of job?	65	51	57
Number of respondents	82	49	79

three contact groups, with reproducibility coefficients of approximately .95. However the position of Question 3 on the scale is different for each group. For the equal status contact respondents Question 3 is tied with Question 1 for the bottom scale position. For the unequal status contact group Question 3 ranks above Question 1—i.e. there are nine respondents who have no objection to sitting next to Negroes in buses or trains, but who would not like to work with them on an equal status basis; while there are only four respondents who accept the latter relationship but are doubtful about the former. (The remaining respondents either accept or reject both relationships.)

For the no contact group Question 3 ranks above both Questions 1 and 2 in scale position. These respondents find working with Negroes on an equal status basis more difficult to accept than sitting down at the same table with them.

Income and Attitudes

We examined the relationship between income and Questions 3, 7, and the social distance score based on the remaining questions. Question 7 and the social distance score proved unrelated to income. On Question 3 there was a marked tendency for lower income respondents to be more willing to work with Negroes than respondents in the higher income brackets. Because of this tendency we undertook a further analysis to determine whether the differences on Question 3 by contact groups would remain significant when differences in income were partialled out.

The results of this analysis are presented in Table 2. The figures in parentheses show the number of cases on which each percentage is based.

Let us examine first the data for equal status contact and no contact groups presented in Table 2. The differences in attitude between these two groups remain significant at the 99 per cent level of confidence. Within each group the difference between upper income and lower income respondents is insignificant. However the unequal status respondents present an entirely different picture. Within this group there is a highly significant difference between the attitude of lower income and upper income respondents. The upper income, unequal status respondents have the same attitudes toward working with Negroes as the no contact respondents; while the lower income, unequal status respondents have attitudes which are as favorable, and perhaps even more favorable

Table 2

Proportion of Respondents Willing to Work With Negroes
on an Equal Status Basis*

Income	Equal Status Contact	Unequal Status Contact	No Contact
Less than $40 a week	76% (38 people out of 50)	89% (16 people out of 18)	52% (17 people out of 33)
$40 a week or more	79% (22 people out of 28)	47% (14 people out of 30)	46% (21 people out of 46)

*The percentages in Table 2 are somewhat higher than the corresponding percentages in Table 1 because of the loss of four respondents in the equal status and one respondent in the unequal status contact group who refused to answer the income question. All of these people had given unfavorable answers on Question 3.

than those of the equal status contact group. Any attempt to explain this difference requires a detailed examination of the work situation and attitudes of the unequal status respondents.

As far as actual work relationships go, the upper income, unequal status respondents seem to be in much the same position with regard to the Negro employees as are their lower income counterparts. A majority in each group are sales clerks in departments in which the only Negro employees are stock girls. The next largest category in each group are supervisors in the bookkeeping and credit departments, in which Negroes are employed as typists, file clerks, and machine operators. All respondents in each group say they get along just as well with the Negroes as with the white workers in their departments. Forty-three per cent of the upper income group and 39 per cent of the lower income group volunteered additional favorable comments about the Negroes they were working with.

The most plausible hypothesis is that a large proportion of the upper income, unequal status respondents see a loss of status for themselves if they were to work with Negroes on a basis of equality, while only a small proportion of the lower income respondents in this group see themselves losing status by going into such a situation. The great majority of Negroes employed in these stores earn between 30 and 40 dollars a week. The lower income, unequal status respondents have jobs whose status is a little higher than that of the Negroes in their own departments, but not much different from that of the majority of Negro employees in the store. The upper income respondents in this group, however, are working at a level which is markedly above that of the average Negro employee. It is not surprising that a majority of them seem to make the tacit assumption that a new job in which Negroes and white people were working together would be a job at a lower level than their present positions.

Two additional hypotheses are required to explain the attitudes of the upper income, equal status respondents and the lower income, no contact respondents. The former group have been working with the minority of Negro employees who make more than $40 a week and who occupy relatively high status positions. Our hypothesis is that these people assume that it is such select, highly paid Negroes with whom they would be associated in a new job.

The lower income, no contact respondents have no reason to expect any loss of status from working on a basis of equality with the typical Negroes employed in these stores. However they do not have the experience of favorable work relationships with Negroes which is common to both the equal status and the unequal status groups. Our hypothesis is that, with the distribution of general attitudes toward Negroes which characterizes all these employees, *both* the experience of favorable work relationships with Negroes *and* the belief that a job in which Negroes and whites work together would be equivalent in status to one's present position are required to produce a substantial majority willing to work with Negroes on an equal status basis. These two conditions seem to exist among the lower income, unequal status contact respondents and among all the equal status contact respondents, but one or the other is lacking in each of the other three groups.

Effects of Equal Status Contact

Let us now turn to a detailed examination of the equal status contact respondents, concentrating on the question: Why has their experience in working with Negroes produced only a greater willingness to accept Negroes in this particular relationship, leaving their other attitudes toward Negroes unaltered? The degree of friendliness with Negroes in their own departments seems to be much the same as in the unequal status contact group. Ninety-two per cent of the equal status contact respondents now working with Negroes said they got along just as well with the Negroes as with the white workers in their departments. Fifty-three per cent knew at least one Negro in the department well enough so that they called each other by their first names.

The presence or absence of first-name relationships seems to depend more on custom and the social climate of a particular department than upon the attitudes of the white employees toward Negroes. Equal status contact respondents who are on a first name basis with Negroes in their departments have slightly more favorable attitudes toward Negroes than respondents who are not, but the difference is not statistically significant. Seventy-six per cent of the former group and 66 per cent of the latter would be willing to take new jobs in which Negroes and whites were on an equal footing. An indication of the superficiality of the personal relationships between whites and Negroes in these equal status contact departments is the fact that only 15 per cent of the white respondents have ever had a Negro as a personal friend. The percentage is the same for those who are on a first name basis with Negroes in their departments and those who are not. (Two respondents say they have had Negro friends in the past, but would not want them now.)

Our initial hypothesis was that employees in the store which had been hiring Negro white collar workers for four years would have more favorable attitudes than comparable employees in the store which had been hiring them for only a year. This hypothesis was based on the assumption that employees in the former store would have had a longer period of association with Negroes, and on the assumption that they would perceive the store management as more firmly committed to a policy of integration. In spite of the plausibility of this hypothesis, there is nothing in our data to support it. There are no significant differences between employees in the two stores on any of the attitude questions. Nor are there any significant differences in attitude among the equal status contact employees as we go from department to department within a particular store.

The most plausible explanation of the attitudes of the equal status contact respondents is that the great majority of them have simply accommodated to a situation in which they found themselves, without any change in their basic orientation toward Negroes. They are willing to continue this accommodation in a new situation of the same type, but this does not affect their reaction to other situations involving Negroes. The reasons given by equal status contact respondents for being willing to work on a par with Negroes in a new job are quite illuminating. Nearly half do not give any reason for their attitude. The great majority of those who do give a reason—25 respondents out of 33—say simply "I've done that and had no trouble," or "I'm doing it now."

Work Relationships Among White Collar Employees

There is a mixture of competition and cooperation in the relationships between employees working at the same level in these department stores. Sixty-four per cent of our respondents said they were making more money than they had been a year previously; however these advances were dependent for the most part on decisions by the store management with regard to each individual employee. They did not result from the automatic operation of seniority, or from a general wage increase negotiated through collective bargaining. In these stores it is possible for a clerk to work for 20 years in a particular department and still make less than $30 a week. Our initial hypothesis was that people who were being left behind in the struggle for advancement would develop less favorable attitudes toward Negroes than people who were getting ahead. This turns out not to be true: there are no significant differences between the two groups on any of the attitude questions. However the fact remains that people who work at the same level in these stores are in a real sense competing with each other for advancement. It is reasonable to assume that this situation puts a damper on the development of genuine friendships among co-workers, both those who are successful in the competition and those who are not.

Work relationships in these stores are probably similar to those found among most groups of white collar employees. The reader will remember that Irish, who was also studying a middle class group, found no differences in attitude among respondents who had and who had not worked with Japanese-Americans, although he found marked differences as a result of residential contact (3). However the situation is somewhat different when we turn to lower class respondents and "blue collar" jobs.

Other Studies of the Effects of Equal Status Work Contact

Brophy (1) found a very marked reduction in anti-Negro prejudice among white merchant seamen who had shipped one or more times with Negro sailors. Thirty-three per cent of those who had never shipped with Negroes were rated as unprejudiced on a ten item attitude scale. This proportion increased to 46 per cent for those who had shipped once with Negroes, 62 per cent for those who had shipped twice, and 82 per cent for those who had shipped five or more times. The situation which Brophy studied was unusually favorable for the reduction of prejudice, because these seamen not only worked together in circumstances requiring a high degree of cooperation but also lived together twenty-four hours a day. An additional factor was that nearly all the men who had shipped two or more times with Negroes were members of a CIO union with a militant anti-discrimination policy.

Merton, West, and Jahoda (4) found a moderate increase in favorable attitudes toward interracial housing projects among lower class white tenants in such a project who had previously worked with Negroes as compared with those who had not had this experience. Forty per cent of the former group, but only 24 per cent of the latter answered "Yes" to the question: "Do you think colored and white people should live together in housing projects?" (In this project Negro and white families were assigned to separate buildings, so that the amount of contact between the two groups within the project was not very great.)

Deutsch and Collins (2), however, found only a slight and statistically unreliable relationship between work experience and attitudes toward Negroes among white housewives in a segregated biracial public housing project. Thirty-one per cent of their respondents who had worked with Negroes favored interracial housing in principle, while 27 per cent of those who had never worked with Negroes favored interracial housing. (By "interracial housing" most of these people meant the arrangement they were familiar with, in which Negroes and whites lived in separate buildings. See Wilner, Walkley, and Cook (5).) Sixty-nine per cent of the housewives with equal status, interracial work experience mentioned Negroes as a group they would not like to have living in the same building with them, and 40 per cent mentioned Negroes as a group they would not like to work with. Among housewives without this experience 72 per cent and 50 per cent objected to Negroes in these two relationships.[2]

The evidence so far available indicates that equal status work contact between whites and Negroes may produce large favorable changes in attitude among the white workers, small favorable changes, or no changes at all, depending primarily on the nature of the work situation and the type of attitude measured. In the department store situation with which this article is primarily concerned equal status work contact produced a large increase in willingness to work with Negroes on an equal basis, but no significant change in willingness to accept other relationships with them.

Notes

[1] The percentages in Table 2 are somewhat higher than the corresponding percentages in Table 1 because of the loss of four respondents in the equal status and one respondent in the unequal status contact group who refused to answer the income question. All of these people had given unfavorable answers on Question 3.

[2] These tabulations were made by the present writers from data kindly furnished by Dr. Deutsch.

References

1. Brophy, I. N. The luxury of anti-Negro prejudice. *Public Opinion Quarterly,* 1946, *9,* 456-466.
2. Deutsch, M. & Collins, Mary E. *Interracial housing: a psychological evaluation of a social experiment.* Minneapolis: University of Minnesota Press, 1951.
3. Irish, D. P. Reactions of Caucasian residents to Japanese-American neighbors. *Journal of Social Issues,* 1952, *8,* No. 1, 10-17.
4. Merton, R. K., West, Patricia S. & Jahoda, Marie. *Social fictions and social facts: the dynamics of race relations in Hilltown.* Mimeographed. New York: Columbia University Bureau of Applied Social Research, 1949.
5. Wilner, D. M., Walkley, Rosabelle P. & Cook, S. W. Residential proximity and intergroup relations in public housing projects. *Journal of Social Issues,* 1952, *8,* No. 1, 45-69.

Black and White Marine Squad Leaders' Perceptions of Racially Mixed Squads[1]

WALTER H. HILL[2]
WILLIAM M. FOX

Allport's (1) contact hypothesis states that intergroup contacts involving shared interests or goals, equal status of participants, and normative support tend to reduce prejudice. This hypothesis has received tentative support from several studies of blacks and whites (2, 3, 4, 5, 6, 7, 8). These studies generally suggest that interpersonal contacts between blacks and whites may result in greater cooperation in task oriented behavior and favorable although limited change in attitudes among whites, but may not affect attitudes and behaviors which are not task prescribed. The purpose of this paper is to present some data which indicate the way black and white supervisors feel and act toward their black, Puerto Rican, and white subordinates on dimensions which are not task prescribed.

Method

As part of a seven-month longitudinal study of leadership effectiveness in the U. S. Marine Corps, a seven item questionnaire was developed and pretested to provide data to test the following hypotheses:
   I. There are no differences between the frequencies with which:
      A. White squad leaders report their black, Puerto Rican and white squad members,
      B. Black squad leaders report their Puerto Rican and white squad members,

Reprinted from *Academy of Management Journal,* 1973, *16*(4), 680-686, by permission of the publisher and the authors.

C. Black as contrasted with white squad leaders report their Puerto Rican and white squad members:
  1. were reprimanded or called down.
  2. were praised.
  3. were uncertain or undecided about what they were to do in their jobs.
  4. were trying to avoid failure (playing it safe) in contrast to looking for sound opportunities to show what they could do.

II. There are no differences in the mean scores reported by:
  A. White squad leaders for their black, Puerto Rican, and white squad members,
  B. Black squad leaders for their Puerto Rican and white squad members,
  C. Black as compared to white squad leaders for their Puerto Rican and white squad members:
    1. for getting along with their subordinates.
    2. for how well they understood their subordinates and their needs.
    3. for subordinate performance.

Subjects

The subjects were drawn from 17 rifle squads of two companies of a Marine training battalion based in the southeastern portion of the United States. The nature of the population, its unique mission, the periodic fluctuations in manpower levels and assignments, and subjects' selective fortitude in completing the questionnaires resulted in more weight being assigned automatically to the perceptions of some of the 29 squad leaders (7 black, 22 white) than others. A decision to exclude subordinates for whom complete personal data concerning age, length of time in squad, length of time in present MOS, and combat service were not available, reduced the sample to 138 squad members (87 whites, 35 blacks and 16 Puerto Ricans). The total number of leaders' responses about subordinates was 591 although individual questions may show varying response frequencies.

Results

Since each part (A, B, and C) of the first hypothesis contains predictions about black and white squad leaders' reactions to their subordinates on the same four dimensions, the discussion will be organized around these dimensions. Since each part (1, 2, and 3) of the second hypothesis pertains to a conceptually different dimension, results relating to each part will be discussed separately.

Reprimanding. The first question asked how many times the squad leaders reprimanded each man, using the following response categories: never, once, 2 or 3 times, 4 or 5 times, several times, and many times. The responses of black and white Marine squad leaders about their black, Puerto Rican and white squad members on this question are reported as Dimension One in Table 1.[3] Hypothesis IA1 was tested by comparing the actual versus expected frequencies with which white squad leaders reported they reprimanded their black, Puerto Rican and white squad members. A chi square test revealed a significant difference ($X^2 = 14.67, p < .01, df = 4$) in white squad leaders' responses about their racially mixed subordinates. Paired chi square tests then were run between the leaders' responses about blacks and whites, blacks and Puerto Ricans, and Puerto Ricans and whites, to determine the source of the variation. These comparisons indicated that the difference arose because white squad leaders gave proportionately more reprimands to whites than to blacks; ($X^2 = 12.90, p < .01, df = 2$); no significant difference appeared when responses to blacks and Puerto Ricans ($X^2 = 3.6, df = 2$) or Puerto Ricans and whites ($X^2 = 1.51, df = 2$) were compared.

Tests of hypotheses IB1 and IC1 indicated that black squad leaders did not differ in the actual versus expected frequencies with which they reprimanded their Puerto Rican and white subordinates ($X^2 = .008, df = 1$) nor was there any difference in the actual versus expected frequencies with which black as compared with white squad leaders reprimanded either whites ($X^2 = 0.00, df = 1$) or Puerto Ricans ($X^2 = 0.00, df = 1$). Thus, the only difference in reprimanding patterns was that white leaders reprimanded whites more often and blacks less frequently than was expected.

Praising. The second questions asked how many times the squad leaders praised each man, using the same response categories as for reprimands. The responses of black and white leaders about their black, Puerto Rican and white subordinates on this particular question are reported as Dimension Two in Table 1. Chi square tests of hypothesis IA2 revealed a significant difference ($X^2 = 32.24, p < .01, df = 6$) between the actual and expected frequencies with which white squad leaders reported they praised their black, Puerto Rican and white squad members. Paired comparisons indicated that differences arose because white squad leaders differentiated significantly in the actual versus expected frequencies by praising whites more and blacks less often ($X^2 = 22.86, p < .01, df = 3$) and praising Puerto Ricans more and whites less often ($X^2 = 9.87, p < .01, df = 3$) than expected; there was no difference in their responses to blacks versus Puerto Ricans ($X^2 = 4.2, df = 3$).

Table 1

Frequencies of Responses of Black and White Marine Squad Leaders
with Regard to Their Black, Puerto Rican, and White Squad Members

Dimensions	Squad Leaders:	Black			White			
Categories	Squad Members:	Puerto Rican	White	Total	Black	Puerto Rican	White	Total
1. *Reprimanded or called down*								
Never		7	15	22	126	20	143	289
Once, or one or more times[a]		6	17	23	28	10	55	93
Two or more times					46	11	107	164
Total		13	32	45	200	41	305	546
2. *Praised*								
Never		9	19	28	111	17	107	235
Once, or one or more times[a]		4	13	17	34	5	62	101
Two or more times					42	11	114	167
More than three times					13	8	21	42
Total		13	32	45	200	41	304	545
3. *Uncertain or undecided about what they were to do in their jobs*								
Never		9	16	25	148	26	183	357
One or more times		3	14	17	49	13	114	176
Total		12	30	42	197	39	297	533
4. Trying to avoid failure (playing it safe) in contrast to looking for sound opportunities to show what they could do								
Avoid failure		7	13	20	60	12	112	184
Look for opportunities		1	4	5	44	6	64	114
Total		8	17	25	104	18	176	298

[a]Since the number of responses from black leaders was small, they were collapsed into two categories: never and one or more times. The large number of responses from white leaders enabled the data to be divided into more categories. Thus the data in this row under black leaders indicate one or more times while the data under white leaders indicate once.

Although there was a significant difference in the frequency with which white leaders praised their Puerto Rican and white squad members, the pattern was not consistent. It appears that this difference occurred because a larger number of Puerto Ricans than was expected were singled out for praise "more than three times" (8 to 3).

Test of hypotheses IB2 and IC2 showed that black squad leaders did not differentiate in the actual versus expected frequencies with which they praised their Puerto Rican and white squad members ($X^2 = .007$, $df = 1$) but white as compared to black squad leaders were more generous than expected in giving praise to white subordinates ($X^2 = 6.22$, $p < .01$, $df = 1$) although no difference occurred in the leaders' praise of Puerto Rican squad members ($X^2 = 1.97$, $df = 1$).

Uncertainty. The third question asked the squad leaders how often they felt their squad members had been uncertain or undecided as to what they were to do, using the same response categories indicated previously. These responses are reported under Dimension Three in Table 1. Chi square tests of hypothesis IA3 revealed a significant difference ($X^2 = 9.78$, $p < .01$, $df = 2$) in the actual and expected frequencies with which white squad leaders reported their black, Puerto Rican and white squad members were uncertain or undecided about their assignment. Further paired comparison tests indicated that the difference arose because white leaders differentiated between black and white subordinates ($X^2 = 9.18$, $p < .01$, $df = 1$). They reported their white squad members as uncertain or undecided more frequently than expected and stated their black members were never "uncertain" or undecided more often than expected; no differences occurred in their responses when blacks were compared to Puerto Ricans ($X^2 = .84$, $df = 1$) or Puerto Ricans contrasted with whites ($X^2 = .18$, $df = 1$).

Tests of hypotheses IB3 and IC3 indicated that no differences occurred in the actual versus expected frequencies with which black squad leaders reported their Puerto Ricans and whites were uncertain ($X^2 = 1.67$, $df = 1$) or between black and white leaders' reports about the uncertainty of their white ($X^2 = .5$, $df = 1$) or Puerto Rican subordinates ($X^2 = .04$, $df = 1$).

Avoiding Failure vs. Looking for Opportunity. The fourth question asked the squad leaders to indicate which of the following their squad members had been most concerned with: avoiding failure (playing it safe), or looking for sound opportunities to show what they could do. Responses to this question are reported under Dimension Four in Table 1. A chi square test of hypothesis IA4 indicated that white squad leaders did not discriminate significantly among their white, black and Puerto Rican subordinates ($X^2 = 1.17$, $df = 2$). Further tests of hypotheses IB4 and IC4 indicated that black squad leaders did not discriminate significantly between their Puerto Rican and white subordinates ($X^2 = .011$, $df = 1$), nor was there discrimination by black squad leaders in comparison to white squad leaders toward either their Puerto Rican ($p = .274$)[4] or white subordinates ($X^2 = .64$, $df = 1$).

Friendliness of Relationship. The fifth question asked the squad leaders to indicate how well they got along with (were friendly with) each subordinate by checking a point on a "best possible"—1—to a "poorest possible"—25—continuum. The responses of black and white leaders for questions five through seven are shown in Table 2. Paired t tests performed on the data shown in Table 2 indicated there was no difference in the responses of white leaders (hypothesis IIA1) when describing their relationships with black, Puerto Rican, or white subordinates. Neither was there any difference in black leaders' descriptions of their relationships with Puerto Rican and white subordinates (hypothesis IIB1). However, hypothesis IIC1 was rejected as black leaders reported a significantly better average relationship with white subordinates ($t = 2.07$, $p < .05$) than did white squad leaders (mean values of 8.48 and 10.13); no difference was found between their reported relationship with Puerto Rican squad members.

Understanding of Subordinate by Leader. The sixth question asked the squad leaders to indicate how well they understood each subordinate and his needs by use of a 25 point scale ranging from "completely"—1—to "not at all"—25. Paired t tests performed on the data in Table 2 provided support for hypotheses IIA2, IIB2 and IIC2, as no significant differences were found in the squad leaders reported understanding of their subordinates and their needs.

Evaluation of Subordinate Performance. The seventh question asked the squad leaders to rate each subordinate's performance by use of another 25 degree scale ranging from "highest possible"—1—to "lowest

Table 2

Black and White Squad Leaders' Perceptions Concerning
Their Black, Puerto Rican, and White Squad Members

Squad Leaders	Squad Members											
	Black			Puerto Rican			White			Total		
	N	x̄	S	N	x̄	S	N	x̄	S	N	x̄	S
Black												
Get Along With				13	10.99	4.2	31	8.48	5.2	44	9.23	5.1
Understand				13	10.53	4.2	31	9.71	5.5	44	9.95	5.2
Rate				13	11.45	4.5	31	11.58	4.7	44	11.54	4.6
White												
Get Along With	200	9.56	4.0	41	10.8	3.8	303	10.13	4.1	544	9.97	4.1
Understand	200	10.46	4.8	41	11.22	4.0	303	10.84	4.7	544	10.73	4.7
Rate	200	9.63	4.7	41	10.22	5.5	301	10.83	4.9	542	10.34	4.9
Total (Black & White)												
Get Along With	200	9.56	4.0	54	10.85	3.9	334	9.97	4.2	588	9.91	4.2
Understand	200	10.46	4.8	54	11.05	4.0	334	10.74	4.8	588	10.67	4.7
Rate	200	9.63	4.7	54	10.52	5.3	332	10.90	4.9	586	10.43	4.9

possible"—25. Paired t tests performed on the data in Table 2 indicated that hypothesis IIA3 should be rejected as white leaders gave a significantly higher mean rating ($t = 2.72$, $p < .01$) to their black subordinates (9.63) than to their white subordinates (10.83). No significant differences were found when hypotheses IIB3 and IIC3 were tested; i.e., black squad leaders did not differentiate in their evaluation of their Puerto Rican and white subordinates nor did black as compared to white leaders differ in their evaluations of Puerto Rican and white squad members.

Conclusion

The results indicate that white squad leaders gave proportionately more reprimands to their white as compared to black subordinates. They also gave their black subordinates better performance ratings and indicated that their white as contrasted with black squad members were more uncertain than was expected. This could indicate that white leaders were maintaining a certain "distance" from their black subordinates and were handling them with "special care" due to recent emphasis on racial harmony in the Armed Forces. The tendency to treat minority group members in a special way may also explain why white leaders seemed to "single out" their Puerto Rican squad members for proportionately heavier doses of praise than their white subordinates. On the other hand, black squad leaders reported that they get along with white subordinates better than white squad leaders reported. Black squad leaders may also be "going out of their way" to make their relations with white members appear free from discrimination.

It does appear that white squad leaders gave proportionately more praise to white squad members than did black squad leaders, but this is the only finding that would support the simplistic assumption that squad leaders in the U. S. Marine Corps at this time will openly express negative racial stereotyping in behaviors relating to their official duties.

Notes

[1]This paper was prepared in connection with research done under the Office of Naval Research, Organizational Effectiveness Research Programs, Contract No. N00014-68-A-0173-0010. The views expressed herein are those of the authors and do not necessarily reflect the views of the U.S. Marine Corps or the U.S. Navy.

[2]Walter H. Hill and William M. Fox were affiliated with the University of Florida, Gainesville, Florida, at the time of publication of this article.

[3]No data on black squad members serving under black squad leaders were available.

[4]Due to the small expected cell frequencies, Fisher's exact probability test was used instead of chi square.

References

1. Allport, G. *The Nature of Prejudice* (Cambridge, Mass.: Addison-Wesley, 1954).
2. Burnstein, E., and A. V. McRae. "Some Effects of Shared Threat and Prejudice in Racially Mixed Groups," *Journal of Abnormal and Social Psychology,* Vol. 64 (1962), 257-263.
3. Deutsch, M., and M. Collins. *Interracial Housing: A Psychological Evaluation of a Social Experiment* (Minneapolis: University of Minnesota Press, 1951).
4. Harding, J., and R. Hogrefe. "Attitudes of White Department Store Employees Toward Negro Co-Workers," *Journal of Social Issues,* Vol. 8 (1952), 18-28.
5. Katz, I., and L. Benjamin. "Effects of White Authoritarianism in Biracial Work Groups," *Journal of Abnormal and Social Psychology,* Vol. 61 (1960), 448-456.
6. Katz, I., and M. Cohen. "The Effects of Training Negroes Upon Cooperative Problem Solving in Biracial Teams," *Journal of Abnormal and Social Psychology,* Vol. 64 (1962), 319-325.
7. Stouffer, S. A., E. A. Suchman, L. C. DiVinney, S. A. Star, and R. M. Williams, Jr. *Studies in Social Psychology in World War II. Vol 1 —The American Soldier* (Princeton, N.J.: Princeton University Press, 1949).
8. Wilner, D., R. P. Walkley, and S. W. Cook. "Residential Proximity and Intergroup Relations in Public Housing Projects," *Journal of Social Issues,* Vol. 8 (1955), 45-69.

Effect of Racial Prejudice on Behavior

The Effect of Reference Group Upon Negroes Task Persistence in a Biracial Competitive Game[1]

HERBERT M. LEFCOURT[2]
GORDON W. LADWIG

This study concerns Negro Ss' avoidance tendencies in competitive achievement tasks. It was predicted that Negro Ss would not show avoidance behavior if they had higher expectancies of being able to gain reinforcements for their efforts. Three groups of Negro reformatory inmates played a competitive game with white stooges who won continuously. One group, designated the high-expectancy group, was comprised of jazz musicians who had been led to believe that the game was related to personal skills of musicians. This group persisted significantly longer than either of 2 control groups. The latter demonstrated the more typical failure-avoidance characteristic of Negroes in previous research.

The results of several recent studies by Katz (Katz & Benjamin, 1960; Katz & Cohen, 1962; Katz, Goldston, & Benjamin, 1958; Katz & Greenbaum, 1963), indicated that Negroes tend to feel inadequate, and orient compliantly toward whites even when they are given objective evidence of equal mental ability. Battle and Rotter (1963) and Lefcourt and Ladwig (1963) have demonstrated that Negro subjects answered questionnaires and performed in achievement tasks in a manner that is characteristic of externally controlled persons. That is, the Negro subjects perceived reinforcements as being unrelated to their own behaviors and therefore beyond their personal control. In these studies Negroes

Reprinted from *Journal of Personality and Social Psychology*, 1965, *1*, 668-671. Copyright © 1965 by the American Psychological Association. Reprinted by permission of the publisher and the authors.

behaved in a predominantly failure-avoidant manner, especially in biracial achievement situations.

In the studies by Katz et al. (1958), and Katz and Benjamin (1960), an attempt was made to alter Negroes' behavior by group prestige techniques in which Negro and white partners were assured that they were competent in classroom ability or had scored highly on certain tests in comparison with fictitious norms. Reversals of predictions or no effects at all were found on a wide range of behaviors in their Negro sample, while whites did show some positive effects from the prestige manipulation.

The present study attempts to manipulate Negroes' behavior through a group prestige technique similar to that used by Katz and his colleagues. The notable difference is that this manipulation utilizes a social role within an already established positive reference group (membership is of high positive reinforcement value to the participants).

From the previously mentioned research it can be tentatively concluded that when Negroes enter biracial, competitive, achievement-motivation eliciting tasks they will have high expectancies of failure and consequently will behave in a failure-avoidant manner. In studies of persistence by Feather (1961, 1963) subjects characterized as motivated to succeed (M_s) were found to persist in an insoluble task longer than subjects described as failure avoidant (M_{af}) if the probability of success was .50 or better. Failure-avoidant subjects, on the other hand, persisted longer when probabilities dropped below .50. In the present study all of the subjects are considered to be M_s to obtain a highly valued incentive (cigarettes). Expectancy of success in securing the reinforcements, however, varies with the prior experience of the subject in the role as a jazz musician. Consequently, subjects who have been defined as having higher expectancies of success regarding their roles as jazz musicians (above .50) will be more apt to persist in an insoluble task related to that role than those who have lower expectancies of success (below .50 level).

Hypotheses

Negroes have usually displayed failure-avoidant behavior in biracial achievement situations. However, when such achievement tasks are construed as related to competence in a role in which Negro subjects have already had some success experience, expectancy of success should increase. It is predicted, then, that Negro subjects will be more persistent in a competitive biracial task when they perceive the task as related to success in a role that has positive reinforcement value for them and in which they have had some success experience.

Method

Subjects

Three groups of Negro inmates were drawn from a correctional institution. The first group (J) was comprised of 20 inmates who had displayed a continuous interest in jazz as demonstrated by at least a 6-months' membership in a jazz club. This club met once a week, held jam sessions, and prepared musical shows for the inmate population. A second group (Q) was comprised of 20 inmates who had joined the jazz club but had quit after attending a few sessions. A third group (C) was made up of 20 inmates who had never joined any music interest groups. Analyses of variance revealed no differences among the three groups in intelligence, age, social class, or types of crimes resulting in commitment. In addition, no differences were found among the groups in regard to the internal-external control dimension (Rotter, Seeman, & Liverant, 1962) or in failure-avoidant behavior on Rotter's Level of Aspiration Board (Rotter, 1942). As reported in a previous study (Lefcourt & Ladwig, 1963), Negroes were consistently more failure avoidant and had greater expectancies of external control than whites. Mean beta IQ was 98.5 and the average age was 21.6 years.

Task

Subjects from the J and Q groups were informed that they had been chosen as subjects for an experiment because of their interest in jazz. The study was described as concerning the interests, opinions, and skills of jazz musicians. Each subject was interviewed regarding his interests in music, his favorite musicians, etc. In addition, subjects were given a scale eliciting their ratings of known jazz musicians. Several other measures were administered at this time, after which the subjects were released. They were told that they would be called in for a second session which would focus on skills of musicians. The C group subjects were merely informed that they had been chosen at random from the inmate population, completed several tests and were released with the information that they would be called back again.

The experimental task was a two-person zero-sum game called NIM. The game, described in *Time Magazine* (The Marienbad Game, 1962), consists of picking up matches until one player is left with the last match, this player being the loser. The outcome of the game can be controlled almost completely by use of a set of combinations.

Negro subjects played against a white stooge who had memorized the necessary combinations. The stooge won each game including a practice trial so that all subjects had a continuous failure experience.

The subject and the stooge were separated by a screen with only their hands visible to each other. The stooge was described as just another inmate who was not a jazz musician. The subjects were instructed:

> This is a simple game but it requires cleverness and skill at outsmarting your opponent. Each of you will take turns picking up matches. You can take as few or as many matches as you wish, even a whole row. [Sixteen matches are initially laid out in rows of 7, 5, 3, and 1.] But all the matches you take in any one turn must be taken from one row. The player who picks up the last remaining match loses. Try one game for practice so you can see how it works. . . . Both of you are starting off with chips worth $2.00. You have 20 chips, each worth ten cents. You will bet ten cents for each game that you play, and you can play any numbers of games you want. Either of you can call it quits at any time. However, if you are the one to give in first then you will only get credit for half the value of your chips. The chips are worth cigarettes at 25 cents a pack, so you can see it is worthwhile to win as many chips from each other as possible. The one who doesn't give in will get paid the full amount that he has won.

Subjects were allowed a maximum of 15 plays after which they were informed that the games would be stopped to insure their winning some reward. Consequently, scores ranged from 0 to 15 games. All subjects were tested during a 2-day period. Four of the 15 subjects tested on the first day were deliberately allowed to win to offset possible effects of communication. No differences were found among J group members tested on the 2 days.

Results

Because of institutional disciplinary actions, 8 subjects of the original 60 were lost for the second session of testing. Consequently, there were slight differences among Ns in the three groups. As Table 1 indicates, significant differences were obtained among the three groups in the predicted directions. The Newman-Keuls procedure was used to determine the significance of mean differences among the three groups (Winer, 1962).

The J group persisted significantly longer than either the Q or C groups. The Q group did not differ significantly from the C group though the difference did approach the .10 level.

Since there were some differences in variance as well as in N and direction of skew among the groups, a Kruskal-Wallis H was computed on the same data. Results indicated an H value of 11.36, $p < .01$. Mann-Whitney U tests revealed similar significance of differences as the parametric tests except that the J + Q group difference was significant at the .06 level rather than the .05 level obtained with the Newman-Keuls test.

Table 1

Analysis of Variance and Mean Differences Among the
J, Q, and C Groups in the Number of Games Played
in the NIM Situation

Group	N	M	SD	F	p	Newman-Keuls Test of Mean Differences Between	p
J	17	12.47	3.76			J + Q	.05
Q	19	8.26	6.68	5.8	.01	J + C	.01
C	16	5.06	6.19			Q + C	ns

Discussion

The results suggest that previous failures of prestige manipulations to alter Negroes' failure-avoidant behavior may have been due to the fact that such manipulations have too often focused on intellectual achievement, an area in which Negroes have low expectancies of success. In this experiment, competence as a jazz musician was emphasized. With a continuous failure experience in a seemingly simple, two-person biracial, competitive situation, subjects who had high reinforcement value for and success in jazz club membership, as demonstrated by the length of time they had remained participants in the club, exhibited more persistence in a task said to be related to competence as a jazz musician. Nearly 50% of the Q group persisted as long as the J group members. In interviews with these subjects, several claimed to have quit attending the jazz club for reasons beyond their control, such as time conflict with required activities. This may explain the greater effect of the jazz cues in the Q than in the C group.

It might be argued that the jazz musician sample is composed of an atypical group of Negro subjects who, having achieved some modicum of success with jazz skills, are more confident of themselves in general. Consequently, it could be hypothesized that these musicians would have displayed the same persistence in competition regardless of the experimental manipulation used in this study. However, it should be noted that only 2 of the 20 subjects in the jazz club sample had any experience performing outside of the institution setting, and their experience was minimal. Therefore, there is little chance that the subjects felt "secure" in the musician role, having no affirmed status except that of novice or amateur. Second, as mentioned above, there were no differences among the three groups in regard to past achievement histories insofar as is indicated by school grades completed, Stanford Achievement Test scores, and intelligence test performance. In addition, the three groups displayed no differences among themselves in failure-avoidant behavior and external control expectancies while each of the groups differed significantly from an otherwise equivalent sample of white inmates.

Another alternative that presents more of a problem is that the subjects in the musician sample may have felt gratified by the investigators' interest in jazz and consequently felt obliged to comply with the experimenters' demands. The control subjects, on the other hand, may have perceived themselves as anonymous guinea pigs who were forced to act as subjects by virtue of the fact that they were reformatory inmates with little right of protest. If such were the case then persistence in the competitive task could be explained by the subjects' perceptions of the experimenters' demands, and by their desire to cooperate with the experimenters.

In follow-up interviews members of the J group frequently mentioned curiosity and interest in the task as an explanation for their persistence. The C subjects, on the other hand, often quoted such maxims as "Bird in the hand . . ." to account for their early withdrawal from the competitive situation. Jazz club members seemed less concerned with the immediate material gains than with the task itself while the reverse seemed to be true of the control groups.

One implication of these findings is that prestige suggestions need to be related to goals towards which subjects have some expectancy of success. A second implication is that Negroes may become more task and achievement oriented when they expect that their behavior can determine the occurrence of reinforcements which are of high value to them. The fact that Negroes have usually performed less adequately than whites on intelligence measures may reflect the fact that middle-class goals which require extensive schooling are customarily unavailable to them. Consequently, such goals may accrue a negative reinforcement value as well as low expectancies of success for Negroes. With gradual changes in Negroes' opportunities for upward mobility it is possible that Negroes will come to expect and value middle-class goals and consequently display more achievement behavior.

Notes

[1]This research was based on the senior author's doctoral dissertation at the graduate school of the Ohio State University. The research was supported in part by the United States Air Force, under Contract No. AF 49(638)-317 monitored by the Air Force Office of Scientific Research of the Air Research and Development Command.

The senior author wishes to thank Alvin Scodel for his suggestions and help in the design of this experiment.

[2]Herbert M. Lefcourt was affiliated with the University of Waterloo, Ontario, Canada, at the time of publication of this article. Gordon W. Ladwig was with the Veterans Administration Hospital, Chillicothe, Ohio.

References

Battle, E., & Rotter, J. B. Children's feelings of personal control as related to social class and ethnic group. *Journal of Personality*, 1963, *31*, 482-490.

Feather, N. T. The relationship of persistence at a task to expectation of success and achievement related motives. *Journal of Abnormal and Social Psychology*, 1961, *63*, 552-561.

Feather, N. T. The relationship of expectation of success to reported probability, task structure, and achievement related motivation. *Journal of Abnormal and Social Psychology*, 1963, *66*, 231-238.

Katz, I., & Benjamin, L. Effects of white authoritarianism in biracial work groups. *Journal of Abnormal and Social Psychology*, 1960, *61*, 448-456.

Katz, I., & Cohen, M. The effects of training Negroes upon cooperative problem solving in biracial teams. *Journal of Abnormal and Social Psychology*, 1962, *64*, 319-325.

Katz, I., Goldston, J., & Benjamin, L. Behavior and productivity in bi-racial work groups. *Human Relations*, 1958, *11*, 123-141.

Katz, I., & Greenbaum, C. Effects of anxiety, threat, and racial environment on task performance of Negro college students. *Journal of Abnormal and Social Psychology*, 1963, *66*, 562-567.

Lefcourt, H. M., & Ladwig, G. W. The American Negro: A problem in expectancies. Unpublished manuscript, Ohio State University, 1963.

The Marienbad Game. *Time Magazine*, 1962 (March 23), *79*, 54.

Rotter, J. B. Level of aspiration as a method of studying personality: II. Development and evaluation of a controlled method. *Journal of Experimental Psychology*, 1942, *31*, 410-422.

Rotter, J. B., Seeman, M. R., & Liverant, S. Internal versus external control of reinforcements: A major variable in behavior theory. In N. F. Washburne (Ed.), *Decisions, values, and groups*. Vol. 2. London: Pergamon Press, 1962, pp. 473-516.

Winer, B. J. *Statistical principles in experimental design*. New York: McGraw-Hill, 1962.

Behavior and Productivity in Bi-Racial Work Groups[1]

IRWIN KATZ[2]
JUDITH GOLDSTON
LAWRENCE BENJAMIN

INTRODUCTION

Field studies have shown that close contact between Negroes and whites in the United States may be marked by tension and conflict, or by harmonious interaction; as yet little is known about the factors that produce one effect or the other. Experiments are needed in which features of the contact situation that are believed to be important are systematically varied, and ongoing social behavior is observed and recorded. The present investigation is of this type. It is concerned with communication and productivity in small groups of Negro and white men working under various conditions of reward and prestige.

Results of a field study by Katz (6) suggest that Negro-white interaction may profitably be regarded as a special case of interaction between persons of high status and persons of low status. Thus, communication in bi-racial groups may be expected to follow patterns similar to those observed in all-white status hierarchies. In experiments by Thibaut (8), Kelley (7), and Hurwitz et al. (4) on groups with status differentials it was found that the direction of communication between participants at different status levels was mainly upward. All of the investigators interpreted the upward communications as being, to some extent, a substitute for blocked upward locomotion. The uniformity of results is particularly striking when it is noted that no two studies utilized the same basis of status differentiation. Both Thibaut and Kelley also reported indications of suppressed inter-level hostility, particularly on the part of

Reprinted from *Human Relations*, 1958, *11*, 123-141, by permission of Plenum Publishing Corporation.

low-status individuals against those of high status, while Hurwitz et al. stressed the cautious, ego-defensive nature of behavior by the 'lows' toward the 'highs,' one manifestation of which was their tendency to talk less than did the 'highs' during discussions.

What do these results suggest regarding Negro-white interaction? We shall consider a relatively simple situation, namely, a small group with the following characteristics: there are in the group equal numbers of Negro men and white men, none of whom have experienced close interracial contact previously; all men have identical task roles and about equal task competence; performance is rewarded on an individual but noncompetitive basis; there are no special 'cohesiveness-building' influences or task-motivating influences acting on the group as a whole. Certain assumptions can be made about the factors governing social behavior in this situation:

1. *Nonhostile withdrawal.* There undoubtedly will exist restraints of a nonhostile nature against interracial communication. Lack of previous acquaintance with other-race persons will create a sense of 'psychological distance' between oneself and other-race men in the group. This feeling will be strengthened by any perceived cultural differences between oneself and them.

2. *Hostile withdrawal.* Interracial hostility will arise from various sources and will inhibit Negro-white interaction. (a) To the extent that they exist, negative attitudes about the other race as a whole will predispose participants to react hostilely to other-race men. In general, hostility will give rise to restraints against all forms of behavior that might create greater interracial intimacy than required in the situation. (b) Fear of status-loss through association with persons of low social status will produce in whites a tendency to ignore Negro group members. (c) Fear of rejection by whites will give rise to a corresponding tendency toward hostile and defensive withdrawal on the part of Negroes.

3. *Inhibition of hostility.* Fear of harmful consequences to oneself will inhibit the direct expression of interracial hostility.

4. *Substitute locomotion.* There will exist a force acting on the Negro men to interact with the high-status whites as a form of behavior in the direction of a more attractive position.

5. *Feelings of inadequacy.* Negroes will tend to feel inadequate when the group is engaged in tasks that appear to require abilities which, according to traditional stereotypes, are possessed in greater degree by the high-status whites.

From Assumptions 4 and 5 it follows that Negroes will direct a larger proportion of their nonhostile behavior to whites than will whites to Negroes. From Assumptions 1 through 5 it follows that Negroes will be in greater conflict about communicating than whites and will, therefore, communicate less. It is not predictable from the Assumptions whether Negroes will talk mainly to one another or to whites. But it does appear that whites will talk mainly to one another, tending to ignore the Negroes.

Effects of a group goal. Deutsch (2) found that group reward, as compared with individual-competitive reward, produced more friendliness, cooperation, and productivity in all-white discussion groups. He attributed these results to the 'promotive interdependence' of participants under group reward. If his interpretation is correct, similar effects should occur when a group reward situation is compared with one of individual but noncompetitive reward, except that the magnitude of some differences might be smaller.

Again referring to the bi-racial work group that we described above, what would be the effects of distributing rewards on the basis of the total group's performance, rather than on the basis of individual performance? First, it is to be expected that under group reward the group as a whole will show more friendliness, cooperation, and productivity than under individual reward. Further, there is reason to believe that the introduction of a group goal will produce specific effects on behavior between races. We have assumed that interracial hostility in the group will be based largely on false beliefs and perceptions. 'Promotive interdependence' will tend to correct false perceptions of other-race men in two distinguishable ways: (1) Cooperative interaction will present the person with *information* about other-race participants. The information will bear upon whatever abilities and personal characteristics are brought into play by the common task. Receptiveness to the information will be high because of its instrumental value in achieving one's own (i.e. the group's) goal. (2) Cooperative interaction will create a *shift in the frame of reference* for perceiving other-race men in the group. They will be seen less as Negroes or whites and more as contributing members of one's 'team.' It is anticipated, therefore, that under group reward, as compared with individual reward, there will be less tendency for whites to talk more than Negroes, and communications of both whites and Negroes will be more evenly distributed between own-race recipients and other-race recipients.

Effects of group prestige. Another condition of groups that is likely to increase friendliness, cooperation, and productivity is that of high prestige. Back (1) endowed two-person discussion groups with prestige by stressing honorific features of membership, and found that this produced a high level of voluntary interaction and receptiveness of members to one another's ideas. It seems likely that when the attractiveness of membership in a group is increased through prestige, the attraction of members for each other will also increase. Hence, with high prestige endowment our hypothetical bi-racial work group ought to show more friendliness, cooperation, and productivity—the last particularly when the prestige endowment involves a belief among members that their work is important and that they have been specially selected for it.

Further, there are reasons why prestige endowment should produce specific effects on behavior between races. As in the group reward condition, it can be assumed that there will occur a *shift in the frame of reference* for perceiving other-race group members. The tendency will be to view them less as whites or Negroes and more as fellow-members of a small *élite*. Since the perceived status of Negroes will be altered in an upward direction, whites will experience *less fear of status-loss* through association with them. The increased communication between races will have a corrective effect on members' erroneous beliefs about other-race persons. Thus, under high prestige, as compared with a neutral prestige condition, there will be less tendency for whites to talk more than Negroes, and communications of both whites and Negroes will be more evenly distributed between own-race recipients and other-race recipients.

THE EXPERIMENT

Overview of the Design

Negro and white men college students were employed to work in groups of four—two Negroes and two whites—on a series of tasks that were described as 'materials that are being developed for vocational aptitude tests.' Each group worked a total of 12½ hours, divided into four or five sessions, under a particular combination of High Prestige (Hi P) or Neutral Prestige (No P) and Group Reward (Grp R) or Individual Reward (Ind R). A two-by-two factorial design was utilized, with four groups in each cell. As dependent variables, social interaction and productivity were measured by means of observers' classifications of behavior and objective measures of output.[3]

The Sample

Subjects were recruited from colleges and universities in New York City. The original intent was to use only Negro and white men who were Northern-born, undergraduate students between the ages of 18 and 25, and who had academic grade averages of C+ or better. Unfortunately, these criteria had to be modified because of the relatively small number of Negro college students in New York City. The Negro sample, as finally constituted, was notably heterogeneous in some respects.

Negro subjects. For the total Negro sample of 32 men the age range was 18 to 33 and the mean was 24·1. Nineteen men were Northern-born undergraduates. Six Ss were Southerners who were enrolled in summer-session graduate courses in New York. (There were two Southerners in each of two treatments and one in each of the remaining treatments.) In addition, seven men were foreign-born undergraduate students—five from the British West Indies and two from Ghana. (There were two foreign-born students in each of three treatments and one in the fourth treatment.)

White subjects. For the total white sample of 32 men the age range was 18 to 31 and the mean was 22 (2·1 years below the Negro mean). All of the white Ss were Northern-born undergraduates. Twenty-one of them were Jewish, six were Catholic, and five were Protestant.

Establishment of the Experimental Conditions

The experimental laboratory consisted of a behavior room and an adjacent observational room connected by a one-way window and a one-way sound system. Floor dimensions of the behavior room were 8½' x 14'. It was furnished with a square table and four chairs. Members of each experimental group had no contact in the laboratory with members of any other experimental group. At the first session the four men of a group were assigned seats around the table so that men of the same race sat adjacent to each other. Thus, each man sat between an own-race person and an other-race person. Seating remained the same throughout the experiment. Arm-bands were worn for identification.

At the outset the men were told that they were to try out various potential test materials and afterwards to describe their reactions to the tasks. It was explained that their performance would be observed by the experimenter and an assistant through the one-way window. If possible, sessions of two and a half hours were scheduled for five successive school days, for a total of 12½ hours.

Reward variable. All groups were told that a bonus of 25 cents an hour, in addition to the base pay of one dollar an hour, could be earned by every man. For induction of Group Reward (Grp R) Ss were told that the bonus would be based on the quality of performance of the group as a whole ('interest and effort shown') and would be awarded uniformly to all men in the group. For Individual Reward (Ind R) Ss were told that the bonus would be awarded to each man individually on the basis of his own performance. It was stressed that the bonus was noncompetitive, i.e. 'Whether or not one man gets the bonus will have nothing to do with another man's chance of getting it.' At the beginning of each new task the men were briefly reminded of the bonus setup.

Prestige variable. For induction of High Group Prestige (Hi P) *S*s were told at the first session that they had been specially selected on the basis of grades and instructors' recommendations and that they were expected to perform better than most of the other groups in the project. (Every man in the sample was at least slightly above the average of his school in scholastic performance.) At the start of the second session and all subsequent sessions these remarks were briefly restated. The No Group Prestige (No P) groups were given no instructions relating to prestige.

The Tasks

Erector. Three construction tasks were used. For each one a box containing enough Erector Set parts to build four identical models was placed in the middle of the table. One picture of the model was placed on top of the box. *S*s were instructed that each man was to build his own model but that they might help each other as much as they liked.

Human relations problems. There were two human relations problems that supposedly tested 'ability to understand other people's feelings and reaction.' The group had 30 minutes to discuss each problem and come to agreement about suitable answers to three questions. Before and after the discussion the men were required to write their own answers to the questions.

Logical problems. Five logical problems were employed which were arithmetically simple but logically 'tricky.' The experimenter read aloud one problem at a time and directed the men to reach unanimous agreement on a solution. Hints were given, if necessary, to prevent prolonged frustration.

Stick puzzles. These puzzles were taken from Katona (5). In each a pattern of squares, made with sticks 4½″ long, was arranged in the center of the table. The group had to reduce the number of squares by moving a limited number of sticks to new positions. There was no restriction on number of practice moves. Hints were given when necessary to prevent prolonged frustration.

Map. The essential features of a small military map had to be projected onto a white poster board measuring 28″ × 40″ that was tacked to a wall. Colored pencils, erasers, rulers, and scratch paper for computations were provided.

Ball-and-Spiral. This task has been used by French (3) and others. The present apparatus was a spiral track 3½″ wide that ascended from a 4′ × 4′ base to a center hole about 24″ above the base. There were 3¾ rotations in the track, the outside edge of which was open, so that a rubber ball could roll off freely. At each corner of the base was a handle.

With one man grasping each handle, a group had to maneuver the ball to the top by tilting the apparatus.

Ball-and-Spiral was the last task administered to each group and was intended to test the effects of the various experimental treatments on ability to work cooperatively during prolonged frustration. Therefore, it was set up as a standard situation, identical for all groups. The instructions were designed to conceal the difficulty of the task, and to persuade the men to risk part of their earnings in a bet which they were likely to lose. Ss were told that every man would win 50 cents each time the group got the ball to the top, but would lose 50 cents if the group did not succeed at least once in 30 minutes. At the end of the first half hour Ss were induced to bet again for a second half hour. No goals were made during the first period, but three groups were able to make one goal each during the second period. Afterwards, all groups were told that they had been deliberately deceived about the true difficulty of the task, and that any 'gambling losses' they had incurred were cancelled.

Rest periods. There were seven rest periods, each about ten minutes long, which were intended to facilitate social interaction.

Measures of Social Interaction

Social behavior was classified by observers as it occurred, according to a set of categories that had been developed in preliminary experiments. In all, three observers were used. One observer was used for all 16 groups, while the other two worked only part of the time for the purpose of measuring inter-observer agreement. The chief observer was familiar with the main hypotheses relating to reward and prestige, but was ignorant of the treatments accorded particular groups. The two auxiliary observers were totally uninformed about the independent variables and the hypotheses. A behavior sampling procedure was used which consisted of ten-minute recording periods alternating with ten-minute rest periods. A running account of all task-irrelevant remarks was kept by the experimenter.

RESULTS

Adequacy of Techniques

Behavior Categories

Thirty-one categories were used to classify behavior in six task situations. Results on one task, Map, were not used because of poor agreement between observers, which resulted from inadequate observational conditions. Some of the categories were so similar in meaning that they produced low inter-observer agreement. These were combined in the analysis of data. The remaining single and combined categories constituted 25 behavior measures which, when duplications on various tasks are eliminated, are reduced to 13 general types of behavior, as follows: (1) Proposes action; (2) Rejects, disagrees; (3) Criticizes objectively; (5) Shows antagonism; (7) Shows disinterest in task; (13) Gives information, help, advice; (14) Asks for information, etc.; (20) Raises other's status; (21) Uses sticks; (31) Gives opinion; (32) Gives suggestion, orientation, information; (35) Asks for opinion, suggestion, etc.; (39) Agrees. The number of categories used for particular tasks varied from three to eight.

Most of the 13 classifications of behavior yielded two types of score: number of communications initiated, and an 'S' score, to be defined later, which has to do with the ratio of communications directed to own-race recipients and to other-race recipients.

Agreement between observers. The main observer and an auxiliary observer independently recorded behavior in the first ten groups. Inter-observer correlations (Rho) of group scores on number of communications initiated were computed separately for Negroes and for whites. Values ranged from ·02 to ·98 for different categories, with a median of ·74. The median is significant at the ·02 level. Inter-observer correlations were obtained also for Negro S-scores and for white S-scores. The range of Rho values was ·13 to ·92, with a median of ·83. Similar levels of inter-observer agreement were found between the chief observer and the second auxiliary observer, who independently classified behavior in the last three groups.

Tests of possible bias in the chief observer. The sign test was used to estimate whether the chief observer, who was acquainted with the experimental hypotheses, was consistently more or less in the direction of predicted results than were the other observers. In tests for every category of behavior no values of Z exceeded ·90 ($p = ·18$), indicating that the chief observer was not measurably biased.

Effectiveness of the Inductions of Reward and Prestige

In order to establish whether the instructions that were given Ss for purposes of inducing Reward and Prestige conditions were understood and remembered, items were included in a questionnaire which Ss filled out at the end of the last session. An open-ended question asked: 'What did you think your bonus depended on?' Two-thirds of the men who had experienced Group Reward (Grp R) answered appropriately and the rest gave ambiguous replies. Only four men under Individual Reward

(Ind R) stated that the bonus depended on the total group's performance, nine answered appropriately, and the rest appeared somewhat confused about the bonus (probably because just before administering the terminal questionnaire the experimenter had always announced identical bonuses for the four group members).

Three questions dealt with the effectiveness of High Prestige (Hi P) instructions: (1) 'Did you really believe you were specially selected for this job?' (2) 'Were you proud to be a member of this select group?' (3) 'Did it make you try harder than you would have otherwise?' Since perfect candor in replying to these questions was hardly to be expected, it is reassuring that only seven men out of 32 denied any effect at all.

Adequacy of Samples

Tests of effects of heterogeneity in Negro sample. It will be recalled that the Negro sample included Northern-born men, Southerners, and foreigners. Since the treatment subsamples could not be equated on Negro geographic characteristics, it was important to know whether these characteristics affected behavior. For each of the four R–P treatments, groups in which both Negroes were Northern-born were compared by means of *t*-tests with those in which at least one Negro was non-Northern. Tests were made for all important categories of behavior and in no case was *t* significant at the · 10 level.

White Ss' previous acquaintance with Negroes. One of the items in a post-experimental questionnaire that was mailed to white Ss inquired about previous acquaintance with Negroes. Uninformed judges placed replies in four categories, indicating degree of intimacy reported. Mean scores for the four experimental treatments were very similar.

A. Effects of the Ethnic Variable

Predictions were made for Negro-white interactions under 'standard' conditions (Ind R–No P treatment). It was not intended that these hypotheses should be tested by the present experiment alone, since the Ind R–No P subsample had only four groups. Replications are to provide the necessary expansion. None the less, it is of interest to know whether the predictions held for *all treatments combined,* and, if so, whether they held despite the occurrence of the predicted 'favorable' effects of Grp R and Hi P.

It was predicted that Negroes would initiate fewer communications than whites under standard conditions.

Values of *F* for effect of Ethnic (E), Reward (R), and Prestige (P) variables on total amount of communication of all kinds are presented in

Table 1.[4] Negro-white differences (i.e. effects of Ethnic variable) were highly significant on every task. In every case white scores were higher than Negro scores (not shown in Table 1). It is apparent that R and P had little effect on total communication: the only notable F was for R on Erector ($F=4\cdot22$, just short of the $\cdot05$ level of significance). There were three trends toward interaction effects, and on Erector there was a significant triple interaction ($F=6\cdot8$, $p<\cdot05$).[5] Regarding the last, cell means indicated that the greatest differences between Negroes and whites occurred under Ind R–No P and the smallest differences under Grp R–No P.

Table 2 presents Ethnic differences in amount of communication by individual categories and tasks. Vacant cells signify that the category listed to the left was not employed on the task indicated. For all F-ratios greater than $1\cdot0$ white scores were higher than Negro scores (not shown in Table 2). Significant values of F were obtained on 16 out of 25 measures. Except for Spiral, a majority of categories on every task yielded significant differences, thus supporting the prediction when applied to *all* treatments.

Some hypotheses have to do with the social direction of communications—i.e. with the proportion of communications directed to own-race persons and to other-race persons. Of the 25 types of behavior that were used, three were non-targeted. To compare the proportions of own-race and other-race utterances in the remaining 22 categories, it was necessary to devise a suitable score. A simple ratio score was inappropriate

Table 1

Values of F for Effect of Ethnic (E), Reward (R), and
Prestige (P) Variables on Total Amount of Communication of All Kinds

| | | | Task | | |
| | | Human | Stick | Logical | |
Source	Erector	Relations	Puzzles	Problems	Spiral
R	$4\cdot2$a	$<1\cdot0$	$<1\cdot0$	$2\cdot6$	$<1\cdot0$
P	$<1\cdot0$	$<1\cdot0$	$1\cdot3$	$<1\cdot0$	$<1\cdot0$
E	$31\cdot1$c	$22\cdot3$c	$22\cdot0$c	$28\cdot8$c	$8\cdot9$c
R/P	$<1\cdot0$	$1\cdot9$	$<1\cdot0$	$<1\cdot0$	$3\cdot0$a
R/E	$<1\cdot0$	$<1\cdot0$	$<1\cdot0$	$1\cdot5$	$<1\cdot0$
P/E	$1\cdot1$	$2\cdot9$a	$1\cdot2$	$<1\cdot0$	$<1\cdot0$
R/P/E	$6\cdot8$b	$<1\cdot0$	$2\cdot0$	$2\cdot2$	$3\cdot7$a

a. $p<\cdot10$; b. $p<\cdot05$; c. $p<\cdot01$

Table 2
Values of F for Effect of E Variable on Amount
of Communication by Categories

Category	Erector	Human Relations	Task Stick Puzzles	Logical Problems	Spiral
1	—	—	—	—	5·5*
2	14·5**	12·2**	—	9·5**	7·9**
3	8·3**	—	—	—	<1·0
5	—	—	—	—	1·6
7	—	—	—	—	<1·0
13	23·9**	—	—	—	—
14	2·0	—	—	—	—
20	—	—	—	—	<1·0
21	—	—	17·9**	—	—
31	—	14·6**	19·4**	24·4**	—
32	7·8**	14·7**	—	14·4**	—
35	—	8·7**	2·4	5·6*	—
39	<1·0	<1·0	—	1·0	—

$* p < ·05;\ ** p < ·01$

for two reasons: it would not take account of remarks directed to the group as a whole, and it would not take account of the fact that each person had potentially two other-race targets and only one own-race target.

A satisfactory measure of 'bias' in communication, the S-score, was devised by Professor Isidor Chein of New York University. The range of possible S-scores is zero to 100, where 100 indicates the maximum possible ethnocentric bias (all responses are directed to the other person of one's own race), 0 indicates the maximum possible opposite bias (all responses are directed to one or both persons of the other race), and 50 indicates the neutral point (responses are distributed according to random expectation). The main steps in the development of the S-score are described in the Appendix, in order to make clear its rationale. Before the decision to use S-scores was made, it was ascertained by means of chi-square tests of association that S-scores were not related to frequency scores.

It was predicted that under standard conditions Negroes would direct a larger proportion of their nonhostile communications to whites than would whites to Negroes.

Table 3 presents the values of *t* for the mean difference between Negro and white S-scores (all R–P treatments combined) on each of 22 behavior measures. None of the Spiral categories yielded a significant difference. On the four other tasks 14 categories out of 17 revealed differences that were significant beyond $p = \cdot 01$. In all comparisons, including those that did not produce significant differences, white S-scores were higher than Negro S-scores, indicating that whites directed a higher proportion of their remarks to one another than did Negroes to one another. Thus, in general the prediction was amply supported when applied to *all* treatments.

It was predicted that under standard conditions the two white men would be biased in favor of each other as recipients of communications.

This hypothesis was tested by evaluating for every category the difference between the mean S-score and S=50 (random targeting of remarks). In Table 4 are presented the results of *t*-tests for all treatments combined. Supporting the prediction, as applied to all treatments,

Table 3
Values of *t* for Effect of E Variable on S-Scores

Category	Erector	Human Relations	Task Stick Puzzles	Logical Problems	Spiral
1	—	—	—	—	1·4
2	4·2**	6·5**	—	6·8**	1·4
3	1·4	—	—	—	<1·0
5	—	—	—	—	<1·0
13	3·1**	—	—	—	—
14	6·6**	—	—	—	—
20	—	—	—	—	1·2
31	—	3·5**	3·3**	4·5**	—
32	—	3·1**	—	4·6**	—
35	—	3·0**	4·6**	6·1**	—
39	2·6*	5·5**	—	<1·0	—

$* p < \cdot 05; ** p < \cdot 01$

Table 4
Values of t for Tests of 'Bias' in White and Negro S-Scores

	Erector		Human Relations		Stick Puzzles		Logical Problems		Spiral	
Category	W	N	W	N	W	N	W	N	W	N
1	—	—	—	—	—	—	—	—	1·4	<1·0
2	2·2b	4·2c	2·2b	7·6c	—	—	3·6c	6·1c	<1·0	2·3b
3	<1·0	1·1	—	—	—	—	—	—	1·1	<1·0
5	—	—	—	—	—	—	—	—	1·6	<1·0
13	2·3b	3·0c	—	—	—	—	—	—	—	—
14	4·5c	5·0c	—	—	—	—	—	—	—	—
20	—	—	—	—	—	—	—	—	—	1·5
31	—	—	1·2	3·6c	<1·0	4·7c	1·4	5·2c	—	—
32	—	—	<1·0	3·2c	—	—	2·3b	5·1c	—	—
35	—	—	1·4	1·9a	<1·0	6·2c	2·2b	6·6c	—	—
39	1·6	1·8a	<1·0	7·5c	—	—	<1·0	<1·0	—	—

a. $p < ·10$; b. $p < ·05$; c. $p < ·01$

whites were significantly biased—always in favor of each other—on seven out of 22 categories.

Negroes were significantly biased—always in favor of white recipients—on 14 out of 22 categories; two additional categories produced trends toward the same type of bias. The strong tendency of Negroes in all groups to ignore each other in favor of white recipients was an unanticipated finding.

B. Effects of the Reward Variable

Amount of Communication

Frequency scores on 25 behavior measures were evaluated by means of analysis of variance with three variables, R, P, and E. Six types of F-ratio that involved R and P were obtained for each set of scores: R, R/E, P, P/E, R/P, and R/P/E. All values of F that correspond to $p < ·10$ are presented in Table 5. The F-ratios for R alone are appropriate for testing the following:

Table 5

Notable Values of *F* for Effect on Amount of Communication
of R, P, and Their Various Interactions

Category		R	R/E	Source P	P/E	R/P	R/P/E
Erector	2	×	2·9a	×	5·0b	2·9a	×
	3	9·8c	×	×	×	×	8·1c
	13	3·1a	×	×	4·8b	×	6·9b
	14	×	×	×	×	3·6a	×
	32	×	×	8·6c	2·9a	6·3b	×
Hum Rel	2	×	×	3·3a	×	×	×
	31	×	×	×	2·9a	×	×
	39	×	4·7b	6·3b	×	×	×
Sticks	21	4·6b	×	×	×	×	3·5a
	35	×	5·9b	×	×	×	×
Problems	2	5·3b	4·4b	×	×	×	3·8a
	32	4·3b	4·0a	×	×	×	×
Spiral	2	4·3b	×	×	×	×	×
	3	×	×	×	×	×	3·6a
	7	3·3a	×	×	×	×	×
	20	×	5·4b	×	×	×	×

a. $p < ·10$; b. $p < ·05$; c. $p < ·01$

The symbol '×' indicates *F* was below $2·9$ ($p > ·10$). Categories that yielded no notable *F*s are not included in table.

It was predicted that under Grp R, as compared with Ind R, the group as a whole would display more behavior of a task-oriented, cooperative nature, and less behavior that was disruptive.

Five behavior measures revealed significant influence of Grp R, all in support of the prediction: Spiral 2—less rejecting of suggestions; Erector 3—more objective criticism; Sticks 21—more using of puzzle sticks; Problems 2—less rejecting of suggestions; Problems 32—more giving of suggestions, orientation, information. The prediction was further supported by one trend: Erector 13—more helping of others.

One trend appeared to contradict the hypothesis: Spiral 7—more task-irrelevant activity under Grp R.

It was predicted that Ethnic differences in number of communications initiated would be smaller under Grp R than under Ind R.

In Table 5 R/E refers to the differential effect of the R variable on Negro and white scores. The prediction was supported by two significant *F*s: Spiral 20—encourages, praises, reassures (under Grp R Negro scores rose more than did white scores); Problems 2—rejects suggestion (white scores fell more than did Negro scores under Grp R). Two trends were supportive: Erector 2—rejects suggestion, and Problems 32—gives suggestion, etc. In both cases Negro scores rose more than did white scores under Grp R.

Two significant *F*s contradicted the prediction: Hum Rel 39—agrees, and Sticks 35—asks for opinion. On both measures white scores rose more than did Negro scores under Grp R.

Direction of Communications

It was predicted that both Negroes and whites would tend more toward purely random targeting of communications under Grp R than under Ind R.

This hypothesis was tested for each racial subsample separately. The S-scores were converted into deviations from S=50 (purely random choice of recipients), and the deviation scores were submitted to analysis of variance with two variables, R and P. In Table 6 are presented all notable values of *F* for the effect on Negro S-deviation scores of R, P, and R/P. The appropriate *F*s for testing the hypothesis are those based on R. Three significant effects supported the prediction: Erector 13—gives help, Spiral 20—encourages, etc., and Spiral 3—criticizes objectively. In each case there was less favoring of white recipients under Grp R.

In Table 6 are presented the corresponding data for the white subsample. Two trends supported the hypothesis: Erector 13—gives help, and Spiral 3—criticizes objectively. On both categories there was less favoring of own-race recipients under Grp R.

C. Effects of the Prestige Variable

Amount of Communication

It was predicted that under Hi P, as compared with No P, the group as a whole would display more behavior of a task-oriented cooperative nature, and less behavior that was disruptive.

Table 5 presents all *F*-ratios for P that attained the ·10 level of confidence. Two categories revealed significant influence of Hi P on behavior. One case supported the hypothesis: Erector 32—more giving of suggestions, etc. The other was contradictory: Hum Rel 39—less agreeing with suggestions. In addition, there was one contradictory trend: Hum Rel 2—more rejecting of suggestions.

It was predicted that Ethnic differences in number of communications initiated would be smaller under Hi P than under No P.

In Table 5 P/E refers to the differential effect of P on Negro and white scores. Two F-ratios for P/E were significant and two indicated trends. All notable Fs contradicted the hypothesis. In every instance white scores rose more than did Negro scores under Hi P, so that the Ethnic difference was greater. The significant Fs were on Erector 13—gives help, and Erector 2—rejects suggestions. Trends appeared on Erector 32—gives suggestion, etc., and Hum Rel 31—gives opinion.

Direction of Communications

It was predicted that both Negroes and whites would tend more toward purely random targeting of communications under Hi P than under No P.

Referring back to Table 6 it can be seen that three values of F for the effect of P on Negro S-deviation scores were significant. All contradicted the hypothesis in that Negroes favored white recipients more under Hi P: Erector 2—rejects suggestion, Erector 14—asks for help, and Human Relations 39—agrees.

In Table 6 are presented corresponding data for the white subsample. Two F-ratios contradicted the hypothesis, with white men favoring own-race recipients more under Hi P: a trend appeared on Erector 2—rejects suggestion, and a significant effect appeared on Human Relations 39—agrees.

Table 6

Notable Values of F for Effect on Negro and
White S-Deviation Scores of R, P, and R/P

Category		R Negro	R White	P Negro	P White	R/P Negro	R/P White
Erector	2	×	×	5·4b	3·2a	×	×
	13	5·4b	3·3a	×	×	×	×
	14	×	×	4·8b	×	5·8b	5·2b
Hum Rel	39	×	×	9·4c	4·9b	×	×
Problems	31	×	×	×	×	5·3b	×
	35	×	×	×	×	5·0b	3·8a
Spiral	3	4·9a	3·4a	×	×	×	×
	20	4·8b	×	×	×	×	×

a. $p < \cdot 10$; b. $p < \cdot 05$; c. $p < \cdot 01$

The symbol '×' indicates F was below 2·9 ($p > \cdot 10$). Categories that yielded no notable Fs are not included in table.

D. Effects of R/P and R/P/E Interaction

No predictions were made about the interaction of R and P. However, it is implicit in the theoretical assumptions that if interaction *were* to occur it would tend to heighten the effects predicted for R and P separately.

Amount of Communication

Values of *F* for the effect of R/P and R/P/E on amount of communication can be found in Table 5. Only two *F*-ratios for R/P were notable: Erector 32—gives suggestion, etc.; there was a significant interaction in which the Grp R–No P treatment yielded the highest scores. Erector 14 —asks for help; there was a trend to interaction in which the Grp R– No P treatment yielded the highest scores.

Triple interaction, R/P/E, was interpreted as showing the differential effects of R/P interaction on Negro and white scores. Two *F*s for R/P/E were significant: Erector 13—gives help, and Erector 38criticizes objectively. In both cases the Grp R–No P treatment produced the smallest Ethnic differences. Three additional categories produced trends in which Grp R–No P minimized Ethnic differences: Sticks 21—uses sticks, Problems 2—rejects suggestion, and Spiral 3—criticizes objectively.

Direction of Communication

Values of *F* for the effect of R/P on Negro S-deviation scores are in Table 6. Three *F*s were significant. In all cases the least amount of bias in targeting communications occurred in Grp R–No P: Erector 14—asks for help, Problems 31—gives opinion, and Problems 35—asks for suggestion.

Table 6 also shows the effect of R/P on white S-deviation scores. One category produced a significant effect: Erector 14—asks for help. On a second category a trend appeared: Problems 35—asks for suggestion. In both instances white men were least biased in their choice of recipients under Grp R–No P.

Findings on Productivity

It was predicted that productivity would be higher for Grp R than for Ind R and higher for Hi P than for No P. Criteria of productivity were of two sorts: objective measures of output or achievement and observers ratings of performance. With the exception of Ball-and-Spiral none of the differences in group productivity that were associated with R, P, or R/P were significant at or beyond the ·20 level. The difficult Spiral task, with its special 'bet' procedure and deceptive instructions, was designed to test the effects of R and P on a group's ability to cooperate during prolonged

Table 7

Treatment Means and F Ratios for Effect of R, P, and
R/P on Weighted Spiral Scores

| | Treatment Means | | | | F-Ratios | | |
| | Grp R | | Ind R | | | | |
	Hi P	No P	Hi P	No P	R	P	R/P
Period I	7·1	15·5	5·0	3·9	2·96	·86	1·48
Period II	21·1	40·7	13·5	12·0	4·82*	1·25	1·23

$*p<·05$

frustration. The measure of group achievement was the sum of weighted scores for all trials. A trial was defined as a sequence beginning with placement of the ball at the starting point and ending when the ball fell off the track. A group was permitted to undertake as many trials as it could in two thirty-minute periods. The raw score for a single trial was recorded as the highest point reached by the ball. To obtain a score which reflected the relative difficulty of attaining various heights on the spiral, we assigned weights that were inversely proportionate to the total number of times designated heights had been reached by all groups combined. In Table 7 are presented cell means and F-ratios for R, P, and R/P effects in the first and second thirty-minute periods. No significant effects occurred during Period I. In Period II Grp R scores were significantly higher than Ind R scores ($F = 4·82, p<·05$), in accordance with the prediction for Grp R.

DISCUSSION

The Tasks

Classified behavior. With the exception of Ball-and-Spiral, all of the tasks brought forth clear-cut differences in Negro and white behavior, with respect to both amount and direction. When the effects of R and P are considered, it appears that the Erector situation was more sensitive than other tasks to the experimental variations. A total of 19 notable effects ($p<·10$) occurred in Erector, as compared with eight effects in Problems, the next most sensitive situation. The relative dearth of behavior effects in Spiral seemed due to the peculiarly limiting nature of the task; i.e. the movements of the ball appeared to control the direction and content of communications. Why did the remaining tasks—Human Relations, Problems, and Sticks—produce so few R and P effects as compared with Erector? Possibly there were special restraints against Negro communication in these situations that tended to 'blanket' R and P influences. The Human Relations discussions focused attention upon the verbal skills of participants. According to traditional stereotypes these are skills which whites possess more abundantly than Negroes. To the extent that the Negro men had been influenced by these stereotypes they would have felt incompetent as discussants and fearful of being judged unfavorably by white participants. Problems and Sticks appeared to require abstract reasoning and numerical ability. As in the case of Human Relations the relative inactivity of Negroes in these situations can perhaps be explained in terms of their sense of incompetence *vis-à-vis* white *S*s. The latter actually achieved significantly more solutions both on Sticks and Problems. Whether this was due to superior ability on the part of white *S*s or to social factors in the situation could not be ascertained, since no independent measures of ability were available.

Productivity. The only task on which either R or P brought forth reliable group differences in productivity was Spiral. Grp R proved to be superior to Ind R. Three factors would seem to be involved.

First, the task was not intellectual in nature, so that Negroes did not experience ego threat and could enter into the activity with zest. (Even Erector, which next to Spiral was the least intellectual activity, had a 'mental problem' aspect in that it was necessary for *S*s to work out important details of construction that were not clearly shown in the pictures.)

Second, the possible 'cooperative increment' in Spiral performance was very high. Each man experienced total dependence upon his three partners. That a factor of involuntary movement—a kind of 'Ouija Board' phenomenon—was crucial for success seems indicated on various grounds. (1) The manifest reward structure (i.e. the 'bet') was identical for all groups. All *S*s stood to win money by cooperating and to lose money by failing to cooperate; it did not 'make sense' for a man to obstruct his partner's efforts. (2) Ind R groups seemingly tried as hard and as persistently as the more successful Grp R groups. Indeed, the former actually spent less time resting (as shown by a statistical trend on Cat. 7, task-irrelevant activity). (3) Ind R men frequently complained to the experimenter of muscular tension and fatigue.

Third, the Spiral task was frustrating. No group scored a goal during the first half hour, and thereby every man lost 50 cents. Over 90 per cent of all *S*s reported on the terminal questionnaire that they had been frustrated by the task. French (6) has shown that on this task 'unorganized' groups (i.e. groups with low cohesiveness) were more susceptible to the disruptive effects of frustration than 'organized' (high cohesiveness) groups.

Reward and Prestige

Reward. This variable produced 12 significant effects and six trends on behavior, and one significant effect on productivity. Except for two significant effects and one trend on behavior all results were consistent with theoretical predictions. Considering the large number of behavior measures that were employed, the influence of R on social interaction appears to have been fairly restricted. The favorable influence of Grp R was stronger on total group behavior than on ethnic differences. There is the possibility that Grp R introduced additional restraints against Negro communication, as well as the additional forces to communicate that were postulated. Under Grp R the Negro S perceived that he was partly responsible for the fate of white Ss respecting the bonus money. If he felt that his own contribution to the discussion (i.e. the group product) was inadequate, he might actually have experienced more tension and embarrassment than did Negroes under Ind R, who felt responsible only to themselves. The only two instances of unfavorable response by Negroes to Grp R occurred on Human Relations and Sticks (verbal-intellectual tasks).

Prestige. The P variable produced eight significant effects and four trends on social interaction. With the exception of one significant finding all of the data contradicted theoretical expectations. Only two effects had to do with total group scores, all of the remaining results refer to unfavorable effects of Hi P on Ethnic differences in behavior. Why did Hi P exercise an adverse influence upon Negro-white interaction? Back (1) observed that high prestige in all-white, two-man discussion groups produced cautious, ego-protective behavior, with a heightening of the tendency to relations of dominance-submission. In our experiment the individual was informed by the experimenter that he had been specially selected to work in a 'superior' group on the basis of his grades and instructors' recommendations. Most of the white Ss probably experienced some initial fear of rejection by the other white group member. For Negro Ss the threatening features of the situation were undoubtedly much greater, and after work began they received little reassurance that they were, in fact, worthy of being in the *élite* group. The white men tended to ignore them, and to display superior ability on intellectual tasks.

This interpretation of the results is presently being tested in an experiment that induces Hi P in such a manner that it appears to Ss to evolve out of group performance.

Relation of Results to Previous Research

The effects of group reward in homogeneous groups. Deutsch (2) found that group reward influenced social behavior and productivity more favorably than competitive reward in all-white discussion groups. The present experiment has extended these findings in three directions: (1) to bi-racial groups (for some behavior variables); (2) to non-discussion tasks (Erector and Spiral); (3) to group reward *per se*—i.e. to group reward vs. a neutral condition of individual, non-competitive reward.

The effects of status differentials in homogeneous groups. The present experiment has broadened the generality of the status notion by yielding results on bi-racial interaction which are similar to those of experiments on all-white status hierarchies (4, 7, 8).

SUMMARY OF FINDINGS

An experiment was performed in which bi-racial groups, consisting of two Negro college students and two white college students, were given a series of varied tasks to perform. Each four-man group worked a total of about 12½ hours in several sessions. Two types of Reward structure were created, Group Reward and Individual Reward, by means of a special bonus. Also, two conditions of Prestige were utilized, High Group Prestige and No Group Prestige. Each experimental group was subjected to the same Reward-Prestige treatment throughout its employment.

Briefly, it was predicted that in situations of contact: communication characteristics of whites and of Negroes would correspond, respectively, to those of high-status groups and low-status groups in general; and both Group Reward and High Prestige would tend to diminish the effects of status disparity, so that Negro-white differences in frequency and direction of communications would be smaller, and productivity would be higher. The main findings are summarized below.

Ethnic Differences. Over all experimental treatments, on a substantial number of communication categories—

Whites made more remarks than did Negroes;

Negroes spoke more to whites than did whites to Negroes;

Negroes spoke more to whites, proportionately, than to one another;

Whites spoke more to one another, proportionately, than to Negroes.

Reward. In general, relatively few behavior categories were influenced by the Reward variable. Grp R produced favorable effects on the frequency of occurrence of some types of behavior in the groups as wholes.

Ethnic differences in frequency of occurrence of some types of behavior was influenced by R, but not always in the predicted direction.

Grp R produced less favoring of white recipients by Negro and white communicators on some categories.

Grp R gave rise to higher productivity on a task requiring cooperation under continued frustration (Ball-and-Spiral).

Prestige. Prestige had little influence on total group behavior. Its effects on Negro-white differences in behavior were almost as numerous as those of Reward and were uniformly unfavorable: on some categories Hi P produced larger Ethnic differences in amount of communication and more favoring of white recipients by both Negro and white communicators.

R and P Interaction. In several cases of R/P or R/P/E interaction the Grp R–No P treatment seemed to be the most favorable condition for Negro-white communication.

APPENDIX

Professor Chein's S-score provides a measure of the social direction of an individual's communications—i.e. his tendency to favor own-race person or other-race persons as recipients—when the group is composed of two persons from each of two ethnic populations, and when a variable portion of total remarks is directed to the group as a whole. Let

n_1=number of responses directed to person of own race
n_2=number of responses directed to persons of other race
n_3=number of responses directed to group as a whole
$N = n_1 + n_2 + n_3$
$N_1 = n_1 + n_2$

Given: one person of own race; two persons of other race

Then, assuming randomness of response direction to own or other race, the expected value of n_1 is

$$E(n_1) = 1/3 \; N^1$$

and 'bias' is indicated by

$$B = n_1 - E(n_1) = n_1 - \frac{N^1}{3} = \frac{3n_1 - N^1}{3}$$

Relative to the total number of responses the 'bias' is

$$\frac{B}{N} = \frac{3n_1 - N^1}{3N} = \frac{3n_1 - n_1 - n_2}{3N} = \frac{2n_1 - n_2}{3N}$$

$$B\% = \frac{100(2n_1 - n_2)}{3N}$$

$B\%$ is not symmetrical in its score possibilities; it reflects the asymmetry of the experimental situation. To correct for this a new score, S^1 was defined, so that

$S^1 = B\%/2$ if $B\%$ is positive, and
$S^1 = B\%$ if $B\%$ is negative

A further transformation yields a score, S, such that the range of possible scores is from 0 to 100, where 100 indicates the maximum possible ethnocentric bias (all responses are directed to the other person of one's own race), 0 indicates the maximum possible opposite bias (all responses are directed to one or both persons of other race), and 50 indicates the neutral point (responses are divided exactly according to random expectation). The transformation is

$$S = 1 \cdot 5(S^1) + 50$$

Notes

[1]This research was carried out under Contract Nonr-285 (24) between the Office of Naval Research and New York University. The project is under the direction of Irwin Katz.

[2]At the time of publication of this article, Irwin Katz was an Associate Professor in the Department of Psychology at New York University, where he had been since 1950. He obtained his Ph.D. in social psychology at Stanford University in 1949. From 1948 to 1950 he taught at the University of Buffalo and served as a psychological consultant to the Board of Community Relations of the City of Buffalo. He is the author of *Conflict and Harmony in an Adolescent Interracial Group*, published by New York University Press in 1955.

Judith Goldston was a research psychologist at the New York Respirator and Rehabilitation Center of New York University—Bellevue Hospital. She was a graduate student in social psychology at New York University and a former Woodrow Wilson Fellow.

Lawrence Benjamin was a graduate student in clinical psychology at New York University and the holder of a United States Public Health Service training scholarship.

[3]Sociometric, attitudinal, and personality data are to appear in another report.

[4]The analysis of variance might appear to violate the assumption of independence, since the Ethnic variable involved two sets of scores, white and Negro, from the same groups. However, the actual correlations (Rho) between white and Negro scores in the 16 experimental groups approximated zero in most cases, and never achieved the $\cdot 05$ level of significance. Moreover, these were inflated estimates of correlation, inasmuch as the 16 groups were drawn from four distinctive R–P treatments.

[5]Throughout, 'trend' refers to cases of $p < \cdot 10 > \cdot 05$, and 'significant result' refers to cases of $p < \cdot 05$.

References

1. Back, K. Influence Through Social Communication. *J. abn. soc. Psychol.*, 1951, Vol. 46, pp. 9-23.
2. Deutsch, M. The Effects of Cooperation and Competition upon Group Processes. In D. Cartwright and A. Zander (Eds.), *Group Dynamics*, Evanston, Ill.: Row, Peterson, 1953; London: Tavistock Publications, 1954.
3. French, J. R. P., Jr. The Disruption and Cohesion of Groups. In D. Cartwright and A. Zander (Eds.), *Group Dynamics*, Evanston, Ill.: Row, Peterson, 1953; London: Tavistock Publications, 1954.
4. Hurwitz, J. I., Zander, A. F. and Hymovitch, B. Some Effects of Power on the Relations among Group Members. In D. Cartwright and A. Zander (Eds.), *Group Dynamics*, Evanston, Ill.: Row, Peterson, 1953; London: Tavistock Publications, 1954.

5. Katona, G. *Organizing and Memorizing,* New York: Columbia Univ. Press, 1940.
6. Katz, I. *Conflict and Harmony in An Adolescent Interracial Group,* New York: New York Univ. Press, 1955.
7. Kelley, H. Communication in Experimentally Created Hierarchies. In D. Cartwright and A. Zander (Eds.), *Group Dynamics,* Evanston, Ill.: Row, Peterson, 1953; London: Tavistock Publications, 1954.
8. Tribaut, J. An Experimental Study of the Cohesiveness of Underprivileged Groups. In D. Cartwright and A. Zander (Eds.), *Group Dynamics,* Evanston, Ill.: Row, Peterson, 1953; London: Tavistock Publications, 1954.

Minority Leadership and Competition 2

Leadership is the process by which one individual influences the behavior of another person or group. Most organizations have recognized the importance of leadership in achieving overall performance effectiveness. An important consideration among today's managers is determining the type of leadership that can lead to high levels of individual, group, and organizational effectiveness.

With the recent attention that a number of organizations have given to affirmative action and equal opportunity, especially in the 1960s and early 1970s, the employment of minority-group members in supervisory- and management-level positions has increased. However, the experiences of these minority-group managers often leave something to be desired. The articles in Part Two illustrate, to some degree, the nature of the problems encountered by blacks in positions of supervision over white subordinates and their means of coping with their situations.

The first reading in Part Two demonstrates the importance of nonwork-related behaviors of black supervisors in their performance evaluations by their employers. Performance evaluations of black supervisors were found not to be related to the job-related behaviors they exhibited. Rather, an employer's perception of a black supervisor's social behavior tended to be the most determining factor in evaluating his job performance.

The second article is an informative, thought-provoking discussion of managerial-leadership failure within neighborhood opportunity centers established during the "War on Poverty" era. A prime dysfunctional factor in many of the centers' operations was the lack of managerial skills exhibited by their indigenous leaders. The authors recommend a project management approach as an organizational strategy for the neighborhood opportunity centers, providing an alliance between indigenous leadership and professional expertise.

The final article, a testimonial of a black man hired into a white man's job, illustrates the fact that equal opportunity coupled with low support is *still* discrimination, and it provides some insight into the ramifications and implications of racial differences in organizations.

Blacks as Supervisors:
A Study of Training, Job Performance, and Employers' Expectations[1]

RICHARD W. BEATTY[2]

This study of a training program designed for the development of black supervisors investigated the relationship of several training and nontraining variables with employers' evaluations of black supervisors' job performance. The results indicated that employers tended to evaluate performance not on factors related to program content or on task-related behaviors, but on other behaviors black supervisors demonstrated while at work.

Today many organizations are involved in some facet of the hiring, training, and promotion of minority workers. However, as Hinrichs (10) suggests, there appears to be only a very minimum of adequate research being published concerning minority employment which could be used as a base for the design of training programs, despite the considerable expenditures of federal and state governments and research foundations. One area, in particular, which appears to be quite neglected is information on the training and performance of minority employees in first-level supervisory positions. Part of the paucity of data on minority supervisors is a result of the manner of reporting by the Census Bureau, which combines foremen with "craftsmen and other kindred workers" (7,13) and does not separate them in such a way that a more comprehensive analysis can be conducted. The need for research on minority supervisors is essential, as is the need for research on other minority problems, if the program design for future efforts to develop

---

Reprinted from *Academy of Management Journal,* 1973, *16*(2), 196-206, by permission of the publisher and the author.

and promote members of minority groups into managerial positions is to be founded upon an empirical base rather than upon social scientists' preconceptions of the needs of minority groups (6).

During the spring of 1971 a training program supported by federal, state, and foundation funds was undertaken to prepare Negro employees for first-level supervisory positions.[3] The present study explores (a) the extent to which this program fulfilled its stated objectives of developing certain supervisory attitudes and cognitive skills, (b) the importance of these attitudes and skills to employers' evaluations of the trainees' supervisory performance, and (c) the nature of the criteria actually used by employers in their performance ratings.

The Training Program

The 48 participants were recruited through industries in metropolitan St. Louis. Of the original 37 men and 11 women, 44 completed the training program.

The first of the program's two phases was a three-day retreat composed largely of affective content using a sensitivity training format under the leadership of a black trainer. The participants explored the emotions and attitudes associated with their roles as managers of both black and white subordinates. The second phase consisted of classroom training—a total of 16 hours during a four-week period—in traditional cognitive first-level supervisory skills such as problem-solving techniques, motivating and training subordinates, and developing positive subordinate attitudes. Role-play techniques, case studies, and lectures were utilized by the four classroom instructors (three white and one black). All instructors participated in the sensitivity training sessions.

Research Procedures and Findings

The research design, following the suggestion of Martin (14), used both internal and external criteria to evaluate the program. Internal measures were defined as those directly linked to the activities of the training program; external measures were designed to assess actual on-the-job behavior.

Two internal measures were used. The first device, the Leadership Opinion Questionnaire (LOQ), is widely used in industry to measure supervisory attitudes by employing a scale for recording information about supervisory consideration and initiation of structure (17). An individual's *consideration* score purports to reflect the degree of trust, respect for ideas, and regard for feelings that characterize his relationships with his subordinates. The individual's score for *initiating structure* involves a supervisor's acts oriented toward defining or structuring the work group toward getting work done and toward goal attainment.

Participants completed the LOQ both before and after the training program. The trainees' LOQ scores were in the "average" range for other groups of supervisory personnel (2), but an analysis of responses (Table 1) revealed that changes during the period of the training program in both consideration and initiating structure were not statistically significant.

A second internal device sought to measure the development of "supervisory skills," [4] or knowledge of supervisory techniques as a result of the classroom phase of the program. To measure this cognitive dimension the Supervisory Inventory on Human Relations (SIHR), was administered to the participants both before and after the training program. The SIHR (1,9,11) measures knowledge of supervisory topics such as problem solving, developing positive employee attitudes, and understanding, motivating, and training employees. Each of these topics was specifically discussed in the classroom, thus establishing content validity of the SIHR as a device for assessing this phase.

The SIHR responses indicated significant increases in the trainees' comprehension of supervisory concepts and techniques (Table 2). However, a breakdown of the overall instrument into specific topics demonstrated that the major increases could be attributed to subjects concerning understanding and motivating employees, and to learning and training (Table 3). These topics together accounted for 65 percent of the SIHR questions.

The first of three external measures was obtained by requesting the trainee's employer to indicate on a Likert-type scale his judgment of the trainee's overall supervisory performance.[5] The posttraining performance ratings were then correlated with both pre and posttraining LOQ and SIHR scores. No significant relationships were found (Table 4), which appeared to indicate that the content of the training program had little to do with employer opinions of the trainees' success as supervisors.

Table 1
Changes on the Leadership Opinion Questionnaire $(N=44)$

Measure	Pretraining		Posttraining		t-score
	$\overline{X}$	σ	$\overline{X}$	σ	
Consideration	49.56	8.00	51.49	7.88	1.13
Structure	52.28	7.74	50.30	9.86	−1.03

Table 2

Changes on the Supervisory Inventory on Human Relations ($N=44$)

Pretraining		Posttraining		t-score
$\overline{X}$	σ	$\overline{X}$	σ	
54.97	11.94	60.11	8.15	2.30*

*$p<.05$

Table 3

Analysis of Subscales of Supervisory
Inventory on Human Relations ($N=44$)

Measure	Number of Questions	Pretraining Percentage of Correct Responses	Posttraining Percentage of Correct Responses	χ^2
Supervisor's role in management	13	69.7	75.0	1.57
Understanding and motivating employees	39	71.3	77.2	6.06**
Principles of learning and training	13	54.1	63.9	5.48**
Developing positive employee attitudes	10	66.5	74.5	2.78
Problem solving techniques	5	88.6	90.9	.11

**$p<.01$

The next task was to use two additional external instruments to discover what task-related behaviors (employers' perceptions of job-related activities) and social behaviors (employers' perceptions of personal and interpersonal attributes) actually were important to employers in their evaluations of black supervisors. Subsequently, each employer was asked to rate his trainee on a series of Likert-type scales designed to record these behaviors. Task-related behaviors included leading and motivating subordinates, making accurate and fair decisions, placing and assigning subordinates, training and developing subordinates, and assisting subordinates in problem solving. The social behaviors measured included acceptance by others, example set for others, self-confidence, friendliness, and open-mindedness.

Table 4

Correlations of Performance with Consideration, Initiating
Structure, Supervisory Inventory on Human Relations
and for SIHR Subscales ($N=22$)

Measure	Pretraining	Posttraining	Reliability of Pre to Posttesting
Consideration	−.31	−.30	.52**
Structure	.08	−.04	.76***
SIHR	−.11	.14	.63***
Subscales:			
Supervisor's role in management	−.25	.20	.39*
Understanding and motivating employees	−.10	.20	.57**
Principles of learning and training	.04	.10	.59**
Developing positive employee attitudes	−.12	.14	.44*
Problem solving techniques	.02	−.35	.40*

*$p<.05$ **$p<.01$ ***$p<.001$

As Table 5 indicates many of the task-related and social behaviors
were strongly related to employers' evaluations of black supervisors' job
performance. However, the task-related behaviors were not related to
the training program's content as demonstrated by insignificant correlations with the major topic areas of the SIHR. In other words, the
supervisor's classroom scores on cognitive content areas such as problem
solving were not associated with the employer's appraisal of the supervisor's task behavior on the same or similar topics. The social behaviors
also failed to show a relationship either with the program's cognitive
content or with consideration and initiating structure. Thus, to explore
the possibility that employers' evaluations of task-related and social behaviors might be relatively independent of the other variables measured,
a factor analysis was conducted.

The method of factor analysis used was a varimax rotation with the
number of factors determined by Guttman's lower-bound theorem
which demonstrated that factors with eigen values having roots less than
one (1.0) were statistically insignificant. Together the five factors which
met this criterion explained 78.6 percent of the total variance.

Table 5

Employers' Evaluation of Supervisors' Task-Related and Social Behaviors Correlated with Performance, Consideration, Initiating Structure and Supervisory Inventory on Human Relations ($N=22$)

Measure	Performance	Consideration		Structure		SIHR		Supervisor's Role	
		Pre	Post	Pre	Post	Pre	Post	Pre	Post
Task-Related Behaviors									
Ability to lead and motivate subordinates	.69***	.00	−.29	.24	.10	−.11	.08	−.17	.15
Ability to make accurate and fair decisions	.48**	.02	−.25	−.01	.06	−.12	−.17	−.20	−.10
Ability to place and assign subordinates	.47**	−.15	−.27	.35	.00	−.34	−.18	−.35	.00
Ability to train and develop subordinates	.16	−.26	−.28	.11	.00	−.26	−.20	−.21	−.03
Ability to assist subordinates in problem solving	.49**	−.15	−.27	.35	.00	−.34	−.18	−.35	.00
Social Behaviors									
Acceptance by others	.52**	.13	.11	.05	−.14	−.13	.00	−.25	−.10
Personal example set for others	.69***	−.21	−.24	.03	−.10	−.12	.02	−.35	.00
Self-confidence	.60**	−.13	−.15	.08	.05	.02	−.07	−.11	−.13
Friendliness and personal interest in others	.59**	−.05	.07	−.03	−.05	−.16	−.11	−.31	−.27
Open-mindedness to other's suggestions and opinions	.38*	.33	.17	−.02	−.24	−.19	−.10	−.19	−.11

*$p<.05$ **$p<.01$ ***$p<.001$

Table 5 (Continued)

Measure	Understanding & Motivating		Learning & Training		Positive Attitudes		Problem Solving	
	Pre	Post	Pre	Post	Pre	Post	Pre	Post
Task-Related Behaviors								
Ability to lead and motivate subordinates	−.14	.16	.23	.09	−.07	.00	−.13	−.33
Ability to make accurate and fair decisions	−.17	−.08	.13	−.21	.00	.04	.00	.04
Ability to place and assign subordinates	−.15	−.08	−.04	−.25	−.27	−.07	−.12	−.47*
Ability to train and develop subordinates	−.27	−.13	−.10	−.21	−.18	−.12	−.33	−.18
Ability to assist subordinates in problem solving	−.39*	−.14	−.03	.02	−.39*	−.25	−.22	−.27
Social Behaviors								
Acceptance by others	−.10	.07	.04	−.10	−.15	.23	−.06	−.20
Personal example set for others	−.13	.04	.12	.02	−.12	.12	−.08	−.40*
Self-confidence	−.02	.08	.20	−.07	.02	.09	.18	.26
Friendliness and personal interest in others	−.22	−.05	.02	−.01	−.08	.11	−.10	−.08
Open-mindedness to other's suggestions and opinions	−.24	−.02	−.14	−.17	−.01	−.03	−.01	−.21

*$p<.05$ **$p<.01$ ***$p<.001$

The factor analysis (Table 6) provided interesting results. The five factors obtained were named social behavior (I), consideration (II), structure (III), knowledge of supervisory techniques (IV), and task-related behaviors (V) respectively. Not only did these factors confirm the expected independence of consideration, structure, and knowledge of supervisory techniques from the task-related and social behaviors, it also indicated that the task-related and social behavior variables were somewhat independent of one another. Furthermore, the job performance variable was loaded heaviest on the social behavior factor which indicated that an employer's perception of a black supervisor's social behavior tended to be the most important influence in evaluating a black supervisor.

Because the factor analysis demonstrated the relative independence of the five factors, and because the job performance variable was more heavily loaded on an employer's perception of a black supervisor's social

Table 6

Rotated Factor Loadings for Personal Behaviors, Task-Related Behaviors, Consideration, Initiating Structure, Supervisory Inventory on Human Relations, and Performance Evaluations

Scale	Factor				
	I	II	III	IV	V
Ability to lead and motivate subordinates	.56	−.12	−.05	−.10	.57
Ability to make accurate and fair decisions	.55	.07	−.18	.04	.69
Ability to place and assign subordinates	.41	.05	.07	.19	.58
Ability to train and develop subordinates	.37	.19	.11	.24	.59
Ability to assist subordinates in problem solving	.43	.06	.19	.19	.51
Acceptance by others	.71	.30	.00	.02	.49
Personal example set for others	.78	.09	−.10	.00	.30
Self-Confidence	.86	−.11	−.03	−.07	.10
Friendliness and personal interest in others	.70	−.06	−.12	.14	.48
Open mindedness to other's suggestions and opinions	.52	.58	−.21	.16	.08
LOQ—Consideration (before training)	.00	.82	−.21	−.04	.28
LOQ—Consideration (after training)	−.11	.76	−.22	−.22	.45
LOQ—Structure (before training)	.02	−.05	.94	−.01	.12
LOQ—Structure (after training)	−.01	.38	.81	.02	.00
SIHR (before training)	−.11	.01	−.16	−.89	.07
SIHR (after training)	−.03	.08	.16	−.89	−.03
Job Performance	.77	.02	−.11	.11	.42

behaviors than upon the supervisor's knowledge of supervisory techniques or the supervisor's task-related behaviors, it was concluded that for a black supervisor to be perceived as successful by an employer it would certainly be helpful for new black supervisors to be aware of the impact that his/her personal and interpersonal attributes may have upon an employer. This conclusion supports many of the "cultural awareness" programs now being used to train the hard-core unemployed in preparation for jobs in primarily white organizations and is consistent with the findings of Senger (16) which indicate that performance evaluations are composed largely of the value orientations of the evaluator.

Policy Implications

What kinds of policy recommendations can be made from a study which indicates that if blacks are given traditional management training which brings about significant cognitive change, and transfer such cognitive changes into on-the-job behaviors, there is little relationship between these behaviors and performance evaluations? If management agrees upon or designs the content of the program and if supervisors have learned the program content, then if evaluations do not correlate with the content variables, the problem cannot be related to the training program, or to the black supervisor, but must be related to the criterion being used by evaluators.

Obviously, this is not a new problem; as every good personnel administrator knows, the measure of any testing instrument or any training program depends upon the prior establishment of *valid* criteria for evaluation. The recent *Griggs* decision of the U.S. Supreme Court concerning the relationship between tests and job-related criteria (8) not only highlights the problem as a crucial management issue, but it brings the issue into the legal arena. As a result of this decision more immediate remedies may be demanded if subjectivity or capriciousness explains as much of the variance in performance evaluation criteria as indicated here. Thus the measure of job performance is as important, if not more important, than the testing issue which the court was addressing. Such measures are bound to come under considerable scrutiny if, as this study suggests, measures of criterion variables may currently be as abstract and ambiguous as the tests the Court was examining in the *Griggs* decision.

In light of all this, what might a company do to ensure fair employment practices, which help minority groups move upward within the organization, while at the same time being fair to itself by promoting employees who can and will make greater contributions to the organization? The results demonstrated here suggest three possible alternatives:

1. Continue to train minority personnel for supervisory positions by training in traditional management skills.
2. Train minority supervisors in the interpersonal skills necessary to determine the evaluator's subjective demands.
3. Mutual adaptation of both organizations and minority supervisors.

The first alternative would be to train blacks in management skills despite the possible subjectivity of the criteria currently used in performance evaluations. This choice has obvious advantages for the company because if the skills acquired by supervisors lead to greater supervisory efficiency and effectiveness the organization is to benefit. However, it appears to be unfair to the black supervisor in that the effort expended both in learning new skills and in on-the-job application of these skills may not be linked to job performance evaluations and the commensurate benefits of salary increases, promotions, etc.

The second alternative would be to ignore the training of blacks in formal managerial skills but to train them in the interpersonal skills necessary to determine the actual, and perhaps subjective, criteria upon which they are being evaluated. This type of training would provide black supervisors the skills to explore with their evaluators actual job demands, what they must do in order to prepare themselves to meet these demands, and the rewards offered for demand compliance. Perhaps a format which concentrates upon overt recognition of the behaviors expected of minority personnel is appropriate in the sense that the actual job demands become better understood, the reward contingencies clarified, and hopefully the subtleties of discrimination minimized. Such a social exchange approach to training minority workers in the essential interpersonal behaviors required by the job context has been suggested previously by Nord (15) who noted the advantage of helping blacks recognize the criteria necessary for them to receive the benefits the organization has to offer. However, this alternative also has the potential disadvantage of not providing for congruence between the subjective demand requirements and the necessary contributions managers need to make for optimum organizational growth and prosperity.

The third alternative follows the suggestions of Friedlander and Greenberg (4) and Triandis and Malpass (18), who suggest that mutual adaptation on the part of both minority employees and employing organizations is essential for satisfying the needs of both groups. This alternative would require the company to clearly specify the task demands of all jobs and the job-related behaviors which contribute to the organization's purpose, and to use these as criterion variables. Minority supervisors then would be trained in the managerial skills necessary to meet criterion demands as well as receive training in the interpersonal skills that would enable them to determine what subjective demands an evaluator is placing upon them. There are several benefits of this alternative. It aids the company by attempting to specify behavior which contributes to company objectives, and then evaluating and rewarding that behavior once it is demonstrated. The black supervisor also benefits because managerial skill training is now designed to meet a specific end—objective criteria for performance evaluations—and he also is prepared with the interpersonal skills needed to cope with whatever subjective components of evaluation that remain.

Summary and Conclusions

The most important implication from this study is that it highlights an age-old problem—the criterion used to evaluate the performance of a manager. Despite the *Griggs* decision and the legal impetus given to the need for relevant selection and performance criteria, there appears to be a very large subjective component in the evaluation of supervisors, especially if they are black. Therefore, the recommendations indicated here attempt to serve the purposes of both an organization and minority supervisors. These recommendations suggest that organizations concentrate upon clearly defining the actual performance expectations necessary for successful organizational functioning, communicating these expectations explicitly to minority supervisors, and holding these supervisors accountable for performance on these criteria. At the same time, the organization must recognize that the social dynamics of the superior-subordinate evaluation has a high probability of subjectivity, particularly if the superior and subordinate are from different cultures. To deal with this bias it may be helpful for minority personnel to be trained in interpersonal skills whereby subjective criteria are made more obvious. These skills would help give explicit recognition to subtle job demands, which may be extraneous to the specific task but critical for his/her organizational survival.

The suggestions made above hopefully are realistic in the sense of attempting to reduce the amount of ambiguity that can exist and serve as a barrier to success on any job for any person, regardless of race. What these proposals offer then is a means of improving organizational performance by focusing upon task performance and actual contribution as well as a means of helping minorities move up more rapidly in the organization. Obviously, these recommendations can help any organization and any individual improve performance and become "successful." However, it is unfortunate that it has taken the experiences of minority employees to reiterate the apparent ambiguity and subjectivity of performance evaluation. If there had been more concentration on identifying and rewarding actual job performance, not only might the problems of discrimination have been reduced, but also other deserving people might be reaping the rewards that organizations have to offer.

Notes

[1] The author would like to thank the Extension Division of the University of Missouri, St. Louis, for their cooperation in presenting the program and Jane Warren for her helpful comments on earlier drafts of this paper.

[2] Richard W. Beatty was Assistant Professor of Organizational Behavior at the University of Colorado, Boulder, Colorado, at the time of publication of this article. He obtained his Ph.D. at Washington University.

[3] This training program was funded under Title I of the Higher Education Act of the Department of Health, Education and Welfare, in cooperation with the Danforth Foundation and the Missouri Department of Community Affairs.

[4] In order to distinguish between skills and abilities, Fleishman's (3) definitions were used. The term skills here reflects a level of proficiency while ability implies a relatively enduring trait.

[5] Because no trainee occupied a supervisory position until after the program, it was not possible to determine the changes between pretraining and posttraining ratings of supervisory performance which could be used to assess the direct on-the-job impact of the training.

References

1. Behling, Gerald L. *A Study of Validation of the Supervisory Inventory on Human Relations* (Master's thesis, University of Wisconsin, 1959).
2. Fleishman, Edwin A. *Manual, Leadership Opinion Questionnaire* (Chicago: Science Research Associates, 1960).
3. Fleishman, Edwin A. "Individual Differences and Motor Learning," in Robert M. Gagné (Ed.), *Learning and Individual Differences* (Columbus: Merrill, 1967).
4. Friedlander, Frank, and Stuart Greenberg. "Effect of Job Attitudes, Training, and Organizational Climate on Performance of the Hard-Core Unemployed," *Journal of Applied Psychology,* Vol. 55 (1971), 287-295.
5. Ghiselli, Edwin E. "Managerial Talent," *American Psychologist,* Vol. 18 (1963), 631-641.
6. Gordon, Jesse E. "What Shapes Poverty Programs," *Manpower,* Vol. 3, No. 4 (April 1971).
7. Gourley, Jack G. *The Negro Salaried Worker* (New York: American Management Association, 1965).
8. *Griggs vs. Duke Power Company,* 91 Supreme Court 849 (1971), *Supreme Court of the United States,* No. 124, 1-12.
9. Hand, Herbert H., and John W. Slocum, Jr., "Human Relations Training for Middle Management: A Field Experiment," *Academy of Management Journal,* Vol. 13 (1970), 403-410.
10. Hinrichs, John R. "Psychology of Men at Work," *Annual Review of Psychology,* Vol. 21 (1970), 519-554.
11. Kirkpatrick, Donald L. *Manual, Supervisory Inventory on Human Relations* (Madison, Wis.: 1967).

12. Korman, Abraham K. "Consideration, Initiating Structure and Organizational Criteria: A Review," *Personnel Psychology,* Vol. 19 (1966), 349-363.
13. Marshall, Ray F. *The Negro Worker* (New York: Random House, 1967).
14. Martin, Herbert O. "The Assessment of Training," *Personnel Management,* Vol. 39 (1957), 88-93.
15. Nord, Walter R. "The Fault Dear Brutus Lies Not in Ourselves But in Our Contingencies: The Application of Exchange Theory to Rehabilitation and the Disadvantaged," in *Rehabilitation, Sheltered Workshops, and the Disadvantaged: An Exploration in Manpower Policy.* (Ithaca, N.Y.: Region II, Rehabilitation Research Institute, New York School of Industrial and Labor Relations, Cornell University, 1970).
16. Senger, John. "Managers' Perceptions of Subordinates' Competence as a Function of Personal Value Orientations," *Academy of Management Journal,* Vol. 14 (1971), 415-423.
17. Stogdill, Ralph M., and Alvin E. Coons (Eds.). *Leader Behavior: Its Description and Measurement* (Columbus: Bureau of Business Research, Ohio State University, 1957).
18. Triandis, Harry C., and Roy S. Malpass. "Studies of Black and White Interaction in Job Settings," *Journal of Applied Social Psychology,* Vol. 1 (1971), 101-117.

The Myth of the Indigenous Community Leader

A Case Study of Managerial Effectiveness Within the "War on Poverty"

ANDRÉ L. DELBECQ[1]
SIDNEY J. KAPLAN

This article presents a detailed description of managerial leadership failure within "War on Poverty" Centers. To overcome leadership "pitfalls," a task-force organization structure is proposed to deal with urban-problem complexities, and to capitalize on unique but selective strengths of Negro managers.

PROGRAM EFFECTIVENESS AND POVERTY LEADERSHIP

In September, 1965, the War on Poverty was formally declared and funded for Midwestern City's regional area.[2] The core of the organizational strategy for community action was the establishment of four Neighborhood Opportunity Centers. Each Center served a geographical area characterized by a severe "poverty syndrome." The purpose of the Centers was: 1) the provision of referral services and 2) program design and community action.[3] (Figure 1 provides an organization chart for the Centers.) One year later, September, 1966, the War on Poverty as conducted by the Neighborhood Opportunity Centers was characterized by apathy, low morale, and a shared feeling of organizational failure.

The purpose of this paper is not to assess the totality of the causes contributing to the demise of effectiveness within the NOC's.[4] Rather, our purpose is to examine the nature of the managerial leadership within the NOC's in order to understand the interrelation between this leadership and organizational deterioration in the Centers. The observations raise some serious questions concerning the viability of the concept

Reprinted from *Academy of Management Journal*, 1968, *11*, 11-25, by permission of the publisher and the authors.

Figure 1

Organization Chart—Neighborhood Opportunity Centers

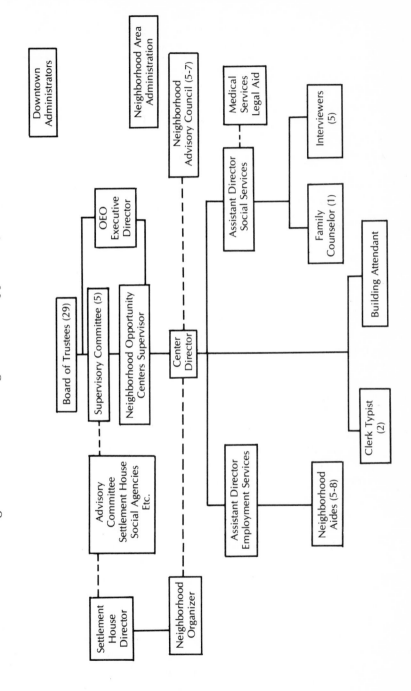

Table 1
Hindrances to Social Change and Program Implementation
(Cited by NOC Personnel)

Personal Conflicts with Leaders (Social-Emotional)	18
Lack of Effective Task-Instrumental Leadership	39
Conflicts Between Subordinate Staff Members	10
All Other Causes	68

Justification for concern with "leadership" as a central causal variable in the demise of organizational effectiveness can be hinted at from Table 1. This table deals with Hindrances to Social Change and Program Implementation taken from questionnaires administered to 44 of the total of 48 subordinates in the Neighborhood Opportunity Centers. Of hindrances cited, fifty-seven or forty-two percent deal directly with leadership inadequacy. For greater statistical detail and analysis of other sources of program failure, see the forthcoming article by the authors: "Perceived Hindrances to Social Change."

of the "indigenous community leader"—the "natural" leader from within an impoverished neighborhood who is to provide *the* managerial leadership in the war against the forces of poverty.

THE INDIGENOUS LEADER CONCEPT

One of the unique characteristics of the original concept of the War on Poverty was the involvement of the poor themselves in their struggle against poverty. Neighborhood Opportunity Center leadership at the director and assistant director level was to be selected from among "indigenous" college-trained residents of the local community served by NOC's.

Several benefits were sought in selecting this leadership. First, it was felt that nonwhite individuals who were members of the local community (for the most part nonwhite) would be more readily accepted as spokesmen for the poor. Second, it was felt that such "indigenous" leaders would be in touch with and sensitive to the realities of living within the inner-city. Third, it was hoped that innovative solutions would be forthcoming from these personnel which would not repeat the failures of former "welfare" approaches to poverty.[5] How successful was this strategy of chosing "indigenous" leadership? What was the degree of their administrative effectiveness in leading the newly created organization in social reform and change?

To answer the above questions, we will examine the ability of directors and assistant directors (1) to provide functional leadership *within* their Centers by

    a) maintaining personal prominence and dominance,

    b) contributing to task accomplishment, and

    c) maintaining a desirable social-emotional climate within their Centers; and

(2) by assessing their leadership *outside* their Centers in terms of

    a) legitimating their Center programs to both the downtown OEO (Office of Economic Opportunity) officials and NOC advisory boards, and

    b) representing their staff "upward" to the OEO hierarchy.[6]

AN ASSESSMENT OF "INDIGENOUS" LEADERSHIP WITHIN THE CENTERS

Maintaining Individual Prominence and Dominance

The "indigenous" leaders faced two difficult problems in maintaining their leadership centrality within their centers. The first problem was one of social-distance and ascribed status. The second related to task-instrumental competence.

In the first problem area, the "indigenous" Negro leadership suffered from prior overexposure within the Negro community. A global personal "stereotype" associated with each of the "indigenous" Center directors and assistant directors seemed to exist. In general, the reputation of each of the Negro administrators tended to be described by employees in terms of his general image within the Negro community (based on familial, social-interpersonal, and sexual behavior). Thus, their image was based in part on life history items and personality idiosyncracies as manifested in behavior prior to the assumption of managerial leadership within the Centers.

The propensity for some separation between "work" behavior and "personal" behavior in conversations concerning a manager—a separation which is typical of middle class assessment of managerial performance[7] —was often absent in the treatment of the "indigenous" administrator in conversations with members of the NOC staffs.[8]

Contributing to Task Accomplishment

Since "indigenous" leaders found it difficult to obtain legitimacy on the basis of ascribed status, for reasons just indicated, there was considerable vying for status and power by means of domination of decision making within the Centers. Here again, however, indigenous leaders faced difficulties. To begin with, the educational and work experience background of the "indigenous" directors and assistant directors did not claim for them the right to dominate the decision processes on the basis of personal expertise. The educational background of the leaders was suspect from several standpoints. First, excepting one director with an M.S.W., the degree of educational attainment (college degrees or partial work toward degrees) was not exceptional relative to the total culture. Second, subordinates often felt that their lesser educational accomplishments were a function of circumstances, rather than a function of differences in ability. Finally, none of the indigenous leaders had training or experience perceived as directly related to the conceptualization and development of proposals for structural reformation of neighborhoods.[9]

Under these circumstances it is not surprising that the directors found themselves in vigorous disagreement with assistant directors, assistant directors with directors, and subordinate staff members with both. Unfortunately, although not surprisingly,[10] two mechanisms for the resolution of this disagreement were generally resorted to: 1) coalition formation, and 2) authority of office. The assistant directors formed coalitions with members of lower echelons in an attempt to pressure the directors into accepting proposals. The directors, viewing coalitions as a threat to their own authority, responded by vetoing proposals on the basis of authority of office. Assistant directors subsequently attempted to by-pass their directors by appealing to the downtown NOC Supervisor for support. Directors, in turn, sought support from selected advisory board members and "put the young turks" into place by closing down open discussion. Directors jointly instituted highly formalized channels for the approval of proposals; the channels contained multiple opportunities for veto.[11]

However, not all the problems of maintaining leadership legitimacy in terms of task accomplishment related to vigorous disagreement with assistant directors. Interviewers, and to an even greater extent, neighborhood aides tended to be activists. They had joined the "War on Poverty" with militant aspirations and desired immediate action— particularly action involving social protest in the form of marches and rallies. To the directors, such demonstrations were problematic since: 1) they represented the last course of action to be taken only after all other courses of action had been closed; 2) such protest action needed to be carefully planned and defended; 3) the downtown office took a dim view of demonstrations and would likely veto them anyway; and 4) for some directors, the whole notion of protest in the streets was "unprofessional." As a result, the directors wanted to hold aides and interviewers to more conventional courses of action.

There were, however, two problems in doing so. First, the aides were hired as "street contacts." As such, their very communication style in dealing with the hard-core made them inept in dealing with middle-class channels of negotiation and discussion. Second, the director himself was often unable to conceive of a sequence of steps necessary to build a viable proposal around which "middle-class" negotiations would center.

As a result, the director was perceived as conservative and unwilling to take the issue to the people, and at the same time as lacking the necessary skills to make his attempt at more moderate negotiation and discussion with community leaders pay off.

There was, in addition, a confounding problem. None of the directors had held prior administrative positions involving negotiation and conflict management. As a consequence, since maintaining "status" and "prerogatives of office" was an important aspect of maintaining self-respect in a new and first administrative post of recognized community significance, directors tended to see vigorous subordinate disagreement as threatening to their own self-esteem and to their image of being "captain of their ships." Thus, protection of "self-image" became confused with analytical disagreement on program proposals.

Maintaining Desirable Social-Emotional Tone

In such an atmosphere, political as opposed to ego-supportive and analytical behavior became the norm within the NOC's. Administration in each of the three Neighborhood Opportunity Centers was described by subordinate staff members as manifesting a conspicuous lack of leadership in project planning and control. This administrative ineptness reinforced randomness in Center activities and the tendency for projects and programs to be pushed on the basis of political skills in marshalling support for one's own project. In the emotional, often bitter political infighting to obtain staff and resources for "pet" projects, ego-support and organizational cohesiveness were sacrificed for political victory in obtaining project approval.

AN ASSESSMENT OF "INDIGENOUS" LEADERSHIP OUTSIDE THE CENTERS

Legitimation of Programs

How effective were the "indigenous" leaders in legitimating their Neighborhood Opportunity Center programs to both the central Office of Economic Opportunity downtown and to their neighborhood advisory boards?

Many of the problems resulting from the lack of separation of personal role behavior from work role behavior were present in the relations between the Negro members of advisory boards and the "indigenous" center leadership. Likewise, the difficulty of establishing administrative "expertise" as a basis for program endorsement was even more severe. When one considers the influence bases[12] of the members of the downtown board of directors who were generally members of powerful and established welfare, civil rights, and service agencies with impressive educational and experience credentials, the relative influence base of the "indigenous" Center directors is seen in perspective.

As a result, the burden of defending and justifying program proposals fell to the downtown officials because the Center directors were not able to verbally or conceptually compete either with the board of trustees or with downtown officials. Programs evolved or were aborted in the absence of representation by articulate and able Center administrators in the downtown decision making. Consequently, subordinate NOC staff members felt that their Centers were on the periphery of policy decision making which indeed was often the case.[13]

A second set of problems developed concurrently. NOC directors and assistant directors, in order to maintain their power position, needed to inaugurate "successful" community action programs. However, in the sphere of community action, the programs were predicated on the collaboration of NOC personnel with community and neighborhood groups. Directors and assistant directors became involved in several "protest" meetings. These protest incidents sought to voice dissatisfaction with existing community services or facilities to community political leaders.

Table 2
Policy and Community Hindrances
to Social Change

EOPA Policy	28
EOPA and NOC Boards	7
Conservative Social Agencies	14
Community Power	4
Employment Policies of Business	15

Table 2 indicates the extent to which policies of the Economic Opportunity Planning Association and its Boards hindered the development of effective programs as perceived by the Neighborhood Opportunity Center Personnel. It is significant to note that internal pressures, seen as a failure of NOC leadership to adequately represent the "real world of poverty" to the more constructive downtown leaders, accounted for a larger percentage of hindrance citations than external community pressures when employment practices are excluded. See authors' article in *Sociology and Social Science.*

Table 3
Sources of Support in Instituting Effective
Community Action Programs*

NOC Directors	1
NOC Assistant Directors	3
Outside Resource People	11

*Taken from author's monograph.
It is significant that in citing effective leadership in providing analytical techniques and solution strategies for specific programs of community action, NOC subordinates mention eleven agents outside the NOC structure as sources of primary support. But only one Director is mentioned.

The lack of leadership from directors in the sphere of community action was shown in interviewing to be a primary source of loss of legitimacy. In instances where real leadership had to come from assistant directors and "outsiders," and especially where the director did not welcome this assistance—which was often the case—the director's legitimacy was seriously questioned. Severe, acrimonious comments in interviews related to this leadership failure were most pronounced.

However, since the NOC staffs did not develop concrete and well-documented proposals, the NOC's were 1) seen as contributing to rabble-rousing by the political leaders, while at the same time they were 2) seen as ineffective by the neighbors in obtaining substantial reform, since the general response of the political leadership was mere placating gestures (see Table 3).

Sponsorship of Subordinates Upward

Highly threatened by their lack of immediate success, under attack from their own staff members, and faced with great internal cleavage of opinion within their staffs relative to appropriate action strategies, directors and to a lesser extent assistant directors were more concerned with their own record and status than with endorsing the capabilities of their subordinates to the downtown office. The usual praise and recognition as well as hopes for organizational advancement were largely lacking for subordinate staff members. Subordinates felt they might just as well "go for broke" in pursuing internal conflict and warfare for personal ends since there was little probability of advancement or organizational reward for conformity and keeping one's place. (Uncertainty concerning refunding reinforced short-term perspectives.) Thus, the formal system of rewards as well as "concern for one's future in the organization" ceased to support directors in their attempt to control subordinate behavior.

SUMMARY OF THE EFFECTIVENESS OF "INDIGENOUS" LEADERSHIP

We can now summarize the effectiveness of "indigenous" leadership in the positions of both directors and assistant directors of the Neighborhood Opportunity Centers within the Poverty Program in Midwestern City. The choice of "indigenous leadership" for these managerial positions contributed to:

Relative to Relationships Within the Centers:

1. The intermingling of personal or private roles with managerial roles. In the small-town, self-contained world of the Negro ghetto, the ability of a native-son to separate his organizational life from his personal life was extremely difficult. As a consequence, the legitimacy of the Center leadership was mitigated by private and remote occurrences outside the organizational decision making.[14]
2. In the absence of secure "legitimacy," excessive competition for dominance of decision making developed. Positional status became confused with decisional dominance. Disagreement with one's analysis was confused with threats to one's positional authority.
3. Lacking expertise based on education or work experience, and lacking training in administration and decision-making processes, leaders dealt with disagreement between staff members poorly. Rather than resulting in creativity and serving as a catalyst for analytical problem solving, this disagreement became the locus of political coalitions, power plays, and hierarchical tyranny.
4. Given the personal insecurities generated by the above variables, and the concern with "making good" in one's superordinate position, personal ascendancy rather than organizational cohesiveness was the primary concern of the administrators.

Relative to Relationships Outside the Centers:

1. The burden of defending Center proposals fell to downtown OEO Administrators, with the consequence of information absorption and negotiation taking place without Center representation.
2. There was an increase in program conservatism because of the inability of Center directors to adequately participate in sponsoring proposals to the downtown Board of Directors.
3. There was a propensity for directors and assistant directors to prematurely align themselves with neighborhood protest groups

and to take "political steps" so as to obtain the endorsement of neighborhood leaders with the consequence that adequate and innovative planning which should have preceded such political action was not undertaken.

None of these problems, of course, is necessarily a unique function of the "indigenous" character of leadership inasmuch as similar administrative pathologies exist in bureaucracies hiring "professional" managerial personnel. However, there is no question that the absence of effective personnel trained in management is in part attributable to this "indigenous" character of the leaders and contributed to a highly consistent pattern of administrative problems across the Centers. The question remains: How might these dysfunctions have been avoided?[15]

RECOMMENDATIONS IF ONE WERE STARTING OVER

A simplistic recommendation would be that the War on Poverty hire more highly trained and "professional" personnel. This is simplistic because it lends to other difficulties.

It is true that a professional manager from outside the immediate neighborhood (White or Negro) with competence in urban and poverty problems and management skills could have avoided many of the problems pointed out above which clearly reflected managerial ineptness and inability to isolate administrative from private roles.

However, even if selected, would the professional manager have been an adequate "leader" for the NOC program? How could the professional manager establish the degree of social-emotional identification needed to enlist the support of the hard-core poor alienated neighborhood leaders, both employed within and serviced by the NOC's, given his position as an outsider? And what professional, whatever his background, portends to have the generic skills of the societal wise man necessary to find innovative solutions to all the problems of poverty?

To put it bluntly, might one not also write a report of organizational failure on the part of many organizations manned by highly professional leaders who, because of their lack of identification and rapport with the "indigenous" population, are seen as inept outsiders acting "on" rather than "with" the community in the quest for social reform?

Seen in light of these questions, the concept of a charismatic professional leader is as utopian as was the concept of a charismatic "indigenous" leader who, in spite of lack of training in the cumulated wisdom of social and administrative sciences, was to have formulated a new kind of effective organizational unit.

The solution, in terms of effective decision making and program implementation, required an organizational strategy that would provide an alliance between the "indigenous" leader and the "professional."

Task-Force Management

An alternative organizational strategy to that of bureaucracy would have been "task-force" or "project management." Composed of several basic decision units, such an organizational structure could have provided for an alliance between indigenous and professionalist savvy. Task-forces, including "indigenous" project coordinators, resource people drawn from the social sciences, professions, the business community, and representatives from appropriate neighborhood groups, could have jointly set about the analysis of various problems central to the poverty issue. Such an organizational strategy has several advantages:

1. Cross fertilization between both the indigenous and resource personnel is provided for.
2. Neighborhood leaders are full participants in the planning process, rather than the passive recipients of organizational programs.
3. The composition of the task-force can be adapted to the specific problem being attended. Presumably, several task-forces would be at work at the same time, each attending a different project and each drawing upon different "indigenous" and "professional" personnel. As one problem is solved, the old task-force would be dissolved and new task-forces formed. Thus, a fluid, dynamic organizational structure could be developed.
4. Since the hierarchical structure is consequently collapsed, vying for positional status based on hierarchical authority would be diminished. Task-intrinsic motivation would be buttressed.
5. Personnel formerly assigned the positions of "assistant directors" as well as subordinate positions would not be artificially specialized. Almost by definition (since "indigenous" personnel were not educated and/or trained for any particular specialty), the contributions of the "indigenous" leaders were insights, community contacts, and community knowledge. These contributions constituted rather eclectic and ill-focused capacities not lending themselves to traditional administrative positions.
6. A fluid organizational network of "task-forces" would allow "indigenous" personnel to drift in and out of decision spheres without isolating their capacities in a particular work function or burdening the organization with selected incapacities within

any particular function. At the same time, as the skills of indigenous personnel development programs become institutionalized, participation in the task-force would provide training for later specialized posts in continuous programs.

7. Given such joint participation, the task-force would avoid the problem of over-identification of a particular program or proposal with any single administrator or neighborhood leader.

Figure 2 presents a diagram of such a task-force organization.

There are a number of excellent treatments of the task-force or project management mode of organization available.[16] What we are envisioning is an NOC in which the middle-management planning functions, both those traditionally assigned to functional specialists and those assigned to staff specialists, are instead undertaken by task-force groups. Responsibility for implementation would still largely rest with the "indigenous" personnel participating in any task-force, since many of the resource personnel would be organizational participants either on a part-time or short-term basis and would be congruent with the felt need for the Negro leader to be in "control" of the program, even though receiving assistance from outside expertise. However, the "indigenous" staff members would be buttressed by "professional" resource people through mediation of both the analytical problem solving and the program planning. Given a well-developed program of action, the "indigenous" leaders would have a firm guideline for implementation.

With the participation of a cross section of "indigenous" and resource personnel in the task-forces, the problem of the Center director in communicating "upward" is made simpler. Programs and proposals would be based on better problem definition and analysis and would contain the implicit endorsement and legitimacy bestowed by the variety of part-time professionals participating in the task-force. Further, given the multiple involvement in the development of the proposal, it is more natural that one or more task-force members would participate in the presentation of the proposal, so that the representational function is shared.[17]

CONCLUSION

The answer to the problem of administration of the Neighborhood Opportunity Centers within the War on Poverty is not the reification of the myth of omniscient "professionalism" nor the enshrinement of the special attributes of the "indigenous" leaders. It is, rather, a challenge for the program to develop a new style of organizational management, based on the "task-force" or "project management" concept.

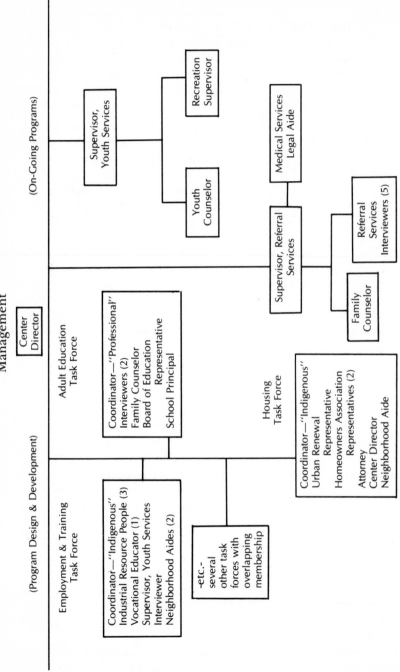

Figure 2
Hypothetical Neighborhood Opportunity Center Using "Task-Force" Management

What must be seen as one primary failure within the four OEO Centers treated in this study is that the admixture of skills possessed within our culture is not being brought to bear on the poverty issues. Rather, the present organization design placing "indigenous" personnel in super-status bureaucratic positions saps the latent potential of the "indigenous" personnel to provide their special brand of "leadership" because of internal conflicts and precludes selective involvement of the "professional" resource person. As Warren Bennis suggests, we must move beyond the anachronism of the bureaucratic model to provide for a more viable management style which brings to bear on organizational decision making[18] the special insights of varied groups.

Notes

[1]André L. Delbecq and Sidney J. Kaplan were affiliated with the University of Toledo, Toledo, Ohio, at the time of publication of this article.

[2]While one hesitates to call any metropolitan regional area "typical," this particular metropolitan area—population 514,000—has been chosen as a test area for several studies since its population and income characteristics are at the median of 20 Northern cities in terms of such variables as percent of nonwhite population, income—white and Negro, unemployment—white and Negro, and other such population and income indices.

[3]As we are using the terms, "referral services" relates to an interviewing program within the Neighborhood Opportunity Centers. The interviews are designed to help direct residents of the neighborhoods to existing welfare and community service agencies in cases where residents are unaware of existing services and/or their eligibility for benefits. "Program design" refers to the development of other programs or services offered by the NOC which meet the needs of area residents, e.g., recreational, adult-education. youth, or employment services. "Community action" refers to the definition of neighborhood needs and the organization of the residents of neighborhoods to obtain from the power structure specific changes, services, or reforms central to the revitalization of neighborhoods.

[4]The observations underlying the following case study are taken from two sources. First, one of the authors participated as a training instructor for NOC staff members during the first nine months of the NOC's operations. Second, both authors conducted a study of training program effectiveness in which 44 NOC staff members completed detailed questionnaires dealing with all phases of NOC staff activities, and in which 16 NOC staff members were interviewed in depth. For a complete report of the data see the authors' monograph: *An Evaluation of a Training Program for Neighborhood Opportunity Center Personnel* (Division of Adult and Continuing Education, The University of Toledo, 1966); and "Perceived Hindrance to Social Change in a Poverty Program," *Sociology and Social Science* (January 1967). While some modest indicative summary tables are included, this article is a distillation of conclusions based both on the data and participant observation with all the attendant risks acknowledged.

[5]Similar concerns with "indigenous" leadership are found in two well-known, prior research studies. In Whyte's *Street Corner Society*, "Doc's Gang" in the North End of Boston felt alienated from agency personnel (William Foot Whyte, *Street Corner Society*, University of Chicago Press, 1943). The youth in "Cornerville" did not patronize local settlement houses because of the social workers' middle class attitudes and the gulf between them and the youth clientele. The implicit argument is that had social workers been indigenous, there might have been more success in attracting the neighborhood youth of a lower class.

Zelznick raises a similar issue. See Phillip Zelznick, *TVA and the Grassroots* (Berkeley: University of California Publications in Culture and Society, 1949), III, 259-264. In this section, Zelznick discusses "Cooptation: A Mechanism for Organizational Stability." This grassroots doctrine used to sell TVA called upon local interests, local people, and local agencies to share power and be involved in decision making in order to legitimize and facilitate the TVA program.

[6]Such a conceptualization of leadership functions parallels several functionalist approaches to leadership; see R. T. Golembiewski, *The Small Group* (University of Chicago Press, 1962), pp. 128-144 and pp. 208-223 for a summary of theoretical conceptualizations.

[7]For research dealing with role separation, see F. Kroupl Taylor, "Quantitative Evaluation of Psychosocial Phenomena in Small Groups," *Journal of Mental Science*, XCLIII (October, 1951), 698.

[8]The classical treatment of separation between "front-stage" and "back-stage" behavior and its social utility in maintaining legitimacy is Irving Goffman, *The Presentation of Self in Everyday Life* (New York: Doubleday, 1959).

[9]This is, of course, no indictment of the "indigenous" leader since even a Ph.D. in an urban studies center rapidly runs to the limits of his expertise in dealing with the complex matters of poverty. Further, each of us can conjure up a stereotype of the "ideal" indigenous leader, a charismatic individual having a great following within the local community or neighborhood, broadly educated in the humanities and social sciences, with a heightened degree of social responsibility and social consciousness, and generic wisdom and common sense. In fact, the selection process quickly pointed up a number of problems. These realities included the fact that: 1) if you are drawing leadership from an impoverished geographical area, you must significantly modify your educational criteria to accept people from areas outside the urban concerns specialty (e.g., with divinity or education degrees), since college degrees are not profused characteristic of such neighborhoods; 2) you must expect that the neighborhood resident who has "overachieved" educationally will be somewhat removed from the hard core poor of his neighborhood and thus will not really be a "neighborhood" spokesman; and 3) broad wisdom and common sense concerning urban problems and poverty are hard to find among the intellectual elite of the social-scientific community, let alone the residents of a limited geographical area within a city.

Further, there is the obvious difficulty of attracting personnel to a new, militant, high risk venture of unspecified duration at relatively low pay, inasmuch as many such potential personnel are often well established in better paying, stable, secure positions within high status organizations. Consequently, those who come forth to apply for positions often represent potential rather than accomplished leaders.

[10]"Not surprisingly" in the sense that these are typical mechanisms for conflict resolution in organizations where appropriate leadership mediation is lacking; cf. Norman R. F. Maier, *Problem-Solving Decisions and Conferences* (New York: McGraw-Hill, 1963) and Clogit G. Smith, "A Comparative Analysis of Some Conditions and Consequences of Intra-Organizational Conflict," *Administrative Science Quarterly* (March, 1964).

[11]These hierarchical responses to innovation and aggression on the part of subordinates are entirely congruent with the mechanisms for power maintenance and conservatism within hierarchical systems as outlined by Victor Thompson, "Bureaucracy and Innovation," *Administrative Science Quarterly* (June, 1965).

[12]Our conceptualization of influence bases is taken from John P. French and Bertram Raven, "The Bases of Social Power," *Group Dynamics*, ed. Cartwright and Zander (Evanston, Ill.: Row Peterson and Co., 1960), pp. 607-624.

[13]It should be noted that the authoritarian posture of the downtown executive director, who did not invite participation by Center administrators, confounded the situation.

However, the Center administrators did not respond to this lack of participation by means of adequate power moves to gain greater visibility.

[14]Similar difficulties were manifest even in lower-level positions. Neighbors were, at times, unwilling to unburden themselves and be candid with interviewers and counselors whom they knew and who "had their own problems."

[15]The student of international business will see some similarities between the problems of management in developing countries and the problems of management in developing neighborhoods.

[16]Cf. John F. Mee, "Ideational Items: Matrix Organization," *Business Horizons* (Summer, 1964), pp. 70-72; Fremont A. Shull, *Matrix Structure and Project Authority for Optimizing Organizational Capacity* (Monograph No. 1, Business Research Bureau, Southern Illinois University, Carbondale, Illinois, 1966); Warren Bennis, "Beyond Bureaucracy," *Transactions* (Summer, 1965).

[17]Kahn et al. point out the value of multiple representation whenever a quasi-independent organizational unit crosses the boundary separating it from either the larger organization or the community at large. See R. L. Kahn, D. M. Wolfe, R. P. Quinn, and J. D. Snock, *Organizational Stress* (New York: John Wiley and Sons, 1964), Chapter 19.

[18]Warren Bennis, *Ibid.*

What It's Like
to Be a Black Manager

*Equal job opportunity is more than putting
a black man in a white man's job*

EDWARD W. JONES, JR.

This author contends that most companies fail to recognize the crucial difference between recruiting blacks with executive potential and providing the much-needed organizational support to help them realize this potential. He cites his own experience in a large company to illustrate the type of lonely struggle that faces a black man in the absence of such support. Then he draws some lessons from this experience that should help management to overcome the subtle ramifications of racial differences within organizations.

Mr. Jones is the manager of an $11-million operating unit of a major company and is responsible for the supervision of 130 employees. After six years with the company, during which he rose from trainee to area manager, he attended the Harvard Business School, where he was graduated two years ago as a Baker Scholar.

When I was graduated from a predominantly black college, I was offered a job in one of the largest corporations in America. On reporting for work, I received a motivational speech from the personnel officer and acknowledged that I agreed with his opinion: the job was going to be challenging in its own right; however, the added burden of prejudice could make it unbearable. In a tone of bravado I said, "I promise you that I won't quit; you'll have to fire me."

At the time, I did not know how important that promise would become. For I was about to begin the most trying experience of my life—

the rise to middle management in a white corporation. During those years, I found myself examining my actions, strategies, and emotional stability. I found myself trying desperately to separate fact from mental fiction. I found myself enveloped in almost unbearable emotional stress and internal conflict, trying to hold the job as a constant and evaluate my personal shortcomings with respect to it. At times I would look at myself in a mirror and wonder whether I had lost my mental balance. Somehow I always managed to answer positively, if not resolutely.

I think that my experiences should prove helpful to companies that are wrestling with the problem of how to move black employees from the entry level into positions of greater responsibility. I say this because the manner in which many companies are approaching the problem indicates to me that a number of well-intentioned efforts are doomed to failure.

Failure is likely because most companies merely substitute blacks in positions formerly filled by whites and then, acting as if the corporate environment is not color-sensitive, consider their obligation over. In short, U.S. business has failed to recognize the embryonic black manager's increased chances of failure due to the potentially negative impact of racially based prejudgments. Gaining acceptance in the organization, which the embryonic white manager takes for granted, can be a serious problem for his black counterpart.

THE JOB OFFER

My story begins when I happened to bump into a recruiter who was talking to a friend of mine. On gathering that I was a college senior, the recruiter asked whether I had considered his company as an employer. I responded, "Are you kidding me—you don't have any black managers, do you?" He replied, "No, but that's why I'm here."

I did well in a subsequent interview procedure, and received an invitation for a company tour. Still skeptical, I accepted, feeling that I had nothing to lose. During a lunch discussion concerning the contemplated job and its requirements, I experienced my first reminder that I was black. After a strained silence, one of the executives at our table looked at me, smiled, and said, "Why is it that everyone likes Roy Campanella, but so many people dislike Jackie Robinson?"

I knew that this man was trying to be pleasant; yet I felt nothing but disgust at what seemed a ridiculous deterioration in the level of conversation. Here was the beginning of the games that I expected but dreaded playing. The question was demeaning and an insult to my intelligence. It was merely a rephrasing of the familiar patronizing comment, "One of my best friends is a negro." Most blacks recognize this type of statement as a thinly veiled attempt to hide bias. After all, if a person is unbiased, why does he make such a point of trying to prove it?

In the fragment of time between the question and my response, the tension within me grew. Were these people serious about a job offer? If so, what did they expect from me? I had no desire to be the corporate black in a glass office, but I did not wish to be abrasive or ungracious if the company was sincere about its desire to have an integrated organization.

There was no way to resolve these kinds of questions at that moment, so I gathered up my courage and replied, "Roy Campanella is a great baseball player. But off the field he is not an overwhelming intellectual challenge to anyone. Jackie Robinson is great both on and off the baseball field. He is very intelligent and therefore more of a threat than Roy Campanella. In fact, I'm sure that if he wanted to, he could outperform you in your job."

There was a stunned silence around the table, and from that point on until I arrived back at the employment office, I was sure that I had ended any chances of receiving a job offer.

I was wrong. I subsequently received an outstanding salary offer from the recruiter. But I had no intention of being this company's showcase black and asked seriously, "Why do you want me to work for you? Because of my ability or because you need a black?" I was reassured that ability was the "only" criterion, and one month later, after much introspection, I accepted the offer.

INITIAL EXPOSURE

I entered the first formal training phase, in which I was the only black trainee in a department of over 8,000 employees. During this period, my tension increased as I was repeatedly called on to be the in-house expert on anything pertaining to civil rights. I was proud to be black and had many opinions about civil rights, but I did not feel qualified to give "the" black opinion. I developed the feeling that I was considered a black first and an individual second by many of the people I came into contact with. This feeling was exacerbated by the curious executive visitors to the training class who had to be introduced to everyone except me. Everyone knew my name, and I constantly had the feeling of being on stage.

The next phase of training was intended to prepare trainees for supervisory responsibilities. The tension of the trainee group had risen somewhat because of the loss of several trainees and the increased challenges facing us. In my own case, an increasing fear of failure began to impact on the other tensions that I felt from being "a speck of pepper in a sea of salt." The result of these tensions was that I began behaving with an air of bravado. I wasn't outwardly concerned or afraid, but I was inwardly terrified. This phase of training was also completed satisfactorily, at least in an official sense.

At the conclusion of the training, I received a "yes, but" type of appraisal. For example: "Mr. Jones doesn't take notes and seems to have trouble using the reference material, but he seems to be able to recall the material." This is the type of appraisal that says you've done satisfactorily, yet leaves a negative or dubious impression. I questioned the subjective inputs but dropped the matter without any vehement objections.

Prior to embarking on my first management assignment, I resolved to learn from this appraisal and to use more tact and talk less. These resolutions were re-emphasized by my adviser, who was an executive with responsibility for giving me counsel and acting as a sounding board. He also suggested that I relax my handshake and speak more softly.

ON THE JOB

A warm welcome awaited me in the office where I was to complete my first assignment as a supervisor. I looked forward to going to work because I felt that subjectivity in appraisals would now be replaced by objectivity. Here was a situation in which I would either meet or fail to meet clearly defined numerical objectives.

There were no serious problems for three weeks, and I started to relax and just worry about the job. But then I had a conflict in my schedule. An urgent matter had to be taken care of in the office at the same time that I had an appointment elsewhere. I wrote a note to a supervisor who worked for another manager, asking him if he would be kind enough to follow up on the matter in the office for me.

I chose that particular supervisor because he had given me an embarrassingly warm welcome to the office and insisted that I "just ask" if there was anything at all that he could do to help me. I relied on the impersonality of the note because he was out on a coffee break and I had to leave immediately. The note was short and tactfully worded, and ended by giving my advance "thanks" for the requested help. Moreover, the office norms encouraged supervisory cooperation, so the fact that we worked under different managers did not seem to be a problem.

When I returned to the office, the manager I worked for called me in. He was visibly irritated. I sat down and he said, "Ed, you're rocking the boat." He stated that the supervisor I had asked for help had complained directly to the area manager that I was ordering him around and said he wasn't about to take any nonsense from a "new kid" in the office.

In a very calm voice, I explained what I had done and why I had done it. I then asked my manager, "What did I do wrong?" He looked at me and said, "I don't know, but whatever it is, cut it out. Stop rocking the boat." When I asked why the note wasn't produced to verify my statements, he said that it "wasn't available."

I left my manager's office totally perplexed. How could I correct my behavior if I didn't know what was wrong with it? I resolved that I had no choice except to be totally self-reliant, since one thing was obvious: what I had taken at face value as friendliness was potentially a fatal trap.

The feelings aroused in this incident were indicative of those I was to maintain for some time. While I felt a need for closeness, the only option open to me was self-reliance. I felt that my manager should support and defend me, but it was obvious that he was not willing to take such a stance. Worst of all, however, was my feeling of disappointment and the ensuing confusion due to my lack of guidance. I felt that if my manager was not willing to protect and defend me, he had an increased responsibility to give me guidance on how to avoid future explosions of a similar nature.

For some months I worked in that office without any additional explosions, although I was continually admonished not to "rock the boat." During a luncheon with the area manager one day, I remember, he said, "Ed, I've never seen a guy try so hard. If we tell you to tie your tie to the right, you sure try to do it. But why can't you be like Joe [another trainee the area manager supervised]? He doesn't seem to be having any problems."

The Appraisal Incident

I directed my energies and frustrations into my work, and my supervisory section improved in every measured area of performance until it led the unit. At the end of my first six months on the job, I was slated to go on active duty to fulfill my military requirements as a lieutenant in the Army. Shortly before I left, my manager stated, "Ed, you've done a tremendous job. You write your own appraisal." I wrote the appraisal, but was told to rewrite it because "it's not good enough." I rewrote the appraisal four times before he was satisfied that I was not being too modest. As I indicated earlier, I had resolved to be as unabrasive as possible, and, even though I had met or exceeded all my objectives, I was trying not to be pompous in critiquing my own performance.

Finally, on my next to last day on the job, my manager said, "Ed, this is a fine appraisal. I don't have time to get it typed before you go, but I'll submit this appraisal just as you have written it." With that, I went into the service, feeling that, finally, I had solved my problems.

Six months later, I took several days' leave from the Army to spend Christmas in the city with my family. On the afternoon of the day before Christmas, I decided to visit the personnel executive who had originally given me encouragement. So, wearing my officer's uniform, I stopped by his office.

After exchanging greetings and making small talk. I asked him if he had seen my appraisal. He answered, "yes," but when his face failed to reflect the look of satisfaction that I expected, I asked him if I could see it. The appraisal had been changed from the one that I had originally written to another "yes, but" appraisal. The numerical results said that I had met or exceeded all objectives, but under the section entitled "Development Program" the following paragraph had been inserted:

"Mr. Jones's biggest problem has been overcoming his own impulsiveness. He has on occasion, early in his tour, jumped too fast with the result that he has incurred some resentment. In these cases his objectives have been good, but his method has ruffled feathers."

I asked the personnel executive to interpret my overall rating. He answered, "Well, we can run the business with people with that rating." I then asked him to explain the various ratings possible, and it became clear that I had received the lowest acceptable rating that wouldn't require the company to fire me. I could not see how this could be, since I had exceeded all my objectives. I explained how I had written my own appraisal and that this appraisal had been rewritten. The personnel officer could not offer an explanation; he recommended that I speak to my old area manager, who had had the responsibility to review and approve my appraisal, and ask him why I had been treated in that manner.

A Bleak Christmas

I tried to sort things out on my way to see my former area manager. My head was spinning, and I was disgusted. The appraisal was not just unfair—it was overtly dishonest. I thought of standing up in righteous indignation and appealing to higher authority in the company, but I had always resisted calling attention to my blackness by asking for special concessions and wanted to avoid creating a conflict situation if at all possible. While the 15-minute walk in the cold air calmed my anger, I still hadn't decided what I was going to do when I arrived at the area manager's office.

I walked into a scene that is typical of Christmas Eve in an office. People were everywhere, and discarded gift wrappings filled the wastebaskets. The area manager still had on the red Santa Claus suit. I looked around at the scene of merriment and decided that this was a poor time to "rock the boat."

The area manager greeted me warmly, exclaimed how great I looked, and offered to buy me a drink on his way home. I accepted, and with a feeling of disgust and disappointment, toasted to a Merry Christmas. I knew then that this situation was hopeless and there was little to be gained by raising a stink while we were alone. I had been naïve, and there was no way to prove that the appraisal had been changed.

I was a very lonely fellow that Christmas Eve. My feelings of a lack of closeness, support, and protection were renewed and amplified. It became obvious that no matter how much I achieved, how hard I worked or how many personal adjustments I made, this system was trying to reject me.

I didn't know which way to turn, whom to trust, or who would be willing to listen. The personnel executive had told me to expect prejudice, but when he saw that I was being treated unfairly, he sent me off on my own.

"What do they expect?" I thought. "They know that I am bound to run into prejudice; yet no one lifts a finger when I am treated unfairly. Do they expect a person to be stupid enough to come right out and say, 'Get out, blackie; we don't want your type here'? This surely wouldn't happen—such overt behavior would endanger the offending person's career."

After the Christmas Eve incident, I went off to finish the remaining time in the Army. During that period, I tossed my work problems around in my mind, trying to find the right approach. The only answer I came up with was to stand fast, do my best, ask for no special favors, and refuse to quit voluntarily.

NEW CHALLENGES

When I returned to the company, I was assigned as a supervisor in another area for five or six weeks, to do the same work as I had been doing prior to my departure for the military service. At the end of this uneventful refamiliarization period, I was reassigned as a manager in an area that had poor performance and was recognized as being one of the most difficult in the company. The fact that I would be responsible for one of three "manager units" in the area was exciting, and I looked forward to this new challenge.

I walked into my new area manager's office with a smile and an extended hand, anxious to start off on the right foot and do a good job. After shaking hands, my new boss invited me to sit down while he told me about the job. He began by saying, "I hope you don't, but I am pretty sure you are going to fall flat on your face. When you do, my job is to kick you in the butt so hard that they'll have to take us both to the hospital."

I was shocked and angry. In the first place, my pride as a man said you don't have to take that kind of talk from anyone. I fought the temptation to say something like, "If you even raise your foot, you may well go to the hospital to have it put in a cast."

As I held back the anger, he continued, "I don't know anything about your previous performance, and I don't intend to try to find out. I'm going to evaluate you strictly on your performance for me."

The red lights went on in my mind. This guy was making too much of an issue about his lack of knowledge concerning my previous performance. Whom was he trying to kid? He had heard rumors and read my personnel records. I was starting off with two strikes against me. I looked at him and said, "I'll do my best."

More Appraisal Troubles

The area's results failed to improve, and John, the area manager, was replaced by a new boss, Ralph. Two weeks after Ralph arrived, he called me on the intercom and said, "Ed, John has your appraisal ready. Go down to see him in his new office. Don't worry about it; we'll talk when you get back." Ralph's words and tone of foreboding made me brace for the worst.

John ushered me into his office and began by telling me that I had been his worst problem. He then proceeded to read a list of every disagreement involving me that he was aware of. These ranged from corrective actions with clerks to resource-allocation discussions with my fellow managers. It was a strange appraisal session. John wound up crossing out half of the examples cited as I rebutted his statements. At the end of the appraisal, he turned and said, "I've tried to be fair, Ed. I've tried not to be vindictive. But if someone were to ask how you're doing, I would have to say you've got room for improvement."

Discussions with Ralph, my new boss, followed as soon as I returned to my office. He advised me not to worry, that we would work out any problems. I told him that this was fine, but I also pointed out the subjectivity and dishonesty reflected in previous and current appraisals and the circumstances surrounding them.

I was bitter that a person who had just been relieved for ineffectiveness could be allowed to have such a resounding impact on my chances in the company. My predecessor had been promoted; I had improved on his results; but here I was, back in questionable status again.

The Turning Point

About six weeks later, Ralph called me in and said, "Ed, I hope you make it on the job. But what are you going to do if you don't?"

At that moment, I felt as if the hands on the clock of life had reached 11:59. Time was running out very rapidly on me, and I saw myself against a wall, with my new boss about to deliver the coup de grâce. I felt that he was an honest and very capable person, but that circumstances had combined to give him the role of executioner. It seemed from his question that he was in the process of either wrestling with his own conscience or testing me to see how much resistance, if any, I would put up when he delivered the fatal blow. After all, while I had not made an issue of my ill treatment thus far in my career, no matter how unjustly I felt I had been dealt with, he was smart enough to realize that this option was still open to me.

I looked at Ralph and any thought about trying to please him went out of my mind. Sitting up straight in my chair, I met his relaxed smile with a very stern face. "Why do you care what I do if I don't make it?" I asked coldly.

"I care about you as a person," he replied.

"It's not your job to be concerned about me as a person," I said. "Your job is to evaluate my performance results. But since you've asked, it will be rough if I am fired, because I have a family and responsibilities. However, that's not your concern. You make your decision; and when you do, I'll make my decision." With that statement I returned to my office.

Several weeks after this discussion, a vice president came around to the office to discuss objectives and job philosophy with the managers. I noted at the time that while he only spent 15 or 20 minutes with the other managers, he spent over an hour talking with me. After this visit, Ralph and I had numerous daily discussions. Then Ralph called me into his office to tell me he had written a new appraisal with an improved rating. I was thrilled. I was going to make it. Later, he told me that he was writing another appraisal, stating I not only would make it but also had promotional potential.

After Ralph had changed the first appraisal, my tensions began to decrease and my effectiveness began to increase proportionately. The looser and more confident I became, the more rapidly the results improved. My assignment under Ralph became very fulfilling, and one of the best years I've spent in the company ensued. Other assignments followed, each more challenging than the previous, and each was handled satisfactorily.

LESSONS FROM EXPERIENCE

My point in relating these experiences is not to show that I was persecuted or treated unfairly by people in a large corporation. In fact, after talking to friends in the company who knew me during the period just described, I am convinced that many of the lack-of-tact and rock-the-boat statements were true. I am also convinced, however, that the problems I experienced were not uniquely attributable to me or my personality and that it is important for companies to understand what caused them.

The manager to whom I reported on my very first assignment made some informal notes which help illustrate my conviction:

"I discussed each case with Ed. As might be expected, there is as much to be said in his defense as against him. He isn't all wrong in any one case. But the cumulative weight of all those unsolicited comments and complaints clearly shows that he is causing a lot of people to be unhappy, and I must see that it stops. I don't think it is a question of what he says and does or a question of objectives. It is a question of voice, manner, approach, method—or maybe timing. No matter what it is, he must correct whatever he does that upsets so many people."

These are not the words of a scheming bigot; they are the words of a man searching for an explanation to a phenomenon that neither he nor I understood at the time. I was not knowingly insensitive to other people or intent on antagonizing them. What this man and others failed to realize was that, being a black man in a unique position in a white company, I was extremely tense and ill at ease. Levels of sensitivity, polish, and tact which were foreign to me were now necessities of life. The world of white business presented me with an elaborate sociopolitical organization that required unfamiliar codes of behavior.

Abraham Zaleznik refers to this phenomenon in *The Human Dilemmas of Leadership:*

> The anxiety experienced by the upwardly mobile individual largely comes from internal conflicts generated within his own personality. On the one hand, there is the driving and pervasive need to prove himself as assurance of his adequacy as a person; on the other hand, the standards for measuring his adequacy come from sources somewhat unfamiliar to him.[1]

My personal pride and sense of worth were driving me to succeed. Ironically, the more determined I was to succeed, the more abrasive I became and the more critical my feedback became. This in turn impelled me to try even harder and to be even more uptight. As a result, I was vulnerable to prejudgments of inability by my peers and superiors.

The Lens of Color

What most white people do not understand or accept is the fact that skin color has such a pervasive impact on every black person's life that it subordinates considerations of education or class. Skin color makes black people the most conspicuous minority in America, and all blacks, regardless of status, are subjected to prejudice. I personally was not as disadvantaged as many other blacks, but to some extent all blacks are products of separate schools, neighborhoods, and subcultures. In short, black and white people not only look different but also come from different environments which condition them differently and make understanding and honest communication difficult to achieve.

Many whites who find it easy to philosophically accept the fact that blacks will be rubbing shoulders with them experience antagonism when they realize that the difference between blacks and whites goes deeper than skin color. They have difficulty adjusting to the fact that blacks really are different. It is critical that companies understand this point, for it indicates the need for increased guidance to help blacks adjust to an alien set of norms and behavioral requirements.

The Informal Organization

One of the phenomena that develops in every corporation is a set of behavioral and personal norms that facilitates communication and aids cohesiveness. Moreover, because this "informal organization" is built on white norms, it can reinforce the black-white differences just mentioned and thus reject or destroy all but the most persistent blacks.

The informal organization operates at all levels in a corporation, and the norms become more rigid the higher one goes in the hierarchy. While this phenomenon promotes efficiency and unity, it is also restrictive and very selective. It can preclude promotion or lead to failure on the basis of "fit" rather than competence.

Chester Barnard recognized the existence of the informal organization in 1938. As he stated, "This question of fitness involves such matters as education, experience, age, sex, personal distinctions, prestige, race, nationality, faith. . . ."[2]

I believe that many of the problems I encountered were problems of fit with the informal organization. My peers and supervisors were unable to perceive me as being able to perform the job that the company hired me for. Their reaction to me was disbelief. I was out of the "place" normally filled by black people in the company; and since no black person had preceded me successfully, it was easy for my antagonists to believe I was inadequate.

I am not vacillating here from my previous statement that I was probably guilty of many of the subjective shortcomings noted in my appraisals. But I do feel that the difficulties I experienced were amplified by my lack of compatibility with the informal organization. Because of it, many of the people I had problems with could not differentiate between objective ability and performance and subjective dislike for me, or discomfort with me. I was filling an unfamiliar, and therefore uncomfortable, "space" in relation to them. Even in retrospect, I cannot fully differentiate between the problems attributable to me as a person, to me as a manager, or to me as a black man.

TOWARD FACILITATING 'FIT'

Because of the foregoing problems, I conclude that business has an obligation to even out the odds for blacks who have executive potential. I am not saying that all blacks must be pampered and sheltered rather than challenged. Nor am I advocating the development of "chosen" managers. All managers must accept the risk of failure in order to receive the satisfactions of achievement.

I do, however, advocate a leveling out of these problems of "fit" with the informal organization that operate against black managers. Here are the elements vital to this process:

☐ *Unquestionable top management involvement and commitment*—The importance of this element is underscored by my discussions with the vice president who visited me during my crisis period. He disclosed that his objective was to see whether I was really as bad as he was being told. His conclusion from the visit was that he couldn't see any insurmountable problems with me. This high-level interest was the critical variable that gave me a fair chance. I was just lucky that this man had a personal sense of fair play and a desire to ensure equitable treatment.

But chance involvement is not enough. If a company is truly committed to equal opportunity, then it must set up reasoned and well thought-out plans for involvement of top management.

☐ *Direct two-way channels of communication between top management and black trainees*—Without open channels of communication, a company cannot ensure that it will recognize the need for a neutral opinion or the intercession of a disinterested party if a black trainee is having problems.

Clear channels of communication will also enable top management to provide empathetic sources of counsel to help the new black trainee combat the potentially crippling paranoia that I encountered. I didn't know whom to trust; consequently, I trusted no one. The counsel of mature and proven black executives will also help mitigate this paranoia.

☐ *Appraisal of managers on their contributions to the company's equal opportunity objectives*—The entire management team must be motivated to change any deep beliefs about who does and doesn't fit with regard to color. Accordingly, companies should use the appraisal system to make the welfare of the black trainee coincident with the well-being of his superior. Such action, of course, will probably receive considerable resistance from middle- and lower-level management. But managers are appraised on their ability to reach other important objectives; and, more significantly, the inclusion of this area in appraisals signals to everyone involved that a company is serious. Failure to take this step signals business as usual and adds to any credibility gap between the company and black employees.

The appraisal process also motivates the trainee's superior to "school" him on the realities of the political process in the corporation. Without this information, no one can survive in an organization. After upgrading my appraisal, Ralph began this process with me. The knowledge I gained proved to be invaluable in my subsequent decision making.

☐ *Avoid the temptation to create special showcase-black jobs.* They will be eyed with suspicion by the black incumbents, and the sincerity of the company will be open to question. Blacks realize that only line jobs provide the experience and reality-testing which develop the confidence required in positions of greater responsibility.

☐ *Select assignments for the new black manager which are challenging, yet don't in themselves increase his chances of failure.* My assignment with John was a poor choice. He was a top-rated area manager, but had a different job orientation and was struggling to learn his new responsibilities. So naturally he would resent any inexperienced manager being assigned to him. Moreover, the fact that he had never seen a successful black manager reinforced his belief that I could not do the job.

These basic steps need not be of a permanent nature, but they should be enacted until such time as the organizational norms accept blacks at all levels and in all types of jobs. The steps will help mitigate the fact that a black person in the organizational structure must not only carry the same load as a white person but also bear the burden attributable to prejudice and the machinations of the informal organization.

CONCLUSION

In relating and drawing on my own experiences, I have not been talking about trials and tribulations in an obviously bigoted company. At that time, my company employed a higher percentage of blacks than almost any other business, and this is still true today. I grant that there is still much to be done as far as the number and level of blacks in positions of authority are concerned, but I believe that my company has done better than most in the area of equal opportunity. Its positive efforts are evidenced by the progressive decision to sponsor my study at the Harvard Business School, so I would be prepared for greater levels of responsibility.

There are differences in detail and chronology, but the net effect of my experiences is similar to that of other blacks with whom I have discussed these matters. While prejudice exists in business, the U.S. norm against being prejudiced precludes an admission of guilt by the prejudiced party. Thus, in my own case, my first manager and John were more guilty of naïveté than bigotry—they could not recognize prejudice, since it would be a blow to their self-images. And this condition is prevalent in U.S. industry.

My experience points out that a moral commitment to equal opportunity is not enough. If a company fails to recognize that fantastic filters operate between the entry level and top management, this commitment is useless. Today, integration in organizations is at or near the entry level, and the threat of displacement or the discomfort of having to adjust to unfamiliar racial relationships is the greatest for lower and middle managers, for they are the people who will be most impacted by this process. Therefore, companies must take steps similar to the ones I have advocated if they hope to achieve true parity for blacks.

Equal job opportunity is more than putting a black man in a white man's job. The barriers must be removed, not just moved.

Notes

[1] New York, Harper & Row, Publishers, 1966, p. 111.

[2] *The Functions of the Executive* (Cambridge, Harvard University Press, 1938), p. 224.

The 3
Minority
Worker

Most individuals have basic beliefs that they apply as guides for their behavior. These beliefs, acquired through experience, formal education, and other influences, provide a framework of thought that guides the behavior of individuals and facilitates their decision-making efforts. Commonly, these basic beliefs are referred to as *values*. Oftentimes the values that people hold, as well as their past experiences, condition the kinds of outcomes that they expect in a given situation. In particular, job behavior is largely influenced by the work values that the individual holds. These values, in turn, may be conditioned by the worker's past experiences, which determine the nature of his subsequent expectancies for certain kinds of outcomes. Hence, the worker's job satisfaction is often affected by outcomes.

Work Values

The first section of Part Three discusses the effects of personal background and attitudes on work values, performance, job satisfaction, and the evaluation of work. The article by Goodale demonstrates that disadvantaged minority workers differ markedly from other employees in their expressed work values because they place more value on working for financial rewards, i.e., the satisfaction of lower-level needs. The study by Milutinovich, which examines the job satisfaction of black and white workers with respect to various aspects of their job (work, supervision, pay, etc.), reveals that neither black nor white employees can be considered homogeneous groups that hold similar attitudes toward work. Rather, occupational level, education, age, sex, and community characteristics must be considered when making comparisons between work attitudes of black and white workers. The subjects in Feldman's study demonstrated work values that were somewhat more mixed and different from those reported by Goodale. Together, the three articles provide useful insight into the complex nature of work attitudes and values of minority-group members.

Work Expectations

The second section deals with work expectations and motivation of the minority worker. Greenhaus and Gavin investigate the racial differences in expectancy-criterion relationships on the job. Their study is a test of the Porter-Lawler theory, which proposes that the amount of effort expended on the job is a function of the expectation that working hard will lead to a series of work rewards, and the importance attached to these rewards by the worker. It was found that blacks perceived a greater connection between hard work and the attainment of work rewards than did whites. In a different vein, Hare examines the nature of black workers' mobility during periods of substantial occupational change, in particular, the period between 1930 and 1960. His results support the positive relationship between the level of education and the mobility of the black worker.

Job Satisfaction

Three different approaches to the study of job satisfaction among minority-group workers are presented in the third section. Behavior that is indicative of low job satisfaction, e.g., absenteeism, is examined by Heneman and Murphy in relation to other demographic and group characteristics, using race and sex as moderator variables of the relationships between absenteeism and these other variables. Champagne and King examine job-satisfaction factors among disadvantaged workers. Their finding that disadvantaged workers place more importance on intrinsic job factors than on extrinsic job factors is in contrast to the findings of the Goodale study noted earlier.

The Ash study reports that female minority-group workers are less satisfied with their jobs than female majority-group workers. The finding holds true even for comparisons within the same occupational grouping. Ash offers several suggestions as to why these differences occur.

Work Values

Effects of Personal Background and Training on Work Values of the Hard-Core Unemployed[1]

JAMES G. GOODALE[2]

This study described how work values of 110 disadvantaged persons differ from those of 180 unskilled and semiskilled employees, identified biographical correlates of work values, and examined changes in work values following training. When compared with regular employees, hard-core trainees placed less emphasis on the tendency to keep active on the job, taking pride in their work, and subscribing to the traditional Protestant Ethic, but placed more emphasis on making money on the job. Significant relationships were found between background characteristics and work values of the hard core. Changes in work values of disadvantaged subjects after 8 weeks of training did not differ from those of 252 controlled subjects (insurance agents and college students).

Persons classified as disadvantaged or hard core represent a subculture of our society with an indigenous life style and value system. One aspect of this value system that is of particular interest to social scientists is the concept of work values—an individual's attitude toward work in general rather than his feelings about a specific job. Many authors have speculated about the development of attitudes of the hard core, but they have presented few data to support their conclusions.

From a series of intensive interviews of 600 middle- and working-class families in Chicago, Davis (1946) identified three factors that may

---

Reprinted from *Journal of Applied Psychology*, 1973, 57(1), 1-9. Copyright © 1973 by the American Psychological Association. Reprinted by permission of the publisher and the author.

produce the behavior and set of values characteristic of the ghetto sub-culture. First, the necessity for survival forces the child of the lower-class family to seek immediate gratification of the most basic physical needs (food, clothing, and shelter), and it inhibits his striving for less urgent goals. Second, Davis argued that when a person becomes accustomed to living at a subsistence level, unemployment becomes an acceptable norm. Third, his lack of adequate income, clothing, shelter, education, and vocational skill makes it impossible for the disadvantaged individual to escape the ghetto. In a similar essay, Himes (1968) observed that under-privileged black children who do not interact daily with employed persons fail to learn that effort leads to advancement in the work situation and remain naive about the language, dress, attitudes, and behavior expected by employers.

Unlike Himes, Schwartz and Henderson (1964) pointed out that most adolescents are exposed to the American work ethic through their experiences either at home or at school. They theorized that the disadvantaged are torn by the contrast between the ideals of the Protestant Ethic (Weber, 1958; e.g., work is good, achievement leads to advancement) and the reality of menial jobs, low pay, and chronic unemployment. They resolve this dilemma by devaluing work and by finding other ways of making money such as stealing, soliciting, and pushing dope. Their choice of solution reflects the rejection of legitimate employment as a means of advancement.

Despite the conclusions of the previous authors, Williams (1968) reasoned that the underprivileged accept the societal work ethic and want to support themselves through employment, but this desire is frustrated in demeaning, low-paying jobs. According to Williams (1968) and Rainwater (1966), most hard-core males work for little money, and as this situation continues over a period of time, employment for low wages becomes aversive, although work itself is still valued. Williams (1968) claimed that since the disadvantaged do not differ from the rest of the labor force in their work values, a well-paying job will transform them into productive employees.

Some authors have measured values of the hard core. In an analysis of alienation scores, Bullough (1967) found that black residents of the ghetto expressed greater feelings of anomie and powerlessness than blacks living in integrated suburban areas. Agreeing with Davis (1946), Bullough concluded that work values of the hard core not only result from ghetto living but also perpetuate the impoverished environment.

Using a sample of disadvantaged persons, Wijting (1969) discovered relationships among work values and demographic information, parental models, early physical surroundings, and early psychological environment. In a canonical regression analysis, high incidence of police trouble in the family, rural residency, and low-family income were associated with emphasis on the social rewards of work and preference for being inactive and uninvolved on the job.⌉

Attempts to Hire the Disadvantaged

Recognizing the vicious circle of unemployment experienced by members of the hard core, the federal government and private business launched a nationwide effort to hire and train the disadvantaged by creating a program named Job Opportunities in the Business Sector and an implementing agency known as the National Alliance of Businessmen (NAB). The NAB set as its goal the employment of 100,000 hard-core individuals by June 1969, and 500,000 by June 1971.

The NAB companies have made sincere efforts to hire hard-core applicants, to improve their skills in specialized training, and to place them on jobs requiring high levels of ability. However, the NAB program has not transformed all applicants into satisfied and productive workers. Of over 400,000 employees hired since 1968, 47% quit their jobs within the first 6 months of employment.[3] In the metropolitan areas that have 100 or more companies participating in the NAB program, turnover rates vary greatly. For example, during the same period, one municipal area in New England reported a 20% turnover rate among the hard core, another in Wisconsin reported a 40% figure, and in Florida, a 56% figure was reported.[4]

High turnover, therefore, may involve the work values of employees. The NAB program has not dealt with these in an effective manner. The work values of disadvantaged employees seem to differ markedly from those held by all other workers in similar jobs, and, in addition, individual differences in attitudes toward work may exist among hard-core employees. In order to determine if these apparent differences are real, the values must be measured.

The Current Study

Although anecdotal evidence and turnover statistics have suggested that the disadvantaged appear to react to work situations differently than do other employees holding the same jobs, there is no research to explain how and why the two groups differ in their work values. This study, therefore, focused on work values of hard-core employees. Since the research was exploratory in nature, no formal hypotheses were formulated. The objectives of the project were as follows: (a) to measure the differences between work values of newly hired hard-core employees and those of other newly hired workers in similar jobs, (b) to identify background characteristics that are related to work values, and (c) to detect changes in work values as a function of orientation programs.

METHOD

Overview

The sample included subjects classified as disadvantaged[5] (hard-core group), regularly employed unskilled or semiskilled workers (comparison group), and middle-class persons (control group). To accomplish objective (a), work values were contrasted beween the hard-core and comparison groups. Objective (b) concerned only the disadvantaged subjects. In meeting objective (c), changes in work values of the hard core were compared with those of the control group.

Subjects

The group of disadvantaged subjects contained 37 females and 73 males, 99 who were black and 11 who were white. They ranged from 18 to 42 years of age with a mean of 23.5, and their educational level varied from 6 to 13 years with a mean of 10.6. The subjects averaged 4.5 years of previous work experience primarily in unskilled jobs. The comparison group included 139 semiskilled and unskilled employees of a midwestern glass manufacturing company and 41 newly hired, hourly workers employed in a southern detergent factory. Serving as control subjects were 137 agents of an eastern insurance company and 115 undergraduates of a small college in California.

The 110 persons classified as hard core were selected from four companies affiliated with NAB. Only 13 subjects terminated before training was finished. Forty subjects hired by a plant in northeastern Ohio produced light bulbs. Thirty-five participants greased and assembled small parts in an automobile training center in northeastern Ohio. In a consortium of 16 companies in southern Ohio, 25 of the disadvantaged received training ranging from manual labor in a steel mill to clerical work in a local bank. Ten additional subjects performed general labor and material handling in a glass manufacturing factory in northwestern Ohio.

Design

The design of this study can be categorized as a nonequivalent control group design (Campbell & Stanley, 1966) in which the control and experimental subjects are not randomly assigned to treatments. Nonequivalent subjects were used as a control group because disadvantaged persons not involved in NAB training were unavailable. In addition, the study must be considered a quasiexperiment because training programs, which differed across companies, were regarded as the same treatment.

Procedure

Participants were told their responses to questionnaires and interviews would provide information about differences in work attitudes, but would have no bearing on their jobs. Participation was voluntary, and subjects were assured that only general results would be reported to their employers. The investigator collected all data from hard-core persons, and questionnaires from other subjects were either mailed to their homes or administered by company personnel and then sent directly to the investigator.

Trainees spent approximately half of each work week in basic education and orientation and the other half in on-the-job training. Hard-core subjects completed the Survey of Work Values (SWV) shortly after they entered training (Time 1) and about 6 weeks later at the completion of the program (Time 2). This questionnaire can be scored on six subscales—Pride in Work, Job Involvement, Activity Preference, Attitude toward Earnings, Social Status of Job, and Upward Striving—and on six clusters—Intrinsic Work Values, Organization-Man Ethic, Upward Striving, Social Status on Job, Conventional Ethic, and Attitude toward Earnings (see Wollack, Goodale, Wijting, & Smith, 1971, for definitions). In the development of the SWV, industrial employees assigned items to their respective subscales with high reliability. When using the scale, subjects are instructed to agree or disagree with each of 54 statements. Scores are obtained by summing responses to items comprising each of six subscales. The test-retest reliabilities of the 9-item subscales range from .68 to .76 despite the fact that the items have been chosen to vary in endorsement level (Wollack et al., 1971). The reading level of the SWV is low enough to permit its use with disadvantaged applicants (Wijting, 1969).

By filling out a biographical inventory at Time 1, each subject supplied information about the physical and pyschological conditions of early home life, the presence of parental work models in the home, the area of the country and size of city in which the person was raised, his work experience, educational and occupational level, financial responsibility, and recent work record. At Time 2, hard-core employees discussed the experiences that were especially satisfying or dissatisfying to them during training in an interview with the investigator.

Comparison employees completed the SWV only once, either shortly after being hired or after an unrecorded amount of experience on the job. Control subjects responded to the SWV once and then a second time about 2 months later. They continued in their usual school or work activities between administrations of the SWV.

Analysis

All analyses involving SWV responses were performed separately for subscale and cluster scores. Absences and incomplete questionnaires created the problem of missing data, often encountered in field research. When cluster or subscale scores were computed, the mean of available responses to items of that cluster or subscale was inserted for missing values (Timm, 1970).

RESULTS

Comparison of Work Values

Discriminant function analysis revealed differences between work values of the hard-core and comparison groups. This statistical technique determined the weighted combination of SWV scores discriminating maximally between the two groups of subjects (Cooley & Lohnes, 1962). The correlations of each variable with the discriminant function (Kelly, Beggs, McNeil, Eichelberger, & Lyon, 1969) and their contribution to the unit variance of the discriminant function indicated the dimensions of work values on which the two groups differed most.

The composite of subscale scores (see Table 1) discriminated between the hard-core and comparison groups with a X^2 of 104.06 ($df = 6$, $p<$ .001). Attitude toward Earnings contributed .48 to the unit variance of the discriminant function, while Activity Preference and Pride in Work accounted for .41 and .07, respectively. Therefore, the main contrast between the two groups was in their preference for activity and deemphasis of money; the hard-core persons scored 5.88 on the discriminant axis, and the regular employees scored 7.12. The subjects were very similar, however, in Job Involvement, Upward Striving, and Social Status of Job.

Analysis of SWV cluster scores (see Table 2) also produced highly significant differentiation between the two groups of employees (X^2 = 81.47, $df = 6$, $p<.001$). Since Conventional Ethic and Upward Striving correlated negatively with the discriminant function, but Attitude toward Earnings correlated positively, the composite reflected an emphasis on wages and a deemphasis of the conventional work ethic. Hard-core subjects scored 7.39 on the composite, while the comparison employees scored 6.30. The two groups were comparable in Social Status of Job, Organization-man Ethic, and Intrinsic Work Values.

Table 1

Discriminant Function Analysis with SWV Subscales as Criteria

Subscale	Hard Core (N = 110)		Comparison (N = 180)		Discriminant Function		
	M	SD	M	SD	b[a]	s[b]	Contribution
Social Status of Job	12.53	2.24	12.89	1.87	.209	.170	.036
Activity Preference	15.85	1.88	17.07	.94	.705	.772	.409
Job Involvement	16.53	1.63	17.03	1.11	−.048	.347	.011
Upward Striving	15.66	1.83	15.87	1.45	.129	.119	.012
Attitude toward Earnings	14.03	2.27	12.39	1.99	−.625	−.685	.484
Pride in Work	16.99	1.63	17.64	.65	.223	.523	.068

Note. Wilks' lambda = .734, X^2 = 104.06, $p<.001$.

[a] Regression weight.

[b] Correlation of variate with its composite.

Correlates of Work Values

Next, the relationships among personal background variables and work values of the hard core were investigated. Since it was decided to combine the biographical information into more reliable and interpretable variates, the 28 background items were subjected to a principal components factor analysis with varimax rotation. After seven factors were extracted, less than 5% of the residual correlations were greater than .10.

Factor 1 (Economic Maturity) was defined by positive loadings on age, years of work experience, marital status, number of persons supported, and by a negative loading on person paying the bills. An individual scoring high on this factor was likely to be old, married with several dependents, to pay most of his family's bills, and to have had much work experience. Factor 2 (Police Trouble) had positive loadings on items dealing with frequency and severity of police trouble by members of one's family and number of arguments with one's parents. Factor 3 (Rural South–Urban North) correlated with the area of the county and size of city in which a person spent his early life. A high score on Factor 4 (Welfare) represented an individual whose father was often out of work and whose family was on welfare. Factor 5 (Socioeconomic Status) summarized the educational level of one's parents and number of family members who drank excessively. Factors 6 and 7 were poorly defined and were not included in subsequent analyses.

Values of the 15 items composing the interpretable factors were converted to z scores and summed to form five clusters. These variates,

Table 2

Discriminant Function Analysis with SWV Clusters as Criteria

Cluster	Harrd Core (N = 110)		Comparison (3N = 180)		Discriminant Function		
	M	SD	M	SD	b[a]	s[b]	Contribution
Intrinsic Work Values	23.06	2.21	23.69	1.17	−.052	−.395	.022
Organization-man Ethic	16.70	2.09	16.97	1.30	−.081	−.171	.015
Upward Striving	8.64	1.40	8.97	.99	−.335	−.295	.075
Social Status of Job	10.25	1.86	10.39	1.64	−.217	−.089	.022
Conventional Ethic	20.39	1.84	21.08	.99	−.403	−.505	.187
Attitude toward Earnings	9.36	1.70	8.13	1.55	.818	.744	.678

Note. Wilks' lambda = .779, X^2 = 81.47, $p < .001$.
[a] Regression weight.
[b] Correlation of variate with its composite.

along with sex and educational level, were included in canonical regression analyses as predictors of SWV subscale and cluster scores. Eleven retrospective variables were dropped because of low variance or high percentage of missing data.

Canonical regression analysis determined the linear combination of the set of predictors and the set of criteria that maximized the correlation between the two sets of variates (Bartlett, 1941; Burt, 1948; Horst, 1961). The correlation of each variate with its composite (Meredith, 1964), and the contribution of a given variate to the unit variance of its composite were used to interpret the canonical analysis. The following interpretations must be considered tentative since cross-validation of the canonical correlations was not feasible because of the small number of subjects. Similarity of the present results to those of previous studies, however, added credibility to the relationships described below.

The first canonical correlation between background variates and SWV subscale scores was .612 (X^2 = 64.33, df = 42, $p < .025$). The predictor composite (see Table 3) showed positive loadings on Economic Maturity (.477), Educational Level (.585), and Rural South–Urban North (.231) and a negative loading on Welfare (−.620). The criterion composite correlated positively with Job Involvement (.880) and Pride in Work (.469) and negatively with Social Status of Job (−.419). The predictor composite described a person from the urban North, who was relatively well educated and economically mature, and whose family had spent

Table 3
Canonical Analysis with SWV Subscales as Criteria ($n = 78$)

Variate	b[a]	s[b]	Contribution
Economic Maturity	397	477	189
Police Trouble	002	046	000
Rural South-Urban North	500	231	116
Welfare	−483	−620	299
Socioeconomic Status	232	239	056
Sex	307	103	032
Educational Level	527	585	308
Social Status of Job	−349	−419	146
Activity Preference	094	452	042
Job Involvement	786	880	691
Upward striving	−089	268	−024
Attitude toward Earnings	−121	−423	051
Pride in Work	197	469	093

Note. Sample included only hard-core subjects. Decimal points are omitted.
[a] Regression weight.
[b] Correlation of variate with its composite.

little or no time on welfare. This type of person values being highly involved in his job and taking pride in his work but deemphasizes the social status of being employed.

The analysis of SWV cluster scores and biographical data ($Rc = .572$, $\chi^2 = 61.53$, $df = 42$, $p < .025$) produced very similar results. The predictor composite in Table 4, composed of Educational Level (.681), Economic Maturity (.406), and Welfare (−.432), described a person of relatively high educational level and economic maturity whose family had spent little or no time on welfare. The criterion function showed positive loadings on Intrinsic Work Values (.724) and Conventional Ethic (.623) and a negative loading on Social Status of Job (−.558). This composite represented a person who values work as its own reward and deemphasizes the social status of being employed.

Modification of Work Values

The next analysis tested the significance of changes in work values experienced by hard-core subjects. Only 65 disadvantaged persons filled out the SWV at Time 2 because of absences, terminations, and refusal of several subjects to take a questionnaire twice in 2 months. Differences

Table 4
Canonical Analysis with SWV Clusters as Criteria ($N = 78$)

Variate	b[a]	s[b]	Contribution
Economic Maturity	459	406	186
Police Trouble	−032	−056	002
Rural South-Urban North	465	222	103
Welfare	−248	−432	107
Socioeconomic Status	128	150	019
Sex	441	263	116
Educational Level	685	681	466
Intrinsic Work Values	449	724	325
Organization-man Ethic	092	100	009
Upward Striving	166	430	071
Social Status of Job	−520	−558	290
Conventional Ethic	454	623	283
Attitude toward Earnings	−084	−252	022

Note: Sample included only hard-core subjects. Decimal points are omitted.
[a] Regression weight.
[b] Correlation of variate with its composite.

were computed by subtracting SWV scores of Time 1 from those of Time 2. Changes in work values of the hard-core subjects ranged from −.25 to .40 and did not differ significantly from those of the control group.

Subjects' Impressions of NAB

Shortly before completion of the orientation, subjects were asked their feelings about the program and what training experiences they found especially satisfying and dissatisfying. Originally, a content analysis of these responses was planned, and frequency of response was to be correlated with changes in work values. This step was dropped when no significant changes in work values were found, but subjects' impressions were still informative. Over 90% said the program was helpful because it provided them with an opportunity to work and earn money. Many with poor work records viewed the training as a second chance to secure gainful employment. Most frequently mentioned as dissatisfying were routine, low-level work, poor condition of training materials, and close supervision by company personnel.

DISCUSSION

Work Values of the Disadvantaged

Results of the two discriminant function analyses strongly supported the premise that the hard core differ markedly from regular employees in their expressed work values. The hard-core subjects scored lower than the comparison group in Activity Preference, Pride in Work, Upward Striving, and Conventional Work Ethic and higher in Attitude toward Earnings. These data indicated that the disadvantaged labor primarily for money rather than for the intrinsic rewards of work. Davis (1946), Himes (1968), and Schwartz and Henderson (1964) also noted the tendency of the hard core to concentrate on immediate gratification and to devalue work for its own sake. Bullough (1967), Killian and Grigg (1962), and Lefton (1968) made similar conclusions because ghetto blacks expressed greater feelings of alienation from the traditional work ethic than did whites or well-to-do blacks. Also supporting this general trend were Centers' report (1949) that lower-class groups strongly valued security and money and Bloom and Barry's finding (1967) that blacks emphasized extrinsic work rewards more than did whites.

The canonical analyses disclosed some important variation in work values within the hard-core sample. Disadvantaged persons of relatively high educational level and economic maturity showed positive attitudes toward the Conventional Work Ethic and the intrinsic rewards of work (Pride in Work and Job Involvement) and placed less emphasis on the social status of employment. Goodale (1970) found that individuals of high socioeconomic status also subscribed to the conventional work ethic. It is interesting to note that Attitude toward Earnings, the work value that discriminated most significantly between hard-core and employed persons, was not related to biographical characteristics of the hard-core sample.

The canonical analyses revealed correlates of work values alien to those held by working members of society. However, longitudinal studies that trace work values developing in children of various socioeconomic classes are needed to identify the time at which the value systems diverge and to suggest determinants of different sets of work values. Until developmental research is done, studies of work values and background information will be more descriptive than explanatory.

Changes in Work Values

An examination of NAB programs that stressed attitude change would have been preferred, but such programs were not available. Perhaps because the emphasis was on acquisition of skill and educational improvement rather than on attitudes, the work values of hard-core subjects were

not significantly altered by orientation. Outlines of the training sched-
ules documented that little time was spent on attempts to modify work
values of the participants.

It is unlikely that 8 weeks of training could have changed work
values that have been formed by many years of experience. A reason for
this may be that disadvantaged persons received training for routine,
unstimulating jobs, while being told that they should regard work as
intrinsically rewarding. The hard core may become disillusioned with
their jobs when expectations formed in training are not fulfilled. Supporting this speculation is the finding of Quinn, Fine, and Levitin (1970)
that the disadvantaged gave poor working conditions most frequently as
the reason for quitting NAB jobs.

Several speculations can be made regarding methods of training
that are likely to produce changes in work values. First, since this study
disclosed specific work values in which hard-core and regular employees
differed, NAB orientation could focus on altering those values. Second,
the variance in work values within the disadvantaged sample indicated
the necessity of having training tailored to individual needs. Counselors
with information about a person's background and initital work values
could develop personalized plans for training. Third, subjects could be
allowed to move in sequential progression toward completion of their
training instead of having to remain in the program for a fixed amount
of time. Fourth, trainees could be placed on jobs after consideration has
been given to abilities and successes demonstrated in training as well
as to the availability of jobs. These suggestions are made as alternatives
to be tried and evaluated, not as rigid guidelines for successful NAB
programs.

A Problem of Measurement

Measurement of values is difficult when subjects are aware of socially
desirable responses. It is legitimate to ask if the differences in work
values of hard-core and comparison subjects were partially due to the
desire of regular employees to gain approval with their SWV responses.
If this is the case, why were the disadvantaged unconcerned with how
their responses would appear? Davis (1946), Himes (1968), and
Schwartz and Henderson (1964) posit that the disadvantaged are not
cognizant of socially acceptable work values because of their isolated
work subculture, and, therefore, cannot pretend to subscribe to them.
Williams (1968) would argue, however, that disadvantaged subjects are
aware of but do not endorse the prevailing work ethic because their current work situations contradict it.[6] Williams (1968) hypothesized that a
hard-core trainee would accept the Protestant Ethic only if he were given
a good job.

Conclusions and Implications for Future Research

Although no changes in work values were detected immediately after orientation in this study, the NAB program may still alter attitudes. Work values of trainees should be measured several months after they have begun their jobs to see if they have accepted a new orientation toward employment. It appears that the hard core are more likely to improve both work values and performance after they have had some experience with jobs more closely matched to their abilities and interests.

Despite problems of measurement, this study gave more precise information regarding the work values of the hard core and ordinary employees in comparable jobs and identified background characteristics that might have produced differences between the two groups. Unfortunately, comparison of performance of hard-core and regular employees on the job was impossible because current high unemployment prevented trainees from moving into full-time work. Relationships between work values and job performance should be examined, however, to discover how different orientations toward work correlate with performance on the job.

Notes

[1] This research was supported under Grant 91-37-70-53 from the Manpower Administration, United States Department of Labor, under the authority of Title I of the Manpower Development and Training Act of 1962, as amended. The author wishes to thank Patricia C. Smith, O. W. Smith, J. P. Flanders, and A. G. Neal for helpful comments on earlier drafts of this article. Appreciation is also expressed to Allen Yates for his assistance in programming and analysis.

[2] James G. Goodale was affiliated with Bowling Green State University, Bowling Green, Ohio, at the time of publication of this article. Requests for reprints should be sent to James G. Goodale, now with the Faculty of Administrative Studies, York University, Downsview 463, Ontario.

[3] Figure presented by Paul W. Kayser, outgoing president of the NAB at the annual meeting in Washington, D.C., March 6, 1970.

[4] The fact that many people quit their jobs does not necessarily mean that the NAB program has failed or that the disadvantaged make unproductive or dissatisfied employees. Individuals may leave their jobs for reasons unrelated to the NAB program (e.g., to move to another city), but their turnover statistics would be included with those who left because they did not like the NAB program or because they did not like work. The statistics were included in the Confidential Progress Report issued by the NAB on January 31, 1970.

[5] A person who is classified as disadvantaged must be a member of a poor family and be unemployed, underemployed, or hindered from seeking work and be at least one of the following: (a) school dropout, (b) minority member, (c) under 22 years of age, (d) 45 years of age or over, and (e) handicapped (Ohio Bureau of Employment Services Letter No. 1055, March 19, 1969).

[6] A simple way to test whether the hard core are aware of socially acceptable work values would be to instruct them to fill out the SWV as they think a white-collar employee would.

References

Bartlett, M. S. The statistical significance of canonical correlation. *Biometrika*, 1941, *32*, 29-37.

Bloom, R., & Barry, J. R. Determinants of work attitudes among Negroes. *Journal of Applied Psychology*, 1967, *51*, 291-294.

Bullough, B. Alienation in the ghetto. *American Journal of Sociology*, 1967, *72*, 469-478.

Burt, C. Factor analysis and canonical correlations. *British Journal of Statistical and Mathematical Psychology*, 1948, *1*, 95-106.

Campbell, D. T., & Stanley, J. C. *Experimental and quasi-experimental designs for research*. Chicago: Rand-McNally, 1966.

Centers, R. *The psychology of social class*. Princeton, N.J.: Princeton University Press, 1949.

Cooley, W. W., & Lohnes, P. R. *Multivariate procedures for the behavioral sciences*. New York: Wiley, 1962.

Davis, A. The motivation of the underprivileged worker. In W. F. Whyte (Ed.), *Industry and society*. New York: McGraw-Hill, 1946.

Goodale, J. G. A canonical regression analysis of work values and biographical information of civil service employees. Unpublished manuscript, Bowling Green State University, 1970.

Himes, J. Work values of Negroes. In L. A. Ferman, J. L. Kornbluh, & J. A. Miller (Eds.), *Negroes and jobs*. Ann Arbor: University of Michigan Press, 1968.

Horst, P. Relations among *m* sets of measures. *Psychometrika*, 1961, *26*, 129-149.

Kelly, F. J., Beggs, D. L., McNeil, K. A., Eichelberger, T., & Lyon, J. *Research design in the behavioral sciences: Multiple regression approach*. Carbondale and London: Southern Illinois University Press and Feffer & Simons, 1969.

Killian, L. M., & Grigg, C. M. Urbanism, race, and anomia. *American Journal of Sociology*, 1962, *67*, 661-665.

Lefton, M. Race, expectations, and anomia. *Social Forces* 1968, *46*, 347-352.

Meredith, W. Canonical correlations with fallible data. *Psychometrika*, 1964, *29*, 55-65.

Quinn, R. P., Fine, B. D., & Levitin, T. Turnover and training: A social-psychological study of disadvantaged workers. Ann Arbor, Mich.: Author 1970. (Mimeo)

Rainwater, L. Crucible of identity: The Negro lower-class family. *Daedalus*, 1966, *95*, 172-211.

Schwartz, M., & Henderson, G. The culture of unemployment: Some notes on Negro children. In A. B. Shostak & W. Comberg (Eds.), *Blue-collar world: Studies of the American worker*. Englewood Cliffs, N.J.: Prentice-Hall, 1964.

Timm, N. H. The estimation of variance-covariance and correlation matrices from incomplete data. *Psychometrika*, 1970, *35*, 417-437.

Weber, M. *The Protestant Ethic and the spirit of capitalism*. New York: Scribner, 1958.

Wijting, J. P. A canonical regression analysis of background variables and work values of underprivileged workers in Toledo, Ohio. Unpublished manuscript, Bowling Green State University, 1969.

Williams, W. Manpower problems in the hard-core ghetto. In N. A. Palombra & E. B. Jakubauskas (Eds.), *An Interdisciplinary approach to manpower research*. Ames, Iowa: Industrial Relations Center, Iowa State University, 1968.

Wollack, S., Goodale, J. G., Wijting, J. P., & Smith, P. C. The development of the Survey of Work Values. *Journal of Applied Psychology*, 1971, *55*, 331-338.

A Comparative Study of Work Attitudes of Black and White Workers

JUGOSLAV S. MILUTINOVICH[1]

Data concerning job-satisfaction differences among whites and blacks were collected from three organizations. The major purpose of this research was to investigate whether cultural-ethnic differences have any important influence on work attitudes of minority and white workers, and to stratify the sample to assess interaction between demographic factors and job satisfaction among races. With the exception of lower satisfaction with supervision by the blacks, no consistent differences in job attitudes were found between the white and minority workers. Stratification by job level and other socio-economic variables did reveal further differences in black and white job attitudes. It also seems that black blue-collar workers have more positive attitudes and black white-collar workers more negative attitudes toward their job than their white counterparts. The relationship between race and work attitudes is very complex. No broad stereotypic assumptions can be stated for all blacks or whites. The intervening variables of occupational level, education, sex, age, tenure, community characteristics, and especially job level must be considered as well as specific determinants of job satisfaction.

As black and other minority-group Americans become integrated into the labor force, the relationship between the minority-group worker and his work has become of considerable interest to behavioral scientists and administrators for practical and theoretical reasons. Negative work attitudes of a worker may result in high turnover, high absenteeism, and

---

This article was prepared especially for this volume. Some of the research described here was presented to the 34th Annual Meeting of the Academy of Management, Seattle, Washington, 1974.

other dysfunctional aspects of job behavior. Emphasis on how best to fit the man and his job has led, among other investigations, to the study of job satisfaction.]

Smith, Kendall, and Hulin (1969) define job satisfaction as "a function of the perceived characteristics of the job in relation to an individual's frame of reference" (p. 361). Thus, job satisfaction results from the interaction of the employee's personality, value system, needs, beliefs, customs, and other internal stimuli that interact with all the external stimuli (i.e., task, place of work, supervisory practice, co-worker attitudes and behavior, community characteristics, etc.). Consequently, differences in frame of reference and environment are expected to produce different job satisfaction for employees.

Several variables relevant to a worker's frame of reference, expressed as job satisfaction, have been found to have affected job attitudes. For example, differences in *sex* (Hulin & Smith, 1964; Smith et al., 1969; Waters & Waters, 1969; Williamson & Karras, 1970; Wild, 1970), *occupational level* (Herzberg, Mausner, Peterson, & Capwell, 1957; Hulin & Smith, 1965; Gurin, Veroff, & Field, 1960; Doll & Gunderson, 1969; Armstrong, 1971), *educational level* (Vollmer & Kinney, 1955; Mann, 1953; Klein & Maher, 1966; Smith et al., 1969), *age* (Bernberg, 1954; Herzberg et al., 1957; Saleh & Otis, 1964; Hulin & Smith, 1965; Altimus & Tersine, 1973; Shapiro & Wahba, 1973), *tenure* (Hulin & Smith, 1965; Gibson & Klein, 1970), *community prosperity* and *environmental characteristics* (Katzell, Barrett, & Parker, 1961; Cureton & Katzell, 1962; Turner & Lawrence, 1965; Hulin, 1966; Blood & Hulin, 1967; Smith et al., 1969; Wild & Kempner, 1972), and *leadership style* (Milutinovich, 1970) were all found to have affected job attitudes.

Despite the publication of more than four thousand articles on job satisfaction (Locke, 1969), there is a dearth of studies that analyze the significant role that racial differences play in the frame of reference as it affects job satisfaction. The most recent research indicates that all blacks or all whites cannot be lumped together (Miller & Dreger, 1973), but must be studied by controlling for relevant demographic variables such as sex, education, income, job tenure, age, job level, etc.

Data from five national Gallup polls (Weaver, 1974) as well as findings by the W. E. Upjohn Institute for Employment Research (1973) indicate that blacks are generally less satisfied with their jobs than whites. Among the few studies involving racial differences in job attitudes were Slocum and Strawser (1972), who found that Negro CPA's assigned more importance to lower-order needs and had more need deficiency on all items than their white counterparts. Bloom and Barry (1967) and Champagne and King (1967) tested Herzberg's two-factor theory on black and white blue-collar workers and found hygiene factors were more important for blacks than for whites. In a hospital study involving only females, O'Reilly and Roberts (1973) found that whites were consistently more satisfied with most aspects of their jobs, although the differences seemed to diminish for the lower job levels. Further, satisfaction with promotion accounted for a significantly greater proportion of the overall job satisfaction variance for whites at the higher-level jobs than for blacks at the same job level. In a study of black and white clerical workers in South Africa, Orpen (1974) found blacks more satisfied with their jobs than whites.

In an industrial setting involving both male and female blue-collar workers, a few minor differences were found between blacks and whites on socio-economic and background variables (Katzell, Ewen, and Korman, 1970). Their major substantive conclusions concerning work attitudes were as follows: (a) on the whole, black employees were somewhat more satisfied with their jobs than were whites, especially in attitudes toward advancement, co-workers, and job content; (b) statistically, race was not a particularly potent factor in explaining differences in job satisfaction; (c) the tendency of blacks to have somewhat more favorable work attitudes than whites, while true on the average, was not uniform among the different companies; and (d) black females were less satisfied than white females, particularly with their pay. However, Katzell et al. (1970) admit that their new measure of work attitudes may lack "sensitivity or reliability" (p. 77).

Gavin and Ewen (1974), using the data from Katzell et al. (1970), performed a single-principle, axis-factor analysis and varimax rotation and found black blue-collar workers were more satisfied than whites with advancement, job and company, pay and working conditions, and total job satisfaction.

Since there have been so few empirical field studies with large samples and adequate consideration of methodological issues examining the significance of the relationship between race and job satisfaction, the purpose of the present study is to re-examine this association. The major objectives of this study are: (1) to investigate whether cultural-ethnic differences have any important influence on job satisfaction for black and white blue-collar and white-collar workers; and (2) to stratify the sample to assess interactions between demographic factors and job satisfaction among races.

Method

Subjects. The sample was composed of 1037 blue-collar and white-collar employees from three organizations. Among the 711 blue-collar workers there were 211 blacks and 500 whites. The white-collar group contained

65 blacks and 261 whites. Organization A, which represented 48 percent of the sample, was a footwear factory in Massachusetts; organization B, which represented 40 percent of the sample, was a water department in a large Eastern city; and organization C, which represented 12 percent of the sample, was a small metal-processing plant in Pennsylvania.

Instruments. The Job Descriptive Index (JDI) developed by Smith et al. (1969) was used to measure job satisfaction with work, supervision, co-workers, pay, promotion, and overall job satisfaction.[2] Very impressive reliability and validity data are given for the measure. Both convergent and discriminant validity of the JDI, as defined by Campbell and Fiske (1959), have been shown by Smith et al. (1969). This measure, according to Vroom (1964), "is without doubt the most carefully constructed measure of job satisfaction in existence today" (p. 100).

Data concerning relevant socio-demographic variables were also collected by self-reports and the sample segmented with respect to job level, sex, education, income, tenure, age, and community prosperity. In selecting these variables for stratification, the criterion used by Smith et al. (1969) was applied—each variable has an influence on the satisfaction norms and on the scores of the five determinants—as data given by Smith et al. (1969) indicate. The same ranges used by Smith et al. for socio-demographic variables were used in this study. In addition, age and job level, which were excluded by Smith et al. (1969), were used in this study. Some changes in our value systems and a larger gap between older and younger generations may have a larger role today on work attitudes than it had a few years ago. Job level was added to separate blue-collar workers from clerical, supervisory, and professional employees.

Procedure. During the administration of the questionnaire in each organization the work process was halted to allow employees time to answer questions without interruption. Employees who were absent during the administration of the questionnaire and members of middle and top management were not included in the sample. Anonymity was assured and explicitly stressed in the introduction to the questionnaire and by the researchers orally during the administration of the questionnaire in order to insure validity of the responses. Participation was encouraged but not required. The response rate of employees present in the room was about 99 percent. About 4 percent of the questionnaires had to be eliminated due to numerous omissions and/or incorrect methods of responding.

Results

Analysis of the JDI scales for the unstratified total sample presented in Table 1 revealed that the black workers were *less* satisfied with supervision ($p<.001$), but were *more* satisfied with promotion than white workers ($p<.001$).[3]

To determine if job level moderates the relationship of race with satisfaction, the total sample was dichotomized into blue-collar and white-collar employees.

According to Table 2, differences in job satisfaction between black and white blue-collar workers are similar to the total unstratified sample. This is not too surprising, because the total sample contained a greater proportion of blue-collar workers. However, total job satisfaction of black blue-collar workers was significantly higher than that of whites ($p<.01$), and no significant differences were found among blue-collar workers for satisfaction with work, co-workers, and pay.

The picture that emerges from the analysis of the white-collar sample is radically different from that of the blue-collar sample as presented in Table 2. White-collar blacks were significantly *less* satisfied than their white co-workers with work itself ($p<.01$), with supervision ($p<.05$), with co-workers ($p<.01$), and with total job satisfaction ($p<.001$). This tendency is also apparent regarding satisfaction with promotion ($p<.075$).

The Omega square (Hays, 1965) tests were employed to estimate the strength of the relationship between race and job satisfaction. Since the largest Omega square was only .07 and the next highest .03, it can be concluded that race, although significant in some cases, accounts for very little satisfaction variance because the Omega square of .07 is equal to a correlation coefficient of about .27, which is hardly significant.

Further stratification of the white-collar sample into clerical, supervisory, and professional employees indicated the additional differences presented in Table 3. A 2×3 ANOVA indicates that both the blacj clerical workers and the black supervisors were *less* satisfied with the work itself than their white colleagues' occupational group ($p<.05$), but the black-white differences in satisfaction with work for the professional group, although in the same direction, were not statistically significant. Consistent with repeated findings in the literature, satisfaction with work itself increased with occupational level.

A significant interaction between job level and race was found for satisfaction with supervision. While blacks in clerical positions indicated *less* satisfaction with their supervisors ($p<.001$) than their white peers, the situation was reversed for the black supervisors, who indicated higher satisfaction with their superiors than their white colleagues. Another significant difference found in this particular analysis was the *lower* overall job satisfaction for blacks as compared to whites ($p<.05$). This difference is pronounced for both the clerical ($p<.01$) and professional ($p<.05$) employees, but does not exist for supervisors. In fact, the black supervisors had the highest overall job satisfaction among the var-

Table 1

Means and One-Way Analysis of Variance of Job Satisfaction Scores Among Black and White Employees for the Total Sample[1]

Determinant	df		MS		Race of Employees		F Ratio	W^2
	Betw.	Error	Betw.	Error	Black $N=276$	White $N=761$		
Work	1	1035	101.0	165015.6	28.71	29.41	<1	.001
Supervision	1	1035	2138.1	178521.5	35.35	38.60	12.40*	.018
Co-Workers	1	1035	45.1	190717.7	38.60	39.07	<1	.002
Pay[2]	1	636	149.5	119176.4	13.42	14.67	<1	.000
Promotion	1	1035	5256.7	274958.5	22.45	17.36	19.79*	.022
Total J.S. (4 Det. pay excl.)	1	1035	44.2	1703845.3	125.17	124.71	<1	.001

[1] The higher the mean value the higher the job satisfaction.
[2] Data for determinant pay were collected only from organizations A and C. Concerning the pay variable the sample consisted of 86 blacks and 552 whites.
* $< .001$

Table 2
One-Way Analysis of Variance of Job Satisfaction Scores Among Blue-Collar and White-Collar Black and White Employees for the Stratified Sample with Respect to Type of Job[1]

Blue-Collar Workers

	df		MS					
					Black	White		
Determinant	Betw.	Error	Betw.	Error	$N=211$	$N=500$	F Ratio	W^2
Work	1	709	552.1	112644.7	28.24	26.31	3.48	.002
Supervision	1	709	801.6	132499.5	34.24	36.57	4.29*	.009
Co-Workers	1	709	160.7	141688.5	39.26	38.22	<1	.002
Pay[2]	1	486	6.53	165.84	13.61	13.30	<1	.000
Promotion	1	709	12109.0	166138.1	23.94	14.90	51.68***	.073
Total J.S. (pay excl.)	1	709	13543.5	1194310.2	125.55	116.00	8.04**	.009

[1]The higher the mean value the higher the job satisfaction.
[2]Data for determinant pay were collected only from organizations A and C. Concerning the variable pay the sample consisted of 82 black and 406 white employees.

*$p < .05$
**$p < .01$
***$p < .001$

Table 2 (Continued)

White-Collar Workers

| | df | | MS | | Black | White | | |
Determinant	Betw.	Error	Betw.	Error	$N=65$	$N=261$	F Ratio	W^2
Work	1	324	1322.56	121.04	30.23	35.27	10.93**	.030
Supervision	1	324	609.26	125.23	38.95	42.38	4.86*	.012
Co-Workers	1	324	867.37	151.92	36.45	40.53	5.71**	.014
Pay[3]	—	—	—	—	—	—	—	—
Promotion	1	324	984.76	304.14	17.63	21.98	3.28[4]	.007
Total J.S. (pay excl.)	1	324	15012.73	1290.81	123.95	140.90	11.63***	.032

[3]Job satisfaction with pay for the white-collar workers was not calculated because the sample was not large enough.
[4]Significant at the .075 level.
  *$p < .05$
 **$p < .01$
***$p < .001$

Table 3
Two-Way ANOVA Means and F Ratios for Job Satisfaction Determinants Among
Black and White Clerical, Supervisory, and Professional Employees[1]

Determinant	Clerical		Supervisory		Professional		df	F Ratio		
	Black $N=38$	White $N=131$	Black $N=11$	White $N=77$	Black $N=16$	White $N=53$		A=Race	B=Job Level	Interaction AXB
Work	27.71	32.33(a)[2]	30.91	37.32(a)	35.75	39.57	1,320	8.93**	7.10***	0.22
Supervision	36.45	42.88(c)	46.27	42.00	39.87	41.68	1,320	.57	2.39	3.18*
Co-Workers	35.90	40.75(a)	39.64	39.70	35.56	41.19	1,320	3.31	0.21	0.81
Promotion	17.53	21.66	25.46	23.35	12.50	20.79	1,320	1.60	2.76	1.23
Total Job Satisfaction	118.13	137.82(b)	144.45	142.79	123.69	145.96(a)	1,320	5.79*	2.63	1.85

[1]The higher the mean value the higher the job satisfaction.
[2]Level of significance for one-way ANOVA analyzed separately for each group of white-collar workers: clerical, supervisory, and professional.
(a) $p < .05$; (b) $p < .01$; (c) $p < .001$.
  *$p < .05$
 **$p < .01$
***$p < .001$

ious black samples. Although their satisfaction with work was found to be lower than their white peers, their overall satisfaction was not significantly lower than that of any other white groups. The only other significant difference was that black clerical workers had *lower* job satisfaction with their co-workers than did their white counterparts ($p<.05$).

Certain concomitants of frame of reference that may somewhat affect job satisfaction are a number of socio-demographic characteristics. The influence of these variables on the various job-satisfaction scales was examined for blue-collar and white-collar workers separately. Table 4 presents the significant F-ratios found for the blue-collar workers.[4]

Table 4

Two-Way ANOVA Summary Table of Significant F Ratios for Job Satisfaction Determinants Obtained by Matching and Stratification of Black and White Blue-Collar Workers

Variable	df	Work	Supervision	Co-Workers	Promotion
A. Race					
B. Sex					
AXF Interaction	1,697	BF < WF, BM 9.35**	BF < WF, BM 7.07**	BF < WF, BM 7.05**	ns
C. Education	4,700	U-Shaped 2.39*	ns	ns	ns
D. Income	2,705	Linear 6.33**	ns	ns	Linear 3.32*
E. Tenure	3,587	U-Shaped 2.61*	U-Shaped 3.79*	ns	ns
F. Age	3,590	Linear 3.89**	Linear 8.89***	ns	ns
AXF Interaction	3,590	ns	ns	B∩-Shaped W U-Shaped 3.54*	ns
G. Community Prosperity[1]	2,705	∩-Shaped 3.17*	ns	ns	ns
AXG Interaction[2]	2,705	BA < Others 4.23*	2.66[3]	BA < Others 5.17**	ns

Note: B=Black; W=White; M=Male; F=Female; A=affluent neighborhood.
[1]There was a significant F ratio for total job satisfaction for this variable (f=3.10*).
[2]There was an interaction effect between community prosperity and race in respect to total job satisfaction (f=5.53*).
[3]Significant at the .068 level.
   * <.05   ** <.01   *** <.001

Stratification of Blue-Collar Sample

Sex. The interaction effect between *race* and *sex* of blue-collar workers revealed some significant differences (see Table 4). Black female workers were *less* satisfied with work, supervision, and co-workers than their white female counterparts ($p<.01$). Black females were also *less* satisfied than black males with the same job aspects. Thus, black, female blue-collar workers were the least satisfied group of workers with respect to work, supervision, and co-workers compared with black male or white female counterparts.

Education. There was no significant interaction effect between education and race. Education, per se, had a significant influence on work. The satisfaction with work was mildly U-shaped. The *less* and the *more* educated blue-collar workers were found to have higher satisfaction with work than the average-educated workers.

Income. There was no significant interaction effect between income and race. However, income as a single variable was linearly related to satisfaction with work and promotion. The higher the reported income level, the higher the satisfaction with work and promotion.

Tenure. The longer their tenure, the more the blue-collar workers were satisfied with work and supervision. However, the curve was mildly U-shaped. After the first three years or less of tenure, satisfaction with work and supervision dropped, only to increase again after seven or more years of tenure. This tendency was more pronounced for the black blue-collar workers than for their white counterparts.

Age. Generally, older blue-collar employees were more satisfied with work and supervision regardless of race. An increase in satisfaction with work and supervision, as a function of age, was noticeable. Blacks, with the exception of those twenty-nine years of age or less, were significantly more satisfied with work in general for each age category. Of special interest was the interaction effect between *race* and *age* with satisfaction with co-workers. The *inversely* U-shaped curve reported by the data indicates that blacks up to twenty-nine years of age and blacks fifty years or older were less satisfied with co-workers than blacks between the ages of thirty to forty-nine. A completely opposite statement can be made about the white blue-collar workers, whose curve of satisfaction with co-workers is U-shaped. Thus there is a significant difference in satisfaction with coworkers between blacks and whites who are thirty to forty-nine years of age, blacks being significantly more satisfied with co-workers than their white counterparts in this age category.

Community Prosperity. The main significant effect of this variable was on satisfaction with work. The curve had a mild *inverse* U-shape because the blue-collar workers from poor and rich communities were less satisfied with their work than the blue-collar workers from middle-income communities. There was also significant interaction between *race* and *community prosperity* in respect to satisfaction with work, supervision, co-workers, and overall job satisfaction. The general pattern which emerged was that the more prosperous the respondent perceived his community, the greater the satisfaction with the above mentioned factors for both blacks and whites. This pattern, however, did not hold up for the blue-collar blacks from the more prosperous communities, because they were the least satisfied group of blacks with regard to work, supervision, and co-workers. Hence, the significant interaction effect.

The data also indicate that blacks from poor and slum neighborhoods were more satisfied with work, promotion, and total job satisfaction than their white counterparts. It should also be noted that blacks from poor and middle-income neighborhoods had higher total job satisfaction than whites from similar types of neighborhoods. However, the blacks from the more affluent neighborhoods were less satisfied than the more affluent whites on total job satisfaction.

Stratification of White-Collar Workers

Sex. Table 5 indicates that white-collar females were, in general, less satisfied than white-collar males with the work itself ($p < .01$), and there was also an interaction effect between *race* and *sex* regarding satisfaction with supervision. Black white-collar females were the least satisfied with supervision. However, there was no significant difference between white and black male white-collar workers with supervison.

Income. The lower the income, the less white-collar workers were satisfied with their work regardless of race. An interaction effect between *race* and *income* affected satisfaction with supervision. Blacks in the low-income group had the least satisfaction with supervision as compared with high-income blacks and low-income whites.

Age. As in the case of blue-collar workers, satisfaction with work also increased linearly as a function of age for the white-collar workers, irrespective of race. White white-collar workers twenty-nine years of age or less were the most dissatisfied group. Blacks were also less satisfied with their work than white workers regardless of age category.

Discussion

Results from this study indicate that neither white employees nor black employees can be considered as homogeneous groups that hold similar attitudes toward work. Comparison of total job satisfaction between blue-collar and white-collar blacks revealed that, although these two

Table 5

Two-Way ANOVA Summary Table of Significant F Ratios for Job
Satisfaction Determinants Obtained by Matching and
Stratification of Black and White White-Collar Workers

Variable	df	Work	Supervision
A. Race			
B. Sex	1,322	F < M 7.31**	ns
AXB Interaction	1,322	ns	BF < BM, WF 5.90*
D. Income	1,302	Linear 10.07**	ns
AXD Interaction	1,302	ns	BLI < BHI, WLI 5.99*
F. Age	2,225	Linear 4.27*	ns
G. Community Prosperity[1]			

Note: B=Black; W=White; F=Female; M=Male; LI=Low income; HI=High income

[1] It was not possible to match the sample on this demographic variable because there were not enough black white-collar workers in affluent neighborhoods and white white-collar workers in the slum and poor neighborhoods.

*p < .05
**p < .01

groups do not differ much from each other, they do differ with respect to the white peer groups in opposite directions. While black blue-collar workers had significantly *more* total job satisfaction than white blue-collar workers, black white-collar employees were *less* satisfied than white white-collar employees. These findings are consistent with the findings of Katzell et al. (1970) and Gavin and Ewen (1974) that black blue-collar workers were somewhat more satisfied than white blue-collar workers. In addition, O'Reilly and Roberts (1973) found that black, female white-collar workers were less satisfied than their white counterparts.

The only black-white difference that was consistent across occupational lines was satisfaction with supervision. All black groups, except for supervisors, consistently rated themselves as having less satisfaction with this determinant. Similar results were obtained by O'Reilly and Roberts (1973) in a study of black females in a hospital setting.

It is very likely that white supervisors, who usually comprise a majority of the supervisory force, are not attuned to the specific needs of minority workers even though they are not consciously discriminating against them. Possibly, the fact that the vast majority of white supervisors are unfamiliar with or unresponsive to the needs of black workers may lead to differential treatment. Blacks may also have a different perception and/or relate to white supervisors differently than do whites. There is a considerable amount of data indicating that black performance suffers under white leadership (Katz & Cohen, 1962; Katz & Greenbaum, 1963; Lefcourt and Ladwig, 1965 (b); Katz, Roberts, & Robinson, 1965; Katz, 1967). It may be assumed that blacks prefer to work under black supervisors; Katz and Benjamin (1960) reported that "Negroes favored one another as future working companions while whites showed no bias" (p. 454). It is not surprising that King and Bass (1970) state that white supervisors are having trouble managing black subordinates in mixed and all-black work groups. These findings point out the necessity of sensitizing white supervisors to the specific problems of minorities and the promotion of qualified minority workers into the supervisory ranks.

Stratification by type of job revealed additional black-white differences in job attitudes. Black blue-collar workers were more satisfied with promotion than the white blue-collar sample. The greater total job satisfaction of the black blue-collar worker is partially attributable to his favorable rating of his promotional opportunities. At first sight this finding is rather odd, considering that until very recently minorities certainly have not been promoted as much as whites (King & Bass, 1970).

The O'Reilly and Roberts (1973) study, cited earlier, which did not find significant black-white differences for satisfaction with promotion for any of their occupational strata, may shed some additional light on this rather interesting finding. Performing separate factor analyses for the black and white samples, O'Reilly and Roberts found that promotional opportunities constituted a much greater component of overall satisfaction for white than for black registered nurses and supervisors. However, Katzell et al. (1970) and Gavin and Ewen (1974) found higher satisfaction of black blue-collar workers with advancement, thus confirming findings of this study in respect to the blue-collar strata. Also relevant are the findings of Stouffer et al. (1949) and Patchen (1960). They concluded that satisfaction with promotion is high when the chances for promotion are poor, and vice versa. Germane in this respect are Rowan's (1968) results, which suggest that "many Negroes entered industry without any expectations of moving up the promotional ladder —[while] most whites enter the industry with expectations of being promoted as rapidly as their seniority would allow" (p. 102). This finding is also consistent with the need-satisfaction construct presented by Locke (1969) in which satisfaction with certain aspects of a job is an inverse relationship between the difference of level of aspiration and level of achievement. Empirical evidence also indicates that minorities, and especially blacks, tend to see events that happen to them as a result of luck or events outside their control. They expect reinforcements to occur as a consequence of actions unrelated to their behavior (Gluskinos et al., 1972; Lefcourt and Ladwig, 1965 (a), 1965 (b); Zytkoskee et al., 1971).

A rather different picture emerges when attention is shifted to black-white differences in job attitudes among white-collar workers. The largest and most consistent black-white difference was satisfaction with work. Although job satisfaction with work increases as a function of job level, as most of the literature reports, black white-collar workers were consistently less satisfied with work than their white co-workers of the same occupational category. This finding is also in agreement with the O'Reilly and Roberts (1973) study reported earlier. It seems that black white-collar workers who have achieved some job status hold higher expectations than their white peers. However, these expectations are apparently often frustrated and what results is a lower satisfaction with regard to work of black white-collar workers than their white counterparts.

The black supervisory sample diverges from the clerical and professional sample on all other JDI scales. The high total job satisfaction, which was the highest for any of the black samples, can be attributed to their favorable evaluation of their superiors and their promotional opportunities. These black supervisors, who probably come from the ranks of the blue-collar workers, held attitudes similar to black blue-collar workers, but "made it" beyond their expectations. However, the black supervisor is not as satisfied with his work as the white supervisor; the significantly lower satisfaction with work itself was counterbalanced by higher satisfaction of black supervisors with their superiors and promotional opportunities, thus equalizing total job satisfaction for both supervisory groups.

On the other hand, the discrepancy in total job satisfaction between the black and the white professionals is noteworthy. This is rather surprising if one takes at face value the current notion that qualified black professionals are at a premium and can make demands concerning specific aspects of their jobs. The data presented here certainly would not suggest that the black professional feels this way. It is possible that "Negro aspirations have risen far more swiftly than Negro advances" (Pettigrew, 1964, p. 179) in general and in relation to their attitudes toward the job in particular. For the professional black, this means lower overall job satisfaction. This finding is also consistent with the Slocum and Strawser (1972) findings concerning need deficiency and lower need satisfaction of black CPAs compared with white CPAs.

The lower satisfaction of females, in general, and of black females, in particular, is consistent with other findings (Hulin & Smith, 1964; Smith et al., 1969; Wild, 1970; Katzell et al., 1970; Shapiro & Wahba, 1973; O'Reilly & Roberts, 1973). This difference may be partially attributed to the entire constellation of variables that co-vary with sex, e.g., job level, income, promotional opportunities, social norms, etc. It is particularly understandable that black females who may be the sole support of the family have lower satisfaction with many aspects of their jobs. The role of a work life may be more important for them than for their white counterparts, who frequently work only to supplement their husbands' income.

Also consistent with the literature was the finding that education and, in particular, income affected satisfaction with work itself (Smith et al., 1969). This is not surprising because the type of work an individual does is clearly related to his education and income. Education and income probably influence the frame of reference of employees especially in terms of their expectations. Workers with high incomes generally have better jobs and consequently more to be satisfied about. This study confirmed the Vollmer and Kinney (1955) finding of negative relationship between level of education and job satisfaction with work, but only for the less-educated blue-collar workers. The U-shaped relationship between education and satisfaction with work also indicates higher satisfaction with work of more educated blue-collar workers, which confirms the Smith et al. (1969) findings. It can be assumed that the more educated employee has a chance to occupy a more desirable job and thus a more positive attitude toward his work role, and vice versa.

The U-shaped relationship found between tenure and satisfaction with work suggests that even a routine blue-collar job initially provides some challenge. Satisfaction will drop when the worker gains mastery over the job, causing him to perceive it as boring and routine. However, satisfaction may increase, perhaps as a result of the necessity to reduce dissonance and to adapt to the situation. Similar relationships have been reported by Herzberg et al. (1957), but have been questioned by Hoppock (1960), Hulin and Smith (1965), as well as Smith et al. (1969). It should be noted that this relationship between tenure and satisfaction was not apparent for white-collar workers, who probably have more challenging jobs and have more opportunity for job mobility. Only the black blue-collar workers had a well-defined U-shaped function between age and tenure. Similar findings were reported by Roderick and Nicholson (1974). For the white blue-collar workers during the last years of tenure there was a slight decline in job satisfaction with work. (This was also found by Shapiro and Wahba (1973).)

The relationship of age to job satisfaction has been a subject of much debate. Herzberg et al. (1957) were the first to report the U-shaped function between age and job satisfaction. Hulin and Smith (1965) and Smith et al. (1969) found no consistent effect over the five satisfaction scales. However, Bernberg (1954), Saleh and Otis (1964), Gibson and Klein (1970), Shapiro and Wahba (1973), and Altimus and Tersine (1973) found a positive relationship between age and job satisfaction. In the present study, age was found to have an effect on satisfaction with work itself, both for blue-collar and white-collar workers irrespective of race. Age also affected satisfaction with supervision. Altimus and Tersine (1973) found a significant difference in job satisfaction with work, but not with supervision among three age groups of blue-collar workers, thus partially supporting the findings of this study.

There is a possibility that the increased generation gap of the last few years widened the values, norms, perception, frames of reference, etc., and may have led to higher expectations or aspiration levels on the part of the young workers. This is particularly true in the case of the young black, where this generation gap is even more pronounced. The high satisfaction with co-workers of the middle-aged, black blue-collar workers and low job satisfaction with co-workers of their white counterparts was somewhat supported by Katzell et al. (1970), who found blacks more satisfied with co-workers in general. The U-shaped relationship between satisfaction with co-workers and age for blacks and the inversely U-shaped relationship for their white counterparts needs further investigation if the significant difference was not due to chance.

The relationship between community prosperity and job satisfaction was rather surprising inasmuch as it conflicts with findings reported in the literature.[5] Kendall (1963), Hulin (1966), Blood and Hulin (1967), and Wild and Kempner (1972) found that job satisfaction is higher in communities with substantial slum conditions as compared to more prosperous communities. Only the blue-collar blacks from the most prosperous communities in this study conformed to the results reported by Hulin (1966) and other researchers in that they actually did report lower job satisfaction. It is possible that even within the past half decade the attitudes of workers from slum and poor communities have changed, insofar as their aspirations and need levels may have risen much faster than their actual achievements, resulting in lower job satisfaction. It is also possible that *objective* measurement of community prosperity based on U.S. Bureau of Census, *County and City Data Book* (1962), used by Kendall (1963), Hulin (1966), and Blood and Hulin (1967), might give different results from *subjective* method of measurement used in this study. A comparative analysis of Kendall's objective method and the subjective method used here would throw more light on this problem of measuring community prosperity and the adequacy of each method.

Although O'Reilly and Roberts (1973) found a relatively strong relationship between job satisfaction and race for the female hospital employees, this study, as well as Katzell et al. (1970) and Gavin and Ewen (1974), could not support the findings of O'Reilly and Roberts. Ethnic differences were only slightly associated with job satisfaction, accounting very insignificantly for the difference in job satisfaction. However, low association between race and job satisfaction does not mean that there are no significant differences in work attitudes between races, as this and other studies indicated.

It may be assumed that minority-group members approach their jobs with different frames of reference, especially with respect to certain specific determinants of job satisfaction, as indicated by the stratified sample. Another important conclusion is that neither ethnic group can be considered homogeneous insofar as work attitudes are concerned. Stratification of the sample by type of job has indicated opposite work attitudes for the same race as well as for different races. It seems that black blue-collar workers have more positive attitudes toward their jobs than white blue-collar workers, as this study, as well as Gavin and Ewen's (1974) study, indicates. On the other hand, black white-collar workers seem to have more negative attitudes toward their jobs than their white counterparts, as this, as well as O'Reilly and Roberts' (1973) and Orpen's (1974) findings, indicates. There are some significant differences among companies, and further investigation of organizational climate and characteristics may be necessary to examine conditions that have contributed to those differences, as Katzell et al. (1970) and this study indicate (see footnote 2). The present study was undertaken to analyze these differences, not to find the cause of the differences.

In summary, it can be concluded that the relationship between race and job attitudes is very complex. No broad stereotypic assumptions can be stated for all blacks. Data analyses presented here generally illustrate the existence of some job satisfaction differences among black and white workers. An explanation of these differences is purely speculative. It can be assumed that minority groups and white workers approach their jobs with different frames of reference. These differences should be verified by further research. In this respect the intervening variables of sex, occupational level, age, tenure, community, organizational characteristics, and especially job level should be considered as well as specific determinants of job satisfaction.

Notes

[1]Jugoslav S. Milutinovich is Assistant Professor of Management, School of Business Administration, Temple University, Philadelphia, Pennsylvania.

[2]It was not possible to collect data on pay in organization B because negotiations with the labor union for extension of the union contract had already started. Data on variable pay are from organizations A and C only. To test the correlation between total job satisfaction with all five determinants and total job satisfaction with four determinants (pay excluded), a simple regression analysis with data from organizations A and C was made. This analysis showed a Pearson product moment coefficient of .95 ($N=661$) with these two variables. Thus, total job satisfaction (four determinants—pay excluded) is nearly as good a measure as total job satisfaction (five determinants).

[3]Analysis of data for individual organizations revealed some differences among companies, as in the Katzell et al. (1970) study. The main deviation from the total sample was in organization B, in which whites were *more* satisfied with work than blacks ($p<.001$), and in which there was no significant difference in job satisfaction with promotion. In organization C, blacks were also *less* satisfied with co-workers than whites ($p<.05$).

[4]Due to the length limit of the original manuscript, mean values, F-ratios, and other pertinent data are not presented for the stratified blue-collar and white-collar workers, but are available upon request from the author.

[5]The main thrust of this paper is on job satisfaction of black and white workers. For an analysis of neighborhood prosperity and its effect on job satisfaction among black and white workers, see Milutinovich and Tsaklanaganos (1974).

References

Altimus, C. A., & Tersine, R. J. Chronological age and job satisfaction: The young blue-collar worker. *Academy of Management Journal,* 1973, *16*(1), 53-66.

Armstrong, T. Job content and context factors related to satisfaction for different occupational levels. *Journal of Applied Psychology,* 1971, *55,* 55-57.

Bernberg, R. E. Socio-psychological factors in industrial morale, III: Relation of age to morale. *Personnel Psychology,* 1954, *7,* 393-399.

Blood, M. R., & Hulin, C. L. Alienation, environmental characteristics, and worker responses. *Journal of Applied Psychology,* 1967, *51,* 204-290.

Bloom, R., & Barry, J. Determinants of work attitudes among Negroes. *Journal of Applied Psychology,* 1967, *51,* 287-292.

Campbell, D. T., & Fiske, D. W. Convergent and discriminant validation by the multitrait-multimethod matrix. *Psychological Bulletin,* 1959, *56,* 81-105.

Champagne, J., & King, D. Job satisfaction factors among underprivileged workers. *Personnel and Guidance Journal,* 1967, *45,* 429-434.

Cureton, E. E., & Katzell, R. A. A further analysis of the relations among job performance and situational variables. *Journal of Applied Psychology,* 1962, *46,* 230.

Doll, R., & Gunderson, E. K. Occupational group as a moderator of the job satisfaction-job performance relationship. *Journal of Applied Psychology,* 1969, *53,* 359-361.

Gavin, J. F., & Ewen, R. B. Racial differences in job attitudes and performance: Some theoretical considerations and empirical findings. *Personnel Psychology,* 1974, *27,* 455-464.

Gibson, J. L., & Klein, S. M. Employee attitudes as a function of age and length of service: A reconceptualization. *Academy of Management Journal,* 1970, *13,* 411-415.

Gluskinos, U. M., Toth, M. A., & Pond, W. L. Alienation of college youth: Black, white, east and west. Unpublished paper, Temple University, 1972.

Gurin, G., Veroff, J., & Field, S. *Americans view their mental health.* New York: Basic Books, 1960.

Hays, W. L. *Statistics for psychologists.* New York: Holt, Rinehart and Winston, 1965.

Herzberg, R., Mausner, B., Peterson, R. O., & Campbell, D. G. *Job attitudes: Review of research and opinion.* Pittsburgh: Psychological Service of Pittsburgh, 1957.

Hoppock, R. A. A twenty-seven year follow-up on job satisfaction of employed adults. *Personnel and Guidance Journal,* 1960, *38,* 489-492.

Hulin, C. Effects of community characteristics on measures of job satisfaction. *Journal of Applied Psychology,* 1966, *50,* 185-192.

Hulin, C. L., & Smith, P. C. Sex differences in job satisfaction. *Journal of Applied Psychology,* 1964, *48,* 88-92.

Hulin, C. L., & Smith, P. C. A linear model for job satisfaction. *Journal of Applied Psychology,* 1965, *49,* 209-216.

Katz, I. Some determinants of racial differences in intellectual achievement. *International Journal of Psychology,* 1967, *2,* 1-21.

Katz, I., & Benjamin, L. Effects of white authoritarianism in bi-racial work groups. *Journal of Abnormal Social Psychology,* 1960, *61,* 448-456.

Katz, I., & Cohen, M. The effects of training Negroes upon cooperative problem solving in bi-racial teams. *Journal of Abnormal and Social Psychology,* 1962, *64,* 319-325.

Katz, I., & Greenbaum, C. Effects of anxiety, threat and racial environment on task performance of Negro college students. *Journal of Abnormal and Social Psychology,* 1963, *66,* 562-567.

Katz, I., Roberts, S. O., & Robinson, J. Effects of task difficulty, race of administrator, and instructions on digit symbol performance of Negroes. *Journal of Personality and Social Psychology,* 1965, *2,* 53-59.

Katzell, R. A., Barrett, R. S., & Parker, T. C. Job satisfaction, job performance and situational characteristics. *Journal of Applied Psychology,* 1961, *45,* 65-72.

Katzell, R. A., Ewen, R. B., & Korman, A. K. The job attitudes of workers from different ethnic backgrounds. U.S. Department of Labor Contract No. 41-8-006-34. New York: New York University, 1970.

Kendall, L. M. Canonical analysis of job satisfaction and behavioral personal background, and situational data. Unpublished doctoral dissertation, Cornell University, 1963.

King, D., & Bass, B. Leadership, power and influence. In H. L. Fromkin & J. J. Sherwood (Eds.), *Integrating the organization: A social psychological analysis.* New York: Free Press, 1974.

Klein, S. M., & Maher, J. R. Educational level and satisfaction with pay. *Personnel Psychology,* 1966, *19,* 195-208.

Lefcourt, H. M., & Ladwig, G. W. The American Negro: A problem in expectancies. *Journal of Personality and Social Psychology,* 1965, *1,* 377-380. (a)

Lefcourt, H. M., & Ladwig, G. W. The effect of reference group upon Negroes' task performance in a bi-racial competitive game. *Journal of Personality and Social Psychology,* 1965, *1,* 668-671. (b)

Locke, E. A. What is job satisfaction? *Organization Behavior and Human Performance,* 1969, *4,* 309-336.

Mann, F. C. A study of work satisfaction as a function of the discrepancy between inferred aspirations and achievement. Unpublished doctoral dissertation, University of Michigan, 1953.

Miller, K. S., & Dreger, R. M. *Comparative studies of blacks and whites in the United States.* New York: Seminar Press, 1973.

Milutinovich, J. S. A comparative study of job satisfaction of Negro and white employees under participative and authoritative supervisory styles. Unpublished doctoral dissertation, New York University, 1970.

Milutinovich, J. S., & Tsaklanganos, A. A. The impact of perceived community prosperity on job satisfaction of black and white workers. Unpublished manuscript, Temple University, 1974.

O'Reilly, C. A., & Roberts, K. H. Job satisfaction among whites and non-whites: A cross-cultural approach. *Journal of Applied Psychology*, 1973, *57*(3), 295-299.

Orpen, C. Discrimination, work attitudes, and job satisfaction: A comparative study of whites and colored in South Africa. *International Review of Applied Psychology*, 1974, *23*, 33-44.

Patchen, M. Absence and employee feelings about fair treatment. *Personnel Psychology*, 1960, *13*, 349-360.

Pettigrew, T. F. *A profile of the Negro American*. Princeton, N.J.: D. Van Nostrand, 1964.

Roderick, R. D., & Nicholson, E. Job attitudes of young men: Some attitudes from the national longitudinal survey. Paper presented at the 34th Annual Meeting of the Academy of Management, Seattle, Washington, 1974.

Rowan, R. L. *The Negro in the steel industry*. Philadelphia: University of Pennsylvania Press, 1968.

Saleh, S. C., & Otis, J. L. Age and level of job satisfaction. *Personnel Psychology*, 1964, *17*, 425-430.

Shapiro, H. J., & Wahba, M. Age and job satisfaction of men and women. 10th Annual Meeting Eastern Academy of Management, Proceedings, 1973, Part C, 1-18.

Slocum, J. W., & Strawser, R. H. Racial differences in job attitudes. *Journal of Applied Psychology*, 1972, *56*, 28-32.

Smith, P. C., Kendall, L. M., & Hulin, C. L. *The measurement of satisfaction in work and retirement: A strategy for the study of attitudes*. Chicago: Rand McNally, 1969.

Stouffer, S. A., Suchman, E. A., DeVinney, L. C., Star, S. A., & Williams, R. M. *The American soldier: Adjustment during army life*. Vol. 1. Princeton: N.J.: Princeton University Press, 1949.

Tukey, J. W. The problem of multiple comparisons. Unpublished paper, Princeton University, 1953.

Turner, A. N., & Lawrence, P. R. *Industrial jobs and the worker: An investigation of responses to task attributes*. Boston: Harvard University Press, 1965.

U.S. Bureau of Census, *County and City Data Book*, 1962.

Vollmer, H. M., & Kinney, J. A. Age, education and job satisfaction. *Personnel*, 1955, *32*, 38-43.

Vroom, V. H. *Work and motivation*. New York: John Wiley & Sons, 1964.

Waters, L. K., & Waters, C. Correlations of job satisfaction and job dissatisfaction among female clerical workers. *Journal of Applied Psychology*, 1969, *53*, 388-391.

Weaver, C. N. Negro-white differences in job satisfaction. *Business Horizons*, 1974, *1*, 67-72.

W. E. Upjohn Institute for Employment Research. *Work in America*. Prepared for the Secretary of Health, Education, and Welfare. Cambridge, Mass.: M.I.T. Press, 1973, 51-56.

Wild, R. Job needs, job satisfaction, and job behavior of women manual workers. *Journal of Applied Psychology*, 1970, *54*, 157-162.

Wild, R., & Kempner, T. Influence of community and plant characteristics on job attitudes of manual workers. *Journal of Applied Psychology*, 1972, *56*, 106-113.

Williamson, T., & Karras, E. Job satisfaction variables among female clerical workers. *Journal of Applied Psychology*, 1970, *54*, 343-348.

Zytkoskee, A., Strickland, B. R., & Watson, J. Delay of gratification and internal versus external control among adolescents of low socio-economic status. *Development Psychology*, 1971, *4*, 93-98.

Race, Employment, and the Evaluation of Work[1]

JACK M. FELDMAN[2]

Two hypotheses derived from need hierarchy theory were tested: (a) Black and/or unemployed men would value material job outcomes more highly than white and/or working-class men. (b) Evaluation × instrumentality of work for material outcomes would correlate more highly with evaluation of work for the black and/or unemployed than for the white and/or working-class samples. The evaluation and instrumentality of 15 job outcomes, working, and being unemployed were gathered from black and white, working-class and hard-core unemployed men in the course of a larger interview. Significant race, social class, and interaction effects occurred, but the direction of the differences was not exactly as predicted. Correlational analyses likewise did not support the hypotheses. Results were discussed in terms of experiential differences leading to differences in the perception of work and unemployment.

The employment problems of racial and ethnic minority group members do not end when integration in a job setting is achieved. Often, these workers find themselves in situations where the reward structures are geared to the norms and desires of the white majority. Discrepancies in the perception of aspects of the work situation produce special prob-

Reprinted from *Journal of Applied Psychology*, 1973, *58*(1), 10-15. Copyright © 1973 by the American Psychological Association. Reprinted by permission of the publisher and the author.

lems. For this reason, it is important to have information on the aspects of work that are seen as desirable and undesirable by different racial and ethnic groups.

Some data are available on this point. Champagne and King (1967) found, in a Southern sample of black and white workers, that somewhat different scale values were assigned to 16 job-related motivational factors (good pay, working conditions, promotion, duty, etc.). Bloom and Barry (1967) factor analyzed 85 black men's responses to a 40-item questionnaire designed according to the Herzberg, Mausner, and Snyderman (1959) two-factor theory. The results were compared to an earlier analysis of the same questionnaire filled in by white blue-collar workers. They concluded that hygiene items were more important to blacks, although their analysis does not support this conclusion.

Maslow's (1954) theory would predict similar results, if one grants the assumption that blacks in general, and unemployed blacks in particular, are relatively more deprived of lower level satisfactions than whites, and thus should value them more highly, other things being equal. It is also true that unemployed people of any race should show this effect and that when social class is varied (in contrast to other studies), a race difference should emerge only to the extent that blacks are relatively more deprived than whites at the same occupational level. In view of the existence of racial discrimination, this is a likely state.

It should also be true that the perceived outcomes of work are differentially related to the evaluation of work in black and/or unemployed, as opposed to white and/or employed, groups of people. According to theory, if work is perceived to lead to material outcomes, those deprived of such outcomes will evaluate it more highly than those not so deprived. If work is perceived to lead to higher order outcomes, those whose material needs are relatively more satisfied will evaluate it more highly.

Thus, this study seeks to test two hypotheses:

1. The hard-core unemployed of both races will evaluate material outcomes more highly than the working class, and blacks will tend to evaluate such outcomes more highly than whites. The black hard-core will evaluate material outcomes most highly.

2. If the evaluation of each outcome for each person is multiplied by its perceived association with working at a steady job (see Graen, 1969, for a full explanation of the instrumentality concept), material outcomes should correlate higher with the directly measured evaluation of work in the black and hard-core samples, while higher level outcomes should correlate highest in the white and working-class samples.

Method

Subjects

Subjects were black and white males, between the ages of 18 and 50, who were living in the St. Louis, Missouri, metropolitan area. They were paid volunteers, recruited from social service agencies (hard core) or from local businesses (working class).[3] Fifty-two black working-class and white hard-core men and 48 black hard-core and white working-class men filled the cells of a 2 × 2 sampling design.

Interviewers and Interview

Interviewers were black and white men, between the ages of 20 and 35, who were from the St. Louis area. All were high school graduates, either working or attending college, and were selected by the author or his associate (Director of Psychological Services, NASCO West, a private drug rehabilitation agency). All interviewers were initially trained by the author, although some replacements were later trained by the field supervisor, who had been specially trained by the author in anticipation of such contingencies.

Data on job outcome evaluation was collected as part of a larger interview taking from 2 to 4 hours (Feldman, 1972). Subjects were paid $8 for a completed interview and the interviewers were paid $10. Interviews were arranged at a time of mutual convenience with interviewers of the subject's own race.

Instruments

The evaluation of 15 job outcomes was assessed. The first 5 outcomes, considered a standard list, were the paraphrased five factor names of the Job Description Inventory (Smith, Kendall, & Hulin, 1969), a well-developed, standard job satisfaction instrument. These 5 outcomes were good pay (pay), working with people you like (co-workers), having a good boss (supervisor), being promoted (promotion), and enjoying the work you do on the job (work itself).

The next 10 outcomes were elicited from a sample of black and white, working-class and unemployed men that was similar to the present sample. These were the 10 most frequent (overall) responses to the question "Name three things you feel you get from working (at a regular job)." Table 1 presents the complete list of outcomes. The evaluations of working at a regular job and being unemployed were also obtained. Unemployment was defined as not having a regular job; thus, doing day work was considered to be unemployed.

Table 1
Mean Evaluation Ratings of 15 Job Outcomes

	Economic Class			
Job Outcome	Hard Core		Working Class	
	Black	White	Black	White
Getting good pay	1.46	1.40	1.13	1.44
	(.82)	(.91)	(.57)	(.95)
Working with people you like[c]	1.54	1.27	1.21	1.79
	(.88)	(.56)	(.71)	(.99)
Having a good boss[c]	1.85	1.46	1.31	1.73
	(1.14)	(.80)	(.79)	(.90)
Being promoted	1.52	1.35	1.19	1.50
	(.97)	(.76)	(.76)	(.91)
Enjoying work you do on the job[c]	1.60	1.44	1.29	1.98
	(1.08)	(.85)	(.84)	(1.18)
Having responsibilities[b]	1.94	2.33	2.50	2.96
	(1.47)	(1.77)	(1.95)	(1.80)
Owing money[b]	6.19	7.29	7.38	7.42
	(2.62)	(2.04)	(2.23)	(1.78)
Saving money[a,b,c]	1.48	1.87	1.33	2.73
	(.80)	(1.22)	(.94)	(1.64)
Buying nice things (car, television)[a]	1.38	2.15	1.65	2.15
	(.71)	(1.46)	(1.29)	(1.27)
Being bored[a]	6.88	7.12	6.60	7.60
	(2.10)	(1.79)	(2.63)	(1.41)
Having family's respect[a]	1.40	1.88	1.23	2.23
	(.80)	(1.53)	(.85)	(1.43)
Having friends' respect[a,c]	1.63	1.69	1.25	2.23
	(1.02)	(1.11)	(.85)	(1.39)
Having fun	1.81	1.77	1.58	1.98
	(1.51)	(1.17)	(.99)	(1.46)
Being tired[b]	5.06	4.79	6.00	5.58
	(2.62)	(2.51)	(2.73)	(1.88)
Supporting yourself[a,b,c]	1.35	1.42	1.21	2.33
	(.67)	(.89)	(.74)	(1.80)

Note. All figures rounded to two decimals: 1 = most positive; 9 = most negative; standard deviations are in parentheses.

[a] Significant univariate race main effect ($p < .04$ or better).
[b] Significant univariate economic class main effect ($p < .03$ or better).
[c] Significant univariate interaction effect ($p < .005$ or better).

Evaluation responses were assessed on the 9-point version of Kunin's Faces Scale (9=most negative, 1=most positive) which yields roughly equal-interval data (Kunin, 1955). Instrumentality ratings were made on a three-choice scale (+1, 0, −1) in response to the question, Would you have _____ if you were working at a steady job? (+1=would, 0=50–50 chance, −1=would not). The scales, which were on flash cards, were presented to the subjects, who responded orally. In order to insure comprehension, all items were decentered and a practice sheet was given before each rating. Subjects who did not perform reasonably well on the practice sheet (e.g., rating outcomes like "a big raise" and "getting hurt in a job accident")—those who could not understand the task or who rated idiosyncratically without being able to justify their ratings—were excused with token payment.[4]

In order to minimize the effects of possible interviewer bias, interviewers were told the purpose of the study only in general terms. They were never aware of the specific hypotheses under investigation. Interviewers were additionally trained through role playing to adopt a neutral tone and manner and thus avoid giving nonverbal cues.

A call-back procedure, in which a randomly selected 10% of the subjects were called and questioned about the interview, further assured the quality of the data.

Results

Validation of Sampling Strategy

A series of demographic and job history questions asked at the end of the interview served to assess the success of the sampling strategy. A two-way (Race × Economic Class) multivariate analysis of variance on job history variables revealed only an economic class main effect ($F=26.51$, $p < .00005$). Univariate tests showed that the hard-core subjects reported that they received more public aid, were employed for shorter periods and unemployed for longer periods, tended to be laid off jobs rather than quit, and received more money per month during layoffs than the working-class subjects. (Complete data may be found in Feldman, 1972). A similar analysis, performed on demographic variables, showed a significant race main effect ($F=6.57$, $p< .00005$), an economic class effect ($F=2.21$, $p < .003$), and a significant interaction effect ($F=1.74$, $p < .03$). Univariate tests showed that black subjects tended to have been married longer, have more children, have lived in St. Louis longer, have parents who worked less often and at less skilled jobs, have been poorer as children, and have less frequently had part-time jobs as children than white subjects. Hard-core, as opposed to working-class subjects, had less skilled parents, but more often had held part-time jobs.

Finally, interaction tests showed that the white working class reported higher educational achievement than any other group. (Full details in Feldman, 1972.)

It may be concluded from these data that the sampling strategy was adequate and that no unusual between-sample differences existed (e.g., a confounding between race and social class), which might have confused interpretation.

It should be realized that causality is not thought to reside in race or social class but in the experiences which one has as a result of his/her race or class. Thus, these data point out some of the experiential differences which may account for any race or social class differences found in other data.

Race and Economic Class Differences in Outcome Evaluation

A two-way (Race × Economic Class) multivariate analysis of variance was performed on the evaluative ratings of the 15 job outcomes. In partial support of Hypothesis 1, two significant main effects and a significant interaction were obtained (race: $F=3.27$, $p < .0001$; economic class: $F=2.11$, $p < .02$; interaction: $F=2.95$, $p < .0004$). As Table 1 illustrates, univariate tests showed that blacks rated saving money, buying things, family respect, friends' respect, and supporting yourself as significantly more pleasant than did whites and being bored as significantly less unpleasant. The univariate economic class tests showed that having responsibilities, saving money, and supporting yourself were rated more pleasant by the hard core than the working class, while owing money and being tired were rated as less unpleasant by the hard core. Univariate interaction effects were found for the outcomes of working with people you like, having a good boss, enjoying the work you do, saving money, and friends' respect. In all but one case, the black working class rated the outcomes as most pleasant and the white working class rated them as least pleasant. Having a good boss was rated least pleasant by the black hard core and most by the black working class.

Race and Economic Class Differences in Correlates of Evaluation of Work

As can be seen in Table 2, Hypothesis 2 was not supported. Although differential correlations are present, they do not fall into the predicted patterns. The black working-class' evaluation of work seems to be related to social, material, and higher order outcomes, while the white working-class' evaluation is not clearly related to any outcomes except that of supporting self and family. The black hard core's evaluation is associated with responsibility, support, and saving money, thereby combining both

Table 2

Correlation of (Evaluation × Instrumentality of Work) for 15 Outcomes
with Directly Measured Evaluation of Work

Job Outcome	Economic Class			
	Hard Core		Working Class	
	Black[a]	White[b]	Black[b]	White[a]
Getting good pay	.18	.24	.25	−.29*
Working with people you like	.24	−.17	.55****	−.04
Having a good boss	.17	−.19	.57****	−.15
Being promoted	−.12	−.02	.31*	−.04
Enjoying work you do on the job	.19	−.03	.33**	−.32*
Having responsibilities	.61****	.08	.18	−.03
Owing money	−.02	.18	−.05	.08
Saving money	.30*	−.13	−.19	.24
Buying nice things (car, television)	.25	.16	.11	−.14
Being bored	−.002	.28*	−.001	.15
Having family's respect	.22	.16	.30*	.05
Having friends' respect	.22	−.06	.13	−.14
Having fun	.17	.12	.02	−.16
Being tired	.03	−.05	.26	.20
Supporting yourself	.55****	.52****	.60****	.30*
Evaluation of unemployment	.19	−.32*	−.26	−.49****

[a] $n = 48$.
[b] $n = 52$.
$*p < .05$. $**p < .02$. $***p < .01$. $****p < .001$.

material and higher order outcomes. The white hard core's evaluation
is most strongly associated with boredom and support, again in contrast
to the need hierarchy prediction.

One of the most interesting findings in Table 2 is the differential
relationships between the evaluation of working and not working. These
are significantly negatively correlated only in the white samples and
positively (though not significantly) in the black hard-core sample. This
seems to suggest a much different conception of work and unemployment in the various samples and especially in the black hard-core
sample.

In addition to the above analyses, a 2 × 2 multivariate analysis of
variance (Race × Economic Class) was performed on the evaluation of
working and being unemployed. Significant multivariate race, economic

Table 3

Mean Evaluation Ratings of Working and Being Unemployed

Item	Economic Class			
	Hard Core		Working Class	
	Black	White	Black	White
Working at a regular job[a,b,c]	1.46	1.85	1.29	2.81
	(.75)	(1.41)	(.86)	(1.88)
Being unemployed[a]	8.19	7.79	8.71	8.00
	(1.54)	(1.77)	(1.04)	(1.74)

Note. All figures rounded to two decimals; standard deviations are in parentheses; 1 = most positive, 9 = most negative.
[a] Significant univariate race main effect ($p < .01$ or better).
[b] Significant univariate economic class main effect ($p < .04$).
[c] Significant univariate interaction effect ($p < .003$).

class, and interaction effects were found (race: $F=13.63$, $p < .0001$; economic class: $F=5.32$, $p < .006$; interaction: $F=4.78$, $p < .01$). Table 3 presents cell means and corresponding univariate tests.

The white working class evaluates working at a regular job more negatively than any other sample, while the black working class evaluates it most positively. The blacks in general evaluate work more positively and unemployment more negatively than the whites.

Discussion

Neither the black nor the hard-core subjects clearly preferred material or lower level outcomes; likewise, the white and working-class subjects did not prefer higher order outcomes. Rather, the pattern of outcome preference is complex, with both material, social, and higher order outcomes rated high by black and white, working-class and hard-core subjects.

The correlational data likewise give little support to the notion of a need hierarchy or to a definite preference by one group or another for extrinsic or intrinsic rewards. Each sample appears to have a unique pattern of outcomes related to the evaluation of work, with only support for one's self and family being important to all groups. These data contradict the conclusions of Bloom and Barry (1967). It is obvious that a relatively simple approach like the motivator-hygiene dichotomy is inadequate to represent differences in work attitudes between race and social class subcultures. These data do seem compatible with Slocum and Strawser's (1972) study of black and white certified public accountants, since the need deficiencies reported by their black sample are similar to the outcomes that correlate with evaluation of work in the black working class. However, since the present data include social class differences as well as racial differences, the current results cannot be interpreted as support for a need hierarchy theory of motivation. Rather, such differences should be explained by looking more closely at the environments of black and white workers, including cultural values, fashions, and economic and political factors, rather than by extending the Protestant Ethic into a universal motivational system.

These results have two separate sets of implications. The first relates to studies of job satisfaction. It is clear that standard job satisfaction instruments will not be valid for all people in all situations. Thus, just as selection devices should be validated in each situation, so should job satisfaction measures. This is not to say that a given instrument is never valid for a given population; since this data refers to a global evaluation of work rather than specific jobs, that statement could not be made in any case. Rather, it is argued that if more information than a global evaluation of the job is desired, the investigation must first be sure that the questions asked are relevant to the employee population.

The second set of implications is more broadly relevant. The white working-class sample in this study fell consistently below the black working class in their evaluation of job outcomes and in the evaluation of work as directly measured. In addition, no strong correlations (and two puzzling negative correlations) were obtained in that sample. The correlations between the evaluation of work and unemployment were, however, highest for the white working class.

This may be a reflection of recent social and economic trends. The recent high levels of unemployment and inflation in the United States may very well have influenced the perceptions of this group in a negative direction. Relative to their previous adaptation level, work may not provide the security and satisfaction it once did. On the other hand, the black working class is experiencing a degree of upward mobility due to minority hiring programs, equal opportunity laws, and the like. Thus, relative to their adaptation level, things are getting better.

The white working class also seems to regard work and unemployment as more nearly opposite concepts than do the other samples. The black hard core, in fact, seems to regard the two as independent, that is, the evaluation of work has little implication for the evaluation of unemployment.

This may also be a reflection of experiential differences. Because blacks are, and have been, more often unemployed than whites, the evaluation of unemployment for blacks may depend on other factors —in each specific instance, what other opportunities there are to make money, and whether welfare payments or unemployment compensation is available, etc. Blacks may have learned, out of necessity, ways to alleviate the hardships of unemployment. Whites, since they have less often been unemployed, might not have developed the necessary skills.

Thus, these data strongly suggest that very different conceptions of work and unemployment exist in different racial and social class groups. Future research should seek to further delineate such differences and explore their theoretical implications.

Notes

[1] This paper is based on a dissertation submitted in partial fulfillment of the requirements for the PhD degree at the University of Illinois. The research reported here was supported by the Social and Rehabilitation Service of the Department of Health, Education, and Welfare (Research Grant No. 15-P-55175/5; Harry C. Triandis, principal investigator). Thanks are due to Harry C. Triandis for his reading of an earlier version of this manuscript and to the rest of the author's dissertation committee, George Graen, Charles Hulin, Roy Malpass, Joseph McGrath, and Martin Wagman for their advice at all stages of the research.

[2] Jack M. Feldman was affiliated with the University of Illinois, Urbana, Illinois, at the time this article was written. Requests for reprints should be sent to Jack Feldman, who is now at the Department of Management, University of Florida, Gainesville, Florida 32601.

[3] The fine work of William Harvey and the staff at the Narcotics Service Council (NASCO) West in locating subjects and coordinating interviews is gratefully acknowledged.

[4] For example, someone who evaluated "being hurt" positively because he saw the possibility of a large insurance settlement would be allowed to continue. For a full explication of this procedure, see Triandis, 1972.

References

Bloom R., & Barry, J. R. Determinants of work attitudes among Negroes. *Journal of Applied Psychology*, 1967, *51*, 291-294.

Champagne, J. E., & King, D. C. Job-satisfaction factors among underprivileged workers. *Personnel Guidance Journal*, 1967, *45*, 429-434.

Feldman, J. M. Race, economic class and job-seeking behavior: An exploratory study. (Rep. No. 15, HEW Social and Rehabilitation Service No. 15-P-55175/5) Champaign, Ill.: University of Illinois, Department of Psychology, 1972.

Graen, G. Instrumentality theory of work motivation: Some experimental results and suggested modifications. *Journal of Applied Psychology Monograph*, 1969, *53*(2, Pt. 2).

Herzberg, F., Mausner, B., & Snyderman, B. B. *The motivation to work*. New York: Wiley, 1959.

Kunin, T. The development of a new type of attitude measure. *Personnel Psychology*, 1955, *8*, 65-78.

Maslow, A. H. *Motivation and personality*. New York: Harper & Row, 1954.

Slocum, J. W., & Strawser, R. H. Racial differences in job attitudes. *Journal of Applied Psychology*, 1972, *56*, 28-32.

Smith, P. C., Kendall, L. M., & Hulin, C. L. *Measurement of satisfaction in work and retirement*. New York: Rand McNally, 1969.

Triandis, H. C. *The analysis of subjective culture*. New York: Wiley-Interscience, 1972.

Work Expectations

The Relationship Between Expectancies and Job Behavior for White and Black Employees

JEFFREY H. GREENHAUS[1]
JAMES F. GAVIN

A recent attempt to understand work motivation has emphasized the importance of expectancies within the work situation. This theory, espoused by Porter and Lawler (1968), proposes that the degree of effort expended on the job is a function of two perceptions: the expectation that working hard will lead to a series of work rewards such as promotion or recognition (effort-reward expectancy), and the importance attached to these rewards by the worker. A person, in other words, will work hard to the extent that he sees hard work as instrumental in attaining important rewards. As Porter and Lawler (1968) predict,

> The greater the value of a set of rewards and the higher the probability that receiving each of these rewards depends upon effort, the greater the effort that will be put forth in a given situation (p. 128).

Several studies by Porter and Lawler have suggested the fruitfulness of the expectancy approach for the prediction of job performance. In an early study, Lawler (1966) had middle and lower level managers indicate the extent to which they felt that their job performance determined their pay. As hypothesized, the stronger the belief that performance determined pay, the better the job performance (as measured by supervisory rankings and self ratings). The relationship between effort-pay expectancy and job performance was replicated in a later study by Porter and Lawler (1968). Extending the research to rewards other than pay, Lawler and Porter (1967) found that effort-reward expectancies were related to

---

Reprinted from *Personnel Psychology*, 1972, *25*, 449-455, by permission of the publisher.

two measures of effort: peer rankings and self ratings. A further investigation by Lawler (1968) suggested that expectancy attitudes tend to determine job performance rather than being the result of performance.

Much of the research conducted by other investigators (Galbraith and Cummings, 1967; Gavin, 1969; Georgopoulos et al., 1957; Spitzer, 1964) lend at least some support to the notion that effort-reward expectancies are related to effort or performance. Most of the research, it should be noted, has concentrated on the prediction of managerial job performance. Perhaps as a consequence, racial or ethnic differences in expectancies or expectancy-criterion relationships have not been reported.

The purpose of the present study was to investigate the relationship between effort-reward expectancy and job performance for whites and blacks. In addition, it seemed useful to explore possible ethnic differences in the magnitude of: (a) the importance attributed to various work rewards, and (b) the level of effort-reward expectancy associated with each reward.

Method

An extensive attitude survey was administered to 390 white and 81 black male, blue-collar employees of a major airline. Criterion information (discussed below), however, was available for only 78 of the blacks. Since it was considered important to control for employees' age and tenure with company (all were high school graduates), a white sample was matched (two whites for every black) with the black sample on these two variables. The mean age for the whites and blacks was 29.9 years and 30.9 years respectively. Average tenure with company for the two samples was 42.1 months and 44.0 months. The final sample, then, consisted of 78 blacks and 156 whites.

A "Survey of Employee Opinions" was administered to all subjects (Ss) in the summer of 1969. In addition to responding to 53 job satisfaction items, S rated the importance to him of each of 12 work rewards on a 3-point scale. S also rated (on a 3-point scale) the chances he would have of attaining each of the 12 rewards if he "did his best" on the job. These latter 12 scores (and their unweighted sum) constituted the effort-reward expectancies.

A supervisory rating form was used to measure job performance. This instrument covered the following 10 dimensions, each measured on a 9-point scale: Quality of Work, Quantity of Work, Attendance, Cooperation with Co-workers, Willingness to Work, Attitude toward the Company, Punctuality, Common Sense, Ability to Follow Instructions, and Overall Job Performance. Intercorrelations among the 10 dimensions ranged from .34 to .87 with a median of .63. Three of the dimensions —

Willingness to Work, Attendance, and Overall Job Performance—seemed particularly relevant to the Porter-Lawler model and were chosen for analysis in the present study.

Results

Table 1 presents the rated importance of the 12 work rewards for the white and black samples. The extremely high means and the small standard deviations suggest that both samples viewed all of the work rewards as very important. None of the differences in importance for the two samples was significant. In fact, the two samples had an identical mean importance rating (across all 12 rewards) of 2.8. It is interesting that the work reward "more say in job" was rated lowest in importance by both groups.

Table 1

Mean Importance and Effort-Reward Expectancies for
White and Black Employees

| | Importance | | | | Expectancy | | | |
| | Whites | | Blacks | | Whites | | Blacks | |
Work Rewards	$\bar{X}$	SD	$\bar{X}$	SD	$\bar{X}$	SD	$\bar{X}$	SD
More pay	2.79	.44	2.76	.46	2.14	.81	2.36	.75*
Say in job	2.56	.58	2.51	.61	2.13	.69	2.29	.68**
Use of special skills	2.68	.54	2.59	.65	2.10	.70	2.26	.74
Respect from friends outside company	2.76	.45	2.68	.57	2.48	.70	2.58	.52
Friendship at work	2.85	.37	2.79	.46	2.81	.45	2.74	.44
Good supervision	2.93	.28	2.96	.25	2.38	.74	2.50	.66
Better benefits	2.92	.30	2.87	.37	2.30	.79	2.52	.61*
Being treated fairly	2.97	.18	2.95	.27	2.38	.72	2.52	.64
More training	2.89	.35	2.87	.37	2.36	.70	2.49	.61
Respect from supervisor	2.93	.28	2.95	.22	2.60	.65	2.67	.57
Respect from co-workers	2.96	.19	2.91	.28	2.72	.52	2.73	.47
A promotion	2.81	.40	2.87	.37	2.33	.70	2.45	.65
Total score	39.60	2.47	39.35	3.05	28.74	5.99	30.12	4.80**

Note.—White N = 156; Black N = 78.
 * $p < .05$.
 ** $p < .10$.

The effort-reward expectancies are also presented in Table 1. The expectancies were lower than the respective importance ratings for all of the work rewards and their standard deviations were higher. Blacks perceived higher expectancies than whites on 11 of the 12 rewards and the total score. Two of the differences—pay and benefits—reached significance ($p < .05$) and two others—more say in job and total score— approached significance ($p < .10$).

Despite the differences in magnitude, the patterns of expectancies were quite similar for blacks and whites. The work rewards, friendship at work and respect from co-workers, had the two highest expectancies for both whites and blacks. Use of special skills and more say in job, on the other hand, had the lowest expectancies for both groups. This similarity is reflected by a Spearman rho of .94 ($p < .01$) between the ranking of work reward expectancies of the white and black samples.

Porter and Lawler (1968), it will be remembered, hypothesized an interaction between expectancy and importance in the prediction of job performance. However, since the work rewards were all rated as very important by both samples (i.e., low item variances), the possibilities of expectancy by importance interactions in the present study were exceedingly remote. Nevertheless, one of the major predictions of the Porter-Lawler model is a positive relationship between effort-reward expectancy and job performance. Table 2 presents the correlations between each of the expectancies and the three criterion ratings. (It should be noted that whites were rated significantly ($p < .05$) higher than blacks on each of the three ratings.) It can be seen that the magnitude of the expectancy-criterion correlations was, in general, low for both samples. It is apparent that more of the correlations were significant for the whites than for the blacks. It must be emphasized, however, that none of the differences in the respective correlations between the white and black samples reached significance.

Discussion

One interesting finding in the present study was the relationship between ethnic group and effort-reward expectancy. Blacks, it was noted, perceived a greater connection between hard work and attaining work rewards than did whites. Although only two of the differences were significant, they were consistently in the same direction. This would seem to suggest that blacks in this study did not feel the relative powerlessness and external control indicated by prior research (Lefcourt and Ladwig, 1965).

Several explanations for this trend may be advanced. First, it is possible that the policies and leadership practices of the company

Table 2

Correlations Between Effort-Reward Expectancies and Criterion Ratings

	Willingness to Work		Attendance		Overall Job Performance	
Work Rewards	W	B	W	B	W	B
More pay	.16*	.07	.16*	.10	.11	−.01
A promotion	.22**	−.03	.23**	.14	.17*	.05
Say in job	.10	.14	.06	.09	.04	.14
Use of special skills	.25**	.03	.19*	.08	.23**	.04
Respect from friends outside company	.04	.22	.05	.24*	−.03	.08
Friendship at work	.07	.01	.12	.01	.11	−.07
Good supervision	.17*	.38**	.08	.21*	.12	.32**
Better benefits	.09	−.02	.12	.02	.09	−.08
Being treated fairly	.12	.04	.06	−.02	.11	−.02
More training	.15	.13	.16	.15	.11	.03
Respect from co-workers	.12	.01	.10	.05	.12	−.01
Respect from supervisor	.16*	.10	.18*	.09	.08	.06
Total score	.19*	.14	.17*	.15	.20*	.13

Note.—W = white (N = 156); B = black (N = 78).
 * Correlation significantly different from zero at .05 level.
** Correlation significantly different from zero at .01 level.

were designed to promote feelings of equity and reward possibilities, especially among its black workers. A second possibility involves the concept of relative deprivation. Perhaps the blacks were so unaccustomed to feelings of influence and control that any degree of effort-reward expectancy was magnified in their eyes. Although these explanations are speculative, they are clearly amenable to empirical test. Effort-reward expectancy may be studied, for example, in relation to perceptions of leadership behavior and organizational climate as well as to prior feelings of control over one's environment.

The similarities in expectancies across ethnic groups, however, must also be recognized. Despite differences in the magnitude of expectancies, the work rewards rated high by the blacks tended to be rated high by the whites, and those rated low by the blacks were rated low by the whites. That is, the ordering of the work rewards with regard to effort-reward expectancy was similar for both ethnic groups. This would suggest that hard work is not rewarded in essentially different ways (i.e., with different rewards) for members of the two ethnic groups.

It was also found that the relationship between expectancy and criterion ratings was generally low for both samples. However, the most predictable criteria for whites were ratings of willingness to work and attendance in that order. Interestingly, willingness to work appears to be the criterion most closely related to Porter and Lawler's notion of effort or work motivation. Also, attendance may indirectly reflect a worker's motivation. It is not surprising that ratings of overall job performance were least predictable. Such factors as ability and accuracy of role perception may intervene between work motivation and actual performance (cf., Porter and Lawler, 1968).

The effort-reward expectancies most consistently related to the criteria for whites were promotion and use of special skills, whereas for blacks they were respect from friends outside the company and better supervision. It is possible that the correlation between a particular effort-reward expectancy and work motivation is an indirect measure of the importance of that reward to the sample under investigation. If, for example, a group tends to be motivated to the extent that it sees a connection between hard work and a promotion, it might then be argued that this group places more importance on a promotion than on other rewards for which there were no significant expectancy-criterion relationships.

If, however, expectancy-criterion correlations are taken as indices of importance, we must be fairly certain that each work reward has a similar "statistical" chance of correlating highly with the criterion. One characteristic that is related to the capacity of an item to correlate with another variable is its variance. That is, the higher an item's variance, the greater its capacity to correlate with an outside variable. It can be seen (in Table 1) that the two expectancies that had the most consistent relationship with the criteria for the whites (promotion and use of special skills) did not possess the highest standard deviations. In fact, pay, better supervision, benefits, and being treated fairly all had higher standard deviations. Among the blacks the standard deviations of respect from friends outside the company and better supervision were not exceedingly high for that sample. Thus, it was not variance, per se, that was responsible for the magnitude of these particular expectancy-criterion correlations.

The attribution of importance to those work rewards with high expectancy-criterion correlations is based on the assumption that expectancies "caused" work motivation in the present study. Although this assumption would appear to have some support (Lawler, 1968), any conclusions must be tentative. Also, as cautioned above, the differences between the correlations in the two samples were nonsignificant. In addition, it would seem unwise to generalize these findings beyond the present study. The subjects were all employed within one job category at one company. Nevertheless, the use of expectancy-criterion correlations as indicators of importance for given samples may warrant future investigation.

Summary

The purpose of the present study was to investigate the relationship between effort-reward expectancy (Porter and Lawler, 1968) and job behavior for white and black employees. It was found, first, that the blacks in this study tended to see a greater connection between hard work and rewards than did the whites. However, the ethnic groups did not differ in the rated importance they attributed to these rewards. It was also found that the relationship between expectancy and work motivation criteria was generally low for both samples. The interpretation of expectancy-criterion correlations as possible indicators of importance was explored.

Note

[1]Jeffrey H. Greenhaus was affiliated with the City College of New York, Division of Research and Testing, at the time of publication of this article. James F. Gavin was with American Airlines.

References

Galbraith, J. and Cummings, L. L. An empirical investigation of the motivational determinants of task performance: Interactive effects between instrumentality-valence and motivation-ability. *Organizational Behavior and Human Performance*, 1967, *2*, 237-257.
Gavin, J. F. Ability, effort and role perception as antecedents of job performance. Unpublished doctoral dissertation, New York University, 1969.
Georgopoulos, B. S., Mahoney, G. M., and Jones, N. W. A path-goal approach to productivity. *Journal of Applied Psychology*, 1957, *16*, 345-353.
Lawler, E. E. Ability as a moderator of the relationship between job attitudes and job performance. *Personnel Psychology*, 1966, *19*, 153-164.
Lawler, E. E. A correlation-causal analysis of the relationship between expectancy attitudes and job performance. *Journal of Applied Psychology*, 1968, *52*, 462-468.
Lawler, E. E. and Porter, L. W. Antecedent attitudes of effective managerial job performance. *Organizational Behavior and Human Performance*, 1967, *2*, 122-142.
Lefcourt, H. M. and Ladwig, G. W. The American Negro: A problem in expectancies. *Journal of Personality and Social Psychology*, 1965, *1*, 377-380.
Porter, L. W. and Lawler, E. E. *Managerial attitudes and performance.* Homewood, Ill.: Irwin-Dorsey, 1968.
Spitzer, M. E. Goal-attainment, job satisfaction and behavior. Unpublished doctoral dissertation, New York University, 1964.

Recent Trends in the Occupational Mobility of Negroes, 1930–1960: An Intracohort Analysis[1]

NATHAN HARE[2]

An intracohort analysis of occupational trends produced more consistent results than did conventional approaches to the study of labor force change. There was a trend of convergence between the occupational distributions of white and Negro males from 1930 to 1940 and, especially, from 1940 to 1950, which did not hold, however, during the fifties. Figures for the South showed a trend of convergence similar to that of the country as a whole during the 1940's, but, in contrast to popular opinion, the Negro lost notable occupational ground in the South during the fifties. The factor of education was found to be of special importance for the Negro's mobility during periods of substantial occupational change.

Recent trends in the occupational distribution of Negroes in the labor force of the United States have been analyzed with contradictory results by several well-known social scientists. There are, to begin with, the static, cross-sectional comparisons by Myrdal[3] and Taeuber and Taeuber.[4] Myrdal concluded that Negroes "usually fail to improve their opportunities by staying in school longer." But Taeuber and Taeuber found, on the other hand, that "there are close associations between levels of education and occupational concentrations," although the "educational levels of nonwhite men in specific occupations are somewhat below those of all men in the same education."

Reprinted from *Social Forces*, 1965, *44*(2), 166-173, by permission of The University of North Carolina Press.

Important trend analyses more recently were made by Bogue[5] and Miller.[6] Bogue suggested that while the occupational differential between whites and nonwhites "is still very large, very substantial changes have been made" since 1940. Miller conversely concluded that "the relative occupational status of nonwhites has not changed appreciably" since 1940. One contribution of the present report—aside from its attempt to illuminate specific trends in the occupational distribution of Negroes, with special reference to the factor of education—is its demonstration that conventional analytical approaches can produce these divergent results.

Method and Data

The pivotal method of this study is the intracohort analysis, which compares a cohort of persons of age x to $x + a$ at a given time t (the initial census year) with the same cohort of individuals, who, at time $t + n$ (the terminal census year), have attained the age of $x + n$ to $x + a + n$. The chief advantage of this approach is its facility for following the movement of a given cohort over a specified period of time, thereby obtaining a record of the change experienced by the same basic set of individuals.

The conventional approach in studies of labor force change compares persons of the same age at two or more different points in time: for example, persons 25-34 in 1950 as against the same age group in 1960. On the contrary, persons who were 25-34 in 1950 were not the same age in 1960; they were 35-44—ten years older. Thus, in ignoring the follow-up device of intracohort analysis and comparing over similar age groups at different times, the researcher actually compares different people. Yet varying historical and socioeconomic circumstances may render incomparable the experiences of individuals comprising distinct cohorts which, though similar in age at the points of comparison, began life a decade or more apart. Persons 25-34, say, in 1940 were born during the decade 1905-14. They entered the job market after the Depression or during its last days and just before World War II prosperity. The older cohorts, on the other hand, began work prior to the Depression but encountered its full impact and World War II later in their occupational careers. Many were newcomers, late in life, to the urban occupational structure.

For an indicator of the disparity at a given point in time—in order to measure the convergence or divergence of recent decades between the races—we used indexes of dissimilarity between whites and Negroes in 1930, 1940, 1950 and 1960. Convergence is here defined as a trend toward similarity of the occupational distributions of whites and Negroes as opposed to divergence, or a trend toward dissimilarity. An index of dissimilarity between whites and Negroes is the sum of the positive (or negative) differences between the two percentage distributions; in this analysis, the amount of redistribution required for absolute occupational parity between the two races.

An initial summary, to illustrate the pattern of the intracohort analysis, is presented in Table 1. Note that these figures disregard the factor of education, which later will be analyzed in some detail. Attention must be given to the manner of reading Table 1, which can be approached in three significant ways: (1) reading from one age group to another, down a single column, gives the pattern for different age groups at the same point in time; (2) reading across rows gives the same age group—but different individuals—at different points in time; and (3) reading from upper left to lower right on a diagonal gives the same cohort at different points in time (the intracohort comparison).

Some of the foregoing observations could easily mislead us to reject the hypothesized trend of convergence, even for the forties. But intracohort comparisons (reading from upper left to lower right on a diagonal) in no case showed divergence during the forties. For all age groups, convergence was apparent and the changes in the size of the indexes of dissimilarity between whites and Negroes were greater between 1940 and 1950 than from 1930 to 1940, indicating an acceleration of convergence during that period. However, there was a notable wane during the fifties in the trend of convergence. In addition, there actually was divergence for the cohort of 1915-24—more about that later.

Admittedly, however, defects in the comparability of the data require caution in making these inferences. The bulk of the data for this study pertain to the Census "major occupation groups" in 1940, 1950 and 1960, unless otherwise indicated. Data for 1930 were somewhat similar but not exactly comparable. Whereas, for the other census years, it was necessary only to combine certain categories to make them nearly comparable, data for 1930, where the Census had used "gainful workers" instead of "labor force," were only roughly similar, and the educational breakdown was not available. Only males were analyzed in this study, since female labor force participation is less stable and complete, for rather well-known reasons.

Some bias may exist in the fact that 1960 data pertain to "experienced civilian labor force with earnings in 1959" rather than "employed males." It was necessary also to compare 1940 data for "native whites" and "Negroes" with 1950 and 1960 data for "all whites" and "nonwhites," respectively. This was due to the fact that education was cross-tabulated with major occupation group for Negroes in 1940, but not for "nonwhites"; for "nonwhites" in 1950 and 1960 but not for "Negroes." However, the inclusion of some foreign-born in these data apparently affects

Table 1
Indexes of Dissimilarity Between White and Negro Occupational Distributions, by Age, United States, for Employed Males, 1930, 1940 and 1950, and Experienced Civilian Labor Force with Income in 1959, 1960

Age	Native White vs. Negro		All White vs. Nonwhite	
	1930*	1940	1950	1960
25-34	45.34	46.02	36.40	35.39
35-44	43.32	43.11	38.85	37.46
45-54	40.99	41.79	39.15	38.27
55-64	39.11	36.04	36.22	38.82

*1930 socioeconomic groups are not exactly comparable to major occupation groups in 1940, 1950 and 1960.

Sources: Alba M. Edwards, *A Social-Economic Grouping of the Gainful Workers of the United States* (Washington, D.C.: U.S. Government Printing Office, 1938), Table 9, pp. 28–29; Table 15, pp. 40–41. U.S. Bureau of the Census, *Population: Educational Attainment by Economic Characteristics and Marital Status* (Washington, D.C.: U.S. Government Printing Office, 1947), Table 21, p. 103; Table 23, p. 117. U.S. Bureau of the Census, *Population, Education* (Washington, D.C.: U.S. Government Printing Office, 1953), Table 11, pp. 5B88–5B91. Unpublished data underlying U.S. Bureau of the Census. *U.S. Census of Population: 1960. Subject Reports, Occupation by Earnings and Education.* (Washington, D.C.: U.S. Government Printing Office, 1963).

the oldest men primarily.[7] Table 2 shows that the conclusion of convergence during the forties held in spite of the foregoing defects.

The intracohort analysis is restricted to the ages 25-34 to 55-64, as younger cohorts were not yet fully in the labor force, and older cohorts were subject to high retirement rates. Employed persons, rather than entire age cohorts, seemed preferable as categories of comparison, as the unemployed and relief workers (in 1940) included in the total labor force are highly subject to the factors of personal health and socioeconomic differences. However, although restricting the analysis to employed males has the effect of sharpening precision, it does not follow necessarily that comparisons of the entire age cohorts would fail to confirm our basic findings. Brief indication of this fact is provided in Table 3, where labor force totals, like employment figures in Table 1, generally indicate a pattern of convergence for all comparisons of a given cohort during the forties.

Changes in Detailed Occupations

Because the foregoing analysis does not take account, except indirectly, of changes in detailed occupations, we used indexes of representational

Table 2

Indexes of Dissimilarity Between Native White and Negro Occupational Distributions, for Employed Males, United States, by Age, 1940, and White and Nonwhite, 1940 and 1950

	1940		1950
Age	All White vs. Nonwhite	Native White vs. Negro	All White vs. Nonwhite
25-34	46.18	46.02	36.40
35-44	43.33	43.11	38.85
45-54	41.42	41.79	39.15
55-64	38.98	36.04	36.22

Source: U.S. Bureau of the Census, *Population, Labor Force, Occupational Characteristics* (Washington, D.C.: U.S. Government Printing Office, 1940), Table 1, p. 11. *Ibid.*, 1950.

Table 3

Indexes of Dissimilarity Between White and Negro Occupational Distributions, for Total Labor Force, United States, by Age, 1940 and 1950

Age	1940	1950
25-34	40.15	33.65
35-44	38.52	36.55
45-54	35.85	35.73
55-64	27.92	30.53

Source: Same as Table 1, for 1940 and 1950.
Note: "Unemployed" (including "on public emergency work" in 1940) and "not in labor force" are regarded as quasi-occupation groups in this analysis.

change to examine individual occupations in which there was less possibility of internal shift. The index of representational change is equal to the proportion Negroes comprised of a profession 1950, divided by the proportion for 1940, multiplied by 100. For instance, Negro males 35-44 years old in 1950 constituted 7.6 percent of all teachers (Negro and white) in that age group which, if divided by 5.6, the percentage for Negroes 25-34 years old in 1940, and multiplied by 100, yields 137 as an index of representational change for that cohort. No change would produce an index of 100.

The problem of sample size presented a problem in those detailed occupations containing few nonwhites even in 1950. Therefore, the occupations selected for Table 4 were those comprising the five in each

Table 4

Indexes of Representational Change, White and Negro Employed
Males, for Selected Occupations, United States, Cohorts of 1905–1914,
1895–1904, and 1855–1894, 1940 and 1950

Occupation	Cohort		
	1905–14	1895–1904	1885–94
Clergymen	136	129	89
Teachers	137	102	83
Physicians and surgeons	123	92	74
Social and welfare workers	194	116	48
Managers, construction	290	380	204
Managers, eating and drinking	107	90	70
Managers, personal service	190	151	105
Managers, retail except eating and drinking	315	211	191
Mail carriers	158	105	125
Shipping and receiving clerks	471	148	196
Messengers	144	73	42
Clerical and kindred	419	194	118
Other salesmen	107	111	123
Brickmasons	182	124	112
Painters, paperhangers	147	112	84
Carpenters	101	112	97
Mechanics, repairmen	137	134	124
Attendants	152	79	68
Laundry operatives	131	90	61
Mine operatives	92	103	89
Welders	504	672	188
Chauffeurs, truckdrivers	150	127	102
Guards and watchmen	122	109	96
Policemen	207	238	132
Barbers	147	133	77
Cooks exc. private household	107	103	93
Lumbermen, woodchoppers	105	109	92
Construction, laborers	157	115	92
Manufacturing, laborers	144	101	200
Railroads, laborers	151	118	119
Wholesale and retail, laborers	124	100	77

Note: Data pertain to Negroes and native whites in 1940.   Source: Same as Table 2.

major occupation group in which Negroes were most represented, except where nonwhites numbered less than 3,000 (100 actual sample cases) in 1950.

The youngest cohort, the cohort of 1905-14, showed net gains in each of the occupations selected, except mine operatives. Some groups, such as welders, shipping and receiving clerks, and clerical and kindred (n.e.c.) showed extreme gains in this cohort. However, these occupations either are not ordinarily jobs for men or contained, in any case, a small base figure of Negroes in 1940. The cohort of 1895-1904 sustained net losses in five of the occupations, while the cohort of 1885-94, the oldest cohort, suffered net losses in more than half of the occupations. Also for each occupation, the size of the index of representational change generally decreased with increases in age as represented by successive cohorts.

The fact that the youngest cohort exhibited most convergence during the forties suggests that young Negroes not only were entering the work force with less dissimilarity (as indicated in previous tables) but also were converging further, once established in the occupational structure. This would seem to indicate accelerated convergence in recent cohorts during the forties.

Regional Redistribution of Populations and Occupational Change

To take account of the fact that Negroes experienced a greater shift from South to North and from rural to urban occupational life during the forties, indexes of dissimilarity were computed for each region and for nonfarm occupations.

In Table 5, the intracohort analysis shows each cohort except for the youngest (25-34) decreasing in dissimilarity in both decades for the North. However the change was generally greater in the forties than during the fifties. In the South, on the other hand, where there was generally some change in the forties, there was divergence or an increase in dissimilarity during the fifties. This no doubt had a significant impact on the ground lost by Negroes for the United States as a whole during the fifties. This leads to the speculation that the convergence during the forties was due to the migration of large numbers of Negroes from southern farms to northern factories.

Table 6 shows indexes of dissimilarity for nonfarm occupations for each region during the forties. For both North and South, there was considerable convergence for each cohort during the forties, although there was generally less convergence in the South where the indexes of dissimilarity were somewhat larger. But the change for each age cohort was at least as large for nonfarm occupations as for major occupation groups in general.

Table 5
Indexes of Dissimilarity Between White and Negro Occupational
Distributions, Major Occupation Groups, by Age and Region, for
Employed Males, 1940 and 1950, and Experienced Civilian Labor
Force Males, with Income in 1959, 1960

Region and Year	Age Group			
	25–34	35–44	45–54	55–64
Non-South				
1940	39.25	46.61	48.60	47.60
1950	34.73	39.88	41.02	36.58
1960	30.03	33.19	36.30	38.68
South				
1940	41.95	39.82	37.64	29.77
1950	40.24	39.10	39.63	35.96
1960	41.07	43.18	41.77	41.68

Source: Same as Table 1 for 1940 and 1950 and 1960.

Table 6
Indexes of Dissimilarity Between White and Negro Employed Males,
Nonfarm Major Occupation Groups, by Age and Region, 1940 and 1950

Region and Year	Age Group			
	25–34	35–44	45–54	55–64
Non-South				
1940	43.68	43.74	45.75	46.18
1950	33.65	38.98	39.67	35.23
South				
1940	49.77	48.87	49.26	49.78
1950	45.45	45.79	47.98	45.60

Source: Same as Table 1 for 1940 and 1950.

It seems apparent then, that, although there were important differences between the South and the North with regard to occupational
segregation, the effect of the regional shift and the urbanization of
Negroes can be overrated. Our figures show that occupational changes
of the Negro male, for the decade from 1940 to 1950, were due to
changes in each region as well as the migration from South to North. If

the same trend for the nation as a whole during the forties was apparent for each region, it is likely that some condition common to the country as a whole was contributing to the change rather than that the change was due alone to the regional shifts of populations. The reader should note, however, that the cohorts in Tables 5 and 6, unlike those for the United States as a whole, are no longer strictly closed, owing to the possibility of migration between regions.

Therefore, a summary indication of the relative impact of the regional shift and occupational changes within regions on the findings for the country as a whole is presented in Table 7. These figures compare expected indexes of dissimilarity for 1950 (based on a weighting or standardization of 1940 occupational distributions for the United States by regional proportions in 1950) with actual indexes of dissimilarity for 1940 and 1950.

The assumption is that, if the expected index of dissimilarity for 1950, representing the change resulting from regional shift alone, is larger than the actual index for 1940, the regional shift was unfavorable to Negroes; if smaller, the redistribution was favorable. If the expected index is smaller, but not so small as the actual 1950 index, then the decrease from 1940 to 1950, was only partly due to regional shift; the remainder of the decrease being due to occupational shift within regions.

For each cohort in Table 7, expected indexes for 1950 are generally smaller than actual indexes for 1940, but not so small as actual indexes for 1950. Hence, regional shift alone apparently does not explain the trend of convergence during the forties.

The Role of Education

The question which ordinarily would now arise is whether the foregoing occupational change (during the forties) merely reflects an improvement in the educational lot of Negroes. But it was possible in this analysis

Table 7

Actual and Expected Indexes of Dissimilarity Between White and Negro Employed Males, United States, by Age Cohort, 1940 and 1950

Cohort (Year of Birth)	Actual 1940	Expected 1950	Actual 1950
1905–1914	46.02	42.78	38.85
1895–1904	43.11	41.13	39.15
1885–1894	41.79	40.58	36.22

Source: Same as Table 6.

to view education as a fixed or nearly closed characteristic. The true educational levels of men 25 years old and over do not change appreciably, although data reveal shifts in the pattern of reporting of education.

Some of the difficulty was caused by the change in the Census question from 1940 to 1950. Unlike the one-step question in 1940, the 1950 question was, as also in 1960, a two-step process designed to determine if the last grade of school attended had also been completed. This led, apparently, to a decrease in the 5-8 year level, as individuals who had attained the fifth grade without completing it were dropped back to the elementary 1-4 year level. The same effect would logically be expected to occur also at the high school level, especially high school 4 years; but, on the contrary, the high school categories constantly increase—starting with the high school 1-3 years for Negroes, and high school 4 years for whites.

Table 8 presents index numbers of white and nonwhite educational attainment for 1950, relative to that of 1940. The index numbers used represent the percentage for 1950, divided by the percentage for 1940, multiplied by 100. An index of 100 would indicate no change in the educational level reported. Table 8 shows Negroes, for all cohorts, overreporting education relatively more than whites at the advanced educational levels (reflecting perhaps their greater necessity, in this society, for upgrading themselves and the increasing value of education), whereas more whites were pushed back into the lowest educational level by the Census question change. However, there was the tendency for both races in all cohorts to overrepresent education in the more advanced educational levels.

This suggests that, supposing 1940 data correct and 1950 data overreported, the top three educational levels of the nonwhite cohorts had been diluted more, compared to the white cohorts, with men whose education actually was lower than reported. This should result in an apparent increase in the handicap of nonwhites at a given educational level. That is, if college men of both groups were equal in educational attainment in 1940, then, in 1950 the nominal college level included proportionately more nonwhites than whites who actually had not attended college. Hence, if nonwhite occupations for college men were closer to whites in 1950 than in 1940, this occurred despite the fictitious introduction of some disparity in their educational levels. Thus the pattern of overreporting works against, not for, the hypothesis, providing reassurance that convergence actually did occur at the upper educational levels in the forties. We may proceed, then, with confidence, to discern the part played by educational attainment in the mobility of Negroes relative to that of whites.

Table 8

Index Numbers of White and Nonwhite Educational Attainment for 1950, Relative to That of 1940, for the Male Cohorts of 1905–1914, 1895–1904, and 1885–1894

Years of School Completed	All White	Nonwhite
Cohort of 1905–1914		
Less than 5 years	206	145
Elementary 5–8 years	89	76
High school 1–3 years	94	112
High school 4 years	102	129
College 1 year or more	114	137
Cohort of 1895–1904		
Less than 5 years	180	149
Elementary 5–8 years	88	70
High school 1–3 years	95	115
High school 4 years	112	141
College 1 year or more	112	128
Cohort of 1885–1894		
Less than 5 years	105	98
Elementary 5–8 years	92	90
High school 1–3 years	98	118
High school 4 years	111	131
College 1 year or more	110	127
	208	208

Source: U.S. Bureau of the Census, 1950, *Population Education, op. cit.,* U.S. Bureau of the Census, *Population, Occupation and Household Relationships of Males, 18 to 44 Years Old* (Washington, D.C.: Government Printing Office, 1940), Tables 1–2, pp. 4–5. U.S. Bureau of the Census, Cohort of 1885–1894, *U.S. Census of Population: 1950,* Vol. II, *Characteristics of Population,* Part I., United States Summary (Washington, D.C.: U.S. Government Printing Office, 1953), pp. 237, 239.

The pattern of educational influence is presented in Table 9, although some of the figures at the lowest educational level may produce somewhat inaccurate results, owing to the factor of immigration.

Note that Table 9 incorporates the findings in Table 1. Thus, reading across by rows in a cross-sectional age-group comparison, we again discover several instances of divergence, i.e., increasing indexes of dissimilarity with increasing age, for the decade from 1940 to 1950. These occur most frequently among the youngest age groups, contradicting the findings to be had by intracohort analysis and making the spurious

Table 9

Indexes of Dissimilarity Between White and Nonwhite Occupational
Distributions, United States, by Age and Education, for Employed
Males, 1940 and 1950, and Experienced Civilian Labor Force with
Income in 1959, 1960

Years of School Completed and Census Year	Age Group			
	25–34	35–44	45–54	55–64
Total				
1940	46.02	43.11	41.79	36.04
1950	36.40	38.85	39.15	36.22
1960	35.39	37.46	38.27	38.82
Elementary 0–8 years				
1940	34.72	35.07	35.00	29.36
1950	27.26	29.84	30.52	32.04
1960	27.89	29.05	32.03	33.80
High school 1–3 years				
1940	40.71	41.11	37.44	38.21
1950	29.17	35.97	39.37	38.25
1960	29.79	31.13	34.16	38.71
High school 4 years				
1940	43.09	45.91	43.37	39.11
1950	32.14	37.05	40.35	36.92
1960	31.72	31.85	34.09	39.55
College 1–3 years				
1940	36.53	38.44	37.01	40.58
1950	30.19	33.54	37.10	29.23
1960	28.06	31.55	31.17	32.02
College 4 years or more				
1940	21.32	23.05	23.78	20.12
1950	11.90	13.01	20.23	17.10
1960	15.29	13.67	14.06	16.33

Source: Same as Table 1, for 1940, 1950 and 1960.
Note: Data pertain to Negroes and native white in 1940.

suggestion that mobility was most consistently achieved by the presumably least mobile, the oldest group.

Most of the educational levels had indexes of dissimilarity (ranging from 11.90 to 45.91) somewhat smaller than the indexes for "total" males (which ranged from 36.04 to 46.02). This reflects an educational inequality as well as an occupational dissimilarity. Dissimilarity was smallest between whites and Negroes at the extreme educational levels in all age groups, and maximal at the high school level in 1940. The same was true, however, for 1950 and 1960, where, moreover, the least dissimilarity at any educational level was among the college graduates (where the largest index was only 16.33). This provides evidence for the special influence of education for Negro mobility.

Apparently, men of extremely low education in either race are prepared for only a limited variety of occupations, and college graduates are prepared for a highly selected group of occupations. Negro men in the high school range, on the other hand, have sufficient training to expect and seek a diversity of employment, but not enough to ensure access to a given occupation; and thus are especially vulnerable to pressures of discrimination.

A college education was especially effective as a means by which the Negro individual managed to break through some of the barriers to equal occupational participation. Mind you, this does not mean that Negroes had attained the level in the economy appropriate to their education. Nor does it mean that, henceforward, their occupational progress will be wholly contingent on their progress through the educational system. It does suggest the special importance, however, of education for Negro mobility. Bear in mind that measures of education do not take into consideration quality of schooling. If the relative quality of Negro and white education has been shifting, then educational changes may account for even more of the variance.

Conclusions

Data indicate, generally speaking, that the decade of the forties comprised a special decade with regard to Negro occupational mobility. For example, the "close ranks" policy in war industry during that period, and the mass migration of Negroes from southern farms to northern industries, where new jobs were available, should be taken into account but not *overrated*. The mobility of Negroes during the forties would appear to have been in part an ecological product of changes in the general economic structure.

In spite of the Supreme Court decision and the passive resistance movement during the fifties, Negroes did not gain appreciably during the fifties. They were able to obtain some jobs symbolizing integration, such as airline stewardess and symphony orchestra bass fiddler, and they moved up, but whites moved up faster. This was in contrast to the forties, when there was a need for them in war industries which launched the great rural to urban shift among Negroes. However, the waning occupational mobility of Negroes in the United States during the fifties appeared to be mainly a result of growing divergence in the South.

Figures for regions and nonfarm occupations generally duplicated the trend of convergence for the forties (though the change was smaller in the South) and confirmed the hypothesis of the special importance of education for the Negro's mobility during periods of substantial occupational change.

Notes

[1] Revised version of a paper read at the Annual Meeting of the American Sociological Association, August, 1963. This report is based on the author's doctoral dissertation at the University of Chicago. Special thanks are extended to Otis Dudley Duncan for helpful suggestions. Acknowledgment also is made to Philip M. Hauser and G. Franklin Edwards, who read an earlier draft of this paper, and to Arnold I. Winard and Mary F. Henson for assistance in obtaining unpublished data for 1960.

[2] Nathan Hare was affiliated with Howard University, Washington, D.C., at the time of publication of this article.

[3] Gunnar Myrdal, *An American Dilemma* (New York: Harper & Bros., 1944), p. 303.

[4] Conrad Taeuber and Irene B. Taeuber, *The Changing Population of the United States* (New York: John Wiley & Sons, 1958), pp. 219-220.

[5] Donald J. Bogue, *The Population of the United States* (Glencoe, Illinois: The Free Press, 1959), p. 504.

[6] Committee on Labor and Public Welfare, United States Senate, Eighty-eighth Congress, Equal Employment Opportunity, First session on S.773, S.1210, S.1211, and S.1937 (Washington, D.C.: U.S. Government Printing Office, 1963), p. 323.

[7] Negroes comprised 95.62, 95.56 and 92.09 percent of nonwhites in 1940, 1950 and 1960, respectively. See: U.S. Bureau of the Census. *U.S. Summary.* Vol. 2. *Characteristics of Population* (Washington, D.C.: U.S. Government Printing Office, 1953), Table 35; U.S. Bureau of the Census. *U.S. Census of Population: 1960. Subject Reports. Nonwhite Population by Race.* Final Report PC (2)-1C (Washington, D.C.: U.S. Government Printing Office, 1963), Table A, p. xi. Note that these figures are without regard to age cohort and labor force status.

Job Satisfaction

Correlates of Absenteeism Among Race-Sex Subgroups

HERBERT G. HENEMAN, III[1]
CHARLES J. MURPHY

Introduction

Investigators have become increasingly interested in the possible differential predictability of organizational behaviors among race and sex subgroups. This interest has been fostered by legislation designed to eliminate such things as discrimination in employment opportunities [e.g., 2], and by the general recognition that the predictability of behavior may be enhanced by subdividing individuals into more homogeneous subgroups. [10]

One important form of employee behavior, absenteeism, has not received much attention in this regard, although the limited available evidence suggests that both race and sex may moderate its relationship with certain predictor variables. Lopez [6] found that race moderated the relationships between absenteeism and two ability tests and structured interview scores. Metzner and Mann [8] found that work attitudes were significantly related to absenteeism among males, but not among females. Finally, Baumgartel and Sobo [1] found that age, tenure and wage rate were not equally predictive of absenteeism for males and females. This encouraging evidence prompted the present study, which examines the role of race and sex as moderators of the relationship between absenteeism and four independent variables.

Reprinted from *Proceedings of the Thirty-Third Annual Meeting of the Academy of Management,* August 19-22, 1973, Boston, Massachusetts, by permission of the authors and the *Academy of Management Journal.*

The independent variables were chosen on the basis of Gibson's [4] framework. According to Gibson, the major determinant of absence behavior is work identification, which is similar to Vroom's [9] notion of the valence or attractiveness of work. Gibson further hypothesizes that numerous variables affect, or are related to, work identification and thus absenteeism. Four of these variables were available in the present study, and their hypothesized relationships with frequency of absences according to Gibson are: age (negative), tenure (negative), skill level (negative), and work group size (positive).

Gibson's framework does not include potential moderating effects of variables such as race and sex. Moreover, there is little empirical evidence of how these two characteristics moderate the relationships between absenteeism and the four independent variables identified above. For these reasons, no explicit hypotheses were made *a priori* regarding possible moderating effects of race and sex in the present study. It was generally expected, however, that the strength and/or direction of relationships might well vary among the race-sex subgroups.

Method

Sample

Subjects were hourly-paid production workers employed by a southern consumer goods manufacturing firm. The firm provided a random sample of approximately seven percent of its total production work force. This procedure resulted in the following race-sex subgroups: white males (n=177), black males (n=115), white females (n=88), and black females (n=29).

Measures

The dependent variable, frequency of absences, was measured by calculating the total number of one-day absences (excluding maternity, military, vacation and jury duty leaves of absence) for each subject over a one-year time period. This is a rather "crude" measure of absence behavior in that it does not differentiate well among various reasons for absence. Specifically, little distinction is made between "avoidable" and "unavoidable" reasons for absence. Lefkowitz and Katz [5] suggest that this distinction be made in studies of employee turnover, and their suggestion seems equally applicable to the study of absence behavior. Unfortunately, the company's absentee records were such that it was impossible to more clearly distinguish between "avoidable" and "unavoidable" reasons for absence than was done by excluding the four types of reasons noted above.

In terms of the independent variables, age and tenure were measured in number of years and months respectively. Skill level was measured by the company-developed job skill index which runs from 1 to 9 in ascending order. Work group size was measured by the number of workers in the department.

Analysis

A zero-order intercorrelation matrix was computed for the total group and for each subgroup. To test for potential moderating effects of race and sex, correlations between absenteeism and independent variables were compared according to Zedeck's [10] recommendations. This involves computing the significance of difference in these validity coefficients between subgroups. [3] Race or sex is considered a moderator variable if the validity coefficients for a given independent variable are significantly different from one another in the two relevant subgroups.

Results

The intercorrelation matrices for the total sample, and each subgroup, are shown in Table 1. In addition, it was found that females had significantly greater absenteeism than males ($r=.26$, $p<.01$), but there was no significant difference in absenteeism between blacks and whites ($r=-.06$, n.s.).

The significance of differences in validity coefficients for the relevant subgroup comparisons are shown in Table 2. Neither race nor sex significantly moderated the age-absenteeism and tenure-absenteeism relationships. Both race and sex significantly moderated the skill level-absenteeism relationship. This was primarily due to the fact that, contrary to other subgroups, there was a strong, positive correlation between skill level and absenteeism for black females. Race and sex also significantly moderated the group size-absenteeism relationship, primarily because this relationship was very different for white females than for the other subgroups.

Discussion

The validity coefficients for the total sample provide minimal support for Gibson's hypotheses. Only one of four variables (skill level) was significantly related to absenteeism in the hypothesized direction. The relationship between age and absenteeism also was significant, but not in the hypothesized direction. Moreover, within the subgroups only six of the twenty validity coefficients were statistically significant, and only four of these were in the direction hypothesized for the total group.

Table 1
Intercorrelation Matrices

Group		Age (1)	Tenure (2)	Skill Level (3)	Group Size (4)	Absenteeism (5)
Total	(2)	87**				
(N=409)	(3)	15**	19**			
	(4)	05	05	16**		
	(5)	09*	03	−22**	−01	—
White	(2)	85**				
Male	(3)	57**	59**			
	(4)	20**	28**	30**		
(n=177)	(5)	−05	−12	−05	−17**	—
White	(2)	83**				
Female	(3)	24*	27**			
	(4)	05	−01	−16		
(n=88)	(5)	08	04	−28**	21*	—
Black	(2)	86**				
Male	(3)	03	14			
(n=115)	(4)	−06	−06	06		
	(5)	−07	−18*	−23**	03	—
Black	(2)	97**				
Female	(3)	02	07			
	(4)	−20	−28	−14		
(n=29)	(5)	00	06	35*	−23	—

Note: decimals omitted $*p<.05$ $**p<.01$

On the other hand, some interesting moderator effects were obtained. First, race and sex moderated the skill level-absenteeism relationship; it was positive and significant for black females and negative and significant for white females and black males. Perhaps this may be explained by way of analogy to March and Simon's [7] model of turnover, since both turnover and absenteeism represent forms of withdrawal from the job. According to March and Simon, decisions to leave the organization are influenced first by the perceived desirability of leaving, which is highly dependent upon one's job satisfaction. The decision to leave is also influenced by the perceived ease of leaving, which is dependent upon one's perceptions of economic forces and personal characteristics.

Table 2
Significance of Difference in Validity
Coefficients Between Subgroups

| | Comparison | | | |
| | Race | | Sex | |
Variable	WM−BM	WF−BF	WM−WF	BM−BF
Age	n. s.	n. s.	n. s.	n. s.
Tenure	n. s.	n. s.	n. s.	n. s.
Skill Level	n. s.	$p<.01$	n. s.	$p<.01$
Group Size	n. s.	$p<.05$	$p<.01$	n. s.

The hypothesized negative relationship between skill level and absenteeism appears to be based on concepts of perceived desirability only. That is, the lower the skill level the lower the job satisfaction and thus the greater the perceived desirability of being absent. On the other hand, March and Simon's model suggests that a combination of relatively high, marketable skills and favorable personal characteristics could lead to greater perceived ease of being absent. This could result in a positive relationship between skill level and absenteeism. In the present study, therefore, it may be that the perceived ease of being absent was much greater for black females than any other subgroup and this is reflected in the positive correlation between skill level and absenteeism for this subgroup only.

Race and sex also moderated the group size-absenteeism relationship. The relationship was positive and significant for white females; it was negative and significant for black females and white males. The relationship for the latter two subgroups is contrary to the general hypothesis and difficult to explain. It is probably reflective of systematic differences (between these two subgroups and the white female subgroup) in personal and/or job characteristics associated with group size and thus absenteeism. The precise nature of these differences, however, is impossible to identify in the present study.

Though the above explanations of the obtained moderator effects are purely speculative, they do illustrate the need for the development and testing of more comprehensive theories of absence behavior. At the very least, the evidence clearly indicates the usefulness of subgroup analysis and suggests that race and sex be utilized as moderator variables whenever possible in future research on employee absenteeism. At the same time, however, the evidence cautions against the expectation of "automatically" obtaining differential validity simply because moderator variables were chosen and utilized *a priori.* In the present study, this is indicated by differential validity for only two of the four independent variables.

Note

[1]Herbert G. Heneman, III, was affiliated with the University of Wisconsin, Madison, Wisconsin, at the time of publication of this article. Charles J. Murphy was with Ohio State University, Columbus, Ohio.

References

1. Baumgartel, Howard and Ronald Sobel, "Background and Organizational Factors in Absenteeism," *Personnel Psychology,* Vol. 12, No. 3 (Autumn 1959), pp. 431-443.
2. Equal Employment Opportunity Commission, *Guidelines on Employment Testing Procedures,* 1970.
3. Ferguson, George A., *Statistical Analysis in Psychology and Education* (New York: McGraw-Hill Book Company, 1959).
4. Gibson, R. Oliver, "Towards a Conceptualization of Absence Behavior of Personnel in Organizations," *Administrative Science Quarterly,* Vol. 11, No. 1 (June 1966), pp. 107-133.
5. Lefkowitz, Joel and Myron L. Katz, "Validity of Exit Interviews," *Personnel Psychology,* Vol. 22, No. 4 (Winter 1969), pp. 445-455.
6. Lopez, Felix M. Jr., "Current Problems in Test Performance of Job Applicants," *Personnel Psychology,* Vol. 19, No. 1 (Spring 1966), pp. 10-17.
7. March, James G. and Herbert A. Simon, *Organizations* (New York: John Wiley & Sons, Inc., 1958).
8. Metzner, Helen and Floyd Mann, "Employee Attitudes and Absences," *Personnel Psychology,* Vol. 6, No. 4 (Winter 1953), pp. 467-485.
9. Vroom, Victor H., *Work and Motivation* (New York: John Wiley & Sons, Inc., 1964).
10. Zedeck, Sheldon, "Problems With the Use of 'Moderator' Variables," *Psychological Bulletin,* Vol. 76, No. 4 (October 1971), pp. 295-310.

Job Satisfaction Factors Among Underprivileged Workers

JOSEPH E. CHAMPAGNE[1]
DONALD C. KING

Sixteen factors dealing with motivation on the job were presented in a paired comparison format to 513 underprivileged adults in a federally supported job retraining project in South Carolina. They were directed to select for each pair the one factor which was more important to them on a job. Analyses were computed for the total sample and for subsamples based on race, sex, and economic environment of residence. The results point out that intrinsic, personal factors are more important than job context factors. Slight differences were found across sex; larger differences were found across race and economic environment.

The past several years have witnessed some major federal anti-poverty legislative actions, among the most notable of which were the Manpower Development and Training Act (MDTA) of 1962 and the Economic Opportunity Act of 1964. As a result of these bills many individuals classed as "underprivileged" either by education or vocational training have been receiving varying amounts of prevocational and vocational training in federally supported programs. In many instances these newly trained individuals are going out into the industrial job market for the first time. One of the immediate questions that can be raised asks: What factors about a job are most important to these people?

Reprinted from *Personnel and Guidance Journal,* January 1967, *45,* 429-434, by permission of the publisher and the authors. Copyright © 1967 by American Personnel and Guidance Association.

A review of the literature pointed out that among the many recent articles on motivation, few were specifically directed to the job needs of underprivileged people, to whom the Office of Economic Opportunity addresses itself. In fact, no article was specific enough to be of significant value in answering the question presented above. Certainly the work of Herzberg, Mausner, Peterson, and Capwell (1957), Herzberg, Mausner, and Snyderman (1959), and Vroom (1964), as well as the need-hierarchy theory of Maslow (1954), is of general value. But the question of how well the work of these men generalizes to the population of underprivileged, disadvantaged workers remained in question. Consequently, this study was designed to extend the literature on job motivation and to answer questions that need to be considered as the underprivileged person assumes a new economic role of stable employment. The study reported here directed itself to this area of investigation and used a sample of trainees classed as underprivileged in an MDTA statewide project called STEP (Special Training for Economic Progress) under the direction of the Committee for Technical Education in South Carolina. What is presented here is only a part of the total study which served as the doctoral dissertation of the senior author (Champagne, 1966).

Method

From a review of the literature on job motivation, 16 motivational factors were determined as representing the primary areas generally investigated. These factors were described by a short phrase and arranged in a paired comparison form. Since the subjects of the study were underprivileged, many had a minimum education. In order to be sure that the wording of the factors would be understood, 25 of the trainees from whom the study sample was selected read the wording of the factors and explained what each meant. Based upon this, certain modifications were made and the instructions for administration were developed. The 16 factors, worded as they appeared in the actual study, were: (1) Good pay; (2) Liking for my job itself; (3) Good working conditions; (4) Fear of getting fired; (5) Praise for good work from fellow workers; (6) Personal satisfaction from doing a job right; (7) Duty to do my best on the job; (8) Steady work; (9) A good company; (10) Chance for a promotion; (11) Praise for good work from the boss; (12) Fear of getting bawled out; (13) Chance for a raise; (14) A good boss; (15) Proving that I can do the job as well as anyone else; (16) Respect for holding a good job from friends and family.

The instrument was administered to 513 STEP trainees throughout the State of South Carolina during June, 1965. They were instructed to pick the one factor in each pair that they considered as more important to themselves when working on a job—that is, which one of each pair had more meaning to them and would help them do their best on the job. Since there were 16 items, a complete pairing of items generated 120 pairs. The pairs were arranged in the order prescribed by Ross (1934) to minimize sequence errors and to achieve maximum distance between sequential presentations of each item.

The responses were analyzed by a least squares solution for a complete paired comparison schedule, and reliability coefficients of agreement and consistency were calculated along with a variance components analysis after the method of Gulliksen and Tukey (1958). The analysis was performed on an IBM 7094 with a Fortran program developed by Gulliksen (1965). An index of temporal stability of the test-retest type was also derived.

Results

The least squares solution gives a normal transform scale value for each item for those groups analyzed. It is a type of "average across individuals" scale value. One group of 30 trainees was given the survey twice, five weeks apart. The scale values for the first administration and for the second administration were correlated, and a Pearson r of .98 was obtained which indicated a high degree of temporal stability.

The analyses reported here were based on the total sample ($N = 513$), the white subsample ($N = 159$), the Negro subsample ($N = 353$), the male subsample ($N = 259$) and the female subsample ($N = 253$). (One respondent was included in the total sample but not in the subsamples because of insufficient coding of the instrument.) The state of South Carolina is neatly divided into three economic and geographic sub-units called the Piedmont which is heavily industrialized, the Pee Dee which is moderately industrialized and moderately agricultural, and the Low Country which is predominantly agricultural. Additional analyses were conducted for trainees from each sub-unit (Piedmont $N = 178$, Pee Dee $N = 70$, and Low Country $N = 264$). Table 1 presents the results of the analysis on the total sample. The items are given in their rank order of perceived importance based on the size of the scale values. Also presented are the coefficient of agreement, R(B), the coefficient of consistency, R(S), and the proportion of total variance accounted for by the scale values, $S^2(S)$. While it may seem that only a moderate amount of the variance is accounted for, it is shown that what is accounted for is far from random. It is very interesting to observe the rank order of importance of the motivation variables. A convenient method of interpreting the results of this paired comparison analysis is to look directly at the different scale values. Differences across scale values indicate differences in relative perceived importance. It is very easy to compare across

Table 1

Motivation Variables in Rank Order of Perceived Importance for Total
Sample of Disadvantaged Workers ($N=513$)

Importance Rank Order	Items	Scale Values
1	Duty to do one's best	.946
2	Personal satisfaction	.518
3	Working conditions	.458
4	Steady work	.344
5	Liking the work	.304
6	Fair boss	.287
7	Proving that one can do the job	.256
8	Fair company	.145
9	Praise from boss	.074
10	Chance for a promotion	.015
11	Chance for a raise	−.094
12	Pay	−.170
13	Peer respect	−.235
14	Praise from co-workers	−.438
15	Fear of getting fired	−1.188
16	Fear of reprimand	−1.223

$$R(S) = .967$$
$$R(B) = .994$$
$$\sigma_s2 = .167$$

groups by merely comparing ranks. Duty to do one's best is ranked as first in importance along with personal satisfaction from doing a job right. The fear of job severance or reprimand is least in importance among these 16 variables and also low is pay, perhaps because the respondents have so long adapted to living in poverty conditions. Finally, it is of interest to note that praise from superiors is more important than praise or respect from peer groups.

Table 2 presents the results of the subgroup analyses based on race. It is seen that the reliability and variance estimates are quite equivalent across race, but there are some noteworthy differences in the rank orders of importance of the motivation variables. For example, while duty to do one's best is first in importance in both cases, the factor of working conditions is more important in rank order to Negroes than to whites and the factor of liking the job is more important to whites than to Negroes. Proving that one can do the job also ranks as more important to Negroes than to whites. The need to prove capability to others

Table 2

Motivation Variables in Rank Order of Perceived Importance for White
and Negro Subsamples of Disadvantaged Workers

Importance Rank Order	White (N=159) Items	Scale Value	Importance Rank Order	Negro (N=353) Items	Scale Value
1	Duty to do one's best	.917	1	Duty to do one's best	1.048
2	Personal satisfaction	.746	2	Working conditions	.513
3	Liking the job	.588	3	Personal satisfaction	.512
4	Working conditions	.518	4	Steady work	.351
5	Steady work	.427	5	Fair boss	.306
6	Fair boss	.369	6	Proving that one can do the job	.305
7	Fair company	.351	7	Liking the job	.242
8	Proving that one can do the job	.244	8	Praise from boss	.125
9	Chance for a promotion	-.002	9	Fair company	.106
10	Praise from boss	-.088	10	Chance for a promotion	.022
11	Peer respect	-.135	11	Chance for a raise	-.089
12	Chance for a raise	-.162	12	Pay	-.161
13	Pay	-.185	13	Peer respect	-.305
14	Praise from co-workers	-.572	14	Praise from co-workers	-.465
15	Fear of reprimand	-1.507	15	Fear of being fired	-1.240
16	Fear of getting fired	-1.510	16	Fear of reprimand	-1.269

R(S)=.968   R(B)=.987 σ_s^2=.228

R(S)=.976   R(B)=.992 σ_s^2=1.82

Table 3
Motivation Variables in Rank Order of Perceived Importance for Male and Female Subsamples of Disadvantaged Workers

	Male (N=259)			Female (N=253)	
Importance Rank Order	Items	Scale Value	Importance Rank Order	Items	Scale Value
1	Duty to do one's best	.897	1	Duty to do one's best	1.131
2	Personal satisfaction	.521	2	Personal satisfaction	.646
3	Working conditions	.486	3	Working conditions	.548
4	Steady work	.416	4	Liking the job	.461
5	Proving that one can do the job	.315	5	Fair boss	.456
6	Liking the job	.236	6	Steady work	.335
7	Fair boss	.201	7	Proving that one can do the job	.245
8	Fair company	.179	8	Fair company	.177
9	Praise from boss	.080	9	Praise from boss	.044
10	Chance for a promotion	.058	10	Chance for a promotion	-.033
11	Chance for a raise	-.008	11	Chance for a raise	-.222
12	Pay	-.107	12	Pay	-.232
13	Peer respect	-.142	13	Peer respect	-.382
14	Praise from co-workers	-.392	14	Praise from co-workers	-.621
15	Fear of being fired	-1.363	15	Fear of being fired	-1.262
16	Fear of reprimand	-1.377	16	Fear of reprimand	-1.293
	R(S)=.972 R(B)=.989 $\sigma_s^2 = .182$			R(S)=.976 R(B)=.991 $\sigma_s^2 = 2.12$	

and to oneself is important to Negroes who have perhaps felt economic discrimination for so long a time.

Table 3 summarizes the data for the male-female analyses. The reliability estimates are nearly identical and the amount of variance accounted for by each subsample is reasonably equivalent. In this case the differences among the motivation variables can be noted in those items ranked fourth through seventh in importance. Men have a greater need to prove themselves while women have a greater need to like their work. Men consider steady work as more important, while women are more concerned about a fair boss.

Finally, Table 4 presents the analyses across the three geographical sub-units described above. While the reliability estimates are very similar, the estimates of the amount of variance accounted for is lower for the Low Country group than for the other two groups. The first three items have the same rank order of importance. But there are some noteworthy differences across groups after these items. It is interesting to note that the Pee Dee hierarchy of items is more similar to the Low Country hierarchy than to the Piedmont hierarchy. But it is also true that the economic conditions of the Pee Dee, while different from the Low Country, are more nearly like those of the Low Country than those of the Piedmont. Pay and job interest are ranked as more important in the Piedmont area than in the other two areas. Since jobs are more plentiful and since the potential employee has a greater choice, it may be that these factors *can* become more important. Steady work was found to be slightly more important in the lesser-developed areas, again perhaps because jobs are harder to find. Proving one's ability is more important in these lesser-developed areas than in the more-industrialized area. Analyses, though not reported here, were computed for race by area subsamples. The differences across race were greater than across area of the state.

Discussion and Conclusions

It has been demonstrated that there is a hierarchy of job satisfaction factors among disadvantaged workers and that this hierarchy can be adequately defined through simple scaling procedures. It has also been shown that within the population of disadvantaged workers, analyses on subsamples brought differences to light and these differences should be recognized by management personnel as they hire and interact with this large labor potential in the Southeast. It is most interesting to note that in all cases the intrinsic factors of duty and satisfaction are generally ranked higher than the extrinsic factors of pay, praise, or respect. In all cases, respect or praise from superiors was more important than from

Table 4

Motivation Variables in Rank Order of Perceived Importance for Piedmont,
Pee Dee, and Low Country Subsamples of Disadvantaged Workers

Importance Rank Order	Piedmont (N=178)		Pee Dee (N=70)		Low Country (N=264)	
	Items	Scale Value	Items	Scale Value	Items	Scale Value
1	Duty to do one's best	.969	Duty to do one's best	1.011	Duty to do one's best	.951
2	Personal satisfaction	.562	Personal satisfaction	.753	Personal satisfaction	.474
3	Working conditions	.526	Working conditions	.470	Working conditions	.444
4	Liking the job	.429	Steady work	.423	Steady work	.303
5	Steady work	.412	Proving that one can do the job	.317	Proving that one can do the job	.275
6	Fair boss	.387	Fair company	.267	Fair boss	.268
7	Fair company	.329	Fair boss	.241	Liking the job	.264
8	Proving that one can do the job	.231	Liking the job	.203	Praise from superiors	.206
9	Chance for a promotion	.069	Praise from boss	.054	Fair company	.023
10	Pay	-.024	Chance for a promotion	-.098	Chance for a promotion	.017
11	Chance for a raise	-.061	Chance for a raise	-.141	Chance for a raise	-.092
12	Praise from boss	-.125	Pay	-.167	Peer respect	-.223

Table 4 (Continued)

Importance Rank Order	Piedmont (N=178)		Importance Rank Order	Pee Dee (N=70)		Importance Rank Order	Low Country (N=264)	
	Items	Scale Value		Items	Scale Value		Items	Scale Value
13	Peer respect	-.259	13	Peer respect	-.260	13	Pay	-.257
14	Praise from co-workers	-.593	14	Praise from co-workers	-.515	14	Praise from co-workers	-.367
15	Fear of being fired	-1.418	15	Fear of reprimand	-1.271	15	Fear of being fired	-1.222
16	Fear of reprimand	-1.434	16	Fear of being fired	-1.288	16	Fear of reprimand	-1.164
	$R(S) = .972$ $R(B) = .987$ $\sigma_s^2 = .211$			$R(S) = .946$ $R(B) = .965$ $\sigma_s^2 = .194$			$R(S) = .956$ $R(B) = .988$ $\sigma_s^2 = .156$	

peer groups. The fear of job severance or reprimand was very low, relatively speaking, indicating to some extent that a fear-inducing, non-employee-oriented management will not be maximally effective with workers similar to those in this study. As this relatively untapped labor resource is made ready for employment through local, state, and federal training efforts, it will become increasingly important that further research on attitudes and motivation be conducted, in order that the transition of this class of worker to stable employment might be more readily effected to the maximum satisfaction of both employer and employee.

Note

[1]Joseph E. Champagne was Director of Research for the Committee for Technical Education, Columbia, South Carolina, at the time of publication of this article. Donald C. King was Professor of Psychology, Purdue University, Lafayette, Indiana.

References

Champagne, J. E. The attitudes and motivation of Southern underprivileged workers. Unpublished doctoral dissertation, Purdue Univ., 1966.

Gulliksen, H. An IBM 7090-94 program for a complete paired comparison schedule, with Fortran listing and trial data. ONR Research Contract Nonr 1858-15, Princeton Univ., 1965.

Gulliksen, H., & Tukey, J. W. Reliability for the law of comparative judgment. *Psychometrika*, 1958, *23*, 95-110.

Herzberg, F., Mausner, B., Peterson, R., & Capwell, Dora. *Job attitudes: review of research and opinion*. Pittsburgh, Pa.: Psychological Services, 1957.

Herzberg, F., Mausner, B., & Snyderman, B. *The motivation to work*. (2nd ed.) New York: Wiley, 1959.

Maslow, A. H. *Motivation and personality*. New York: Harper, 1954.

Ross, R. T. Optimum orders for the presentation of pairs in the method of paired comparisons. *Journal of Educational Psychology*, 1934, *25*, 375-382.

Vroom, V. H. *Work and motivation*. New York: Wiley, 1964.

Job Satisfaction Differences Among Women of Different Ethnic Groups

PHILIP ASH[1]

The present research compares the job satisfaction of black, white, and Spanish-surname female production and clerical employees. In one study, 112 white, 63 Spanish-surname, and 47 black female clerical and production workers in an electrical components company completed a Science Research Associates employee attitude survey. In the second, 56 white and 14 black female non-academic clerical employees in a university took the Job Description Index. In both studies, black women were more dissatisfied than white. Spanish-surname employees (in the first study) were generally more satisfied than blacks but less satisfied than whites.

Although the relationships between numberless variables and job satisfaction have been reported in the psychological literature, few studies have dealt with the effects of ethnic group membership on job satisfaction and worker morale. Indeed, of the three major reviews of job attitude research encompassed in well over 500 studies published prior to 1967 (Brayfield & Crockett, 1955; Herzberg, Mausner, Peterson, & Capwell, 1957; Vroom, 1967), neither Brayfield and Crockett nor Vroom mention ethnic comparisons, and Herzberg cites only four studies on the issue. In the latest two of an annual series of summaries of job satisfaction literature, only one citation was found among 113 studies in 1968-69 (Pallone, Hurley, & Rickard, 1971) and only 3 among 103 studies in 1966-67 (Pallone, Rickard, & Hurley, 1970).

Reprinted from *Journal of Vocational Behavior*, 1972, *2*, 495-507, by permission of the publisher and the authors. Copyright © 1972 by Academic Press, Inc.

203

The reason is generally not hard to identify: Until very recently the doctrine of "merit employment" imposed a color-blind constraint on most industrial psychological research, compounded, in attitude surveys, by a strong effort to achieve credibility in the almost-always-made commitment to guard and protect respondent anonymity. Disclosure of ethnicity, however, can be made without compromising anonymity, and minority-group members are increasingly insisting on such group iden-tification, rather than hiding it, to ensure that their particular problems and grievances come through clearly. This is also the thrust of the civil rights movement, which requires detailed reporting by ethnic groups. Among civil rights groups today the attitude is frequently expressed that "color-blind" reporting was much more often a refuge for bias than a principle of equity.

The research reported to date, however, which is summarized below, is still fragmentary and occasionally contradictory (a character-istic shared with most employee attitude studies!).

OVERALL MINORITY GROUP ATTITUDES

Cole (1940), on the basis of a random sample of workers in five occupa-tional groups in Philadelphia, reported that Negroes showed very wide variations in job satisfaction (and that foreign-born workers on the whole had negative attitudes). In a study reporting on the effects of experience of discrimination, Saenger and Gordon (1950) gathered over 500 interviews from a "representative sample of New Yorkers." Job satisfaction was lower among minority-group than among majority-group persons, and was lowest among blacks. Among all minority groups, the people with the lowest job morale were those who reported that they had actually personally suffered from discrimination. A *Fortune* (1947) survey, in which workers in a national sample were asked to rate the interest they had in their jobs, found that only 42% of the black group reported their work as "interesting," as compared with 52% of a "poor white" group and 92% of a "prosperous white" group. A larger propor-tion of blacks than of the white United States population was then, and still is, in lower-class occupations, however, and the *Fortune* survey results need to be qualified. The clear relationship between job satisfaction and occupational level (e.g., Ash, 1954) may easily account, at least in part, for the *Fortune* finding. Blacks may have found their jobs uninteresting not because they were black, but because the majority of them held unin-teresting jobs.

However, even when occupational group is held constant, differ-ences in job satisfaction are usually, but not always, found. For example,

Slocum and Strawser (1972), using a questionnaire based upon Maslow's needs hierarchy theory, attempted to find out whether attitudes toward intrinsic job factors such as self-actualization and ability to make decisions, and extrinsic factors such as pay and job security vary as a function of race. Their study was based on a sample of 218 certified public accountants, 87 black and 131 "other." The results indicated that the self-actualization and compensation needs categories were the most important and most deficient areas for both black and non-black CPAs. However, the blacks reported more need deficiency than nonblacks in all categories.

However, in a study of the relationships between belief systems and the job satisfaction of migratory workers, ul Hasson (1968) found no interracial differences and no relationship between the content of respondent's belief systems and job satisfaction. For those workers at lower socioeconomic levels, job satisfaction was positively related to family adjustment, home ownership, and the extent of participation in community life.

In a study focused on leadership style, King and Bass (1970) noted that differences in black and white superiors and subordinates are reflected in leadership and followership styles. More than the average white, the black is concerned with such injustices as rejection for jobs and denial of promotional opportunities.

In 1969, the Committee on Equality of Opportunity in Psychology conducted a survey of American Negro psychologists (Wispé, Ash, Awkard, Hicks, Hoffman, & Porter, 1969). A six-page questionnaire containing items about family background, undergraduate and graduate education, occupational history, and present earnings was mailed to 429 persons identified as Negro psychologists. After many follow-ups, a response rate reached 81%. Most of the Negro psychologists received undergraduate training in Negro schools, and then continued on for graduate degrees in primarily white institutions, since few graduate study programs were offered at the Negro schools. Of those who found employment with colleges and universities after obtaining a doctorate, 154 had returned to Negro institutions and only 46 were employed in white institutions. One individual was noted as replying, "recognizing the limitations of a segregated society, I protect my ego by seeking employment only in Negro institutions." The fact that 85% of the sample held doctorate degrees or master's degrees while only 27% were members of APA, was another reflection of their isolation. Nearly half of the respondents claimed that their race limited their professional opportunities.

ETHNIC GROUP AND THE TWO-FACTOR THEORY

Few studies have yet been reported concerning the *structure* of the attitudes of minority workers. A pair of studies related to the Herzberg two-factor theory give conflicting results.

Bloom and Barry (1967) tried to determine whether the work attitudes of Negro blue-collar workers could be explained by Herzberg's (1959) two-factor theory.

Using the "Work Attitude Study" designed by Malinovsky and Barry, 180 questionnaires were distributed to male Negro blue-collar workers. Eighty-five were completed and returned. The findings suggested that the work motivations of Negroes are too complicated to be explained by the two-factor theory. However, item-response data can be interpreted to suggest that hygiene variables are more important to the Negro than motivator variables.

Gendel (1965) found, however, that among 119 housekeeping workers (90% of them black) in two VA hospitals, recognition, advancement, and responsibility were related to job satisfaction, while job dissatisfaction was generated by hospital policies and administration, wages, working conditions, and job-related interpersonal problems, lending support to the applicability of the two-factor theory.

It is clear that much work remains to be done to pin down the similarities and differences in job satisfaction and morale as among majority white, black, and other minority-group workers. In the studies reported here, one compares the job satisfaction of blacks and whites, while the other compares the job satisfaction of blacks, Spanish-surname employees, and others (whites). The main analysis is limited to female employees.

STUDY 1—FEMALE EMPLOYEES IN AN ELECTRICAL COMPONENTS MANUFACTURING FIRM

Subjects and Procedure

The ABC Company manufactures small precision electrical components. Although located in a suburban community, its labor force draws heavily upon the central metropolis' ethnic minority groups, particularly in its largely female production worker group. With a total workforce of just under 440, approximately 386 employees completed a SRA Attitude Inventory (Science Research Associates, 1969). The Inventory was administered on company time, to groups of about 50 employees each, under conditions guaranteeing employee anonymity. To avoid the possibility of identifying any employee by too-detailed a cross-tabulation, respondents were classified *independently* by occupational group and sex and by ethnic group and sex.

These classifications are reported in Table 1. It will be noted that of 167 male employees, only eight (5.0%) were either black or Spanish-surnamed, while among female employees 21.2% were black, 28.4% were Spanish-surnamed, and 50.4% were "other" (majority white).

Over three-quarters (76.6%) of the females were production workers, 17.1% were clerical, and 5.4% were supervisory. No women in the company held a supervisory position higher than first-level production supervisor. The 12 female supervisors, who were known to be divided about equally among the three ethnic classifications, were probably divided about equally among the survey respondents. Female clericals in the survey sample were also distributed proportionately to their representation in the total work force.

The analysis centers upon the female work force. Data for males are included in the tables, but are not considered comparable even with "other" (white majority) women because of the heavy weighting in the male sample by professional and management personnel, who would be expected to show greater job satisfaction than lower-level employees.

The SRA Inventory included 78 questions (responded to by *Agree, ?, Disagree*) grouped into fourteen job-related scales and a fifteenth measuring "Reactions to the Inventory." Widely used in industry, extensive norm data are available to permit comparison of a particular company or subgroup of employees with norm populations of various kinds. Although a number of factor analyses of the SRA Inventory indicate that the 14 given scales are not independent, and may be described more compactly by three or four major "common" factors, and perhaps as many specifics (e.g., Ash, 1954; Baehr, 1954; Wherry, 1954) they are

Table 1

Sex, Ethnic, and Occupational Group Classification of 389 Employees in a Precision Electrical Components Plant

	Male		Female	
	No.	Pct.	No.	Pct.
Black			47	21.2
Spanish-surname	8	5.0	63	28.4
Other	159	95.0	112	50.4
Hourly	44	26.3	170	76.4
Managerial and supervisory	63	35.9	12	5.4
Professional	63	37.7	0	0
Clerical	0	0	38	17.1
Total	167	100.0	222	100.0

as they stand useful points of departure for investigating the issues that make employees discontent or satisfied in particular company settings.

Results

The standard computer analysis procedure used to analyze Inventory responses yields normalized group scale scores and percent favorable response figures for each question, but not scale scores for individuals or other moment statistics (means and standard deviations). However, category means can be reconstructed from the percent-favorable responses to item choices.

This has been done for the analysis reported herein. For each item, the favorable response was given a weight of 2, the ? response a weight of 1, and the unfavorable response a weight of 0. The maximum possible score for a scale is therefore two times the number of items in the scale.

Although the scale mean scores, each based upon the same people within an ethnic group, are not independent, an analysis of variance over repeated measurements was made over the 15 scales, treating each ethnic group scale score mean as a data point. Only the three female groups were included in the Anova; it is obvious from Table 2 that the (white) male group manifested higher satisfaction on every one of the fourteen job-related dimensions, but the high representation among male employees of professional and managerial employees makes it difficult to interpret these differences.

Analysis of variance over the scales means yields a highly significant effect for scales ($F = 53.1$; expected on the basis of the range of possible maxima), and for ethnic group ($F = 18.8$) well beyond the 0.1% level of confidence.

Over the 15 scales, there were four orderings of job satisfaction. First, for eleven of the scales, "others" (white, nonSpanish) scored highest, Spanish-surnamed employees scored next, and blacks scored lowest. This ordering applies to working conditions, employee benefits, supervisor-employee interpersonal relations, confidence in management, effectiveness of administration, adequacy of communication, security, status and recognition, identification with the company, opportunity for advancement, and reactions to the Inventory. Overall, then, on most dimensions, majority-group white employees are most satisfied, and blacks are least satisfied. As late-comers into the industrial scene, facing an alien culture across a language barrier (many of the Spanish-surname employees know almost no English; they took the Inventory in Spanish), they are somewhat more accepting of things as they are, but still feel that, relative to majority-group whites, they are frequently recipients of less-than-equal treatment.

Table 2

Mean Category Scores on the SRA Attitude Inventory for 222 Female
Production and Clerical Workers and 159 Male Workers (Production,
Technical, Clerical, Sales, and Supervisory Combined): Electrical
Components Manufacturing Company

| Scale | Maximum Possible Scores | Females | | | Males |
		White	Spanish-Surname	Black	White
1. Job demands	10	6.05	6.17	5.97	7.81
2. Working conditions	12	8.09	7.80	6.50	8.51
3. Pay	8	2.46	2.29	2.68	4.45
4. Employee benefits	8	4.20	3.50	3.04	6.41
5. Friendliness and cooperation of fellow employees	8	5.00	3.67	4.44	6.14
6. Supervisor-employee inter-personal relations	16	10.41	9.40	8.28	12.04
7. Confidence in management	14	8.14	6.58	6.37	11.37
8. Technical competence of supervision	12	8.30	7.62	8.01	8.91
9. Effectiveness of administration	10	5.93	5.71	5.31	6.75
10. Adequacy of communication	12	6.62	5.92	5.14	8.41
11. Security of job and work relations	14	7.57	6.65	5.35	10.39
12. Status and recognition	12	7.23	6.48	6.27	9.41
13. Identification with the company	8	6.09	7.78	4.67	7.00
14. Opportunity for advancement	8	4.80	4.73	4.48	5.99
15. Reactions to the inventory	4	3.58	3.44	3.43	3.41
Total inventory score	156	94.47	85.74	79.80	117.00
No. cases	—	112	63	47	159

Second, on the scale for *Job Demands,* Spanish-surname females
were least dissatisfied while blacks were most dissatisfied. Interviews
with a sample of employees indicated that, in comparison with working
conditions in cultures from which they migrated (Puerto Rico and Mex-
ico primarily), factory conditions here are better than there.

Third, Spanish-surname employees were less satisfied with their
pay than either majority-group whites or blacks, while blacks were *more*
satisfied than whites.

Finally, Spanish-surname employees were less satisfied than either blacks or majority-group whites with the friendliness of fellow employees (extensively documented in interviews, and stemming, in large part apparently, from the language barrier), while whites were most satisfied. Attitudes toward the technical competence of supervision followed the same trend. Interview data suggests that the distrust of Spanish-speaking employees of the competence of their supervisors also stems from the language barrier: the supervisor, frequently unable to communicate, is viewed as incompetent and unhelpful.

An analysis was also undertaken of the extent of interethnic differences among the 78 items on the Inventory. For each item, a chi-square was computed based upon the numbers of employees in each ethnic group giving the favorable response. Thirty items were found to discriminate at or beyond the 5% level of confidence. These are summarized in Table 3. The male percent favorable response is also given, but it did not enter into the analysis since, as indicated above, the occupational distribution of males is not comparable to the occupational distribution of females. There were no items on scales *IX. Effectiveness of administration; XIV. Opportunity for growth and advancement; or XV. Reactions to the Inventory* on which significant ethnic group differences were found. Since the item frequencies are, of course, not independent, the true power of the tests is unknown. The observed differences, however, are generally of a magnitude that cannot be dismissed. The item differences contribute to, and provide a basis for interpreting, the scale score differences.

In summary, in this Company there are significant differences in job satisfaction and morale as among black female employees, Spanish-surname female employees, and "other" (white nonSpanish-surname employees). It is suspected, at least, that these differences are not atypical. Discrimination—the frequent experience of minority-group workers—not unexpectedly leads to dissatisfaction. It remains to be explored whether this relative dissatisfaction results in other costs to the enterprise, such as higher turnover and lower productivity.

STUDY II—FEMALE CLERICAL EMPLOYEES IN A UNIVERSITY

Method

In another attempt to evaluate the effect of membership in a minority group upon job satisfaction, a small study was conducted among female clerical employees at the metropolitan campus of a major state university.

The Job Description Index (JDI) (Smith, Kendall, & Hulin, 1969) was chosen as the measure of job satisfaction. This questionnaire has

Table 3
Percent Favorable Response on SRA Inventory Items on Which
Significant Interethnic Group Differences Among Female
Employees Were Found

| | Percent Favorable Response | | | |
| | Females | | | Males |
Scale and Item	Black	Spanish-Surname	"Other"	"Other"
I. Job demands:				
They expect too much from us around here.[b]	28	27	49	77
II. Working conditions:				
Poor working conditions keep me from doing my best in my work.[a]	32	54	54	67
Some of the working conditions here are annoying.[b]	11	30	36	38
I have the right equipment to do my work.[b]	70	43	66	65
III. Pay:				
I'm paid fairly compared with other employees.[a]	38	17	32	58
IV. Employee benefits:				
I understand what the company benefit programs provide for employees.[b]	23	29	46	89
Compared with other companies, employee benefits here are good.[a]	23	27	42	77
V. Friendliness and cooperation of fellow employees:				
The people I work with help each other out.[a]	36	38	56	72
The people I work with get along well.[b]	64	35	71	74
The people I work with are very friendly.[c]	66	41	75	84

[a]Chi-square value significant at the 5.0% level.
[b]Chi-square value significant at the 1.0% level.
[c]Chi-square value significant at the 0.1% level.

Table 3 (Continued)

| | Percent Favorable Response | | | |
| | Females | | | Males |
Scale and Item	Black	Spanish-Surname	"Other"	"Other"
VI. Supervisor-employee interpersonal relations:				
My boss is always breathing down our necks; he watches us too closely.[a]	60	70	80	90
My boss lives up to his promises.[b]	51	37	49	67
My boss ought to be friendlier toward employees.[a]	34	37	55	69
VII. Confidence in management:				
If I have a complaint to make, I feel free to talk to someone up the line.[a]	47	27	45	88
Management here is really interested in the welfare of employees.[b]	38	21	44	77
Most of the higher-ups are friendly toward employees.[c]	51	30	75	92
VIII. Technical competence of supervision:				
My boss keeps putting things off; he just lets things ride.[a]	57	54	63	70
My boss lets us know exactly what is expected of us.[a]	64	60	56	59
X. Adequacy of communication:				
Management tells employees about company plans and developments.[b]	40	40	63	88
I know how my job fits in with other work in this organization.[a]	53	43	65	86
Management keeps us in the dark about things we ought to know.[b]	36	41	46	69

[a]Chi-square value significant at the 5.0% level.
[b]Chi-square value significant at the 1.0% level.
[c]Chi-square value significant at the 0.1% level.

Table 3 (Continued)

| | Percent Favorable Response | | | |
| | Females | | | Males |
Scale and Item	Black	Spanish-Surname	"Other"	"Other"
XI. Security of job and work relations:				
Changes are made here with little regard for the welfare of employees.[a]	15	30	38	76
You can get fired around here without much cause.[a]	26	37	50	76
I can be sure of my job as long as I do good work.[c]	40	59	72	85
You always know where you stand with this company.[a]	26	21	38	48
XII. Status and recognition:				
Compared with other employees, we get very little attention from management.[a]	34	30	50	69
I have plenty of freedom on the job to use my own judgment.[a]	40	25	47	77
XIII. Identification with the company:				
The longer you work for this company, the more you feel you belong.[c]	38	67	68	75
I really feel part of this organization.[a]	34	27	48	70
I'm proud to work for this company.[b]	57	67	82	90

[a]Chi-square value significant at the 5.0% level.
[b]Chi-square value significant at the 1.0% level.
[c]Chi-square value significant at the 0.1% level.

been designed to measure satisfaction with five areas of a job: Type of work, pay, opportunity for promotion, supervision, and the coworkers on the job. A list of adjectives or short phrases is presented for each job satisfaction scale, and the subject is asked to indicate (by answering, Yes, No, or ?) whether each word or phrase describes his or her job.

One hundred and fifty questionnaires were distributed, with the notation that all information was to remain confidential, and that the completed questionnaires should be returned unsigned. The respondents were asked to identify their ethnic group as Black, White, or Other.

Of 99 questionnaires returned, 24 were not completed correctly and could not be scored (17 from white respondents and 7 from black respondents). In addition, five respondents did not identify their ethnic group. Fifty-three white respondents and 14 black respondents correctly completed the questionnaire. The three questionnaires returned by "Other" respondents were included with the white questionnaires to make a total of 56 in that group.

Results

The questionnaires were scored using the weights recommended by Smith et al. (1969), and the mean scores for each of the areas of job satisfaction and ethnic group mean differences were computed for each scale.

In each case, the mean score of the black employees is lower than the mean score for white employees. A difference significant at the 0.5 level of confidence using a two-tailed t-test was found for the *Type of Work* and *People on your Present Job* scales; a difference significant at the .005 level of confidence was found for the scale *Present Pay*. The other two mean differences, while not statistically significant, were in the same direction.

These results agree to some extent with the conclusions of the study reported above. Blacks have a noticeably less favorable attitude toward their jobs than do whites. There was, however, one outstanding disagreement between the two studies. In the SRA study, female blacks were *more* satisfied than the whites on the Pay scale, while female black clerical workers, on the JDI, were significantly *less* satisfied than whites.

In both studies white employees were more satisfied with opportunities for growth and advancement than black employees, but in neither case was this difference statistically significant. In the factory study, several of the item differences on the scales relating to supervision were significant (e.g., items on supervisor-employee relations and on technical competence of supervision); in the university clerical worker study, the difference (on the JDI) was in the same direction, but not statistically significant at the 5% level of confidence.

Table 4

Mean Scores on the *Job Description Index* for White and Black Female
Clerical Workers in a University

| | Group | |
	White	Black
1. Work on present job	26.07	19.92[a]
2. Present pay	8.98	3.35[b]
3. Opportunities for promotion	7.89	6.64
4. Supervision on present job	41.84	37.71
5. People on your present job	36.05	28.42[a]
No. cases	56	14

[a]Difference significant at the .05 level of confidence.
[b]Difference significant at the .005 level of confidence using a two-tailed *t*-test.

SUMMARY AND CONCLUSIONS

Previous research has suggested that minority-group workers are less satisfied with their jobs than majority-group (i.e., nonSpanish-surname white) workers. The two small studies reported herein, and a few of the earlier studies, suggest that this difference persists even when workers in the same occupational groups are compared.

The *reasons* for this difference have not yet been pinned down, however. On the one hand, it might be argued that minority-group workers would have a frame of reference based on discrimination experienced that would lead them to *expect less* from their jobs. Hence, they ought to be *more* satisfied than majority-group whites. Almost all research results run counter to this hypothesis, however. The alternative hypotheses are that these persisting differences reflect either negative effects of continued experiences of a discriminatory nature from either fellow employees or supervisors or both, or that minority-group employees come to work with a set of expectations different from those of whites, which are not as well-fulfilled as the expectations of white employees, or that both of these phenomena occur. Further research should be directed toward more accurately pinpointing the reasons for lower job satisfaction among minority-group workers than among majority-group employees, and policies and programs should be devised to reduce this differential. It would be quixotic to hope that any set of prescriptions could eliminate job dissatisfaction altogether.

Note

[1]Philip Ash was affiliated with the University of Illinois at Chicago Circle at the time of publication of this article. Requests for reprints should be directed to Philip Ash, University of Illinois at Chicago Circle, Box 4348, Chicago, Illinois 60680.

Grateful acknowledgement is made to Mary Wilkinson for assisting in completing the data analysis involved in the two studies reported herein.

References

Ash, P. The employee inventory—a statistical analysis. *Personnel Psychology,* 1954, 7, 337-364.

Baehr, M. E. A factorial study of the SRA Employee Inventory. *Personnel Psychology,* 1954, 7, 319-336.

Brayfield, A. H., & Crockett, W. H. Employee attitudes and employee performance. *Psychological Bulletin,* 1955, 52, 396-424.

Bloom, R., & Barry, J. R. Determinants of work attitudes among Negroes. *Journal of Applied Psychology,* 1967, 51, 291-294.

Cole, Remson J. A survey of employee attitudes. *Public Opinion Quarterly,* 1940, 4, 497-506.

Fortune Survey. A self-portrait of the American people—1947. *Fortune,* 1947, 35, 51-54.

Gendel, H. L. *The motivation to work in hospital housekeeping workers.* Ph.D. dissertation, Western Reserve University, 1965.

Herzberg, F., Mausner, B., Peterson, R. O., & Capwell, D. F. *Job attitudes: review of research and opinion.* Pittsburgh: Psychological Service of Pittsburgh, 1957.

Herzberg, F., Mausner, B., & Snyderman, B. B. *The motivation to work.* New York: John Wiley & Sons, 1959.

King, D., & Pass, B. *Leadership, power and influence.* Institute for Research in the Behavioral, Economic, and Management Sciences, Paper No. 280. Lafayette: Herman C. Krannert Graduate School of Industrial Administration, June 1970.

Pallone, N. J., Hurley, R. B., & Rickard, F. S. Emphasis in job satisfaction research: 1968-1969. *Journal of Vocational Behavior,* 1971, 1, 11-28.

Pallone, N. J., Rickard, F. S., & Hurley, R. B. Job satisfaction research of 1966-1967. *The Personnel and Guidance Journal,* 1970, 48, 469-478.

Saenger, G., & Gordon, N. S. The influence of discrimination on minority group members in its relation to attempts to combat discrimination. *Journal of Social Psychology,* 1950, 31, 95-120.

Science Research Associates. *The SRA Attitude Inventory.* Chicago: Science Research Associates, 1969.

Slocum, J. W., Jr., & Strawser, R. H. Racial differences in job attitudes. *Journal of Applied Psychology,* 1972, 56, 28-32.

Smith, P. C., Kendall, L. M., & Hulin, C. L. *The measurement of satisfaction in work and retirement.* Chicago: Rand McNally, 1969.

ul Hasson, R. *The belief systems and job satisfaction of rural migrant workers in an urban area.* Ph.D. dissertation, Auburn University, 1968.

Vroom, V. *Work and motivation.* New York: John Wiley & Sons, 1967.

Wherry, R. J. An orthogonal re-rotation of the Baehr and Ash studies of the SRA Employee Inventory. *Personnel Psychology,* 1954, 7, 365-380.

Wispe, L., Ash, P., Awkard, J., Hicks, L. H., Hoffman, M., & Porter, J. The Negro psychologist in America. *American Psychologist,* 1969, 24, 142-150.

Minorities in the Organization 4

One would have hoped, at this late date and after all the lessons of the civil rights movement, that the approaches of most major corporations toward the employment of minorities would have reached a stage at which it is no longer a problem. However, it remains a problem because the mid 1970s witnessed the loss of momentum that was prevalent prior to the recent economic downturn. Rather than showing an increase in the number of minorities employed, many organizations reflected a decrease due to the need to lay off a number of employees. Hopefully, however, not too much ground has been lost.

Integrating Blacks into White Organizations

The first section of Part Four contains three articles concerning the integration of minorities into organizations and the problems associated with this process. The article by Hope, written in 1952, provides an enlightening perspective of the initial beginnings of the equal-opportunity-employment movement. Juxtaposing the Hope article with the Aiken article, which was written twenty years later, the reader gets a true sense of the speed at which the problems of integrating minorities into predominantly white organizations have been tackled. Taken together, both articles provide a good indication of the nature of progress made in their respective eras. The article by Triandis and Malpass provides a very good review of a number of studies that were largely concerned with training programs for minorities and the social and psychological aspects of interpersonal interaction between blacks and whites in on-the-job settings.

Employment Programs for Minorities

The focus of the second section is on the efforts that companies have exerted in terms of special employment programs for minority-group members in order to make their entry and assimilation into the organization's work force a successful experience. The article by Burack, Staszak, and Pati identifies key organizational variables and external environmental factors that influence the efforts of organizations to incorporate minorities, especially the disadvantaged, into their work force. Pati and Fahey, in the second article concerning affirmative-action programs, examine a number of the problems faced by many companies in complying with federal minority hiring regulations and legislation. They also review some of the particulars of certain specific pieces of legislation. The final paper in this section, by Nason, explores some of the factors that have been roadblocks to upward mobility of blacks into management positions within organizations and provides insight for companies to help them develop programs designed to overcome these roadblocks. Nason provides helpful suggestions to corporations that wish to design employment programs, responsive to the special needs and requirements of minorities.

Testing and Evaluation Procedures

The third section contains three articles that are concerned with a specific aspect of employment programs for minorities—employment testing and evaluation. The articles by the APA Task Force and by Schmidt et al. discuss the validity of employment tests that are used as selection procedures for minority-group members. The disadvantaged often encounter some biased, unfair, and inappropriate uses of employment and promotion procedures, particularly in the use of tests. The APA Task Force offers helpful suggestions concerning the proper use of certain employment and promotion procedures.

The article by Schmidt et al. discusses the methodological requirements for demonstrating the differential validity of employment tests for blacks and whites. They conclude that differential validity is probably less of a reality and more of an illusion. The final article, by Boehm, offers further insight into the issue of differential validity. Boehm concludes, as do Schmidt et al., that there is little evidence to support the notion of differential validity when objective criterion measures are used as opposed to subjective measures.

Integrating Blacks into White Organizations

Industrial Integration of Negroes: The Upgrading Process

JOHN HOPE, II[1]

When the top-management minority utilization policy of an industrial firm changes from one which gives preference to some racial, religious or national origin group or groups, to one which assures equality of employment opportunity to all without regard to minority status, rather profound and not readily reversible changes are set in motion. These changes involve the internal relationships of the major parties concerned in the production process—management, its employees as individuals, and, if organized, the union or unions which act as the employees' bargaining agents.

The social and economic forces activated by such a change have a definite impact upon the manpower management functions of the employer—recruitment and hiring; allocation, utilization, and progression of employees; company sponsored training, etc. These, in turn, may affect the cost of manufacturing the product, its volume of output and sales, and consequently the prospect of profit for the entrepreneur. Likewise, the nature of the manifestations of these forces is likely to influence employee productivity, the degree of harmony or friction existing between labor and management in their plant relationships and, therefore, the level of the employees' real income and standards of living.

The nature of the expected results of such a change in policy for employer and employee—whether they appear to be positive or negative, productive of profit or loss, increase or decrease in real wages—

Reproduced by permission of the Society for Applied Anthropology from *Human Organization*, 1952, *11*(4), 5-14.

strongly influences the pattern of implementation of a non-discrimination policy. It affects the speed and ease with which the transition is made, and the size and character of the obstacles which retard the ultimate realization of a fully integrated labor force, in which the minorities' status ceases to be a factor in decisions of management or cooperating unions, or in the actions of individual employees of the dominant group.

Such a change involves a process of adjustment over a period of time, encompassing the following general stages: (1) complete exclusion of the minority; (2) restricted utilization, in which minority status is a factor in choice, manner and extent of utilization; (3) utilization of the minority on the basis of objective efficiency qualifications alone.

In some cases, the time period involved in the first phase may be negligible, but theoretically it is the initial stage since it represents the "purest" form of discriminatory employment policy. During the second phase, elements of the two extremes—exclusion and complete disregard of minority status—are intermingled in an uneasy state of incompatibility in which under-utilization of the resources of the minority is the rule.

Thus, one cannot accurately or fairly appraise the cost of integration by measuring the transitional costs alone, whether pecuniary or non-pecuniary. Rather, one must await the completion of the process and appraise the ultimate results. However, it may be fruitful to examine in detail the technique used during the process of reaching the final stage of non-discrimination, and study the problems which interfere with its full application. The changes in internal relationships between the major parties involved may be observed, and insights gained as to the nature and magnitude of the cost of change—the probable balance between advantage and disadvantage which must ultimately determine the success or failure of such a plan of employing manpower in the production process.

Minority Utilization Practices in Transition

In this paper we shall be concerned with the consequences of management's efforts to apply a non-discrimination policy in its employment of Negroes to only one of its manpower management functions, that of upgrading and transfer as a means of achieving full utilization of present employees. The plants studied include three southern plants of the International Harvester Company. They are large-scale industrial installations operating under a common minority utilization policy, national in scope, and determined solely by their parent firm. Despite the fact that the prevailing pattern of Negro utilization in each of these communities is directly contrary to that of the Company, top-management countenances no qualifications or adjustments of its minority policy to fit local industrial mores and conventions. However, it recognizes the peculiar problems faced by its plant management groups in implementing this policy in such a social environment and gives them full and realistic counsel and support.

The Company minority policy states that "there shall be no discrimination against any person because of nationality, race, sex, political or religious affiliation." While this policy was originally espoused and its implementation initiated before any union had obtained bargaining rights in any of these plants, virtually all of the union locals, both CIO and AFL, which subsequently became representatives of the employees, have accepted the non-discrimination policy and have incorporated it within their contracts with management.

In compliance with this policy, hundreds of Negroes have been employed in a wide variety of semi-skilled production jobs. Through the normal exercise of their seniority rights under their union-management contracts they have received promotions to higher job classifications on the basis of their qualifications and seniority, without regard to their race. Production workers constitute about four-fifths of the plant labor force and Negroes were found widely diffused among the many production departments in job classifications ranging from unskilled to the lower levels of skilled occupations.

Their entrance into the ranks of the non-managerial professional class has been less spectacular, though they have been utilized in such capacities in two of the three plants studied. On the other hand, with the exception of one maintenance shop at the Louisville Works, no Negroes have been employed as journeymen in the apprenticeable trades in the maintenance departments, nor have any been enrolled in apprenticeship training courses or as journeymen's helpers in any of these plants.

Through the persistent application of this minority policy, the Negro's share in the total employment of these three plants has continuously increased, and the percentage of Negroes engaged in job classifications above the unskilled level has grown significantly.[2]

Within the framework of a non-discrimination policy, in each of these plants the effective and persistent joint application by both management and local unions of the contractual rule governing the promotion and transfer of old employees to open jobs, on the basis of their length of service and qualifications, has contributed significantly to the upward vertical mobility of Negro employees with a minimum of internal friction. During 1950, roughly one-fourth of the Negro employees in each plant were upgraded,[3] and virtually all of these promotions were within the ranks of production workers.

Through the application of the Company's promotion and transfer policy, during the life of the Louisville and Memphis Works, Negro production workers have attained a job level comparable to that of their white associates.[4]

Among the day work occupations, Negro penetration of the semi-skilled labor grade was about equal to that of whites, while among the skilled classifications, white workers in both of these plants were employed in four labor grades above the highest attained by Negroes—labor grade 9.[5] White workers were still dominating the ranks of skilled production jobs during the Summer of 1951, as they did skilled maintenance occupations, but Negroes had obtained a foothold in the former group.[6] Consequently, it is not apparent that promotion and transfer among Negro employees has been a significant factor in progression within the non-managerial professional or maintenance categories in any of the plants studied.

Despite these limitations, a fundamental change in the job status of Negro employees relative to whites has come about through non-discriminatory upgrading practices.[7]

Methods of Progression

In the plants studied, the great bulk of the numerous semi-skilled and many skilled production jobs are filled by upgrading current employees from lower classifications in the same department, or by voluntary transfer of workers from other departments. Old employees may move from one job to another by two main methods: first, by seeking "open jobs," and second, by "bumping," when employees with higher seniority and the ability to perform a particular job take that job from a person with a lower period of service.

An employee may bid on any open job in his department, or may file a "request for transfer" to a job he desires and feels he can perform in any other department within the same bargaining unit. He is entitled to it if his period of service is the longest of the eligible applicants and he can perform the job. Where applicants for a job include persons working both within and outside the department, those inside are given preference over those in other departments.

The second method of movement, bumping, is not used as widely as the first and is less frequently a means of advancement. It is used generally in the event of a plant-wide reduction in force. If one person bumps another with lower seniority for a particular job, he must be capable of performing the job to which he has been assigned after a brief "breaking-in" period. In practice, it is seldom possible for an employee to qualify for a job during this short time unless the job is in his department and he has had an opportunity to "pick up" the skill necessary for its performance beforehand.

Undoubtedly, the coincidence of these seniority provisions and the non-discrimination clause has materially contributed to the vertical

mobility of current Negro employees. Any restriction upon these seniority rights is a violation of contract as well as an impediment to the full
utilization of labor. Thus, it is appropriate to examine some of the racial
implications of this manpower management function—their impact
upon the plant, and some problems which have arisen.

In describing their upgrading experiences, it is important to note
that all three plants began the application of their non-discrimination
policy in new plant situations and thus did not have precedents of contrary practices to combat, although each was surrounded by companies
having such practices.[8]

Progression Problems and Their Disposition

It is probably neither an accident nor mere coincidence that most of
the racial incidents of more than very limited scope have involved some
aspect of the non-discriminatory progression policy.[9] This is a focal
point in the conflict between the discriminatory and non-discriminatory
policies.

Harvester management and unions are committed by contract to a
non-discriminatory promotion and transfer policy, while the prevailing
progression pattern of the communities surrounding each of these
plants is the opposite. The normal application of this Company's policy
tends to challenge the *status quo*. When a Negro moves to a new job by
virtue of his qualifications and seniority, the questions inevitably arise
of whether such a job raises him to a status equal to or above that of his
white associates, and whether it may give him supervisory authority,
however limited, over white workers. The ultimate success of the application of the non-discriminatory policy may depend upon the ability of
management and union leadership to find answers which will foster the
white workers' acceptance of their equalitarian promotion policy with a
minimum of transitional tension and interference with production.

It is inevitable that the application of such a policy in unsympathetic
community surroundings would cause some problems. Therefore,
through the recital of actual cases, it is appropriate to consider some of
the problems involved and how they were handled. Our purpose is to
describe some of the more striking incidents and developments that
reveal the forces of change at work, rather than merely to recount the
more representative, but perhaps less complex, manifestations of routine promotion and transfer practices.

The first two cases involve upgradings which gave Negroes a job
status equal to that of whites in their immediate vicinity. The second
group describes situations in which Negroes were elevated to skilled jobs

hitherto considered "white jobs." The next treats instances in which progression of Negroes placed them in positions involving some supervisory
responsibilities. Finally, the result of a Negro's effort to advance by "bumping" a shorter service white employee in his department is described.

Working Together as Equals

The first case involves the refusal of a white drill press operator to work
beside a Negro of comparable status. During 1948, the first year of
operation at the Memphis Works, a Negro grinder was employed in
the machine shop and was assigned to work beside a white drill press
operator. The operation required that materials processed by the Negro
grinder be passed along to the white driller next to him. After they had
been working side by side for several days, the latter became angry and
stated that he refused to work beside a Negro, and that he would not
continue until this particular Negro was removed.[10] The industrial relations manager talked with the white worker in an effort to persuade him
to change his mind and, being unsuccessful, advised him to take the
remainder of the day off, hoping that he would change his mind and
return to work the following day. The next morning the white worker
returned to work at the beginning of the shift, but finding the Negro at
his job, he again refused to work. Others left their jobs until the whole
plant, with the exception of the foundry, was stopped by an unauthorized walk-out.

When the union was advised officially of this violation of contract,
according to the industrial relations manager it gave firm support to
management in its efforts to get the workers back on the job.[11] The
Company demanded that the union get its members back to work in
compliance with the contract, which required that the Negro be maintained on the job and that the white worker in question return to his
job. Union representatives spoke to the employees at the plant gate,
firmly supporting the company position that the Negro had a right to
stay on his job and attempting to persuade the workers to return to
work. After a stoppage of about two days, plant operations were resumed
and all workers returned to their former positions, including the two in
question. (The Negro remained in the machine shop as a machine
operator from July 20, 1948 to May 30, 1949, when he was transferred
voluntarily to the foundry department.)

Directly after this incident, he requested another job in the same
department but removed from the white worker who had precipitated
the stoppage. The industrial relations manager states that since this incident, they have rarely had a Negro apply for a job in this department.
He adds the opinion that in addition to the problem of acceptance by

white workers, the low number of Negro applicants for jobs in the machine shop arises from the limited training opportunities available to them in the Memphis area. Although the Company has had no training program in this department, there was such a scarcity of trained personnel for the new foundry that when it was opened a training course was established in which Negroes as well as whites participated.

Sometime prior to June, 1949, at the Evansville Works, a Negro helper in the press room was promoted by his foreman to press work and assigned to a press with a white employee for "breaking-in." The assignment was made about 11:00 a.m.; after lunch the other press men would not return to their jobs.

> "Didn't you understand the non-discrimination policy when you were hired?" these men were asked by management officials.
> "Yes, but we didn't think it would apply to our department," the workers said, or, "We thought it meant Negroes would have their own departments."

At this point, management realized that the educational program had to be repeated, and set about doing so. A statement was issued to employees saying that the policy "gave those who would do the best work the chance to do it." After this restatement and discussion of the non-discrimination policy by management officials, the workers thought the matter over and eventually returned to their jobs, except for one man who did not feel that he could work under these conditions and thus was terminated.[12]

As in the previous case, management maintained its non-discrimination policy by its resolute determination to put it into operation despite the opposition of a considerable number of white employees. Gallagher has the following to say about the role of management in the latter instance:

> Cooperation of all levels of management, especially the foreman, is important to the Evansville program. . . . Only where these men agree with and fully implement the policy can it be successful. Other foremen in these positions might have said nothing or let the irritation continue and eventually explode the whole action of the policy.[13]

A "White Man's Job"

The next case concerns the result of elevating a Negro to a skilled job which had traditionally been considered a "white man's job." During August, 1951, at the Memphis Works a white crane operator was transferred at his own request to a stock-keeper's job, leaving his former job vacant. There were two men eligible for this job on the basis of their seniority and qualifications, one white and one colored, the white man having a longer period of service than the colored. However, the former did not want to bid on the job, so under the contract the Negro was entitled to and requested it. The Company upgraded him to the classification of crane operator. When he went on his job, the white workers walked off in a body. Management firmly held its position that the Negro was entitled to the job and advised the union concerned that the wildcat strike constituted a violation of its contract. The union took the same position and vigorously worked to persuade its members to return to their jobs. The industrial relations manager recalls that on the morning after the stoppage began, he observed a union official speaking to the workers in the rain at the plant gate in an effort to persuade them to comply with the contract and return to work.

This stoppage attained considerable size and led to high tension and some violence. It lasted about two days and involved almost half of the employees of the plant. The statements as to the nature and extent of the violence are conflicting but it is agreed that there was some rock-throwing and scuffling between white and colored workers and that some were hurt. The intervention of company and union representatives working together to separate the two groups and avoid further clashes was important in minimizing the extent of the damage done. Despite these pressures, both union and management officials insisted that the Negro was entitled to the job and were determined to see that he was not removed from it. As a result, plant operations were reestablished with the Negro performing his new functions as a crane operator. At the time of the writer's interview almost a year later, he was still on the job and no further difficulties had been experienced.

In this case as in the other two described above, the promotion rights of qualified Negro applicants under the terms of the contract were fully and, in some cases, dramatically protected by the determined joint efforts of management and union leadership to implement this phase of their contract without procrastination or qualification.

The next case indicates some of the consequences of less unified and decisive action. Since March, 1948, a Negro welder whose qualifications were unquestioned by either management or union has intermittently tried unsuccessfully to obtain a transfer to a job as welder. Both management and union agree that his seniority and qualifications entitle him to such a job. Repeated attempts have been made to persuade him to withdraw his request temporarily on the ground that the rank-and-file opposition to his entrance to the welding department is so intense that he might experience harm or even death if he tries to occupy the position to which he is entitled by the contract. The elements of this case are described in detail because this case so clearly shows the various types of reactions of the interested parties, and the hazards involved in the transition from a preferential to a fair employment program of utilization.

In March, 1948, Mr. B filed an application for a job at the Memphis Works stating his qualifications as a welder. The foreman asked him whether he could weld and said that he would send for him and have him take a test. The test occurred in April, 1948. At that time the foreman gave the applicant the material and torch for the welding test and showed him what was required of him. The test was completed and the plates and papers were returned to the personnel department.

When they heard that a Negro might be coming into their department, the 10 or 13 welders in the department at that time sat down in protest for about one hour.

After Mr. B finished his test the foreman told him to come back the next day at about 4:00 p.m. to start work on the second shift. Mr. B got there a little early and was told by the foreman that there was no booth ready and asked whether he would take a labor job until one could be prepared for him. Mr. B states that he accepted a labor job, but found himself continually being "put off" on the ground that there was no available booth. All of these incidents occurred before any union had bargaining rights so that the Company had total responsibility.

Mr. B states that when a union (CIO) did obtain bargaining rights, he placed the matter before them, and, as he put it, the union "kept promising and promising and promising me. I filed a grievance with the union and they kept putting it off."

According to a union official, this union obtained bargaining rights in about April, 1949, and the delay in handling this grievance arose because it was lost and thus did not go through the usual grievance steps. Because of this failure to process the grievance, the Negro union members requested that a representative of the International Union Fair Employment Practice Department be brought into the case. The co-director of the International Union FEP Department met with union officials and the complainant, and as a result of their discussion, it was decided that Mr. B should not insist upon taking the welding job at that time because, they argued, the union was young and such action might break it up.

During the late spring of 1951, Mr. B filed another grievance with the union alleging that two new white welders had been hired in spite of the fact that he had filed a prior request for transfer to a welding job in this department. The Company expressed its willingness to place him in the job, but the union was unwilling because of their fear of violence against him.

Both union and management officials state that the danger of undetected foul play in this department is greater than usual because of the nature of the work. Each welder works alone in a closed booth with a hood over his head. As a result, an assailant could approach him unobserved from the rear in comparative privacy. With the filing of Mr. B's latest grievance, the threat of violence was again made by the white welders in the much enlarged department. The industrial relations manager stated to the writer that the Company was willing and ready to place this Negro in accordance with his rights under the contract, but that it was genuinely fearful that he might become a victim of serious violence. He stated, however, that they put the whole matter up to the union. When the union demurred, the Negro union leaders protested to the union president, asking that the matter be brought before the membership. The local president objected to a rank-and-file meeting with members of both races but suggested a meeting with a group of Negro members.

It was agreed that they pick from all over the plant a list of Negro members to whom letters of invitation be sent for a meeting. It was held on a Sunday afternoon in the Summer of 1951 and much discussion of this case took place. The president attempted to persuade the Negro members not to insist upon having Mr. B placed on the welding job despite the fact that he was admittedly qualified and had full rights to the job. He feared that the rank-and-file would take the path of violence and if they did he, the president, would feel personally responsible for the results. He added that he did not believe that the job was worth what might happen to Mr. B if he attempted to work on it. In short, he inferred the danger of violence and probably even death. He asked that the Negroes wait a while longer.

It is the writer's understanding from the Negro leaders present that they agreed to wait 20 days for the president to do the necessary job of education in the welding department in order that the provisions of the contract could be applied without danger of violence. No further information has been obtained beyond this point.

At the time of the writer's visit, Mr. B was still working as a coremaker in the foundry, having been promoted from the labor grade originally given him. He is now earning the same wage rate and holds the same labor grade as he would had he been given the job in the welding department to which he aspired.

From conversations with management and union leaders, the writer was impressed with their failure to comprehend the importance to Negro workers of job status and employment at one's highest skill. Both emphasized the fact that the applicant who is pressing so vigorously for a job as a welder is now in the same labor grade and making the same wage rate as he would make if he were transferred to the job of his choice. On the other hand, Mr. B expressed to the writer his pride in being a qualified welder and his desire to make his contribution doing the type of work for which he is best equipped and to which he is entitled, regardless of the remunerations of his present job.

This time, unlike the previous cases described, timid and vacillating practices, first on the part of the Company, and later on the part of the union, have nurtured and strengthened the resistance of a small but determined and strategically-placed minority and, thus, have jeopardized their control of the situation in this plant area. The worker believes that through disunity in its actions, the position of the union has been weakened rather than strengthened by this procrastination.

Parenthetically, it might be added that as a result of earlier weaknesses in the handling of grievances, as shown in this case, the procedure has been strengthened and corrected. The danger of losing official, written grievances or the destruction or withholding of grievances by careless or unsympathetic committeemen or union officials is no longer possible under the present union-management grievance procedure.

The next case involves a situation in which the Negro concerned was apparently hired at an occupational level below his highest skill. It demonstrates how he progressed toward a position where he could fully employ his previously-attained skill despite his racial identity. He rose from a position of dishwasher to that of chef by the sheer weight of his continually demonstrated superiority, and without the support of the protective contractual provisions and organization available to Harvester employees. The catering facilities of the Louisville plant are leased to a large industrial catering concern which has sole responsibility for its operation. Consequently, the manager of this department is not bound by the contract between the Louisville Works and its employees.

The story of Mr. D's progression from dishwasher to chef, the top position in the kitchen, demonstrates what a man can do through patience and quietly efficient persistence, mixed with a personality that gained for him acceptance by the majority group in the department where he worked. He began working at the Louisville Works about five years ago. Prior to that time he had worked for 19 years at a tavern in Louisville where he had performed a variety of tasks. He indicated that at the time he changed jobs there had been no financial advantage in his new job, but as he had grown older he had become more and more tired of the atmosphere of the tavern and, since he neither drank nor smoked, he wanted to work in a more wholesome environment. He started as a dishwasher at $30 per week and worked at this job for about two years. At the end of that time, he was promoted to the position of supervisor of the dishwashers.

About a year later, the white chef got drunk one day and could not perform his duties. The supervisor told Mr. D that he was disturbed, that the meal had to be cooked and there was no one to do it. Mr. D volunteered to fill in and he did so well that the manager, Mr. O, was impressed by his work. The writer was told by Mr. D that the manager of the cafeteria came to him and reproached him for not having told him that he could cook, to which Mr. D replied, "You never asked me."

He was first hired to cook on Saturdays on an overtime basis while performing his duties as dishwasher supervisor during the remainder of the week. In about January, 1950, after about six or eight months with this status, he was promoted to the position of cook on a full-time basis. The manager observed that the chef did not seem to be able to supervise the kitchen crew well and that the quality of his work was deteriorating. During this period, being a cook himself, Mr. D recognized that certain necessary functions were not being performed and, on occasions, did some of these on his own initiative. Unknown to him, the manager, who had highest seniority in the kitchen, was watching his work quite closely and with much interest. Finally, Mr. O decided that the chef would have to be relieved of his supervisory duties and his observations of Mr. D had convinced him that he could do the job.

According to the manager, during April, 1951, he called the white kitchen employees together and stated that the present arrangement was not working well, that he was going to place Mr. D in charge of the kitchen, and that he expected them to cooperate with him. He indicated that if they did not, it would mean their jobs. In answer to this statement, the oldest white cook in the kitchen said, with his arms flying, "Why sure we'll cooperate with Andrew! Didn't we cooperate with him before when he was working with us, and when he was in the dishwashing department? We'll cooperate with him now!"

Says Mr. O, "This settled everything." Since that time, he reports, the kitchen has been running very well and he is quite happy about it.

This conversation took place in the kitchen of the plant. As we went out into the main cafeteria in the early afternoon, I saw the Negro chef sitting in the midst of his staff on the "white" side[14] of the dining room, all of them happily eating lunch together.

Later, in a conversation with Mr. D, I asked whether he had any difficulty with his crew when he took over his duties as chef. He stated that he had had no trouble at all with the other workers because they all knew that he had been carrying this load while he was classified as a cook; that they came to him and told him, "that's what should have been done before," and that "we'd all work together." This conversation also gave an interesting clue to the chef's technique of leadership. He finds that by getting all the cooks together and planning jointly, they get along all right. Sometimes they sit down and plan menus for a week at one time. Another day they'll plan something else. All make suggestions and

they take the best of these, he continued. As a result, the speed of preparation has been increased, and, whereas in the past they had hardly
finished preparing the food before it was time to serve it, now the meal
is ready by 10:00 a.m.

It is Mr. D's job to see that all food is properly prepared and con-
veyed to the steam table for serving. From that point the supervisor of
the waitresses is responsible. At the present time, according to Mr. D,
there are 32 persons including day and night shifts under his supervision. Among these are two bakers, four cooks, one kitchen helper, and
five women in the salad department (all white).

This case indicates the wholesome influence wrought by continuous
association of workers of different races in preparing members of the
majority group for full acceptance of the minority as equals on the basis
of their qualifications. This is probably a significant factor in the total
absence of unfavorable incidents or objections to this unusual elevation
of a Negro to a supervisory position over several white skilled kitchen
employees.

Supervising "White Folks"

The third type of case reveals some of the problems raised and some
of the forces operating when the promotion of a Negro places him in
a position in which he will supervise the work of white employees or
where such a supervisory responsibility is a prospect through future
advancement. The case chosen describes the promotion of a Negro to
the position of checker, where he was required to pass on the work of
approximately five production employees. There had never been a
Negro checker at the Memphis Works before the spring of 1951, at
which time a Negro with the seniority and qualifications entitling him
to such promotion placed his bid for an open job as checker in the
department in which he worked.

According to a member of the executive board of the union involved,
as the job was set up, this checker would have had under his supervision
three white workers and two Negroes. Thus, his promotion would not
only have upgraded him to a higher level of skill, but would have put
him in a supervisory capacity over white workers. According to the
industrial relations manager, the management was willing to open this
job to the Negro applicant because he was entitled to it under the terms
of the contract. Union leaders were called in, advised of the decision,
and asked to prepare the workers in that department for the change. In
this informal conference, the union took the position that management
was moving too fast and tried to persuade the industrial relations manager not to act at that time. The Company would not depart from its
position.

In the face of these signs of equivocation on the part of union leadership, the colored union leaders took the position that they would not "back down on this case as they had in the case of the Negro welder because there was not the same danger of violence in this case and, if violence came, (the checker) would be in a position to see it coming." Thus, efforts to persuade the Negro complainant to withdraw his application failed. A formal grievance alleging discrimination in upgrading was instituted, and it began to move through the normal grievance channel. Finally, the Executive Board of the union officially considered the case and declared that under the terms of the contract the Negro applicant was entitled to the job whether he supervised white or colored employees.

Union officials were instructed by the Board to transmit their ruling to the union membership and to prepare them for the change. On the basis of this ruling, negotiations between company and union officially began. Management was asked to rearrange the work assignments of checkers in this department so that all of the five workers under the supervision of this Negro checker would be Negroes. According to a union official, the Company agreed to make this change within two weeks. On these terms, it was mutually agreed that the applicant would be upgraded to the job of checker within the terms of the contract, but the conditions of work were changed in such a way that the taboo against Negroes supervising white workers would be maintained—temporarily, at least. From conversations with various principals in these negotiations, it seems apparent that both Company and union recognized that it is only a matter of a short time before this taboo will be breached. But they preferred to make the transition gradual in order to temper the expected opposition and contribute to a more peaceful transition to a completely non-discriminatory promotion practice. One member of the union committee indicated that there were four or five other colored employees who had the necessary seniority to bid on each subsequent open job as checker, and that shifting work assignments in this way would not indefinitely keep Negro checkers from supervising white workers.

Nevertheless, this compromise solution was mutually agreed to by union, management, and the complainant, and was scheduled to be carried out after a brief period during which union leaders were to prepare their white members for the change. Despite these precautions, the elevation of a Negro to this minor supervisory status precipitated the largest wildcat strike of a racial origin that had occurred at the Memphis Works up to that time. Some 1,350 employees (three-fifths of the total) were involved in the walkout, which lasted a little over two days. Thereafter, all workers returned to their jobs and the Negro checker remained at his post and has performed his functions since that time without incident.

Company officials state that this strike was precipitated and nurtured by deliberately "planted" false rumors about the job in question, and that had the employees known the facts it is unlikely that any stoppage would have occurred, except perhaps for a few workers in the department where the checker was to work. This would have been of minor importance. According to the president of the union, the rumor was disseminated that a Negro had been upgraded to a job as foreman and that he had 20 white workers under him. He states that when the workers knew the facts, all came back to work except those in the department concerned, and they could not possibly hold out long. The union did not support this strike but rather made vigorous efforts to get its members to return to work.

The letter written by the plant manager to employees on May 8, 1951, explaining the nature of this strike confirms the importance of rumors in some degree. The letter states in part:

> It seems that a misunderstanding over a job assignment in Service Parts started this stoppage. More checkers were needed in that department, and three more checkers were added. These were new jobs, jobs which had not existed before. No bumping was involved. Union officials discussed the matter with us in advance and were in accord with us.
>
> One of the three checkers' jobs went to a Negro employee. There is no doubt he is entitled to the job. He has the seniority. He is qualified. And we have a contract. You are as familiar with that contract as I am. You know it clearly states seniority and qualifications will determine who is entitled to fill jobs which are open.
>
> That's the story. Rumors had a lot to do with starting and spreading this unnecessary stoppage.

It is apparent, however, that there is some conflict between the letter and the statement of union leaders as to the nature of this job. According to the union leaders, it was an open job which had been filled previously so that there were specific persons who were to work under this party originally. The letter states that this is a new job. It is a question whether this discrepancy is a real one or whether it involves a part of the final adjustment in the story which was to be made public in order to temper the shock of transition from a discriminatory to an equalitarian supervisory pattern.

"Bumping White Folks"

The previous cases have described situations in which Negroes have been upgraded to open jobs. The final one is concerned with a case in which a Negro employee at one of the plants aspired to a higher job which required the displacement of a lower seniority white worker. In

1951, according to the industrial relations manager, a Negro drill press operator, Mr. E, put in a bid to "bump" a white worker of lower seniority from a higher rated job in another department of the same bargaining unit. Bt this means, he sought a promotion from day work labor grade 5 to 6. The job classification desired was gear tester, G 95A.

The peculiar significance of this case is that the long range prospects available to Mr. E through this promotion, had he been successful at this stage, were particularly favorable. A responsible management official describes the circumstances in the following way:

The gear tester classification has two categories G 95A and G 95B. The A category involves random tests made in the shop and is in labor grade DW 6; the B category involves laboratory testing, requires a much higher level of skill and is classified as labor grade DW 10. Because these two jobs are closely related by their nature, and the tasks involved require a close relationship between the men in the laboratory and those working with gear testing in the shop, once Mr. E had attained the lower gear testing classification he would have had an excellent opportunity to qualify for an open job in classification G 95B in a short time. Furthermore, there were only four men in the classification G 95A, and the length of Mr. E's service period would have given him the highest seniority rank of this group. Consequently, despite the fact that he would have been the last person to enter this job classification (G 95A), he would have been the first eligible for advancement to an open job in the higher classification, G 95B, because of his higher seniority rank. In this way, it would have been possible for him to rise from labor grade DW 5 to 10 in a relatively short period of time.

Mr. E's longer service period gave him the right to a trial at this job (95A) for the three-day breaking-in period required by the contract, at the end of which he had to qualify by a performance test. According to the foreman, he failed and consequently was denied the job he sought. The industrial relations manager states that the Negro applicant admitted that by and large the test was fair. Nevertheless, a grievance was filed by his union alleging that the Company had discriminated against his right to upgrading because of his race.

By the final settlement of this grievance, Mr. E's classification was raised from labor grade DW 5 to DW 7 by placing him in the classification G 79 as a gear matcher. This gave him a 15¢ per hour raise over what he would have received had he qualified for G 95A.

According to the industrial relations manager this settlement was in the nature of a compromise, taking into account the realities of the racial situation as seen by management, and the political implications involved in the union grievance. He states that the management was well aware that the union was using the race issue politically to gain the

support of Negro employees, and that although they could have supported the foreman's rejection of the complainant completely, this
would have contributed to the propaganda objective of the union. On
the other hand, he felt that because the person attempting to bump the
white man was a Negro, the objections of the workers in classification
G 79, all of whom were white, would be abnormally vigorous and a
grievance with acute racial overtones would soon follow.

The industrial relations manager recognized if Mr. E had been promoted to G 95A, in a short time he would probably have "jumped"
ahead of 47 gear matchers then in a higher labor grade—DW 7. This
would have been possible because although in a higher labor grade, this
operation (G 79) is essentially repetitive and less closely related to job
classification G 95B than G 95A, so that his chances of meeting the qualifications for the former within the brief breaking-in period would have
been better. Under the settlement upgrading him to job classification
G 79, Mr. E's seniority made him the fifth in line to be upgraded to G
95B, instead of the first had he been promoted in the first instance to
G 95A. Thus, this official felt that through this compromise the aspirations of the Negro for upgrading were partially realized, the possibility
of racial tension arising from the obvious bumping of a white worker by
a Negro, and his progression at a more rapid rate than his white associates were avoided, and the assumed political objectives of the union
were at least partially neutralized. This settlement was accepted by all
parties concerned and must be assumed to represent a mutually satisfactory solution to the problem.

The industrial relations manager cited this case to show that the
combination of the Negroes' lower level of educational attainment, and
the rigid seniority rules of progression which govern management
actions, have in some cases led to charges of Company discrimination,
whereas the real problem was the inability of Negroes to perform the
tasks to which they aspired.

It is not the purpose here to discuss the merits of the settlement, but
rather to indicate the complexity of the real issue that may be involved
in a single charge of racial discrimination. We also wish to point out the
nature of the background against which many such cases are settled
in the day-to-day operation of a plant which uses a bi-racial labor force
and operates under a fair employment policy. The basic elements
involved in this case are at work in varying degrees in all three of the
plants studied; it is likely that similar cases have arisen and will continue
to arise from time to time in each plant.

The problem of deciding whether a man is qualified or not, when
he is on the margin, is difficult at best. In the southern economy,
particularly, the racial issue introduces an added factor; the differential

system of formal educational opportunities for white and colored in the region, although neither set nor controlled by the local plant, tends to contribute a moral background element in such cases; as a result, a decision based solely upon the objective facts of the case is difficult at best, and made even more troublesome in the face of the possible aspirations of a militant industrial union with an equalitarian minorities policy. As one industrial relations manager put it, the rather explicit rules governing progression, applied in the framework of a non-discrimination policy, tend to "push" Negro employees up the ladder of consecutive labor grades. At the same time, the differential training opportunities available to them tend to restrict the limits of their capacity for upgrading compared to those of white workers of comparable intellectual capacity. As a result, as they move up from grade to grade, frequently on the basis of superior seniority rights, the difficulty of qualifying for the job in a short time, in the face of limitations in their general educational attainment as well as vocational training, comes up to plague them.

Although the following figures are not conclusive, because they do not take into account qualifications arising from vocational training or experience, they throw some light upon this problem. At the Louisville Works on a randomly-chosen day in the summer of 1951, 29.8 percent of all white production workers and 20.4 percent of the Negroes had completed their elementary school education. At the same time 52.0 percent of these white workers had completed their elementary and high school education, while only 35.4 percent of the Negroes had gone this far. If the comparative positions of these racial groups are considered for the machining department in which the parties involved in this case were employed, the same situation is apparent: 28.3 percent of the white and 17.9 percent of the colored employees had attained an elementary school education, while 51.5 percent of the white and 37.2 percent of the colored had finished high school.

Thus, the stresses and strains which are reflected in grievances such as described in this case, with which management must deal from day to day, arise in part from some elements outside the control of local plant management or union. However, they cannot be completely ignored by either in their consideration of grievances which involve either direct or indirect allegations of racial discrimination or differentiation.

Assuming that the union concerned in this case is in fact using the racial issue politically to win the support of the minority group, this case raises the very real question of whether the company decision in the grievance involved should have been influenced by this fact or by the fact that the complainant involved happens to be a Negro. The political implications simply intensify the racial character of the issue, but their absence would not eliminate the racial element. On the other hand, one may question whether company decisions should take into account the very probable hostile reactions of a group of white workers whose lethargy or lack of desire for the job allows a worker outside of their group to attain a preferred position over them, even though it is highly probable that the racial difference will cause protest of greater than normal intensity and that this might adversely affect immediate plant operations. The Company may reasonably assume that the "bumping" of a white worker by a Negro under present conditions is anathema and expect the counter-use of the race issue by white workers to offset such an advantage. Nevertheless, it remained a question of whether this element should be a factor in the settlement of such a grievance.

Conclusion

It is apparent from the foregoing description of the growth in quantity and the rise in job status of Negro employees, and from the changes in the relationships between management and union, Negro and white workers, and Negro union members and their unions, that the day-to-day minority utilization practices are persistently, though sometimes haltingly, shifting. They are moving from the intermediate stage of limited minority advancement towards the final state of color-blind upgrading of workers on the basis of their efficiency qualifications and period of service, though the latter phase has not been fully attained. This process is taking place primarily through the normal, unspectacular machinery of union-management jurisprudence established by union-management agreement which governs all relationships between these parties. This machinery is rendered applicable to secondary disputes involving alleged discrimination against minorities by the mutual acceptance of a policy of non-discrimination by employer and employees.

Within this formal structure, the importance of informal education in effectively handling minority-majority relations, which union and management officials achieve in the normal prosecution of their day-to-day responsibilities, cannot be over-estimated. This provides a major channel through which attitudes of leadership and, indirectly, rank-and-file are changed. Such informal and sometimes grudgingly accepted education paves the way for ever-widening acceptance of the non-discrimination policy of those working under it, and thus contributes to the stability and harmony of its application.

Notes

[1]John Hope, II, was an Industrial Relations Consultant for the Race Relations Department of the American Missionary Association, Social Science Institute, Fisk University, at the time of publication of this article.

The thesis developed in this article was worked out while the writer was on loan to the Committee of the South of the National Planning Association to participate in its survey of racial employment practices in certain areas of southern industry. His part is a case study of three plants entitled *Bi-racial Employment Practices of the International Harvester Company South.* This paper is in no sense a summary of the studies of the National Planning Association, which, of course, bears no responsibility for the ideas and point of view put forth in the preceding pages. However, the writer expresses his appreciation to this Association and the International Harvester Company for the opportunity to obtain the data used herein. The case studies in racial employment authorized by the Committee of the South had not been completed when the article was first published.

[2]Between 1946 and the end of 1950, Negro employment grew from 4.2 percent to 14.1 percent of total employment at the Louisville Works, and from 4.4 percent to 8.1 percent at the Evansville Works, while the Negro population of these cities was approximately 15 percent and 7 percent, respectively. Likewise, in Memphis where Negroes constitute about 34 percent of the population (1950), their employment at the Memphis Works rose from 12.2 percent in 1947 to 23.1 percent in 1950.

Of the total number of Negroes employed at the respective southern plants, the percentage engaged in job classification above the common labor level rose from 22.4 percent to 43.2 percent at Louisville, and from 12.8 percent to 68.8 percent at the Evansville Works from 1946 through 1950. Similarly, between 1947 and 1951, this group of Negroes increased from 22.4 percent to 66.8 percent at the Memphis Works. Negroes were found in skilled and apprenticeable trades at the Louisville Works, in non-managerial professional categories at the Louisville and Evansville plants, and in office clerical classifications at the Evansville Works.

[3]Of the 10,187 Negroes employed by the International Harvester Company, at the end of 1950, 1,714 or 16.8 percent were upgraded during that year. Similarly, 235 or 25.9 percent of those employed at the Louisville Works, 187 or 28.0 percent of those at Memphis and 96 or 27.0 percent of those at Evansville were upgraded.

[4]Comparable information about the Evansville plant was not available. Within the piecework category, no more than one percent of the workers was classified above labor grade 10 in the summer of 1951, and Negroes were represented in labor grade 10 or above it in both plants.

A larger percentage of Negro than white workers was employed in the "upper-half" of the 14 piece-work labor grades, the difference being larger at Memphis than at Louisville, e.g., at Louisville 31.4 percent of the white and 37.2 percent of the Negro piecework employees; and at Memphis, 17.5 percent of the white and 41.4 percent of the Negroes.

[5]At the Louisville Works, 8.2 percent, and at the Memphis Works, 4.8 percent of the white production day workers were in labor grades above the highest attained by a Negro, i.e., labor grades 10 to 14.

[6]At the Louisville Works, 29.5 percent of the white production day workers and 2.8 percent of the Negroes were in skilled labor grades, while at Memphis 23.5 percent of the white and 1.9 percent of the Negroes were similarly classified.

[7]In other plants in each of the communities where the Harvester plants studied are located, Negroes have enjoyed improved wage rates and earnings as well as better treatment in recent years, but changes in the range of job opportunity and the inclination to use them at their highest skill were limited. In these plants, Negro workers as well as other workers are sharing in a general improvement due to such factors as general business expansion, increasing labor scarcity, and gains from collective bargaining through increased labor organization. But in no other plant observed was management aggressively challenging the prevailing standard of job status as in these Harvester plants.

[8]In the first place, white and colored employees entered these plants at the same time so that white employees could not feel or seriously allege that Negroes were taking white people's jobs—a not uncommon rallying point of opposition to Negro integration. Next, the incurably prejudiced workers tended to be screened out by the Company's practice of making acceptance of the non-discrimination policy virtually a condition of employment. (Gallagher, "Harvester Equality Is Good Business," *American Business*, June, 1949, p. 32.)

In the third place, when these plants were recruiting their initial labor force, conscious diffusion by management of Negro employment among many job classifications and departments fostered the adjustment of white workers generally to the presence of Negroes, and provided a basis for the accumulation of seniority by Negroes in widely scattered areas. This, no doubt, facilitated the harmonious implementation of the subsequently negotiated rules governing upgrading and transfer. Finally, the first Negroes hired in any department were selected so that they would be "superior both in qualifications and personality" to the white workers with whom they were to be associated in order to further insure their acceptance. (Southall, *Industry's Unfinished Business*, p. 155.)

[9]Of the four racial incidents which culminated in unauthorized work stoppages during the life of these plants, all involved changes in the job status of Negro employees relative to whites, and three out of four involved upgrading *per se*. The challenge to the prevailing division of labor between white and colored workers in the community at large became more direct and fundamental with each successive incident, so that each constituted a higher hurdle to the attainment of non-discriminatory practices in the plant. (For details see cases on pp. 9-29.)

As a result of these racial stoppages, an average of about one day per involved employee was lost during a period of approximately four years. The average loss for all employees on the plant rolls was about one-half day. Likewise, such stoppages accounted for only about 2.2 percent of the total number of man-hours lost from unauthorized strikes from all causes. Wages lost from such strikes amounted likewise to 2.2 percent of the total wage losses from all unauthorized stoppages.

[10]The incident described did not occur until these men had been working side by side for about a week. One official ventures the opinion that the Negro was probably working faster than his white associate so that the parts were piling up in front of the white worker.

[11]Report of Stoppage, July 27, 1948, Memphis Works, International Harvester Company.

[12]Gallagher, *Op. Cit.*, p. 32.

[13]*Ibid.*, p. 32.

[14]When the International Harvester Company acquired these facilities, it found that the previous tenants had maintained segregated cafeteria, washroom, and toilet facilities. It has not yet de-segregated the cafeteria though the other services have been progressively integrated since Harvester began operations.

Studies of Black and White Interaction in Job Settings[1]

HARRY C. TRIANDIS[2]
ROY S. MALPASS

The 1969 APA Convention was characterized by desperate efforts by psychologists to find social relevance in their work (Nelson, 1969). It appears that many psychologists find themselves in conflict when contemplating the problems which they find scientifically exciting and attempt to relate them to social problems; others are concerned with the "publish or perish" pressures which favor the smaller laboratory studies as opposed to the broader social-problem-oriented investigations. We submit that the conflict between "pure science" and "social problems" can be resolved and the larger social problems can be fractionated to become manageable.

This paper is intended as an illustration of an approach which combines the examination of scientifically interesting problems with studies of considerable social relevance. The scientific focus concerns the antecedents and consequences of what has been called "subjective culture" —i.e., a cultural group's characteristic way of perceiving its social environment.[3] The problem of social relevance concerns jobs for blacks.

The problem on which we are focusing provides examples of integration of concerns with social issues and social phenomena occurring in natural environments with more esoteric theoretical interests. At the social level, our concern for greater employment opportunity for and greater employment effectiveness of blacks (and potentially other ethnic groups) has obvious contemporary relevance, and the reasons behind it do not need much elaboration. The observation that many of the problems in black-white intergroup and interpersonal relations are as yet

Reprinted from *Journal of Applied Social Psychology*, 1971, *1*, 101-117, by permission of the publisher. Copyright © 1971 by Scripta Publishing Company.

poorly understood is, however, a challenge both to our personal understanding of our social world as persons and citizens, and to our encyclopedic knowledge and our epistemological algorithms as scholars and scientists. Faced with this social problem, not only do we wish to find solutions, we wish also to find abstract modes of approaching and conceptualizing this class of problems. Social concern and scholarly curiosity can move together. There are many instances of the integration of social concern and theoretical inquiry that could be presented, and no doubt many will suggest themselves to the reader as we proceed. However, there are theoretical issues that have remained unyielding that may be clarified particularly well in combination with social intervention research in general, and with the research outlined here in particular.

Unemployment and low income may be the most significant problems facing black Americans today. Granted that there are important problems in the area of housing and education, the problem of employment seems even more central. Holding a good job may allow a black person to solve some of the other problems, but without a good job it seems difficult to see how he will. Solving the problems of employment may have profound effects on the structure of the black family, as well as a number of related significant problems. Fleisher (1966), for instance, did a regression analysis of delinquency rates in 101 cities across the United States using as independent variables income, unemployment rates, racial composition, residential mobility, family stability, and region. He concluded that in "delinquency prone groups" a 1% rise in income may result in a 2.5% reduction in delinquency, and a 10% rise in income in a 20% reduction in delinquency. An extrapolation would suggest that if the average black family income was the same as the average white family income, delinquency in the ghetto would be lower than in middle-class white neighborhoods! Granted that such extrapolations are not justifiable, because relationships between variables may not be linear for the whole range of the variables, this is a striking illustration of the extent to which income level may be related to social problems.

But further, the question raised concerns theoretical issues about "delinquency," normative behavior and motivation of the following form: To what extent is our understanding of these phenomena likely to be clarified by means of an analysis of: (1) dynamic-personality phenomena, present by virtue of certain tendencies formed during child rearing; (2) contra-attitudinal phenomena in which persons are forced by economic and other environmental pressures to behave in ways inconsistent with the norms they accept or prefer; (3) reflections of behavioral dispositions that respond to environmental stimuli and that were acquired through specific interactions of person characteristics and environmental conditions? To be sure there are more alternatives than these three, and the questions have to be formulated at much more concrete levels for empirical analysis. But the theoretical issues are of long-standing concern in psychology. They can be clarified most effectively when empirical study is mounted on the scale we are prepared to undertake in the study of contemporary social phenomena.

The present paper is an attempt to illustrate how practical concerns derived from social problems can be combined with theoretical interests. It may serve several functions: (1) suggest how other social problems might be examined, while at the same time theoretical interests may be served and fundamental progress can be made in the scientific study of social behavior; (2) arouse the interest of other psychologists in the particular area of investigation; (3) provide a summary of some relevant literature; (4) suggest particular research problems that need investigation. The paper also makes suggestions about particular kinds of actions that might be encouraged by persons concerned with black employment opportunities and the success of blacks in job settings. Some of these actions are reforms that need to be evaluated, in the manner suggested by Campbell (1969).

BROAD CONSIDERATIONS

It is well documented that blacks have experienced higher rates of unemployment than whites. The causes of this phenomenon are many. Among the major causes are stereotypes of blacks held by some whites, as well as certain real differences between blacks and whites which make the adjustment of blacks in white job settings less likely. Turnover rates among blacks are very high, and this is in part the result of the hostility they experience in the strange environment of a white factory. If we are to explore some of these phenomena we need to obtain adequate data concerning the actual differences between blacks and whites and the nature of black-white interaction in job settings. We need also to learn how we can train people in such settings to increase the probability of a black person's success, and to reduce turnover.

Relevant Characteristics of Blacks and Whites

Recent reviews of the literature (e.g., Dreger & Miller, 1960; 1968) have summarized black-white differences on a number of variables. For our present purpose it is sufficient to point out four major kinds of differences.

Motivational differences. Black ghetto residents appear to have lower self-esteem, shorter time perspectives, and to see little connection between their own behavior and the reaching of goals (weak means-ends connections), when compared with middle-class blacks and whites.

According to a personal communication from H. Rosen, who has done much research on the hardcore unemployed in the Detroit area, low self-esteem is positively correlated with job stability. One of the problems of the new image of the black is a high self-esteem relative to already developed skills, hence a disappointment with promotion opportunities and job quitting. It is necessary to research precisely how much of this disappointment is traceable to inadequate skills leading to low prestige jobs, or white employer prejudice leading to such jobs, in different kinds of regions, industries, and levels of jobs in American industry. Under what conditions, in short, is a low self-esteem functional from the point of view of adjustment to the American environment and under what conditions is it dysfunctional?

Differences in the use of time. Ghetto blacks use time in a way which suggests to middle-class blacks or whites that they are *unreliable, lazy,* and *tardy.* There is little objective evidence on these matters, but the impression (stereotype) exists. They also appear to socialize too much on the job. On objective indexes of "loitering on the job," absenteeism, and turnover, there is a good deal of evidence that ghetto blacks differ from lower-class whites; poor attendance was identified as the major cause of dismissal of blacks (APA Symposium, 1969).

Differences in interpersonal behavior. The ghetto produces patterns of social behavior characterized by low interpersonal trust, low ingroup boundary stability, high suspicion, hostility toward and competition with outgroup members, and a good deal of "rapping" (Kochman, 1969). There seems to be an underdevelopment of cooperative behavioral skills (e.g., how to reduce conflict without resorting to overtly hostile acts), and there is much difficulty in accepting the expectations of white supervisors. Simple behavior patterns, such as knowing when to ask for help, seem to be undeveloped, so that the black employees either do not ask for help when they should do so or, when trained to ask for help, become overdependent (APA Symposium, 1969).

On the other hand, blacks appear to be very high in affiliation, as in the U.S. Department of Commerce report on black-white differences in geographic mobility (Ferman, Kornbluh, & Miller, 1968) which indicated that the lower mobility of blacks is due to their emotional ties with persons and places.

There are certain contradictions in the data, which require further research. One possible way to reconcile these contradictions is to assume that blacks are somewhat more attached to a few persons and places that are sources of emotional security than are whites. Their ingroups may be relatively small, consisting mostly of a few friends and relatives and members of the opposite sex with whom they have formed a liaison, while most of the other members of the black ghetto are perceived as outgroup members. Research now in progress will examine the ingroup boundaries of ghetto blacks and lower class whites to clarify this issue.

Differences in behavioral norms. Some differences in behavioral norms are superficial, such as the use of "inappropriate dress," but some are fundamental, such as black and white conceptions of proper on-the-job behavior. It appears that some ghetto blacks conceive of jobs as "Boss says do X, I do X," while some whites have a broader conception, doing "X, most things related to X, and if I finish before the end of the shift, I should tell the boss and even ask for an additional job." If this observation is correct, research is needed to determine the causes of such differences. Are these differences in the degree of "identification with the organization," differences in the extent to which orders are obeyed literally, or cultural differences traceable to differential rewards for taking the initiative?

Additional Needed Research

There is also a need for broad research programs that will explore the frequency, extent, and antecedents and consequences of the cultural differences mentioned in the previous sections. Several research programs are needed. For example, programs might test:

1. Rainwater's (1965) argument that there are different family structures in rural and urban black culture. If he is correct, there should be corresponding differences in family role perceptions and role behaviors among newcomers and oldtimers in the ghetto.
2. Silberman's (1964) argument that blacks have more trouble than others in answering the fundamental question "Who am I?" If this is true, this should be reflected in the self-perceptions of whites and blacks, and in race differences in self-esteem.
3. The argument that blacks see that there is little sense in trying to succeed. If this is true, there should be lower strengths in the connections between means and ends.
4. The argument that apathy, lack of motivation to increase education and income, and low levels of aspiration (Roach, 1965) are characteristic of blacks; if this is true, what are the antecedent conditions?
5. The state of interracial attitudes in broad surveys of blacks and whites, such as that conducted by Marx (1967). Such studies need to be done, periodically, to assess longitudinal trends suggesting changes in such attitudes.

For our part, we have started with considerable skepticism about differences in the perception of the social environment by blacks and whites. We first examined methodological issues and ways to exclude competing hypotheses, that such observed differences are due to artifacts, or to broad perceptual habits, or other variables, such as social class. In Triandis and Malpass (1970) we examined strategies for research which will exclude such competing hypotheses. In Triandis, Feldman, and Harvey (1970, 1971a, 1971b, 1971c), there is considerable evidence that there are genuine racial differences in the perception of the social environment. However, much more needs to be done to establish the antecedents of these differences. Given that such differences exist, what kinds of social experiences are likely to reduce interracial conflict in job settings?

Considerations Concerning the Training of Blacks and Whites

Most of the traditional thinking in this area has used the "rehabilitation model," which essentially states that in order to solve the problem of unemployment you must change people, through appropriate training, to adjust to the existing environment. For example, Ginzberg (1967) writes: "Without understanding employers, foremen and fellow workers, many of the newly trained workers will not be able to make it" (p. 20). Without questioning the need for increasing such understanding we have to examine whether such efforts will be sufficiently productive, or whether changing the environment might not be *more* effective.

Skepticism about the effectiveness of training the hardcore unemployed can be derived from several sources, including H. Rosen's (personal communication) comment that hardcore employees do know what is "correct" behavior in the factory and refuse to behave according to it because they find it incongruent with their basic values. It may well be that after an extensive period of intensive negative affect associated with whites, all institutions, including industry, that are associated with whites elicit negative affect. A strategy of change, then, may be to attempt to show that industrial life has a logic of its own, which can be found in Japan or Nigeria just as much as in the U.S.A. Blacks who accept this argument may then be willing to behave as required by the institution. This line of investigation is at least worthy of further exploration. However, the more promising line of exploration involves changing the environment.

The social environment of the newly trained employee consists of managers, fellow workers, and immediate supervisors. Is X amount of change in the new employees as productive of integration of the disadvantaged into the mainstream of American economic life as a similar amount of change in the foremen, fellow workers, and managers? If we are to consider such a question, we need to establish some clear criterion.

We propose to adopt the criterion "percent of the disadvantaged who hold income-producing jobs for one or more years." A number of criteria reflecting individual behavior, such as disciplinary actions, tardiness, absenteeism, and turnover should also be included. But from a societal viewpoint, if we modify either the employees or the environment and observe a significant increase in the percentages of the disadvantaged who hold jobs for one year, we will consider this modification successful. We can, in the final analysis, simplify the problem and ask how much change in the criterion is obtained with the expenditure of what resources directed at changing the employees *or* the environment, or what balance in such training is optimal.

There are several lines of research which suggest that changing the environment will be more economical than changing the employees:

1. There are several studies which suggest that the poor are alienated, less susceptible to group pressures, and more resistant to change than middle-class individuals. Roach and Gursslin (1967) quote almost a dozen studies which document these points (see p. 388, footnote 22).

There is also a rather general agreement that the effects of discrimination, as experienced by blacks, result in low self-esteem. In fact, many social analysts have seen the black power movement as a means to increase self-esteem. Attitude change research (e.g., reviews by McGuire, 1969; Triandis, 1971) strongly suggests that there is a curvilinear relationship between attitude change and self-esteem, with moderate amounts of self-esteem being most conducive to attitude change. In short, there is a strong suggestion that we cannot "reach" the alienated, the isolated, and the disadvantaged to change them and prepare them to live in the middle-class environment of the majority culture as easily as we might reach the middle-class who are more likely to develop the kinds of attitudes needed to understand and accept the blacks.

2. It has been suggested that middle-class behavior is much more under the influence of normative factors than lower-class behavior. Here a model of behavior developed by Triandis, Vassiliou, Tanaka and Shanmugam (1971) may be useful. Figure 1 shows this model. Behavior is conceived as being under the influence of a number of "psychological systems," each of these systems being shown as a chain of influences. One such system includes the perceived probabilities that certain kinds of behavior will lead to desirable or undesirable outcomes; another consists of certain cognitions and the affect attached to these cognitions concerning the "other person"; another consists of normative influences; still another of previously established habits, which involves behavior without awareness; etc. The percentages of variance of behavior controlled by each of these systems may differ for different groups of people. Thus, it is argued, rigid, authoritarian, middle-class adults may

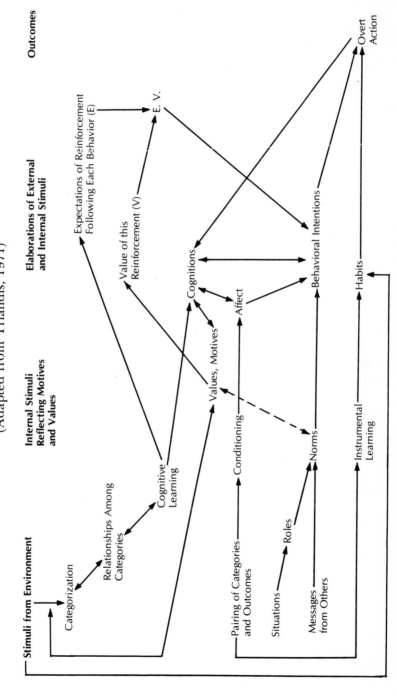

Figure 1

Behavior is a Complex Function of Several Psychological Systems
(Adapted from Triandis, 1971)

behave primarily under the influences of norms and roles; lower lower-class individuals may behave more impulsively, under the influence of a minimum number of cognitions. If this speculation is correct, it would follow that it is more difficult to train a lower lower-class individual to behave according to the "white rules," simply because less of his behavior, in general, is under the influence of norms.

On the other hand this speculation is ethnocentric, since it does not allow for the operation of different *kinds* and *sources* of norms. Further research is needed to determine if what appears as nonadherence to norms is due to (1) adherence to different kinds of norms; (2) adherence to different sources of norms; (3) acceptance of a greater range of behavior as consistent with particular norms; (4) rejection of various kinds of norms; (5) ignorance of norms; or (6) different instrumentalities for various kinds of norms for the various groups with which the individual interacts. Further explication of Figure 1 will be provided in a later section.

One could anticipate from data collected by Hunt and Dopyera (1966) in a study of "conceptual level" of junior high school students and its relation to behavior in different classroom environments that there is a greater heterogeneity of conceptual level in the lower-class population.

With greater variance of lower-class students as compared with middle-class students, and with rule-oriented behavior and deference to authority being characteristics of only the middle range of this conceptual level dimension (where the middle-class distribution was more peaked), one would expect relatively fewer lower-class young adults to be easily influenced by unilateral assertion of rules and authority. Further, those who are not so influenced are heterogeneous in response to various environmental pressures. Hunt (1966a) provides other data suggesting an interaction between person type and certain features of the environment with respect to conformity. An implication that is theoretically interesting, but operationally difficult, is that the environment into which a trainee is placed should optimally be changed contingent on certain characteristics of the trainee and the nature of the criterion variable(s), requiring a diagnostic system for trainees and considerable control over the flexibility of the social environment. This is a classic concept in social psychology: $B = f(P, E)$.

3. A major characteristic of the ghetto is the lack of interpersonal trust. Strodtbeck (in the conference mentioned in Footnote 1) pointed out that a person who has very limited resources cannot afford to trust others. For example, if going to work involves getting a babysitter, and the babysitter eats the food available in the house, one may have to do without food. In short, the babysitter cannot be trusted. Friends, in the

ghetto, can be severe burdens since if they get into trouble they may require your help, but if you help them you will not have enough for yourself. The lack of resources leads to rare interpersonal reinforcement by means of material exchanges. The high frequency of crime and interpersonal exploitation make trust responses dysfunctional. Certain black groups, such as the Panthers, have developed self-protective norms which permit relatively more trust within the group, but in general one cannot trust another. (See Cleaver in *The Black Panther*, August 16, 1969.)

Research evidence seems consistent with these observations. For example, Erksine (1969) reports the results of a recent poll (NORC, February 1964) which asked national samples: "Do you think most people can be trusted?" The national total was 77% "Yes," 21% "No"; the corresponding black percentages were 59 and 40. Suspicion seems characteristic of urban populations with an agrarian background, such as the Greeks (Triandis & Vassiliou, 1967b), the Southern Italians (Banfield, 1958), and the Peruvians (Whyte & Williams, in progress). Thus, it is conceivable that the black responses reflect the agrarian background of the American Negro rather than ghetto culture as such. This is of little practical importance, however, since the main point is that as long as such high levels of suspicion exist, it is difficult to reach people through interpersonal appeals.

4. There are objective characteristics of the ghetto environment which make job adjustment difficult. From an extensive study of a California ghetto, Maruyama (1969) gives an example. A young black returns from his job with $130. A policeman searches him and finds the money and takes it away, saying: "Punk, I know you couldn't have gotten this money unless you stole it. Well, I'll let you away easy this time, I'll give you $20 back. Make sure you keep your black mouth shut." Under such conditions, is it worthwhile for the black man to go to work? Here is a case in which, no matter how well trained, he cannot cope with his environment unless the environment is changed.

In fact, Jacobs (1966) presents an unbelievable picture of the relationship of ghetto blacks to the government agencies of a major California city, which suggests the need for intensive training of policemen, social workers, and welfare officials in understanding black culture rather than training the blacks. Maruyama (1969) presents several examples of behaviors which are "totally unacceptable" in the white middle-class world which are rationally desirable and obviously functional within the ghetto. For example, violence has a different function in the ghetto from that in middle-class neighborhoods. Consider this excerpt from an interview:

> The ghettos that I have grown up in are, if you did not fight, I mean, you are in trouble, so ah, beat up every day. Your lunch money was taken. Your mother sent you to a store, you know, and you didn't fight, and they knew you wouldn't fight, and the, the money was taken and after money was taken you might get a whip when you get home. (Maruyama, 1968, p. 21).

In such environments violence appears a logically defensible way of life. Similarly, "kindness" is often dysfunctional in the ghetto. The logic of the ghetto may not be the same as the logic used by the middle class. For instance, the consequences of prostitution to the middle-class white are more money, but also degradation. To the black ghetto member they may include financial independence—hence, self-assertion and self-respect. Maruyama points out that regularly employed women, such as prostitutes, have more prestige in the ghetto than seasonal laborers. Thus, a pimp, who has some control over prostitutes, may gain status by accepting such an occupation. It is a research question of considerable importance to determine the effects of understanding the logic of the ghetto on the behavior of policemen and government officials. Behaviors may be classified as criminal or not depending upon the interpretation of the intention behind them. It follows, then, that teaching officials about ghetto logic could improve their ability to make correct inferences about intentions.

THE NATURE OF NEEDED TRAINING

The first part of this essay established that there are probable important differences in the way ghetto blacks and middle-class whites perceive their social environment. We also suggested that middle-class whites might be easier to train than ghetto blacks. The next section considers the nature of training that is needed for each side. The purpose of such training, in all cases, is to increase the probability that each side will "understand" the other. This involves developing skills in making the correct inferences about intentions and in predicting the behavior of members of the other group. However, given the nature of the cultural differences discussed above, each training target must receive a different kind of training. We now turn to the types of training targets.

There are three major potential targets of training. First, we might train the economically disadvantaged. The nature of such training may well be designed to increase self-esteem, to teach how to take advantage of the facilities provided by different kinds of environments (e.g., how to make complaints specifying that policemen have behaved unfairly), and may require counselors whose job it will be to reinforce interpersonal trust responses.

Second, we might train the members of the employee's social environment—foremen, managers, fellow workers. Training them to develop greater flexibility in judging others, to appreciate that different social environments may require different kinds of logic, to suspend judgment when they see behaviors which they do not understand, and to see the legitimacy of the point of view of the other culture may lead to improvements in our criterion scores.

Third, we might consider innovations in the kinds of people and organizations that may be brought into play to improve problems of employment. For example, we might consider the use of volunteers (or if this is insufficient, federal employees) to be called "race relations commissioners" (RRCs). The RRCs should be high-status members of the establishment committed towards changing it (for example, top executives of companies or lawyers with a social conscience). The job of these volunteers would be to spend a half-day in the ghetto, listening to the special problems of the members of the ghetto. They should then use whatever means of redress might be available, including presentations in front of state legislative committees, to modify the inequities which they find in the ghetto, to develop new welfare laws, new controls on policemen, new policies for social workers, etc. It is clear that our proposed training would be most beneficial to the RRCs, since they would need to understand the basic features of black culture before they begin their work. These RRCs would *not* be black. They need to be high-status persons within the white establishment, whose opinions are likely to convince white legislators or members of the federal executive. They should not appear to have any "axes to grind." Several other innovations in organizational arrangements are in order. For example, the buddy system employed by some industrial organizations to facilitate the induction of ghetto residents, school counselors, and many other categories of individuals would find our training relevant.

It should be clear that we advocate a different training approach for each of the three targets of training. The black ghetto resident, for instance, should be trained primarily by counselors, using reinforcement of specific behaviors, etc. The fellow workers may require training to "appreciate the need for further training" and develop positive attitudes toward the ghetto dwellers before the final phase of "cognitive training," such as is provided by a culture assimilator.[4] Other trainees may be selected to have positive attitudes and hence may require only the "cognitive training." This will be true most frequently with the RRCs.

On the other hand, certain kinds of training may be common to all groups. Perhaps all trainees can profit from training designed to bolster their security, so that they may increase their openness to different points of view and different values. It is probable that all can profit from the development of a greater ability to suspend judgment when evaluating the behavior of others, and greater flexibility in evaluating the contextual appropriateness of different behaviors. Information about the expectations of various subgroups in one's society and greater ability to discriminate different kinds of people, situations, and levels of appropriateness of behavior in different settings would be valuable for any trainee. This would also involve greater ability by the trainees to behave differently toward different kinds of people (greater role differentiation), particularly in making themselves understood by others. At a higher level of accomplishment among trainees we might hope for the development of empathy as well as of some skills in changing the attitudes of their coworkers in matters that are of great importance to them but of lesser importance to their coworkers, and also a greater ability to express themselves, to understand their own feelings and to communicate them to others. The development of skills which would allow an optimal coordination of their behavior with the demands of their environment and the expectations of those with whom they work would be the ultimate goal of training.

How is this training to be accomplished? Certain major types of training can be distinguished: (1) affective training—control of one's own affect and the affect of others; (2) cognitive training—learning what goes with what; (3) behavioral-transactive training—learning through face-to-face contacts, simulated contacts, or programmed simulated interaction. The types of cultural training now available are very large. A recent compilation of information concerning such training by Wight (1969) resulted in a handbook of over 700 mimeographed pages. Different purposes may be served best by adopting different combinations of types of training.

There are several research questions in the training area that must be answered in the near future. Among these questions are such matters as whether one trains inductively—by providing a lot of experiences out of which the trainee forms his own theory of appropriate behavior— or deductively—by providing the trainee with a tested theory of appropriate behavior in different roles, situations, and conditions. Probably the answer to this question will be some kind of compromise, but there is a real question then, in determining the optimal level of training between the most inductive and the most deductive.

Another question is the extent to which one emphasizes *similarities* between cultures in his training, thus providing opportunities for the development of positive affect, but also risking that the trainee's disappointments in intercultural contact will lead to negative responses, or emphasize *differences,* thus developing a rather affectively negative trainee, whose level of adaptation is so low that he will not be surprised by any "shocking" intercultural events.

In order to produce trainees who can adapt to changes in their working environment, it seems reasonable that training should provide: (1) discriminative skills, to discriminate among social contexts, appropriate role behaviors, person types, etc.; (2) some manipulative skills, to permit modification of environments, people, and differential behaviors of the trainees in different environments; and (3) adaptive skills, changing the trainee's own behavior in response to evaluation of the effectiveness of his previous behaviors, with respect to different kinds of people and in different kinds of environments. This scheme is partly derived from the component analysis of the training of training agents given by Hunt (1966b).

To develop such training it is clear that we need to learn precisely what variations in subjective culture occur in different kinds of people and in different kinds of settings, what particular roles operate, and how are different roles integrated (e.g., the roles *old man* and *unskilled laborer* result in conflicting tendencies on the behavioral intention "to respect"; how is such conflict resolved in different subjects?). We need to learn the diagnostic cues which will permit appropriate behavior in different settings. We need to learn more about the coordination of information about people and about environments to produce more effective social behavior.

In Conclusion

Tests of various aspects of the nomological network suggested by Figure 1 would make a contribution to our scientific understanding of social behavior. Many of the studies suggested by our analysis of black and white interaction in job settings can supply information about the links of this network. At the same time, the kinds of training that may emerge from the present effort may lead to improved employment histories among black Americans. Thus, a problem of theoretical interest *can* be combined with problems of social significance.

Notes

[1]This paper was supported by the Vocational Rehabilitation Administration of the Department of Health, Education and Welfare, under Project No. RD-2841-G (H. C. Triandis, Principal Investigator). The following persons attended a conference in Monticello, Ill., in April 1969, in which many of the ideas discussed here were presented and further developed. We are grateful to Philip Brickman, Northwestern University; Joan H. Criswell, Division of Research, Rehabilitation Research Branch, Department of Health, Education and Welfare; Roy D'Andrade, Stanford University; James M. Jones, Yale University; Irwin Katz, University of Michigan; James Scott, State University of New York, Plattsburgh; Fred L. Strodtbeck, University of Chicago; June Tapp, University of Chicago; James Taylor, Menninger Clinic, Topeka; Allan Wicker, then University of Wisconsin, Milwaukee (now at the University of Illinois); Judith Ayer (now at Miami University);

Fred Fiedler (now at University of Washington, Seattle); Terence Mitchell (now at the University of Washington, Seattle); Stanley Nealey (now at Colorado State); Jacquetta Burnett, James Davis, Jack Feldman, Robert Ferber, Martin Fishbein, Michael Lewis, Joseph McGrath, Charles Osgood, Tulsi Saral, Steven Schwartz, Clarence Shelley and John Symonds, all from the University of Illinois.

Helpful comments on an earlier draft were received from H. Rosen of Wayne State, and several of the above.

[2] Harry C. Triandis and Roy S. Malpass were affiliated with the University of Illinois at the time of publication of this article. Requests for reprints should be sent to Dr. Harry C. Triandis, Department of Psychology, University of Illinois, Champaign, Illinois 61820.

[3] A summary of previous work in the analysis of subjective culture can be found in Triandis, Feldman, & Harvey (1971a, 1971b, 1971c) and Triandis, Vassiliou, V., Vassiliou, G., Tanaka, & Shanmugam (1971). This work is an extension of previous studies of the relationship between culture and cognition (e.g., Brown and Lenneberg, 1954; Landar, Erwin, & Horowitz, 1960; Lenneberg & Roberts, 1965). Several new techniques have been developed (Davis & Triandis, 1965; Triandis, 1959, 1964a, 1964b; Triandis, Kilty, Shanmugam, Tanaka, & Vassiliou, 1968; Triandis & Vassiliou, 1967a; Triandis, Vassiliou & Nassiakou, 1968) which permit the analysis of subjective culture. The data are analyzed through some multivariate model, such as factor analysis, multidimensional scaling (Torgerson, 1958), or the models proposed by Kruskal (1964) and Shepard (1962). Once the basic attributes underlying a domain of meaning are known they can be further tested with one of the deductive models, such as Guttman's (1959) facet analysis (Foa, 1965), or Osgood's (1968) feature analysis. For certain domains of meaning componential analysis is very useful (Wallace, 1962). The broad theoretical framework used by Triandis et al. (1971) has much in common with Dulany's (1968) and Ryan's (1969) theories of intentional control of behavior. Such intentions are organized in "maps of subjective culture" which are exemplified in Triandis and Vassiliou (1967b). The prediction of behavior from various kinds of subjective culture information was presented by Davis and Triandis (1965) and Triandis and Vassiliou (1968). The use of subjective culture information for cross-cultural training (Fiedler, Mitchell, & Triandis, 1971) and several other implications of such studies are discussed in Triandis et al. (1971).

[4] Culture assimilators are programmed learning experiences in which a trainee is presented with an incident involving cross-cultural interaction. He selects one of several possible interpretations of the incident and receives reinforcement and explanations concerning the relative merits of each interpretation, in the light of known differences in the social behavior of the various cultural groups (see Fiedler, Mitchell, & Triandis, 1971).

References

Banfield, E. C. *The moral basis of a backward society.* Glencoe, Ill.: Free Press, 1958.

Barton, A. H. *Measuring the values of individuals.* New York: Columbia University Bureau of Applied Social Research, No. 354, 1965.

Brown, R. W., & Lenneberg, E. H. A study of language and cognition. *Journal of Abnormal and Social Psychology,* 1954, *49,* 454-462.

Campbell, D. T. Reforms as experiments. *American Psychologist,* 1969, *24,* 409-429.

Davis, E. E., & Triandis, H. C. An exploratory study of intercultural negotiation. (Tech. Rep. No. 26) Urbana, Ill.: Department of Psychology, University of Illinois, 1965.

Dreger, R. M., & Miller, K. S. Comparative psychological studies of Negroes and whites in the United States. *Psychological Bulletin,* 1960, *57,* 361-402.

Dreger, R. M., & Miller, K. S. Comparative psychological studies of Negroes and whites in the United States, 1960-1965. *Psychological Bulletin,* 1968, *70* (3, Pt. 2), 1-58.

Dulany, D. E. Awareness, rules and propositional control: A confrontation with S-R behavior theory. In T. R. Dixon and D. L. Horton (Eds.), *Verbal behavior and general behavior theory.* New York: Prentice-Hall, 1968, pp. 340-387.

Erksine, H. The polls: Negro philosophies of life. *Public Opinion Quarterly,* 1969, *33,* 147-158.

Ferman, L. A., Kornbluh, J., & Miller, J. A. *Negroes and jobs.* Ann Arbor: University of Michigan Press, 1968.

Fiedler, F. E., Mitchell, T. R., & Triandis, H. C. The culture assimilator: An approach to cross-cultural training. *Journal of Applied Psychology,* 1971, *55,* 95-102.

Fleisher, B. The effects of income on delinquency. *American Economic Review,* 1966, *56,* 118-137.

Foa, U. G. New developments in facet design and analysis. *Psychological Review,* 1965, *72,* 262-274.

Ginzberg, E. Advice to the urban coalition. *The Reporter,* September 1967.

Guttman, L. A structural theory of intergroup beliefs and action. *American Sociological Review,* 1959, *24,* 318-328.

Hunt, D. E. A model for analyzing the training of training agents. *Merrill Palmer Quarterly,* 1966, 12, 137-156. (a)

Hunt, D. E. A conceptual systems change model and its application to education. In O. J. Harvey (Ed.), *Experience, structure and adaptability.* New York: Springer, 1966, pp. 277-302. (b)

Hunt, D. E., & Dopyera, J. Personality variation in lower class children. *Journal of Psychology,* 1966, *62,* 47-54.

Jacobs, P. *Prelude to riot: A view of urban America from the bottom.* New York: Random House, 1966.

Kochman, T. "Rapping" in the black ghetto. *Transaction,* 1969, *6,* 29-34.

Kruskal, J. B. Multidimensional scaling by optimizing goodness to fit to a non-metric hypothesis. *Psychometrika,* 1964, *29,* 1-28.

Landar, H. J., Erwin, S. M., & Horowitz, A. E. Navaho color categories. *Language,* 1960, *36,* 368-382.

Lenneberg, E. H., & Roberts, J. M. The language of experience: A study in methodology. *International Journal of American Linguistics,* 1965, *22* (2, Suppl.).

Maruyama, M. Trans-social rapport through prison inmates. *Annales Internationales de Criminologie,* 1968, *7,* 19-46.

Maruyama, M. The ghetto logic, 1969. (Mimeo).

Marx, G. T. *Protest and prejudice.* New York: Harper & Row, 1967.

McGuire, W. J. The nature of attitudes and attitude change. In G. Lindzey and E. Aronson (Eds.), *The handbook of social psychology.* Reading, Mass.: Addison-Wesley, 1969, pp. 136-314.

Nelson, B. Psychologists: Searching for social relevance at APA meeting. *Science,* 1969, *165,* 1101-1104.

Osgood, C. E. Interpersonal verbs and interpersonal behaviors. Technical Report No. 64. Urbana, Ill.: Department of Psychology, University of Illinois, 1968.

Rainwater, L. Crucible of identity: The Negro lower class family. In T. Parsons and K. Clark (Eds.), *The Negro American.* Boston: Beacon Press, 1965, pp. 160-205.

Roach, J. L. Sociological analysis of poverty. *The American Journal of Sociology,* 1965, *71,* 68-75.

Roach, J. L., & Gursslin, O. R. An evaluation of the concept of "culture of poverty." *Social Forces,* 1967, *45,* 383-392.

Ryan, T. A. *Intentional behavior: An approach to human motivation.* New York: Ronald Press, 1969.

Shepard, R. N. The analysis of proximities: Multidimensional scaling with an unknown distance function, I and II. *Psychometrika,* 1962, *27,* 125-139; 219-246.

Silberman, C. *Crisis in black and white.* New York: Vintage Books, 1964.

Symonds, J. D. Culture differences and social class in the Negro community. (Tech. Rep. No. 1, SRS No. RD 2841-G) Urbana, Ill.: Department of Psychology, University of Illinois, 1969.

Torgerson, W. S. *Theory and methods of scaling.* New York: Wiley, 1958.

Triandis, H. C. Categories of thought of managers, clerks and workers about jobs and people in industry. *Journal of Applied Psychology,* 1959, *43,* 338-344.

Triandis, H. C. Cultural influences upon cognitive processes. In L. Berkowitz (Ed.), *Advances in experimental social psychology.* Vol. 1. New York: Academic Press, 1964. (a)

Triandis, H. C. Exploratory factor analyses of the behavioral component of social attitudes. *Journal of Abnormal and Social Psychology,* 1964, *68,* 420-430. (b)

Triandis, H. C. Person perception: A review of the literature and implications. (Tech. Rep. No. 3, SRS No. RD 2841-G) Champaign, Ill.: Department of Psychology, University of Illinois, 1970.

Triandis, H. C. *Attitudes and attitude change.* New York: Wiley, 1971.

Triandis, H. C., Feldman, J., & Harvey, W. Person perception among black and white adolescents and the hardcore unemployed. (Tech. Rep. No. 5, SRS No. RD 2841-G) Champaign, Ill.: Department of Psychology, University of Illinois, 1970.

Triandis, H. C., Feldman, J., & Harvey, W. Role perceptions among black and white adolescents and the hardcore unemployed. (Tech. Rep. No. 6, SRS No. RD 2841-G) Champaign, Ill.: Department of Psychology, University of Illinois, 1971. (a)

Triandis, H. C., Feldman, J., & Harvey, W. Job perceptions among black and white adolescents and the hardcore unemployed. (Tech. Rep. No. 7, SRS No. RD 2841-G) Champaign, Ill.: Department of Psychology, University of Illinois, 1971. (b)

Triandis, H. C., Feldman, J., & Harvey, W. The perceptions of implicative relationships among black and white adolescents and the hardcore unemployed. (Tech. Rep. No. 8, SRS No. RD 2841-G) Champaign, Ill.: Department of Psychology, University of Illinois, 1971. (c)

Triandis, H. C., Kilty, K. M., Shanmugam, A. V., Tanaka, Y., & Vassiliou, V. Cultural influences upon the perception of implicative relationships among concepts and the analysis of values. (Tech. Rep. No. 56) Urbana, Ill.: Department of Psychology, University of Illinois, 1968.

Triandis, H. C., & Malpass, R. S. Field guide for the study of subjective culture. (Tech. Rep. No. 4, SRS No. RD 2841-G) Champaign, Ill.: Department of Psychology, University of Illinois, 1970.

Triandis, H. C., & Vassiliou, V. Frequency of contact and stereotyping. *Journal of Personality and Social Psychology,* 1967, *7,* 316-328. (a)

Triandis, H. C., & Vassiliou, V. A comparative analysis of subjective culture. (Tech. Rep. No. 55) Urbana, Ill.: Department of Psychology, University of Illinois, 1967. (b)

Triandis, H. C., & Vassiliou, V. *Journal of Applied Psychology,* 1971, in press.

Triandis, H. C., Vassiliou, V., & Nassiakou, M. Three cross-cultural studies of subjective culture. *Journal of Personality and Social Psychology,* 1968, *8* (4, Pt. 2), 1-42.

Triandis, H. C., Vassiliou V. & G., Tanaka, Y., & Shanmugam, A. V. *The analysis of subjective culture.* New York: Wiley, 1971.

Wallace, A. F. C. Culture and cognition. *Science,* 1962, *135,* 351-357.

Wight, A. R. *Handbook of cross-cultural and community involvement training.* Estes Park, Colo.: Center for Research and Education, 1969.

The Black Experience
in Large Public Accounting Firms

WILLIAM AIKEN[1]

Black accountants began to enter the public accounting profession in significant numbers in 1969 as barriers against hiring blacks began to fall. Members of minority groups aspiring to enter the profession cannot yet say that the door is open, but they can observe that it is now ajar. Many of those who have entered the profession are now determined to be a positive force in implementing genuine commitments to equal opportunity.

In 1970, a small group of black accountants in New York organized NABA, the National Association of Black Accountants, to provide a vehicle to make good that determination. The organization has grown rapidly and now has members and chapters in several parts of the country. It has initiated numerous programs for the benefit of its members and the community, but its primary purposes are to encourage and assist members of minority groups who are interested in pursuing accounting careers and to make available volunteer consultants for minority businessmen who are unable to pay consulting fees.

This article reports on and evaluates the results of one of NABA's first undertakings, a questionnaire survey to ascertain how black accountants employed by large public accounting firms view their experiences.[2] NABA plans to sponsor follow-up surveys periodically to monitor progress or retrogression.

The results of the current survey are important because the experiences of the black pioneers who have been employed by large public

---

Reprinted from *Journal of Accountancy*, August 1972, pp. 60-63, by permission of the publisher and the author. Copyright © 1972 by the American Institute of Certified Public Accountants, Inc.

accounting firms will either encourage or discourage other blacks aspiring to careers in the profession.

Scope of the Survey

During April and May 1971, confidential questionnaires were mailed to 314 black accountants who were employed by several large accounting firms. Large public accounting firms were selected for the study because at the time of the survey only these firms had begun to employ a significant number of blacks, and because most NABA members were employed by large firms. Six large firms provided the names of black accountants on their staffs. Names of staff assistants from the New York offices of two other large firms were obtained through NABA members employed by those firms.

Respondents were asked to indicate their age, year employed and sex and to provide data on educational background (colleges or universities attended, degrees earned and year of graduation). They were then asked to rate several aspects of their experience.

The respondents were classified, as far as possible, by regions, based on the postmarks on the responses.

The 168 respondents consisted of 147 professionals who had earned degrees in accounting and 21 interns and preprofessionals who had not earned degrees in accounting. Interns and preprofessionals were excluded from evaluation of work experiences, promotions, etc.

Profile of Respondents

Most of the 168 respondents were young men in their twenties who had earned bachelor degrees in accounting in 1969 and 1970 and who had been hired by public accounting firms in those years; 85 per cent were men, 11 per cent were women and 4 per cent failed to indicate sex. The respondents reported 144 bachelor degrees and 13 advanced degrees. Forty-three per cent of the respondents had attended traditionally black colleges or universities, and 57 per cent had attended predominantly white colleges or universities.

Tables 1, 2, 3 and 4 identify the respondents by region, age and year hired. Some respondents did not answer all questions in the survey.

Appraisal of Work Experiences

Respondents appraised aspects of their work experience on a simple value scale as shown on Table 5. The responses were analyzed on the

Table 1
Responses by Region

Region	Number of Responses	Percentage
East	91	63
Midwest	29	20
West	18	13
Southwest	6	4
Total	114	100

Table 2
Postmarks on Envelopes Received from Respondents

East	Midwest
Atlanta	Akron
Baltimore	Chicago
Birmingham, Ala.	Cincinnati
Boston	Cleveland
Charlotte, N.C.	Des Moines
Memphis	Detroit
New Haven	Indianapolis
New York	Lansing, Mich.
Newark	Milwaukee
Philadelphia	Minneapolis
Pittsburgh	Pontiac, Mich.
Washington, D.C.	Saginaw, Mich.

Southwest	West
Baton Rouge	Long Beach, Calif.
Dallas	Los Angeles
Denver	Oakland
Houston	San Francisco
Kansas City, Mo.	San Jose, Calif.
New Orleans	
St. Louis	

Table 3
Age Groups

Ages	Number of Responses	Percentage
20 to 24	66	42
25 to 29	60	38
30 and above	31	20
Total	157	100

Table 4
Year Hired

Year	Number of Responses	Percentage
1970	74	50
1969	47	32
1968 and prior	26	18
Total	147	100

Table 5
Work Experiences—Summary (in percentages)

	Poor	Fair	Good	Excellent	Outstanding
Work experience (overall)	9	30	36	21	4
Promotions	10	36	35	17	2
Salary advancements	5	35	46	13	1
Firms' efforts to motivate black staff	29	37	23	9	2
Firms' attitudes toward blacks	13	31	45	8	3
Social relationships—black and white staff	23	38	27	11	1

basis of sex, region, year hired and school attended to determine whether significant differences were apparent on these bases. Only the analyses on the bases of sex and region appeared to reveal any significant differences (see Tables 6 and 7).

Appraisals on some matters give some indication of the character of the black experience in public accounting, as well as simple evaluation. It is interesting to note that the respondents rated their firms' atti-

Table 6
Work Experiences—Female and Male

	Female		Male	
Rating	Number of Responses	Percentage	Number of Responses	Percentage
Outstanding	—	—	6	6
Excellent	—	—	30	23
Good	4	22	49	33
Fair	11	61	33	26
Poor	3	17	10	8
Total responses	18	100	128	100

Table 7
Work Experiences by Region

Rating	East	Midwest	Southwest	West
Outstanding	2%	7%	—	12%
Excellent	19	39	16%	12
Good	43	25	—	29
Fair	26	29	68	41
Poor	10	—	16	6
	100%	100%	100%	100%
Total responses	90	28	6	17

tudes toward blacks better (56 per cent good to outstanding) than their firms' efforts to motivate blacks (only 34 per cent good to outstanding).

The social relationship between black and white members of professional staffs appears to be representative of our society—61 per cent of the respondents reported poor to fair relationships.

Comments by Respondents

The questionnaire sent to the respondents asked, "In your opinion how can your firm best improve its relationship with its black professional employees?" Approximately 7 per cent of the 125 responses to this question indicated complete satisfaction, with no improvement necessary.

On the other hand, 93 per cent indicated a desirability for improvements in the following areas:

Work experience	37%
Racial attitudes	29
Hiring policies	12
Motivation efforts	7
Promotions	3
Counseling	2
Performance ratings	2
Greater training	1
Unfavorable	93%
Favorable	7%
	100%
Total responses	125

Some comments follow which illustrate the tone (both strong and mild) of the criticisms in the two most frequently mentioned areas in need of improvement—work experience and racial attitudes:

"Upper management is not aware of the _____ we must take from seniors in order to survive with the firm."

"I have noticed that white seniors take an interest in white juniors and point out small things that will help the juniors. No senior takes such an interest in blacks. Our little mistakes are remembered, our good points are overshadowed by our small errors."

"The accountant's mentality (one of suburban egotism) could and should be changed to something approaching urbanity."

"Blacks appear to represent a disproportionate percentage of the unassigned during slack periods. We can least afford to be unassigned."

"Everyone, blacks and whites, appears to be treated the same."

The Usefulness of the Survey—An Interpretation

NABA hopes that the views expressed by these black pioneers will be seriously considered by management in all public accounting firms employing blacks or preparing to do so. As one respondent said, "The firm can only hope to understand and effectively deal with our problems by realizing *first* that they exist."

Blacks entered public accounting with the hope that recruiters' pronouncements of equal opportunity would come to fruition. Many people believe that the unprecedented surge of interest in blacks during the 1968-69 recruiting season was due largely to government pressure. Others argue that it was due to a shortage of accountants. Whatever the reason, the firms in this survey have, in the aggregate, shown substantial progress in the hiring of black professionals.

However, hiring is only the first step toward providing equal opportunity. The primary concern of a large percentage of the respondents is whether or not they are going to have meaningful work experiences. It is encouraging that 61 per cent of the respondents report good to outstanding experiences. However, every effort should be made to bring a large number of those reporting poor to fair work experiences (39 per cent) into the mainstream by affording them meaningful work experiences.

Blacks can least afford to be unassigned or to spend a large portion of their time in "busy work." Black CPAs are too few in number. The black community needs them, and the only real hope of getting them in the near future lies in the ability of blacks in public accounting firms to have meaningful work assignments and complete their experience requirements. This will also effectively prepare them for the business world.

Negative feedback reaching blacks on the campuses, regarding work experiences, causes the students to ask some searching questions about the role they would be playing if they were employed by a large public accounting firm. On the other hand, the positive multiplier effect of good work experiences leading to CPA certificates for black accountants cannot be minimized.

The respondents showed special concern regarding the attitudes of some supervisory staff personnel. It is at this level that blacks feel that the greatest impediment to their progress exists. It is reported that in some quarters seniors have the power to decide who their assistants will be. Blacks are not likely to fare well under such a system because of the racial attitudes that exist in our society. Top management's commitment to equal opportunity is not being effectively communicated below the management level.

Perhaps there is a need to establish machinery for the airing of grievances which would otherwise not be heard. In this way, blacks could be afforded some measure of protection or redress against those who are so prejudiced that objectivity plays a small part in their evaluations. People take advantage of those whom they view as powerless and without recourse.

As a group, the black female respondents, from all areas of the country, rated their experience in all categories from poor to good, with none reporting excellent or outstanding experiences. This kind of unanimity clearly indicates a need for greater focus on the problems encountered by persons who happen to be both black and female. They should be shown that their race and sex are not factors in progress—only their competence.

Any recruit to public accounting, black or white, needs a minimum of two years in order to prove himself. The first year's experience is often not challenging and can hardly be used as a conclusive measure of anyone's potential (with the rare exception of the totally incompetent person). Two years' experience is also crucial from the standpoint of the CPA experience requirement in New York and other states.

And the two years of experience is especially vital to blacks. If blacks are terminated before they complete their CPA experience requirement, where can they go to complete it? Would any other large public accounting firm be interested in hiring a black who has been terminated? Our white counterparts are obviously more mobile. Some have relatives with CPA practices. Blacks don't enjoy such relationships.

From Economic Violence to Equal Opportunity

In our society there is much talk about the periodic violence—physical violence—that arises out of frustration, and there is every reason for concern about this problem. However, seldom is real consideration given to the social and economic violence visited upon segments of our society ad infinitum. The underutilization of a black professional is a form of economic violence. Underprivileged blacks no longer have a monopoly on the frustration, anger and despair brought about by inequality. Few middle-class blacks continue to believe that all one need do is become educated in order to "make it." This distrust results from decades of unfulfilled promises—a historical pattern of deception that continues to permeate our society.

The public accounting profession has some of the most brilliant minds in the world. CPAs successfully assist clients in the solution of the most intricate business problems. With this kind of talent, the public accounting profession should be able to provide leadership in the quest for equal opportunity in the business community and indeed in the nation. The fact that 96 per cent of the respondents to NABA's survey rated their firms "fair to outstanding" overall offers much hope for the future.

Notes

[1]At the time of publication of this article, William Aiken was Senior Accountant at Arthur Young & Company in New York City. He served on the Community Affairs Committee and the Insurance Committee of the New York State Society of CPAs. He was also president of the National Association of Black Accountants and a member of the AICPA. Mr. Aiken received his M.B.A. degree from the Bernard M. Baruch College in New York City.

[2]The complete study, entitled *The Black Experience in Large Public Accounting Firms*, may be obtained from the National Association of Black Accountants, P.O. Box 726, FDR Post Office Station, New York, N.Y. 10022 for $5.

Employment Programs
for Minorities

An Organizational Analysis of Manpower Issues in Employing the Disadvantaged

ELMER H. BURACK[1]
F. JAMES STASZAK
GOPAL C. PATI

This paper draws attention to the relevance of factors in both the external and internal environment on organizational efforts to incorporate the disadvantaged into the workforce.

Of particular importance to the success of such endeavors is an awareness of the differences which arise from institutional affiliation. Institutional differences exert a major influence on policies and procedures relating to manpower planning, e.g., recruitment, selection, and training.

INTRODUCTION

In recent years, increasing attention has been directed to the problems of employing the disadvantaged; unfortunately, many of these attempts have been accompanied by considerable tension and inept approaches. Problems in this area are multidimensional [9, pp. 144] and need rational, systematic analyses [26, p. 1] to reduce the economic hardships of the underprivileged living in crisis cities [18, pp. 7-10] and to facilitate their assumption of a stable role in the "world of work." In general, the word "disadvantaged" refers to an individual who possesses most of the following characteristics: he is poor and has relatively little or no income; he has no job skills; he is undereducated; he is a member of a minority group; and he is probably from a ghetto. Thus, deprivation may move along any combination of economic, educational, and social lines.

Reprinted from *Academy of Management Journal,* 1972, *15*(3), 255-271, by permission of the publisher and the authors.

Although there are numerous individuals representing various minority and ethnic groups who possess the above characteristics, the word "disadvantaged" refers primarily to Blacks in the context of this paper.

FOCUS OF PAPER

This paper focuses on identifying key organizational variables and relationships which influence attempts to assimilate successfully the disadvantaged employee into the workforce of a particular firm. By successful, we mean that they are assimilated to the point that they become a part of the *stable* workforce. Conceptual models are proposed which facilitate identification of those variables important for analysis in various institutional settings and which enhance effective manpower planning and programming. Improvement of performance in this area promises better selection and manpower training from heretofore untapped sources of labor and also responds to deep-seated moral and ethical issues. Clearly, "Manpower planning means considerably more than executive development, multicolored replacement charts, and organizational planning" [30, p. 103]. "Organizations which limit themselves only to these activities will face a paradox" [14, p. 217]. On the one hand, many firms may be experiencing difficulty in acquiring a sufficient supply of skilled and unskilled workers; while on the other hand, unskilled individuals with potential abound in our social and organizational reservoir. In addition, some firms which have employed disadvantaged workers have not been able to retain them or have not been able to establish a motivational basis for good performance. For some employers, plus others who have participated in federal manpower supported programs and some in conjunction with the National Alliance of Businessmen, organized approaches are signaled which preserve the dignity of job applicants and raise the chances for their success. However, unfortunately, failures or inadequate programming abound, and it will be one of the purposes of this paper to identify some of the underlying difficulties.

Techniques currently being applied by many officials in business and government in recruiting, selecting, and utilizing the disadvantaged are inadequate [23, p. 66]. And, the problems continue—for example, the topics discussed at a large, recent (Summer 1971) meeting on problems of the disadvantaged confirm that these problems continue to persist. Lack of prior experience and attempts to apply existing prescriptions and knowhow compound the difficulty in developing operational programs tailored to the specifics of a given concern. Generalization of existing knowledge and perspectives is limited, for what has been successful in one situation may not be applicable in another (our research supports this contention).

The subject matter of this paper is developed in the following order: first, environmental external variables are identified which impinge on an organization and affect the incorporation and utilization of the disadvantaged; next, employee interaction patterns and relationships are examined; third, models are set forth which incorporate the elements of the initial analysis and which facilitate the interpretation of preliminary findings from our research. Finally, some implications are drawn for officials and managers in manpower planning, programming, and the administration of human resources—e.g., "personnel."

Preliminary findings from three different organizational settings (in-service units, manufacturing, and government) assist in developing the subject matter of our analyses.

The Influence of Legislation

The philosophy and activities of the government have been instrumental in establishing the milieu within which organizations operate. During the 1960's, 27 programs [13; 25] were established—to an important extent these provided this basis of our nation's posture on manpower policy. Important acts included the Area Redevelopment Act (1961) and the Manpower Development and Training Act (1962) [6, p. 1]. The passage of the Civil Rights Act (1964), with its equal opportunity clause, further crystallized the national posture toward a national manpower policy. Of particular interest here was the freeing-up of governmental funds to support private sector programs, compliance-reporting under "equal opportunity," and the establishment of groups such as the National Alliance of Businessmen (NAB) to encourage the participation of private enterprise.

Although several notable programs were established by private firms without the "assistance" of the government or NAB, groups such as NAB have emerged as a potent force in the growing pressure on private business organizations to adopt a posture of increased social consciousness and responsibility, as well as economic return (*albeit,* a modest one), by participation in federally funded efforts.

Labor Market

Company (institutional) employment policies and practices are influenced to a great degree by the characteristics of the labor market. The numbers, composition, and location of the labor force greatly affect the type and magnitude of problems confronted by a particular firm in employing the disadvantaged.

Organizations located in small cities or in suburban areas often encounter problems which differ from those of their counterparts in large urban centers. Typically, the poor and unskilled do not live in the suburbs; thus, they must be transported to these locations—mobile middle- and upper-class families are a frequent source of labor supply in these areas. Travel time, cost of travel, and availability of adequate transportation are matters of concern to the institution and to the disadvantaged workers. Hiring and travel problems are reinforced by area unemployment patterns. Frequently, the composition and intensity of unemployment varies between the urban center and suburbs or smaller municipalities. Organizations located in smaller cities may face labor shortages at a time when unemployment prevails in the big cities.

It is widely recognized that periods of labor shortage or labor surplus exert an important influence on an organization's employment policies. During periods of labor shortages, firms frequently lower their selection criteria; whereas, in periods of labor surpluses, firms are usually more selective. Consequently, the condition of the labor market influences the organization's general hiring policies as well as its selection criteria and posture toward employing the disadvantaged. Although these environmental considerations bear significantly on employing the disadvantaged, internal institutional forces are equally significant.

INSTITUTIONAL VARIABLES

It seems clear that the successful incorporation of the disadvantaged into the organization is closely related to the outlook and understanding of company policymakers and management officials. The groups are instrumental in defining the character of daily work activities and establishing the broader features of the work environment. Figure I illustrates the system of relationships and the role of top management, first-line supervisors, and the disadvantaged employee.

Figure I clarifies the importance of top management support and commitment to the success of a company's manpower program for the disadvantaged. Positive cues, deeds, and active support are central to confronting procedural and attitudinal problems. Lack of top management policy and support frequently results in dual recruiting standards for unskilled and managerial personnel [2, pp. 818-822]. A notion persists among many managers and recruiters that minority people are something "less" and that they are poorly motivated for successful performance. Consequently, many minority members remain undiscovered at the bottom of the organizational hierarchy or in the ghettos. For those who are discovered, "tokenism" is not an infrequent result.

Figure I

Influence of Important Organizational Groups on Behaviorally Related Problems of the Disadvantaged

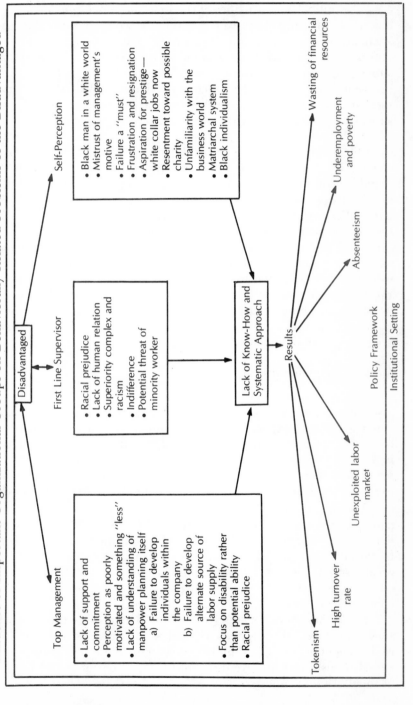

The outlook and activities of the first-line supervisor form a second link in rationalizing the pressures within the work environment. Lack of adequate personal training; insufficient budget support for training recruits; poor individual understanding of a company's program; and a supervisory outlook/attitude which is antagonistic to Black/minority problems [9, pp. 144-152] are factors which clarify "halfway" supervisory measures. Figure I also makes it clear that the situation at the worker-supervisor interface is further strained by the prevalence of attitudes which the minority (disadvantaged) worker manifests. A Black, for example, coming from a ghetto culture characterized by a matriarchal system [18, pp. 7-10] may not be culturally prepared to cope with demands encountered in a predominantly white work environment. The disadvantaged employee often exhibits an attitude of suspicion and mistrust reflecting his perception of the "world of work" in a white society; his lack of motivation reflects frustration and resignation; his pride is hurt; and it is difficult for him to understand why he should cooperate with management when failure is (appears to be) imminent. Some Blacks would like to be placed in a white collar prestige job immediately [22, pp. 101-132] or on realistic job paths leading to promotion rather than working on a blue collar unskilled job with little chance to move up. However, the manpower problems of skill development and promotion are shared with many other workers irrespective of racial considerations.

A More Comprehensive View

The following tabulation (Figure II) brings together key items from this discussion of problems emerging from self-perceptions of the disadvantaged and from expectations of the supervisor and, frequently, the co-worker. Perhaps it need not be said, but the "outcomes" suggested here easily engender racist sentiments among members of the dominant white work force. Although some points may seem obvious, it is instructive to view the entire set to grasp the full impact of the issues involved.

The six points depicted in Figure II made it clear that the sources of poor performance in the work place reflect a multiplicity of considerations and, consequently, require enlightened understanding for their resolution. Elements of tension and frustration, the work ethic of the greater society, and the latent (at times blatant) racist feelings of many of those in the work situation lead to a complex (sometimes explosive) situation in many concerns.

In the next series of discussions, the dynamics of the interactions among management, supervisory, and worker groups within the work environment are examined more closely to further clarify problems here and also to suggest positive directions for improvement and resolution of some of these issues.

Figure II
Some Key Sources of On-the-Job Tensions
and Frustrations for the Disadvantaged Worker

Area of Concern	Outcome
Time orientation	Tardiness, absenteeism, and fall-down on priority projects
Lack of prior job experience and job skills	Extended training time, frustration, seeming lack of interest
Norms and values ascribed to work	Different patterns of language, behavior and dress. Potential alienation from co-worker groups and the social organization
(Myth of) failure syndrome	Easily discouraged, high vulnerability at early point of employment—sulen or apparent, don't-care attitude
Antiestablishment (white) sentiment	Belligerency or sullen compliance
New racial pride	Remaining aloof, fear of "Uncle Tomism"

Interaction Pattern

The successful incorporation of the disadvantaged worker into the organization's workforce hinges on work and social interrelations among the following roles: a) general management, staff member, supervisor or boss; b) co-worker; c) customer-client; d) union official; and e) worker. Thus, the interrelationship between the supervisor and the worker has obvious importance because the supervisor is most often the key in the day-to-day support, operating relationships, expectancies, training, and frustration. The first-line supervisor, in his role of authority figure and trainer, exerts a major influence on the degree of support and confidence felt by the worker. Co-workers and other supervisors often will take their cues from the outlook and conduct of the supervisor of the disadvantaged worker. Co-workers also occupy a vital role in determining the degree of success that the disadvantaged employee achieves. The co-workers, by virtue of their close proximity to and frequent contact with the disadvantaged worker, can extend or withhold support, training, encouragement, assistance, and acceptance.

Clearly, empathy among fellow workers and the presence of a minimal number of (other) disadvantaged workers who can share problems and frustrations constitute basic ingredients for success.

The nature of the tasks to be performed in terms of required education, learnable skills, and physical demands influence the type of employees that the organization will seek to utilize. Interpersonal relationships
and the logic of the work technology determine work dependencies and,
thus, the nature, type, and frequency of problems which emerge. Staff
or support groups and the union constitute additional groups within
company environments which may have to be reckoned with in particular units.

Where worker elements are organized (union), another "partner" is
added to the role system of the organization and, thus, represents an
additional party with which to contend. However, the union is subject to
its own pressures and frustrations; actions (even supportive ones for the
disadvantaged) are subject to the scrutiny of union membership. In
some cases this scrutiny has led to criticism by union members and claims
of "favoritism." In this instance, the presence of unions (especially in
manufacturing) may compound the effects of change through the impo-
sition of selection criteria, transfer provisions, and (traditional) emphasis
on seniority as a basis for training, promotion, transfer, and layoff.
Enlightened approaches are indicated here if the disadvantaged are to
survive and grow. Union-management commitment must be translated
into tangible contract provisions, and conflicting issues must be resolved
prior to employing the disadvantaged.

At a more general level, the relative importance of particular (roles
and) role relationships reflects the relative numbers of personnel
involved in these activities and the contribution of the relationship or
work activity to goal achievement in particular organizational environments. It is important to keep in mind that the focus in probing role relationships pertains to such matters as training needs, conflict potential, or
approximating the extent to which individual change is required. Viewing job roles and role systems within particular institutional settings provides a basis for establishing models which assist in crystallizing problems
and provides directions for remedial approaches. Some of the important
points of this discussion are summarized in Figure III, which depicts
combinations of institutional settings and job demands and, thereby, the
work-related interactions emerging in these environments. One of the
points that emerges from Figure III suggests, for example, that banks
and insurance companies tend to impose similar job demands in terms
of intellectual and physical requirements and social interaction/com-
munications. Yet, both of these institutional settings differ from those
often found in retailing and manufacturing settings—however, both of
these in turn differ in dominant interaction patterns, especially as these
patterns pertain to the client or consumer. Admittedly, these are general
characteristics, but they do suggest the close scrutiny required of vari-

Figure III
Taxonomy of Jobs in Different Institutional Settings

Institutional Settings	Intellectual	Job Demands+ Physical	Social Interaction and Communication	Good Housekeeping*
	Hi - Lo	Hi - Lo	Hi - Lo	Hi - Lo
Banks	X	X	X	X
Insurance	X	X	X	X
Retailing	X	X X	X	X
Manufacturing	X	X	X	X

*Good Housekeeping refers to timeliness and punctuality, how to get to work, etc.

ous job attributes to the extent that these are affected by institutional mission.

A final point concerns additional factors which apply irrespective of institutional or job circumstances. It has already been noted that the supervisor plays a critical role in heightening tensions or ameliorating pressures which abound within the work environment. This observation is part of a more general point—various organizational personalities at all organizational levels are influential in establishing climate characteristics and receptivity in the organization. For example, the supervisor's boss often has a dominant, sometimes pervasive influence on the posture of the supervisor.

In the next section, the models and observations which have been developed are extended, based on several pilot studies we have carried out in: (a) a large firm producing heavy equipment based on mass production principles; (b) a large food retailer with numerous outlets; and (c) a governmental agency.

Extending the Models

In the food retailer example (as well as in department stores and other similar service settings), work-related interaction patterns on the selling floor were characterized by frequent contacts with supervisors, co-workers, and clientele. This is an area of work activity where the disadvantaged worker is highly visible. *Direct and frequent contact* with the organization's clientele places additional pressure on the trainee, his co-workers, and supervisors, especially in a white community or where important segments of the (influential) customer clientele are white. Lack of experience or finesse in socially acceptable dress and mannerism contribute to these tensions. Customers, accustomed to prompt and efficient service, often lack patience and consideration. At the same time, the store in its zeal to place minority/disadvantaged workers in store work, may convey a "visible image" of compliance with Fair Employment Practices and community norms of desired action, but may fail to properly train these new work-force entrants. Consequently, higher intellectual, social (at times), and housekeeping requirements (see Figure III), compounded by the direct relationship with the clientele, add a critical dimension to the service organizations contemplating the initiation of a program to employ the disadvantaged.

On the other hand, the work system of manufacturing organizations is often characterized by unskilled, manual duties requiring less educational inputs and heightened physical requirements (see Figure III). Of course, various departments of service organizations also may stress operations requiring less qualified people. Note that in back-end operations or supportive units of service operations, such as docks and warehouses, client interactions are not part of the needed communication patterns. In this sense, interaction demands are reduced in this area. Work-related interactions, limited to co-workers and the immediate supervisor, closely parallel the technology or work flow.

In both department stores and retail food stores, female employees dominate the selling operations, whereas male employees dominate the supportive services (such as warehousing where physical requirements frequently preclude the use of female employees). Also, large numbers of male employees are found in the heavy work or unattractive (to whites) areas of manufacturing organizations. Females generally are more committed to the "world of work" because of their matriarchal-cultural background; they are more stable employees, and they display relative disinterest in promotional opportunities. Thus, female disadvantaged workers may achieve measurably greater acceptance than the male.

The manufacturing organization may display widely varying cross-currents in the utilization and acceptance of disadvantaged workers. It is not unusual for a workforce to embody a good number of minority workers (in lower level jobs). Consequently, the enculturation process for entry level jobs may be eased in some manufacturing organizations where minority employees are already workforce members. Of course, in some cases, although minority groups may be employed, lines have been sharply drawn to restrain mobility and social interaction. Moreover, those who have worked with the NAB in seeking new employers for the disadvantaged would be quick to suggest that most of the inroads are in the name companies with high community or society visibility. The large mass of medium- and small-sized firms remains largely untouched.

Physical Dispersion of Organization

The physical deployment of facilities is another factor affecting the type and number of problems arising in employing the disadvantaged. Decentralization is a characteristic of many service organizations, reflecting the geographical dispersion of their markets which necessitates establishing semiautonomous units in both urban and suburban areas. The problems which can arise from the existence of multiple outlets are illustrated below:

> *Large retail food chains* represent a case in point, albeit an extreme case of decentralization, as these chains may have more than 100 outlets in a relatively limited geographical area. The exaggerated decentralization of these retail food stores poses significant difficulties in the placement and training of the disadvantaged. The initial placement, as well as subsequent changes in assignment of disadvantaged workers emphasizes the logistics problems confronting decentralized organizations. The large number of dispersed outlets poses difficulties in training as it is common practice for retail food organizations to provide training at individual outlets, yet with each phase of the training provided in a different outlet. In addition to the logistics problem, several other problems compound the provision of training in a centralized facility. First, outlets are usually open for 70-80 hours per week, which necessitates staggered work scheduling. It is unlikely, therefore, that all trainees will have identical work schedules because their schedules will have to be co-ordinated with those of other employees. Secondly, retail food store operations are characterized by a low profit margin which obviates the hiring of "extra" personnel to cover for employees undergoing training—typically, training is on-the-job and emphasis is placed on "paying their own way as soon as possible."

The exposure to a new environment in the course of training may be viewed as a challenge and an opportunity to advance by the employee who has developed positive work attitudes and has had the family, cultural, and educational background to be self-supportive and confident in a new environment. However, to the disadvantaged employee the prospect of leaving a familar environment, in addition to the demands of learning new duties and establishing new relationships, presents an almost insurmountable task.

Also, pressures from being located in a predominantly white community provide added complications. Thus, the institutional setting and demands of the service organization impose rather severe pressure on the disadvantaged trainee.

This section completes our description of environmental considerations, institutional mission, and structure and interaction patterns viewed as providing insights into the problems of employing the disadvantaged. In the next section, some implications of these analyses are presented.

IMPLICATIONS

One of the important perspectives to develop in seeking more structured approaches to employing the disadvantaged is to assume a systems perspective and to consider the achievement of stable employment as a goal of a manpower delivery process.

Figure IV presents a broad view of a manpower "delivery" process which serves to identify major stages where expectations and performance of the disadvantaged are shaped by various organizational groups. This exhibit also depicts some of the many formal and social relationships previously discussed that have to be established, or strengthened, in order to gain a permanent workforce member. The ability *successfully* to deliver appropriate numbers and types of hirees suitably trained to assume roles in the permanent job structure defines the needs of this manpower processing system. For example, in the initial stage (A), the male-female mix is adjusted to meet requirements of the job mix, but also with an eye toward absenteeism and turnover. Yet, it is important to note that in this stage management establishes initial employee expectations of job demands and possibilities, as well as possible hostility, support, or congeniality in the organization's environment. These clearly have a direct bearing on the character of manpower problems subsequently encountered in the job system. In prejob or preemployment processing (B), akin to some areas of "vestibule" training, major strides may be made in orienting new workforce entrants to the social and job milieu. This can provide the needed basics (orientation and work habits for example) in the "world of work" and elementary educational skills to help solidify chances for job-holding, let alone mobility and promotion. This stage is featured by many social and employment imperatives which are generally applicable, plus other imperatives which are particular to specific institutional needs. Development of a support system concept is a key to successful incorporation of the disadvantaged into the permanent workforce because it helps ensure the identification of key tension points, program objectives, and the necessary policy support and program relationships for success. Support systems include orientation procedures, training, counseling on personal matters, and opening up communication channels to various institutional personnel and offices. Participants in the support system include coaches, counselors, "buddies" [21, p. 230], training instructors, personnel managers, recruiters, supervisors, co-workers, and, most importantly, top management. Top management support is crucial for employment success, because, as one company representative stated, "We tend to do what is *in*spected, not what is *ex*pected." Participants in the support system, particularly the training instructor, frequently assume the role of counselor and must develop a rapport with the trainee in order to achieve an atmosphere of

Figure IV

The Employment Cycle and Manpower Planning for the Disadvantaged

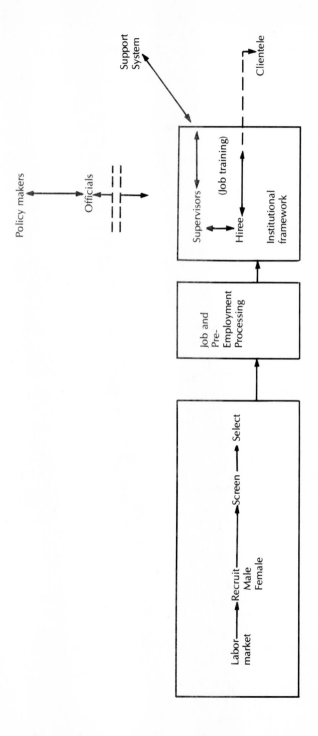

acceptance, trust, and confidence. It is well to note that the supervisor frequently guides training, and substantial variation can emerge in employee preparation due to the competence of various supervisors and their attitudes towards trainees.

Thus far, efforts to recruit "hard-core" have been singularly unsuccessful. Most successes reported have been with those who, in addition to meeting government classification criteria, also possess positive work attitudes and are frequently heads of households [11, pp. 148-156]. This concentration on seeking out the disadvantaged with sought-for work habits is often termed "creaming"; the procedure is necessarily limited, and private industry and the government will soon face the task of recruiting the real "hard-core."

Recruitment and Selection

If organizations are to be successful in confronting employment problems, they must develop effective recruiting and delivery systems, along with a capability to effectively communicate with disadvantaged personnel.

The selection process, as well as the assumptions underlying this process, must be reviewed. The focus of the selection process in the past had been to *screen out* those who lacked the necessary qualifications, often through multilayered interviews and testing procedures. A shift to a *screening-in* posture is imperative if the disadvantaged are to be recruited and given an opportunity to become permanent employees. Interview sessions may be utilized as an orientation vehicle to explain fully the program and potential problem areas to the disadvantaged; emphasis is needed on diagnostics and development. Thus, the emphasis in interviewing is changing from information gathering to providing information—an early developmental training experience.

Another reason for re-examining selection criteria is that experience in dealing with the disadvantaged has proved to professionals in testing and to job analysts that past selection and job criteria were unrealistically established. The following examples illustrate this fact well.

> The results of one study indicate that 80 percent of the 209 disadvantaged employees who entered Lockheed's training program were employable, yet would not have been considered for employment if "regular" selection guidelines had been followed [11, p. 150].

> In the same study, most supervisory complaints concerned poor attendance, whereas supervisors were quoted as saying "Best-trained and most productive men I have ever received," and "These men really want to work, they work hard, and the quality of their work is very good" [11, p. 150].

Personnel officials of a large manufacturing organization when preparing to participate in the program under the auspices of the National Alliance of Businessmen, estimated that the productive efficiency of the disadvantaged employees would only be two-thirds that of regular hires, and their scrap rates would be 50 percent greater. Evaluation of the program after one year revealed that there were little, if any, differences in either production efficiency or scrap rates between the two groups. In general, our own research observations in the three field sites previously described indicated that personnel officials, work analysts, and managers had distorted expectations regarding performance and often poor ideas of the "actual" requirements of office and factory jobs.

It is important that techniques be developed to diagnose effectively each trainee's individual needs. Although the disadvantaged seem to encounter little, if any, difficulty in learning job skills, they frequently bring problems to the work place (adjusting to work, financial problems, or transportation) which require sensitivity and understanding on the part of the employing organization.

Training

It is important to recognize that training needs frequently encompass broader areas than those previously encountered in the past. These requirements may include work skills, basic educational development, technical training, and enculturation requirements. Government-assisted programs have been a major factor in meeting educational requirements in such areas as basic math and linguistic skills. On-the-job training and training in "pilot operations" or under-simulated conditions have been important approaches in teaching technical skills—new training technologies such as programmed instruction also evidence possibilities for these accomplishments. Interestingly, new training approaches which have been sought-out have proved to be, in some cases, highly effective for all workforce entrants and have been adopted.

The process of enculturation is a major challenge which is not readily accomplished. No small part of the problem related to deep-seated racism on the part of supervisors and co-workers. Practical compromises have often evolved where top management has made it clear to the organization that it intends to actively support and develop a successful employment program. This approach acknowledges that attitudes may be slow to change, but it establishes a middle ground which is based on performance of the disadvantaged worker. In short, where training and support lead to acceptable work patterns on the part of the new employee, this constitutes the basis for success or acceptance—unrealistic objectives are (temporarily) set aside regarding attitudinal shifts.

Providing programs for upgrading incumbent personnel is necessary for "it is understandable that employees who have worked in the industry for a long time with little or no advancement up the career ladder might oppose recruitment of 'outsiders' and resent special help given new recruits to assist them in adjusting to jobs" [15, pp. 130-144]. One of the most notable programs for upgrading incumbent employees was pioneered by the steel companies and leaders in the steelworkers union [15, pp. 130-144]. In short, both training and upgrading must be viewed in a broad sweep, undertaking manpower planning and programming which has the promise of major benefits for all employees.

Manpower Planning and Programming

Programs to employ the disadvantaged dramatize deficiencies in effective manpower planning. New dimensions to "old" problems require that top management establish a manpower policy and program which seeks to provide meaningful jobs and well-prepared people. A major feature of the manpower planning approach is that of contending with change by analyzing its thrust and communicating to top management how the scope of duties, responsibilities, and relationships of various positions will be affected. Then appropriate programs must be formulated. Thus, the organizational variables and interrelationships which uniquely influence a particular organization's success in attempting to incorporate disadvantaged employees into their permanent workforce can be more effectively delineated through the systematic analysis of both the organization's institutional setting and its technical and work systems.

SUMMARY AND CONCLUSIONS

The intent of this paper is to provide a method for more systematically analyzing organizational variables and interrelationships critical to the effective assimilation of the disadvantaged into the organization's permanent workforce. The institutional setting determines the environment within which the organization will conduct its operations; the nature of its relationships with external groups, such as clients or customers; and the manner in which the organization is influenced by the activities of political, social, economic, and competitive groups.

Internally, the technical and work systems characterizing the organization influence the composition of the work force, the content of work assignments, and the nature and frequency of the trainees' interaction patterns. Thus, organizational variables and interrelationships which uniquely influence a particular organization's success in attempting to incorporate disadvantaged employees into their permanent workforce can be more effectively delineated through systematic analysis of the organization's institutional setting, key role participants, and its technical and work systems.

In retrospect, it appears that the only organizations that have initiated programs to employ the disadvantaged thus far have been either large private organizations or government agencies. The costs incurred in training, as well as the staffing requirements, impose serious economic constraints on the smaller organizations seeking increased involvement.

To date, only nominal success has been achieved in the employment of the disadvantaged. Success has been achieved in that many disadvantaged, who would be unemployed in the absence of these programs, are working today. To this extent, the programs have been successful. However, a significant portion of the success achieved thus far has been with the "soft-core"—those who possess positive job attitudes and are on the threshold of being productive employees, needing only the opportunity afforded by these programs.

Many questions remain unanswered. What are the chances for attracting the hard-core? What problems must be resolved before the hard-core can be attracted? What internal support systems will be required if the hard-core are recruited? Possibly the only way to achieve meaningful answers is to establish an advisory group composed of those possessing experience in this area. However, this would require several changes in the existing structure, not the least of which is a change in the legislation to encourage, rather than forbid, collaboration by competing organizations.

Note

[1]Elmer H. Burack was Professor of Management, Stuart School of Management, Illinois Institute of Technology, at the time of publication of this article; F. James Staszak was Associate Professor of Management and Dean of the College of Business Administration, Lewis College, Lockport, Illinois; Gopal C. Pati was Assistant Professor of Business Administration at Lewis College.

References

1. Ackley, Gardner, "The Corporation and Government," *Proceedings Report of a Symposium on the Corporation and Social Responsibility* (Chicago: University of Illinois, 1967).
2. Adams, Patricia, and Alice E. Kiddler, "The Black MBA—Not Qualified—or Misunderstood?" *Personnel Journal* (1969).
3. Bell System and the City, "Ghetto School and Ghetto Youth," "The Study Helpers," "Wrong Ways to Find Jobs for Negroes," *1* (1968).
4. _____, "Remedial Education for Those Who Need It," *2* (1969).
5. Burack, Elmer H., and Gopal C. Pati, "Technology and Managerial Obsolescence," *MSU Business Topics, 18* (1970).
6. Doeringer, Peter B., *Programs to Employ the Disadvantaged* (Englewood Cliffs, N.J.: Prentice-Hall, 1969).

7. Elwart, B. E., "Can Business Respond to the Social Needs?" *Proceedings Report of a Symposium on the Corporation and Social Responsibility* (Chicago: University of Illinois, 1967).

8. Gilmer, B. S., "Business Involvement in Urban Problems; A Look at One Company's Search for a Solution," *Business Horizon, 11* (1968).

9. Goeke, Joseph R., and Caroline S. Weymar, "Barriers to Hiring Black's," *Harvard Business Review, 47* (1969).

10. Hearns, Jakie P., "New Approaches to Meet Post-Living Difficulties of Disadvantaged Workers," *Proceedings of the 21st Annual Winter Meeting, Industrial Relations Research Association* (1968).

11. Hodgson, James D., and Marshall H. Brenner, "Successful Experience: Training Hard-Core Unemployed," *Harvard Business Review, 46* (1968).

12. Litterer, J. A., *The Analysis of Organization* (New York: John Wiley and Sons, 1965).

13. Mangum, G. L., *The Emergence of Manpower Policy* (New York: Holt, Rinehart, and Winston, Inc., 1969).

14. Marks, Samuel B., "Employers' Techniques for Upgrading Low-Skill People," *Proceedings of the 21st Annual Winter Meeting, Industrial Relations Research Association* (1968).

15. McCauley, J. Scott, "The Corporate Steel Industry Education Program," in Peter B. Doeringer, ed., *Programs to Employ the Disadvantaged* (Englewood Cliffs, N.J.: Prentice-Hall, 1969) 130-144.

16. McFarland, Dalton E., *Management: Principle and Practices* (New York: Macmillan Co., 1970).

17. Miller, Arjay, "The Corporation and Society: Private Purposes and Public Responsibilities," *Proceedings Report of a Symposium on the Corporation and Social Responsibility* (Chicago: University of Illinois, 1967).

18. Moore, L. W., "Urban Unrest—Whose Problem Is It?" *California Management Review, 11* (1969).

19. *New York Times, 4* (January 11, 1970).

20. "Opening a New Horizon," *Nation's Business* (1970).

21. Pagano, Jules, "Union-Management Adaptation to Needs of Disadvantaged New Employees," *Proceedings of the 21st Annual Winter Meeting, Industrial Relations Research Association* (1968).

22. Piore, Michael J., "On-the-Job Training in the Dual Labor Market: Public and Private Responsibilities in On-the-Job Training of the Disadvantaged Workers," in Weber, Cassel and Ginsberg, *Public-Private Manpower Policies, Industrial Relations Research Association Series* (1969).

23. Purcell, Theodore V., "Breakdown Your Employment Barriers," *Harvard Business Review, 46* (1968).

24. Raskin, A. H. "The Labor Movement Must Start Moving," *Harvard Business Review, 48* (1970).

25. Rezler, Julius, *Automation and Industrial Labor* (New York: Random House, 1969).

26. Stanford Research Institute, "Minority Manpower Planning," Report #342 (1968).

27. Stetson, D., "Builders and Unions Here Offer Minority Training," *New York Times* (March 22, 1970).

28. Taylor, David P., "Discrimination and Occupational Wage Differential in the Market for Unskilled Labor," *Industrial and Labor Relations Review, 21* (1968).

29. "Technology and the American Economy," *Report of the National Commission on Technology, Automation and Economic Progress* (Washington, D.C.: U.S. Government Printing Office, 1966).

30. Vetter, Eric W., "How to Forecast Your Manpower Needs," *Nation's Business* (1964).

31. Weigle, Lester J., "The Growing Problem of Executive Obsolescence," *Dun's Review and Modern Industry* (1965).

Affirmative Action Program:
Its Realities and Challenges

GOPAL C. PATI[1]
PATRICK E. FAHEY

With the advent of governmentally-imposed affirmative action plans, it is hoped that minorities will receive a greater share of the national economy. However, companies operating under such plans face never-before-encountered problems in accomplishing their duties. Where does one find qualified minority employees? Must incompetents be hired to satisfy the specified goals? What is the cause of the hostility and resentment some recruiters receive when contacting potential minority employees? Add these questions to the simmering internal discontent of the company's own middle line supervisors and the end result can approach panic—a lost federal contract is an economic blow. The authors examine the situation faced by modern business in complying with federal minority hiring goals.

Managers in many business organizations are increasingly feeling the impact of public policy in many functional areas of management.[2] This has created an unusual fermentation of mixed feelings of hope and frustrations. It has been further compounded by the complexities and ineptness of the technological society which has demanded an unprecedented emphasis on human resource utilization and development.[3] As a matter of fact, in the last several years it has been the area of manpower planning and development in general, and equal employment opportunities in particular, where the role of government has been increasingly observed.[4] Many government-initiated and supported programs to

Reprinted from *Labor Law Journal*, June 1973, *24*(6), 351-361, by permission of the publisher and the authors.

ameliorate poverty, unemployment and wastage of human resources have generated numerous kinds of anxieties, debate and bewilderment among educators and practitioners. The affirmative action program is that part of the public policy which has induced many organizations to undertake a more vigorous approach to reach out for members of the minority groups, who have been traditionally left out as a consequence of socio-economic deprivation. More specifically the objective here has been to provide them with training, jobs and an opportunity to share the fruits of our economic system, thereby enabling them to assimilate themselves better in the greater participating democracy.

The experience of the last several years in the area of affirmative action program has been characterized by learning, relearning, and adjusting to things unheard of before, and clearly indicates the ineptness of many approaches to meet the great challenge. This has also required tremendous change in internal organization, values, climate and many organizational adjustments that were not thought of before. Consequently, the objective of this paper is not only to point out these changes and challenges, but also to point out the bumpy roads and detours that have been encountered by managers within the last several years. The issues to be examined will not only have implications for traditional personnel functions and practices but also for an unprecedented philosophical change that a corporation will have to undertake in order to keep up its commitment to the government and society.

LEGAL REQUIREMENTS IN PERSPECTIVE

On July 2, 1965, Title VII of the Civil Rights Act of 1964 became effective. Title VII "Equal Employment Opportunity" covers companies, labor organizations, and employment agencies. It *prohibits* discrimination because of race, color, religion, sex or national origin. During the 1971 Fiscal Year, the Equal Employment Opportunity Commission (EEOC), established by Title VII as the primary federal enforcement agency for the Civil Rights Acts, received 22,920 new charges. This was a substantial increase over the 14,129 charges received during the previous fiscal year.[5]

Under the 1964 law, the EEOC was limited to "informal methods of conference, conciliation and persuasion" unless the Department of Justice concluded that a person or practice of resistance to Title VII was involved. If the employers refused to accept the conciliation conditions, it was the individual victim of discrimination who carried the burden of obtaining an enforceable court order.

Under the recently signed "Equal Employment Act of 1972," the EEOC, if unable to secure an acceptable agreement within thirty (30) days, may bring action in a U.S. District Court. In addition to the above, other provisions of the "Equal Employment Act of 1972" include: coverage of state and local government agencies, coverage of educational institutions, coverage of employers of fifteen (15) or more persons and labor unions with fifteen (15) or more members. The latter coverage is effective March 24, 1973.

The changes enacted by the "Equal Employment Act of 1972" will make increasingly stringent demands on employers in the future.

The other federal agency with jurisdiction in the field of employment discrimination is the Office of Federal Contract Compliance (OFCC). The authority of the OFCC is derived from Presidential Orders 11246 and 11375. These orders resulted from the government's decision to use its immense purchasing and regulatory powers to enforce equal employment opportunity.

A federal contractor, which term includes virtually every employer with a contractual, financial, or regulatory relationship with the federal government, is required to go beyond the prohibition to discriminate under the Civil Rights Act. The contractor must take "affirmative action," that is, results-oriented activities, not mere passive compliance.

The Office of Federal Contract Compliance has shifted the burden of proof from the government to the contractor and made eligibility for government contracts, services, financing, etc., dependent on compliance with OFCC guidelines.

Previously "Order #4" and currently "Order #14" set forth the components of an acceptable written affirmative action program, the basis for the compliance review.

An acceptable affirmative action program must include an analysis of minority and female participation in all levels of the organization to determine if minorities or women are being underutilized. Underutilization is defined as "having fewer minorities or women in a particular job category than would be reasonably expected by their availability."[6] Once the deficiencies are identified, the contractor must set goals and time-tables to which good-faith efforts will be directed to increase the utilization of minorities and women at all levels where deficiencies exist.

Despite the confusion caused by President Nixon's declaration against quotas in his renomination speech on August 24, 1972, it is improbable that the current method of goal setting will be abandoned. Though the difference between goal and quota might be subtle, it is generally accepted that a goal is a reasonable objective based on the availability of qualified people and a quota would restrict employment opportunities to members of a specific group without regard to qualification.

Emerging Trend

The above material provides a framework and perspective for understanding the role of government in the personnel decisions and suggests the kind of direction a manager will have to take in reexamining his own values and then reconciling these with those of corporate philosophy and posture in the area of manpower planning and development. Furthermore, it definitely indicates the emergence of more stringent rules and regulations as an answer to the partial failure of many organizations in achieving the result-oriented goals of the affirmative action program. The spirit and the realities of the regulations require that it is not just the personnel manager or department that has to carry the burden, but line and operating managers will also have to do their share to achieve the company objectives. In other words, it does affect the whole organization.

More specifically, this means that the operating manager will have to do things that he has never done before and yet his organization is demanding that he: (1) modify his recruitment, selection and testing policies; (2) vigorously and systematically reassess his training needs and criteria; (3) rechannel his training and developmental facilities and faculty; (4) become involved in better manpower inventory, manpower audit and control. He is further responsible for doing these things within the limitation of budget, without duplicating effort and coordinating better with the federal and state program without annihilating organizational climate. This requires not only broadening the knowledge base of individual managers, but also a serious effort in defrosting old ideas, relearning new developments and refreezing this newly learned knowledge to be useful in organizational growth. Thus, this challenge can only be met by more aggressive consolidation of managerial expertise supplemented by a strong corporate commitment.

RECRUITMENT

The immediate impact of AAP and the EEOC regulations has necessitated broadening the base of manpower supply. The basic objective of a traditional recruitment and selection policy has been to get the most qualified people at the least cost from those traditional sources which would be consistent with the organizational way of life in meeting the needs of the available job openings. The frequently used external sources have been (1) employee referrals, (2) private employment agencies, (3) walk-in recruiting, (4) newspaper ads, (5) major senior colleges and universities, (6) (to a lesser extent) vocational and correspondence schools. The traditional internal sources have been (1) transfer, (2) promotion, (3) job upgrading, without giving much attention to the potential of minority manpower within the organization.

Indeed, these sources once served their purpose in the past and still are doing so; however, in light of the developments in the area of reaching new elements of manpower these traditional sources may not be adequate. Consequently, the following sources are emerging as the kind of places that the employers are increasingly contacting to find people as required by the law:

1) Urban league offices,
2) Individual ministers and local religious organizations,
3) Minority-oriented media,
4) Senior and junior colleges with large minority populations,
5) Schools in the inner cities,
6) Local Spanish-American organizations,
7) Trade schools (more vigorously used now),
8) Women's organizations,[7]
9) Agencies dealing with correctional manpower.

As a consequence of this enlargement of the recruitment base, companies are definitely seeing more people to meet legal requirements as well as corporate ethic.

However, the rejection rate is usually high which can lead to many uneasy moments during a compliance review.

One company provided the following information which illustrates the difficulties that might arise as organizations appeal to minority-oriented agencies to fulfill their affirmative action commitments. During the effective period of an affirmative action program, the rejection rate for black female hourly applicants was 80 per cent while the rejection rate for white female hourly applicants was 68 per cent.

Though it certainly does not account for the entire disparity in rejection rates between black and white applicants, one statistic does give some insight into the depth of the problem employers are currently facing. In job categories for which a typing test meets the OFCC requirements for testing, the average black female applicants ($N = 70$) typed 30 WPM—approximately 25 per cent below the average typing speed of the remainder of the applicant population.

Furthermore, many agencies do refer people without any skills who miserably fail to meet even the minimum requirements of the company. When qualified individuals are available, frequent lack of transportation to a suburban plant location may prevent them from even appearing for an interview. In addition, many agencies are often speculative about their knowledge of job availability and send applicants to plants without any job openings, creating frustration for many individuals. Needless to say, there is a steep competition among the companies themselves to attract the best qualified personnel available. Consequently, some companies in the area are facing difficulty even in gaining entrance to an organization or institution which might have qualified minority manpower.

Confrontation with the new types of manpower and the sources has also caused reconsideration of the qualification of company recruiters. Today, a recruiter has to be a person who understands the minority culture; if not, at least make an attempt to understand and be sensitive to the needs of divergent groups. Several examples will clarify this point. In one instance a company representative went to a Spanish-American organization meeting to recruit. Ironically, no one spoke English and the entire meeting was conducted in Spanish. The recruiter could not communicate with the prospects and he returned to his office, of course, without recruiting anyone. The second example is of the case of a recruiter who went to a prominent black educational institution only to be asked "what the hell are you doing here?"[8] In another instance at a female dominated institution, a recruiter was asked about the real intention of the company for recruiting females. More specifically, a question such as, "Why, Honey, suddenly are you interested in us?" baffled the recruiter.

The implications of these examples are crucial. There exists a tremendous amount of mistrust about the real intent of the corporation in hiring minority groups. They are not sure about their future in these organizations where organizational posture of active recruitment is being considered as the ultimate consequence of severe government prodding and pressure rather than a genuine attempt by the organizations to hire them on an equal basis in any real sense. Accordingly, it is imperative that a recruiter know the sensitiveness of the issue, understand the dilemma, and is prepared to represent the corporation and carry on its objectives in spite of the realities of complex attitudinal crisis.

EMPLOYMENT TESTING

One employment procedure that has come under close scrutiny since the 1966 EEOC published guidelines is employment testing.

The field of industrial testing has grown substantially since World War II. Far too often, testing programs have been incorporated in the selection process based only on the "professional judgment" of personnel executives with little or no expertise, or on the recommendation of consultants motivated more by their fee than by the service they provide to industry.

Though the professionals in the field have for decades been recommending validation of personnel tests for their intended purpose, the widespread failure to establish criterion-related validity has resulted not only in the denial of employment to minorities but also in a waste of money. Contrary to generally accepted business practices, top corporate executives have been approving expenditures for testing programs that screen out people who would be productive employees and select people who will be marginal employees at best. Funds are allocated to production, advertising, research, etc., only if a reasonable return is anticipated but this requirement is lacking in the allocation of funds to personnel department testing programs in most cases.

In the U.S. Supreme Court decision *Griggs v. Duke Power Company*,[9] the Court adopted the interpretative guidelines of the EEOC that tests must fairly measure the knowledge or skills required in a job in order not to unfairly discriminate against minorities.

> Nothing in the Act precludes the use of testing or measuring procedures; obviously they are useful. What Congress has forbidden is giving these devices and mechanisms controlling force unless they are demonstrably a reasonable measure of job performance.[10]

The Supreme Court decision in upholding the EEOC guidelines settled much of the confusion centered around test usage. A test can be used only if professionally developed and validated against job performance in accordance with the standards found in *Standards for Educational and Psychological Tests and Manuals*[11] and the burden of proof is placed on the employer in the area of business necessity.

Government contractors subject to the Rules and Regulations of Order #14 are required to provide an analysis of testing practices used in the past six months to determine if equal employment opportunity is being offered in all job categories. This will include the number of men and women acceptable on the test, the number of men and women not acceptable on the test, the same information for Negroes and Spanish-surnamed Americans, American Indians, Orientals and others when the group constitutes 2 per cent or more of the labor market or recruiting area for non-minority men and women. If there is a disparate rejection rate the test must be validated in accordance with the OFCC Testing Order (except for language arising from different legal authority, this order is the same as the EEOC guidelines).

Test validation will not bring about equal employment opportunity but will allow the employer to determine the relationship between the test and job performance and determine the significance of the test as a predictor of job performance for racial, sex or national origin groups. A test that has been validated against job performance, used with other selection or assessment tools, can significantly aid in the development and maintenance of an efficient work force. Such a test does not violate the civil rights law nor is it forbidden by the executive orders.

At this point it seems appropriate to discuss the validation study recently completed by one industrial organization.

A test battery was administered to 165 applicants over a four-month period. Though the battery included five, short, professionally-developed tests and the tests were chosen only after a thorough job analysis by an individual with a graduate degree and experience in both job analysis and testing, only one of the battery met the requirements for test usage.

The job is an inspection job that requires a background in electrical circuitry. The applicants selected for employment are enrolled in a company training school program for eleven days prior to actually starting on the job. During this period each employee is paid approximately $300.00. The selection tools used prior to the test validation study were considered unsatisfactory and the company considered it necessary to find additional tools to reduce the failures in the training school and the turnover on the job. (It should be noted that the training school evaluation was also validated against subsequent job performance by the Pearson product moment coefficient method with a coefficient of .4965.) The sample size was sixty-seven and the coefficient .4965 is significant at the 1 per cent level and satisfies the requirements of both the EEOC and OFCC.

The test was one of the Purdue Vocational Tests with two forms. In the study, Form B was used and Form A would be available for retesting purposes. Though the test carries a twenty-five minute time limit, this was disregarded and it was considered a work limit test.

Number Tested	Mean Score	Race	Enrolled in Training School
108	38.75	Caucasian	52
41	24.92	Negro	13
1	—	Oriental	1
1	—	American Indian	0
14	29.53	Spanish-American	5

The above clearly indicates that the classes protected by Title VII are adversely affected, that is, 48 per cent of Caucasians tested were subsequently enrolled in the training program but only 32 per cent of Negroes and 36 per cent of Spanish-Americans. As there is a disparate rejection rate, the test must be validated. The related criteria considered were (1) training school evaluation and (2) job performance criteria.

The training school evaluation consists of four paper and pencil tests on the subject matter taught during the eleven-day program. As noted previously the correlation coefficient between Training School Evaluation and job performance criteria is .4965.

I. Validity—Test Correlated to Training School Evaluation

$N = 67$
Mean = 39.7
Standard Deviation = 10.2
Correlation Coefficient = .4877

The Pearson product moment method results in a .4877 coefficient which is significant at the 1 per cent level and satisfies the testing requirements.

II. Validity—Test Correlated with Job Performance Criteria

In this case the performance criteria consisted of a thirteen-week average percentage of a standard set by the Time-study Department.

$N = 38$
Mean = 41.2
Standard Deviation = 10.05
Correlation Coefficient = .3788 which is significant at the 5 per cent level and satisfies the requirements of the order and the guideline.

Therefore, it is considered that the above meets the requirements set by the OFCC and EEOC. The authors are aware of the issues not considered above, that is, differential validity, etc. These were part of the study but not noted here.

III. Reliability

The method chosen was the split half estimate. The number in the sample was 158, none of which were retests. The scores of the odd number items were correlated against the even number items by the Pearson product moment correlation coefficient. The resultant correlation coefficient .857 was corrected by the Spearmen Brown formula to correct the reliability coefficient for the full length test to .9229, certainly in the acceptable area for continued test usage.

The test was validated in a period of economic downturn as clearly indicated by the number who successfully completed the training school (59) and the number included in the efficiency study (38). Nineteen employees were transferred out of the inspection group prior to the time meaningful proficiency data was available.

In view of the above, expectancy charts were constructed but a cut-off score was not determined until a later date and was based on "need" for inspectors as well as test score.

Though a complete explanation of the statistical data is not included here, it is obvious that the efforts generated to validate the test will not only reduce costs of failure and turnover, it will also be a more objective evaluation of prospective employees which is expected to increase the chances of minority group members to be selected.

There was not a disparate rejection rate for female applicants and the test validity study did not report validity correlation coefficients by sex.

PROMOTION

Promotional opportunities for minorities and women have been thus far a neglected subject primarily because of the initial emphasis on economic opportunities and its delivery system rather than vertical mobility within the organizational structure. Since some progress has been made in the employment opportunity area, the promotional aspect becomes the next logical step. This is a recent phenomenon and has been effectively dramatized in those organizations with a large population of female employees. An example of this was the recent EEOC charge against the Bell system for lack of females in management level jobs.[12] As a result of this charge and consequent negotiations, Illinois Bell has agreed to promote 2,500 women employees by 1974. On the national level, the AT&T system has agreed to promote 50,000 women into higher paying jobs, including 10 per cent into management posts. Furthermore, 6,600 members of the minority groups will be promoted into higher paying jobs, 12 per cent of them into management. Before specifying the regulations for government contractors in this section, one must pause to consider the significance of the AT&T agreement. If it took eight long months for AT&T to conclude an agreement such as this, other organizations traditionally less committed to equal employment opportunity must now recognize that they cannot ignore this enormous responsibility they are charged with.

The emerging government regulations require government contractors to insure that minority and female employees are given equal opportunity for promotion. Suggestions for achieving this result include: (1) post or announce promotional opportunities, (2) take inventory of current minority and female employees to determine academic skill and experience level of individual employees, (3) initiate remedial training and work study programs, (4) develop and implement formal employee evaluation programs, when apparently qualified minority or female employees are passed over for upgrading and require supervisory personnel to submit written justification, (5) establish formal counseling programs and hold supervision responsible for having qualified and promotable minority or female employees in their organization.

The question of promotional opportunity is a twofold question.

One, minorities have been historically hired in the least desirable jobs, if hired at all. It appears that recruiting minorities for supervisory, technical and clerical jobs is a step in the right direction. It will only be after qualified minorities are on the payroll that the question of promotion will occur. Promotions of minorities must be made on the basis of qualification and potential, not on how well they measure up to some undefined profile that has no proven relationship to job performance. The problem in this area is also related to the structural condition of the economy and the labor market in particular. During recent years there has been little turnover in managerial jobs and new jobs have not been created as anticipated. This has been further compounded by the lack of manpower planning and developmental efforts within organizations and the lack of consideration for people with potential within the organizational reservoir, particularly women and minorities.

Two, qualified women have always been hired but often not on jobs that truly utilize their abilities. To alleviate this problem organizations must open up their training program for females with management potential. Failure to open the facilities to women or minorities will invite stringent rules and regulations imposed by governmental authorities. This means that the burden of proof will not only affect personnel people but other line personnel who will be required to spend a great deal of time in manpower inventory and audit. This will be an additional burden to the line organizational personnel who will have to spend more time and energy in developing human resources, a task for which they are seldom trained.

SUPERVISORY AND CORPORATE ATTITUDE

Perhaps it is the preoccupation with our own frustrations that emotionally isolates us from one another. This is particularly true for many supervisors and foremen who are frustrated because they feel that they are being "left-out" from some of the action of the great society. Affirmative action programs are a traumatic experience for them. To them government pressure signals the practice of dual standard; company commitment appears phony in view of his usual assumption of the role of responsibility without accompanied authority. His own values and his inability to understand the motivation of youth, women and black employees; his own changing neighborhood, his own employer's emphasis upon his reeducation for organizational mobility or survival; increasing economic demand on him to make any significant headway in the inflationary economy—all these baffle him and place him in a very defensive mood. Thus, when the personnel department tries to select people *in,* the foreman seems to select them *out.* The supervisory groups just do not believe that "equal employment opportunity" is really happening and do not believe that the company is serious.

An unprecedented amount of attitudinal modification on the part of the top as well as supervisory groups is necessary if this program has to succeed. A strong support system within the organization is a necessity if any significant progress is intended to be made. And that support system can be developed if,

1) A vigorous organizational renewal program is pursued (at least partially),
2) an organizational development effort is seriously launched,
3) company reassurance of supervisory job security is strengthened,
4) 100 per cent company commitment is demonstrated, and
5) reward is given to the supervisory and various support personnel for their cooperation in an effort to create a better organizational climate.

If the above-mentioned is not being done (and in most cases that we studied it is not), then we should not be surprised about the dubious impact of the action-oriented affirmative action program. First line supervisors in most instances do not know what it takes to make a good worker and performer out of an individual. Under this condition it is very unlikely that a person without training and previous work experience will survive in an organization once hired.

IMPLICATIONS

One, increasingly stringent goals and timetables as well as increased pressure from municipal Human Relations Commissions will emerge in the future. Only with specific goals derived from factual analysis will a company be able to carry the burden of proof against the OFCC and sell the program internally to non-persuaded upper management.

Two, the proposed regulations to require federal contractors to keep records of employees' religious and ethnic background will eventually be adopted in spite of protests from groups that consider such regulations an invasion of privacy.

Three, federal contractors will find it necessary to appoint a full-time Compliance Officer. An effective affirmative action program requires a strong results-oriented executive, not the average impotent personnel executive nor the unqualified token minority, too often administering programs at present.

Four, a considerable amount of money has been spent in recent years to fund neighborhood agencies to train and assist minority group members to secure employment. Many of these organizations have failed miserably. In the future, business organizations must take an interest, both financially and with their training expertise, to ensure that qualified applicants are available from the sources an affirmative action program requires companies to contact.

Five, this indeed is a very sensitive area and will continue to be a serious problem for those organizations who are passive. A strong corporate commitment supplemented by an internal support system will have to be undertaken to live up to the real spirit of the equal employment practices.

Six, in light of our experience in the Midwest it is very clear that recruiting a few warm bodies to meet the legal requirements is not enough. The real spirit of the law requires reevaluation of corporate philosophy, changes in traditional personnel practices, modification of attitude of the operating managers and a type of complete involvement which will help minorities to retain a job and grow within the organization. Otherwise, more interesting laws will be forthcoming.

And finally, with regard to continued progress by minorities in all job categories, comparative data for about 31 million employees covered by 1970 EEO-1 employment reports indicate that since 1966, Negro employment as a proportion of total employment is up 1.9 per cent in total employment, 1.0 per cent among officials and managers, 1.2 per cent in professional category, 2.1 per cent among technicians, 1.9 per cent among sales workers and 3.7 per cent in office and clerical category. Spanish-surnamed Americans and women also showed increases in each of these job categories. While it can be assumed that the percentage gains would have been higher in a more dynamic economy, that is, minorities remain in a great many cases "last in," "first out," our conclusion is that minorities remain grossly underrepresented in the more desirable jobs in industry in spite of law and moral suasion. Furthermore, if we are to use our human resources to their potential, organizations must make total commitments to expend time, money, energy and expertise at least to the extent imparted to the other factors of production, for example, finance, plant acquisitions, technology, etc. If this is not done, the chances of living up to the real spirit of the burgeoning laws is very slim.

Notes

[1] Gopal C. Pati was a senior assistant professor of industrial relations and management at Indiana University Northwest at the time of publication of this article. Patrick E. Fahey was manager of manpower planning and compensation with the Stewart-Warner Corporation.

[2] Leon C. Megginson, *Personnel; A Behavioral Approach to Administration,* Homewood, Illinois, Richard D. Irwin, Inc., 1972, pp. 244-245.

[3] Elmer H. Burack and Gopal C. Pati, "Technology and Managerial Obsolescence," *MSU Business Topics,* Spring, 1970, Vol. 18, pp. 49-56.

[4]Robert A. Gordon, *Toward a Manpower Policy,* New York, John Wiley and Sons, Inc., 1967, also see Garth L. Mangum, *The Emergence of Manpower Policy,* New York, Holt, Rinehart and Winston, Inc., 1968, Elmer H. Burack, *Strategies for Manpower Planning and Programming,* New Jersey, General Learning Press, 1972.

[5]Equal Employment Opportunity Commission, *6th Annual Report,* CCH, Chicago, June, 1972, p. 25.

[6]*Federal Register,* Section 60-2.11, Vol. 36, No. 234, October 4, 1971.

[7]For example, National Organization for Women, Professional Women's Caucus, Talent Bank from Business and Professional Women.

[8]Descriptive adjectives have been omitted in the interest of scholarship.

[9]*"Griggs v. Duke Power Company,"* Labor Law Reports, Commerce Clearing House, Inc., p. 15, 1971. (39 U. S. L. W., 4317)

[10]Ibid.

[11]*Standards for Education and Psychological Tests and Manuals,* Washington, D.C., American Psychological Association, 1966.

[12]Chicago Sun-Times, Thursday, September 21, 1972.

The Dilemma of Black Mobility in Management

Discrimination Still a Problem

ROBERT W. NASON[1]

Increasingly, corporations are feeling pressure to·employ a representative number of blacks (and other minorities) at all levels of management. However, they claim that the limited supply of capable blacks impedes sufficient progress to ease the pressure. This article presents an analysis of the causes of the black mobility problem in an attempt to help corporations develop adequate insight and programs to meet this dilemma. The legacies of overt racism in terms of institutional behavior and deprivation of capability are both subtle and pervasive in their effects on black mobility. If progress is to be made in resolving this dilemma without increased external intervention, then management must understand, with much greater sophistication, their own corporate barriers to black mobility as well as encourage the kind of governmental and private action which will eliminate the roots of black deprivation.

In recent years, considerable discussion has centered on the paucity of blacks in management and their stunted upward occupational mobility. Emotion has often distorted arguments, and symptoms have been held up as causes. Blacks have charged whites and their organizations with discrimination, racism, ignorance, lack of sensitivity, and inhumanity. On the other hand, white employers have complained of the scarcity of qualified blacks, of the inability of blacks to fit productively into their organizations, and of the difficult economic situation which precludes

---

Reprinted from *Business Horizons,* August 1972, pp. 57-68. Copyright © 1972 by the Foundation for the School of Business at Indiana University. Reprinted by permission.

the hiring of more blacks. Both sets of allegations have roots in the immediate problems facing each group, yet both also lack sufficient depth and breadth of understanding to form a sound basis for improvement of the situation.

The objective of this article is to present the parameters which affect the black man and his relationship to the American economic enterprise. It is hoped that a clarity of thinking will result which will bypass the emotion and shallowness that have characterized the debate thus far, for it is misunderstanding of the basic problem that prevents formulation of a sound strategy for resolution. Indeed, the largely ill-founded attempts to achieve equal opportunity in management have often further polarized attitudes and reinforced preexisting biases which continue to obstruct black managerial fulfillment and the utilization of this country's scarce human resources.

Why should business become involved in the correction of such a social problem? Some argue it must become involved because of its social responsibility; others note business' role in the creation of the problem as justification for involvement. As valid as these arguments may be, the increasing pressure of governmental agencies, civil rights agencies, and the general public leave business little option but to become involved.

Before going beyond the allegations leveled on both sides, it is useful to place the problem of black mobility in perspective. The obvious yet little exposed facts are that, relative to nonwhite representation in the population, nonwhites hold a miserly portion of the jobs with managerial content, and those who do hold managerial jobs are paid less than whites, even those with similar educational backgrounds.

The extent of these inequalities is simply demonstrated. Of all managers, officials, and proprietors in 1969 only 3.2 percent were nonwhite. To put this another way, 11.1 percent of the white working population had managerial jobs in 1969, compared to only 3.0 percent of the nonwhite working population. Further, there are few blacks in senior positions. In 1970, in fifty of the nation's largest corporations only three out of 3,182 senior officers and directors were black, and all three were nonofficer directors.[2]

As for the rewards for managerial activity, the accompanying figure shows for 1960 both regional and educational differences between salaries of whites and nonwhites of managers, officials, and proprietors. It should be noted that the average income of college graduate nonwhite managers in the North barely surpasses the average income of white managers with no more than six years of education. Further, for similar levels of education, the average white manager in the six-year education group earns $2,000 more than the average nonwhite manager, and at the college graduate level the average white manager earns $7,000 more than his black counterpart.

Income in Thousands

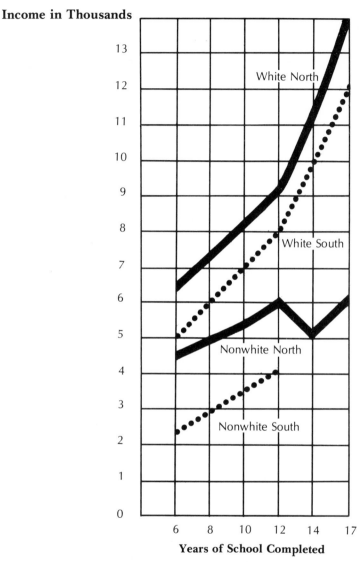

Years of School Completed

SOURCE: Paul M. Siegel, "On the Cost of Being a Negro," in Edwin M. Epstein and David R. Hampton, eds., *Black Americans and White Business* (Encino, Calif.: Dickenson Publishing Company, Inc., 1971), p. 108.

Whatever the reasons, nonwhites, relative to their population, attain vastly fewer managerial positions and earn substantially lower remuneration than do whites. It is the analysis of why this situation exists that forms the thrust of this work. Before proceeding I would like to note that the reduction of the problem to basic units for analysis creates generalizations which do not represent all individuals. Further, I will limit the analysis to blacks and not all minorities as blacks are numerically predominant on the one hand and face somewhat unique forces in America on the other.

ONE STEP BEHIND THE SYMPTOMS

The foundation for the lack of black upward occupational mobility is America's history of individual and organizational discrimination which has kept the growing ranks of the professional manager almost entirely white. Though past managerial discriminatory practices are an accepted fact of our corporate heritage, their current repercussions are generally overlooked.

These repercussions are manifested in current corporate barriers to black mobility through overt discrimination; through the institutionalization of rules, procedures, and behaviors, which has the same effect as overt discrimination though it is indirect and may not be intended; and through impairment of black capability which is essential to upward mobility. Each of these aspects of the problem will be discussed in turn.

Overt Discrimination

It is slowly becoming socially unacceptable today to hold racist attitudes and beliefs, yet such attitudes with strong historical strength are difficult to change in human nature. Thus, it is unrealistic to expect that white managers' attitudes have changed sufficiently in recent years to end overt discrimination in the American corporation.

More likely, the social pressure for civil rights from all sources has modified the observable behavior of white managers. The result is that racism is exerted at a more subtle level and is more difficult to combat. For example, it is easier to combat racially based hiring or promotion policies if they are translated into formal policy by the organizations' managers than if they are informally agreed upon and covered by rationalizations of job qualifications and seemingly objective screening tests.

Institutional Racism

A more subtle deterrent to black mobility is what has become known as institutional racism. In this case, individuals may justifiably feel that they and their fellow managers hold no personal prejudice against blacks, yet there are real barriers to black admission and mobility in management.

It is not the purpose of this article to discuss this topic fully, but it is necessary to illustrate what is meant.

First, most employment tests and screening criteria are standardized for white subjects and subtly place the inner city or rural Southern black at a disadvantage. SAT college entrance examination (to be discussed later) is one example. Also, many of the items on such quantifiable criteria are not relevant to job performance, yet discriminate against minority backgrounds.

For instance, common to almost every job description is the specification of minimum level of formal education. This credential often has little meaning for job performance and may even be dysfunctional where over-education is a requirement. The result is that those with less formal education and certification are needlessly excluded from consideration.[3]

Second, most management blacks do not have access to the informal organization of a firm in the same way as do their white counterparts. Thus, while evaluations become more subjective as more managerial content enters the job, the black has fewer advocates and is often outside the social system which leads others upward.

Third, the mobility of management blacks is stunted by their predominant use in nonline jobs when they do get into management. This is a result of three factors: the white view of the black individual as a representative of his race and thereby its spokesman; the need for the guise of integration because of civil rights organizations, government, and public pressure (for example, tokenism); and the white perception that in many cases blacks can deal with other blacks more easily than can whites, a view that assigns blacks to advisory functions relating to black personnel, black markets, and the community.

Such titles as "Special Assistant to," "In Charge of Special Markets," "Director of Urban Affairs," and "In Charge of Equal Opportunities Employment" clearly show the tangential nature of the jobs and the likely dead end to upward mobility. Even blacks in more central occupations are asked to devote considerable time to public and community relations.

Fourth, the corporation often requires a black applicant to have higher qualifications than comparable whites. It is, at first thought, amazing that even many management blacks join with whites in this search for the "superblack," though on reflection this phenomenon is perfectly logical. The use of higher standards is due to the stigma in our society which has been placed on being black. A white employee who misperforms casts a negative light only on himself, but a black who makes a mistake or is inappropriate for the job for which he was hired casts aspersions on all blacks and reinforces the negative stereotypes leveled against his race.

Thus, a black personnel man in a firm consciously or unconsciously feels that each black he hires must be a sure bet so that the quality of his race and thus his own image will be upheld. Blacks who have sought jobs in management know that the black placement officer is usually tougher on his race than most white personnel interviewers. This dilemma, one not easily resolved, works to the detriment of black upward mobility.

Finally, to the extent that seniority influences promotion, blacks who are generally newer to management are discriminated against. This phenomenon is more visible at operative levels where blacks tend to be laid off first due to lack of seniority.

In summary, for most firms to date, institutional and overt racism renders the commonly used claim "An equal opportunity employer" a mockery. At best, this means that an employer will consider blacks for employment, but that equal opportunity is a long way off. Of course, few blacks would tell an employer directly how he views his mobility potential within the firm for fear of being penalized as a troublemaker, especially since the employer usually feels he has gone out of his way to have the black there in the first place.

However, his thoughts would probably closely parallel the analysis of James Spain in a paper delivered to the Conference on the Role of Black Managers in Society in February, 1970. Spain views the modern corporation as analogous to a plantation where the operatives are the field hands and the management is equivalent to the plantation owner. After discussing the use of black labor, he moves to management:

> Now come up from the fields and raise your sights to the "big house," as it were, comprised of corporate headquarters, business offices proper and executive suits. [*sic*]. Here, in this privileged domain, you will find examples of the subject of this talk, the so-called black managers, pseudo executives and professionals, in other words, the "house niggers." For the most part, lacking any real authority or responsibility, but rather assigned to perform a number of peripheral, sometimes useful but more often merely decorative functions, which have extremely little to do with the really important operations of the corporation, these "good and faithful servants," nearly faceless and all but nameless in the corporations' table organization, daily make their appointed rounds.[4]

Spain goes on to conclude that all that has really changed in the past few years is that corporations have shifted the point at which they begin to apply discriminatory practices against their black management employees. Rather than excluding blacks altogether from the ranks of management, the current practice by the overwhelming majority of corporate employers is to prevent the aspiring black manager from advancing beyond the first or second level of supervision.

The Rape of Talent

Thus far we have dealt with only one side of the problem, as pervasive as it may seem. The other side involves the complex interaction of social, economic, political, and educational forces which deprive most blacks of the tools needed to be competitive in the job market. An examination of the environment which black managerial talent must come from will provide insight into the shaping of black capability.

Blacks come primarily from the rural South and urban ghettos—increasingly the latter. These environments, though different, exert similar influences on the maintenance of their deprivation. The Kerner Commission on Civil Disorders states: "What Americans have never fully understood—but what the Negro can never forget—is that white society is deeply implicated in the ghetto. White institutions created it, white institutions maintain it, and white society condones it." [5]

It is obvious that this statement applies also to the rural South where legal, economic, educational, political, and social institutions have openly practiced discrimination. It is not the place of this article, however, to deal with why white America has over the centuries chosen to withhold the rights, privileges, and prosperity of this rich land from blacks and other minorities, but to examine the consequences. [6]

The point is that not only have most blacks been excluded from management, but most have also been systematically deprived of those achievements which are considered by the corporation as necessary qualifications for managerial positions and mobility. Though inequality has been pervasive in all areas of existence for blacks, three broad categories have had particular impact on their managerial competitiveness: financial deprivation, background deprivation, and educational deprivation.

Financial Deprivation. The first of these deprivations stems from economic discrimination which, since the inception of slavery in this country, has denied most blacks access to the responsible and better paying jobs in American society. In addition, blacks were not, by and large, paid equal wages for equal work, and had little job security. Thus, the black community has not been able to amass resources which might have been used to overcome other aspects of discrimination.

For example, because they were historically precluded from business except as laborers and operatives, blacks could not develop competing businesses even to serve their own needs. It is a myth that ghetto businesses are predominantly black owned. The majority are owned by whites and on the average the best capitalized are white owned. For example, in Newark, N.J., about half of the population is black but only 10 percent of the licensed businesses in the city are black owned. In Los Angeles, where blacks comprise about a quarter of the population, less than 1 percent of the licensed businesses are black owned. In Washington, D.C., where blacks represent 63 percent of the population, only about 13 percent of the businesses are black owned.[7]

The indoctrination of inferiority has been so complete that many struggling new black businesses are finding out that black customers often prefer products made by whites because they feel that these products are better. This deep-rooted sense of inferiority has been pointed out many times by Jesse Jackson as one of the major obstacles to overcome in the Chicago Operation Breadbasket which he heads.

Combined with the limited income from unequal employment opportunities and inadequate business development is the other side of the coin—living costs. Generally, inner city ghetto residents pay more for rent, property taxes, food, transportation, manufactured products, services, and credit than do non-ghetto whites. The added strain on already limited income is added pressure against any accumulation of financial resources.[8] The lack of capital thus means that not only can blacks not compete through black-owned business, but also that there is an almost complete lack of strength to fight the white-imposed deprivation.

Deprivation of Background. In terms of management access, the lack of black business and black managers has meant that few blacks have had experience in management and many have only a limited perspective of business and its operation—that of a laborer and consumer. It takes little reflection to realize that this fact causes competitive disadvantage for blacks.

The lack of experience with business throughout childhood shows up in the lack of understanding upon which to build further analytic and conceptual tools and behavioral patterns. Ghetto blacks often have little familiarity with the business terminology that is assumed to be generally known. Ghetto blacks often have no background understanding in the divisions of business, the various functions of departments, capitalization, and bank relationships, even at rudimentary levels. Ghetto blacks have little familiarity with the life styles of managers and salaried white collar workers, with the social patterns which often get things done outside the formal organization, and with the use of contacts and influence, though it is questionable whether many of these models of behavior are desirable in business.

These background deficiencies can indeed be overcome, but they take training where none is now offered and an effort on the part of the black individual which is not expected of most whites. The ghetto black is at the same disadvantage in the business environment as the white middle-class suburbanite would be if he were suddenly required to survive in the ghetto. His language, behavior patterns, and understanding would be largely irrelevant.

I doubt whether the white affluent suburbanite, aged 18-25, could effectively learn what the street kid has been taught all his life. The pre-college training of managers has usually been considered as a constant and a given in the study of business. The desire of business to have black managers in increasing quantities brings attention to the absurdity of this assumption which was even erroneously applied to the more homogeneous white Americans.

Deprivation of Education. To the deprivation of background and economic power must be added the inequality of formal primary, secondary, and higher education. Despite allegations to the contrary, it is fact that the separate schools in the South were, and are, far from equal in quality of education. This is being overcome to some small degree by the start of school integration. However, it is clear that the lack of jobs available to blacks after education results in a lack of incentive to become educated. This fact, coupled with the inadequate educational funds allotted black schools over generations, have given the blacks a very weak educational platform from which to move into managerial positions.

Theodore Cross puts the education problem in perspective:

> Most cities base their educational expenditures per pupil on the assessed property values of the school district. For example, in the Robbins ghetto of Chicago, which is 99.1 percent Negro, the assessed property value per child is $7,300. The tax rate is $2.02 per hundred dollars of valuation, and the annual expenditure per pupil is $300. In the city's affluent Kenilworth section, the assessed property value is $55,000 per child, the tax is less than $2 per hundred dollars of valuation, and the annual school expenditure is $800 per pupil.[9]

The recent 6 to 1 decision of the California Supreme Court, which held that the constitutional rights of school children to equal protection under the law was violated by the current means of educational financing, may spark some movement toward more equitable school financing mechanisms. The promise of change, however, is small consolation for those who have already endured years of deprivation.

As swelling numbers of blacks have moved to urban areas in search of jobs, the problem has been compounded by the worsening plight of large urban areas. The shrinking tax base matched with increasing costs of services, increasing needs for services, and inept city political-managerial structure have rendered the quality of education in the ghettos near the bottom of this country's quality distribution. It was no accident that most inner city schools soon turned all black with the tremendous influx of blacks.

First of all, the quality of education was already deteriorating as the more affluent whites flocked to private schools or the suburbs.

Second, black immigration caused neighborhoods to become black quickly because of discrimination, ruthless realtor tactics, and fear of loss of property value. Third, blacks were not allowed to seek housing in areas with better schools and were not allowed to leave the city for the suburbs because of housing discrimination.

The flow of blacks into and whites out of central cities is dramatically shown by the percent of each group living in these areas over a recent 19-year period. In 1950, 43 percent of all Negroes and 34 percent of all whites lived in central cities; in 1969, the figures had changed to 55 percent of all Negroes and 26 percent of all whites.[10] The result was that the blacks concentrated in areas where schools and neighborhood conditions were worse than those they had left behind in the South.

Finally, college education has increasingly dominated the access route to management positions. Indeed, even master's level training is becoming more the rule than the exception for upward mobility in management. Yet blacks have been turned away from college because of the inferiority of their primary and secondary schooling, by discriminatory admissions policies, by the historical lack of opportunity to use educational level attained in employment, and by the unavailability of financial support. Each of these factors will be briefly discussed.

Colleges and universities, when challenged on the number of black students they have, are quick to point out the inadequate preparation of blacks. This condition, coupled with the institution's dedication to academic excellence as a goal, cannot help but skew the student body in favor of the whites. Admissions officers currently lament this seemingly insoluble dilemma in black admissions: on the one hand, a directive to increase black admissions substantially, and on the other hand, the directive to maintain and improve the academic quality of entering classes. As has been pointed out, there is no question that the average black precollege education is relatively deficient compared to that of the average white.

However, the admissions offices often add to their problem through the selection criteria used, and thus needlessly deny blacks admission. The most widely used and heavily weighted admission criterion for most institutions of higher education is the SAT. Many admissions officers admit that, even for white middle-class applicants, the SAT does not effectively predict future success. However, for blacks, the SAT is a highly inaccurate predictor of their ability or potential success in college. This inaccuracy is based on the fact that the SAT has been standardized for the traditional college students and their backgrounds. This means relatively affluent whites with college preparatory high school background. It also means that the test was standardized on middle-class values, aspirations, and behavior patterns. Thus, able black applicants have a severe handicap if they come from other walks of life and environments.

Another widely used criterion is the quality of high school that the applicant has graduated from. Naturally, most of the inner city schools are not given much weight. Coupled with quality of high school is rank in class. It is difficult to support school rankings as meaningful, particularly since the stilted and disciplinary educational process of inner cities drives many of the bright students to drop out or not study for lack of incentive.

Other factors play restrictive roles as well. For example, ghetto schools have fewer student activities where leadership can be exercised, and many of the real leaders end up on the streets. Extracurricular activities somehow seem less important relative to the other problems of inner city life. Thus, for the most part, applications from black students do not list the activities so cherished as indicators of breadth of person. Another restrictive factor is that blacks do not have the same access to referrals and references as whites. Most are not the sons and daughters of alumni, and they do not have access to prestigious alumni or other prominent members of society.

Though admissions offices are now scurrying to admit more blacks, the traditional evaluation criteria are being modified only slowly in the attempt to seek out true black potential. It is a tough job, and there are few tested guidelines. It is all too easy, particularly in this time of tight university budgets, to revert to the easily quantifiable traditional criteria.

Finally, admission is an empty gesture for someone without the means to pay for costly higher education. Most private schools require more than $4,000 per year for tuition, living expenses, books, and general maintenance. State schools generally require in excess of $2,000 per year. Thus, for most blacks, meaningful acceptance must be coupled with financial aid. Not only are scholarship funds needed for a large proportion of blacks but their need is on the average much greater than the average for whites.

The crisis in financial aid, created by increasing numbers of scholarship students, increasing costs of education, and current budget realities, is in direct conflict with the cry for more black students. Thus, the super-black is in high demand, but the average black has severely limited access to college relative to the average white.

In addition to restrictions on admissions, the incentive for blacks to get a college education has been dampened. Only in the last decade have entry level management jobs been made available to blacks. Previously, there were few outlets for black college graduates other than the few posts in black colleges. Many college-educated blacks were forced to abandon their dreams and accept unskilled or semiskilled work to provide for themselves and their families.

Thus, limited access to college, paired with the lack of meaningful jobs, made the sacrifice for college education seem a waste. The result was a lack of college aspiration among blacks which until recently kept application pressure off colleges. The inertia from generations of experience of this kind still keeps many blacks from applying for college and for scholarships even where their chances for admissions have improved and entry level management jobs are opening up.

Thus, for many reasons there have been few blacks passing through the conduit of college to management positions. What is critical is the fact that today a college degree is part of the set of credentials necessary for entry level management, yet there is little chance that the output of black graduates will be substantially increased beyond the currently best qualified, even with all the concern of employers and colleges.

Reasons have been noted for why blacks are not in college. Given the level of resources in the black community and the level of resources committed by whites and their organizations, the trend is not reversible. Resolving the crisis of our cities' schools alone depends on reform of our cities' financial and political structures, which depends on regional, and in turn, national reforms. The cost of education of increased black enrollment is well beyond the resources of educational institutions and to overcome it again requires state and federal shifts in priorities.

Indeed, if all Americans could today erase all personal prejudices due to race and color, the disadvantages of the blacks would continue due to this country's legacy of systematic exclusion of blacks from the resources and tools needed to be competitive with whites. The protracted period which will be necessary for personal prejudice to be nullified effectively makes the picture even more dismal.

BUSINESS INVOLVEMENT NEEDED

Before discussing what actions might be instituted by business, it is necessary to return to the question of why business should tackle such a problem, one that extends well beyond the traditional realm of its activities. Is not this a problem for individuals and governments? Business has no expertise in the area of race relations. Should it not stick to its function of creating a standard of living for the American people?

The answer is simple. Business has little choice but to become involved. This is not because businessmen are more humanitarian than they were in the past, or because they fear the loss of profits due to riots, civil war, or the breakdown of the values of our society (though that may occur), or because they feel blacks are so productive. They have little choice because they occupy the same middle ground they did when the public condoned and indeed required discrimination to the point of legal and profit reprisals.

Business has, in its own interest, simply mirrored the public value system without thought or malice. It was the path of least resistance. The table is now turning. The company which is exposed as racist is embarrassed and feels it has lost in public relations. More important, government, responding to the civil rights movement and to the mounting evidence of injustice and inequality, has instituted human relations legislation and commissions, has insisted on black representation in firms, and has set up quota systems for government contractors. Firms desire to have blacks because it is less painful than the consequences of not having blacks. The number of blacks in large corporations represents a clear barometer of the balance between the teeth in public and governmental pressure and the willingness of corporations to devote energy to include blacks in management.

There is a long way to go, but a start has been made, and the handwriting is clear. Firms are now going to have to pay to rectify what they passively condoned in American history. The dilemma is between the staggering costs of remedial action on the one hand and the mounting public and legal pressure on the other. Clark has summarized this burden somewhat differently:

> First, a substantial proportion of the tax dollar paid by industry goes to support public schools. Second, inner city public schools are producing human casualties who cannot be effectively integrated into the industrial and economic segment of society without the expenditure of additional funds by business and industry to compensate for the inefficiency of the public schools. Business and industry are, in fact, subsidizing inefficiency if they continue to permit public education to spawn hundreds of thousands of functional illiterates each year. . . . Business and industry are being offered shoddy products and being asked to use them as if they were not.
> This is an unnecessary burden.[11]

It is clear that the more lethargic the response of business to current pressures, the greater the pressures are likely to become. Whether the pressure is social or legal, it restricts freedom of business action which can only be distasteful to the decision makers within the corporations. Suggestions are now being taken more seriously to force business conformity to societal objectives in many areas, and race relations is no exception.

For example, a recent article, responding to the fact that 96 percent of all jobs in America with salaries of over $15,000 are held by white males, has suggested that within a ten-year limit minorities and women be included in all positions and salary levels in ratios which represent their proportions in the work force.[12] By insufficient action does business want to precipitate the acceptance of such a plan by government? The vise is closing and business will attempt to thread a path of least resistance.

Levels of Action

There are three levels of action which can help business to comply with society's changing values concerning racial discrimination. These proposed actions are no panacea, but they will ease the pressure by moving business toward the societal goals while attempting to gain the necessary partnership of government. The three levels of action are as follows:

> Internal examination, analysis, and correction of racial barriers to black mobility, for example, elimination of irrelevant job qualifications and biased application of criteria
>
> Development of short-run programs to bridge the gap between the demand for black managers and the supply, for example, compensatory management development
>
> Initiation of aggressive effort to influence governments at all levels to shift priority toward ameliorating the deprivation of the blacks, particularly in the inner cities.

Internal Analysis

The most difficult and fundamental task facing business is that of self-analysis. This is true for two reasons. First, self-criticism is always painful, particularly when time-worn loyalties, biases, and power have built up within organizations. Second, on top of this basic resistance to critical evaluation of the rules and practices of any bureaucracy is the shallow perception of the problem on the part of the organizational investigators conducting the self-analysis. This is to say, the white members of the organization do not perceive the subtle racism, intended or not, that retards black managerial mobility.

Few whites have had the curiosity or taken the time to try to view the organization from the black vantage point. Of course, whites cannot ever see through the black man's eyes, but an honest attempt to do so is a shaking experience. There is also help available to the organization from outside; however, much like psychoanalysis, the outsider can guide and evaluate, but there must be self-realization and understanding for there to be a basis for health. This self-understanding must be shared by all managers in the firm; otherwise, those who do not understand will perpetuate the barriers as before.

Further, understanding is not sufficient. It is simply not enough for top management to issue a directive against discrimination. There must be a strong sanction against discrimination which competes with the rewards for profit, service, or output. Policy statements rarely move those whose rewards are based on other performance criteria. Performance criteria must also be changed with the self-analysis.

What is implied, then, is a program of analysis carried out at all levels of management by those in charge to uncover overt and, particularly, indirect barriers to managerial mobility of blacks and then the institution of organizational and incentive reforms to implement needed change. The process of this analysis will involve the creation of understanding within the organization which can lead to enlightened internal and external racial practices. It cannot be overstressed that the managers themselves must perform the analysis, though guidance may be necessary from those sensitive to the various forms and shapes of racism.

In this regard, many whites and blacks have devoted years to understanding the subtleties of racism. Black consultants are more likely to have a greater depth of knowledge because of their own personal experience. On the other side, white consultants may have less difficulty convincing white managers of the necessity for change and the reality of discrimination versus what many consider as black paranoia. As one comprehends the scope of the problem and its causes, one also realizes the importance of having the white man clean his own house. If one realizes what the black man must endure because of the color of his skin, one can hardly ask him to take on yet another burden—that of enlightening those whites who do not believe in the current extent of unfairness.

Institutional understanding of its own racism is the foundation on which the other levels of action can be built. Without this foundation the other programs are likely to be empty and to fail, thereby wasting the organization's and society's resources. The often repeated thought by managers: "We hired some of them but they just didn't pan out," or "Sure, we hired some black MBA's but they didn't fit into our way of doing business," or "All the blacks we hire to management posts soon leave; they want to get ahead too fast," and so on.

All of these comments originate out of ineptness of program attempts based on ignorance of the racial dimensions of business. Each experience so conceived has added to the insults of the black man and to the arrogance and ignorance of the whites involved. The "inferiority" of blacks is a self-fulfilling prophecy.

Transition Programs

Thus, if this first level of action has been successful, the second can be attempted. This second stage is the relatively short-run building of effective programs for the development of black managers. If progress has been made in the organization's self-understanding and procedures, blacks will be more willing to join management and will progress more rapidly in it, which moves the firm toward the desired alleviation of pressure.

However, the organization will also have to seek out and develop black capability to fill the demand. With the understanding it has gained, it is in a position to mount such programs with a greater degree of success. The program options open to business are many and varied. Only a few will be mentioned here as illustrations.

In direct financial realms, business could ease the burden on colleges by sponsoring black student scholarships. This would help open the pipeline of black graduates seeking entry level management positions.

Another type of business involvement would be support of both the talent and financial resources of programs designed by community organizations, high schools, and colleges to overcome deficiencies in educational backgrounds of blacks. Such programs in their various forms all have the common goal of increasing black capability. In addition, business could well make significant inputs in helping develop specialized training of blacks for eventual management entry. For example, programs could be developed for present company blacks to help them in their upward mobility.

Finally, experience should be provided blacks in the opening of greater numbers of managerial positions. This can be achieved both within the corporation and through third-party contracts which foster the development and strengthening of black business. All such programs are cosmetic in that they do not attack the root of the problem but deal with trying in some small way to overcome the resultant deprivation.

Two words of caution are in order. First, whatever programs are chosen, be sure that those affected are in key positions of direction and execution. This will help avoid the all too often insensitive white failures. This does not mean burdening present black managers but involvement of the community from which you are drawing.

Second, speak with action, not public relations. Nothing is more galling to blacks and sensitive whites than the massive media campaign showing token blacks in "important" positions, and token social programs. To an increasingly wary public this smacks of insincerity and deception. How many blacks could that campaign educate in college or what programs could have been improved or started for the same resources? To show off the few blacks in management or the small programs (in terms of profits) is but to use blacks again to keep them in their place. To use blacks for public relations is to sabotage the participating blacks and destroy the credibility of the company with civil rights organizations, the government, and the public. It is from these people that the pressure is coming and they will not be fooled.

National Influence

No matter how well-conceived and executed, such programs cannot possibly rectify the situation and its pressure on business because these programs do not hit at the core of the problem. The core is the self-perpetuating deprivation of the ghetto and rural South, which lack resources and education. To tackle the result of three hundred years of overt and indirect discrimination, major shifts in national state and local financial and political priorities will have to be achieved.

At the base of these shifts must be the complete revitalization of the education to which blacks are allowed access. The traditional political and resource allocation process must be pressured into action, reorganization, and responsiveness to the root inequities and deprivations. Only through such reorientation can government assume its share of the cost and thus relieve business from continued aggravation and pressure to attempt what it cannot alone achieve.

Business can help the necessary reorganization by using its new base of racial understanding as a platform from which to lobby aggressively for the needed change. Though businessmen disclaim the weight of their voices, there is no doubt that when they feel strongly, their voices are heard with strength. Witness the oil interests, attempts at taxation of insurance, and so on. The businessman must be an advocate of constructive change to his friends, colleagues, and political associations if his burden is to be eased. In this longer-term effort, it is not enough to campaign alone for educational reform. Business must also participate in and advocate reform in the areas of housing, political representation, welfare, and civil rights to give general support to the increasing capability of blacks.

Notes

[1] At the time of publication of this article, Robert W. Nason was a faculty member at Wharton School, University of Pennsylvania, and a director of the Community-Wharton Education Program.

[2] Statistics for 1969 from *Monthly Labor Review*, U.S. Department of Labor, Bureau of Labor Statistics, XCIII, No. 2 (Washington: U.S. Gov't Printing Office), p. 44.

Figures for 1970 from Edwin M. Epstein and David R. Hampton, eds., *Black Americans and White Business* (Encino, Calif.: Dickenson Publishing Co., Inc., 1971), p. 93.

[3] For expansion of this topic, see Ivar Berg, *Education and Jobs: the Great Training Robbery* (New York: Praeger Publishers, 1970).

[4] James Spain, "Career Mobility for Black Managers," published in the conference proceedings of the *Conference on the Role of Black Managers in Society*, Fisk University, Feb. 2-4, 1970, pp. 27-28. Spain is the president of the Council of Concerned Black Executives, New York, and is a manager in a large corporation.

[5] *Report of the National Advisory Commission on Civil Disorder* (New York: The New York Times Company, 1968), p. 2.

[6]For information on the perpetuation of discrimination for white benefit see *Racism in America and How to Combat It*, U.S. Commission on Civil Rights, Clearinghouse Publications, Urban Series No. 1 (Washington: U.S. Gov't Printing Office, January, 1970), and Louis L. Knowles and Kenneth Pruit, *Institutional Racism in America* (Englewood Cliffs, N.J.: Prentice-Hall, Inc., 1970).

[7]The "1968 Annual Report of the Interracial Council for Business Opportunity," as reported in Theodore L. Cross, *Black Capitalism, Strategy for Business in the Ghetto* (New York: Atheneum, 1969), p. 60-61.

[8]See Theodore L. Cross, *Black Capitalism, Strategy for Business in the Ghetto*, Part II (New York: Atheneum, 1969), and David Caplovitz, *The Poor Pay More: Consumer Practices of Low-Income Families* (New York: Free Press, 1969).

[9]Theodore L. Cross, *Black Capitalism, Strategy for Business in the Ghetto* (New York: Atheneum, 1969), p. 33.

[10]*The Social and Economic Status of Negroes in the United States*, Bureau of Labor Statistics Report 375, U.S. Department of Labor (Washington: U.S. Gov't Printing Office, 1969), p. 7.

[11]Kenneth B. Clark, "Efficiency as a Prod to Social Action," *Monthly Labor Review*, Bureau of Labor Statistics, U.S. Department of Labor, XCII (Washington: U.S. Gov't Printing Office, August, 1969), p. 55.

[12]John Kenneth Galbraith, Edwin Kuh and Lester C. Thurow, "The Galbraith Plan to Promote the Minorities," *The New York Times Magazine*, Aug. 22, 1971.

Testing and Evaluation Procedures

Job Testing and the Disadvantaged

APA TASK FORCE ON EMPLOYMENT TESTING
OF MINORITY GROUPS[1]

In an ideal world each individual would pursue activities perfectly suited to himself and to his society. Each person would use his capabilities in the most productive and self-enhancing fashion, and his society thereby would make the wisest and most humane use of its manpower resources.

Such a goal is not easily realized. Its attainment may be blocked sometimes by the personal maladaptive tendencies of the individual. More generally, however, it is society that often thwarts the matching between an individual's capabilities and his vocational role. The reluctance or inability of our industrialized society, over nearly a century, to use fully the country's manpower resources testifies to the difficulties in achieving an ideal congruence between the individual and his work performance. The personal, social, and economic ills resulting from such an inappropriate usage of manpower are apparent even to the most casual observer. Allowed to continue, they can destroy the essential fabric of a society willing to accept them.

Intensified national concern that all sectors of the population have equal opportunity for employment has focused attention on techniques for evaluating personal abilities and insuring their use. For example, in September 1968, after considerable study of the use of employment tests for the selection of employees from among minority group applicants, the Department of Labor issued regulations concerning the

Reprinted from *American Psychologist*, 1969, *24*, 637-650. Copyright © 1969 by the American Psychological Association. Reprinted by permission of the publisher and the authors.

validation of employment tests by government contractors and sub-contractors. Underlying the regulations was

> the belief that properly validated and standardized tests, by virtue of their relative objectivity and freedom from the biases that are apt to characterize more subjective evaluation techniques, can contribute substantially to the implementation of equitable and nondiscriminatory personnel policies.

This article is concerned with certain important elements in the chain of events that can lead to the inappropriate use of manpower and unfair and self-defeating personnel practices. Tests and related sources of personnel data—whether application forms, biographical data sheets, questionnaires, or interviews—long have been of special concern to large numbers of psychologists. This professional interest, together with unequivocal support of the policy of equal employment opportunity and a desire to share responsibility for its implementation, underlies the present statement. It was prepared to indicate major considerations in fair employment appraisal, particularly of the disadvantaged, and to suggest constructive action, especially with regard to job testing. Throughout, it is assumed that full manpower usage and full conservation of human resources are esssential ingredients of a healthy society, and that without them demoralization and economic insecurity are certain. This central concept governs the findings, conclusions, and recommendations of the overall statement.

Sequence of Procedures in Employment and Promotion Decisions

Decisions regarding employment and promotion inevitably involve a variety of structured and unstructured elements of management-employee relations, all of which—as will be shown in the next section—are liable to bias and unjust discrimination.

In the quest for a job, an applicant's first encounter is typically with a receptionist. After completing an application form, the candidate generally will encounter next the more formalized and systematic information-gathering procedures used in the personnel selection process. Three information sources are usually drawn upon by the potential employer: biographical data, interview impressions, and test scores. The first two are almost universally used in selection, and, although tests are used less frequently, their role can be a potent one in determining the job applicant's fate.

In many instances, personal background information may not be requested in written form, but may be elicited during an interview. Often, the interview is little more than a vehicle for collecting biographical data. Facts revealed by the application form and/or the interview frequently are verified by reference checking. Such checks, of course, can extend beyond the simple verification of previously obtained information; they may be the occasion for extracting opinions about the applicant's honesty, ability, motivation, or the quality of his job performance.

When a job requires a specific skill—for example, typing or shorthand—a specific test of that skill might be used. Or, when an applicant claims to have specialized experience or knowledge in a given field—for example, in plumbing or auto repair—a direct test such as an oral trade test may be administered to gauge the extent of his proficiency. Aptitude tests also may be used to estimate the applicant's capacity for learning the tasks he will need to perform on the job. Some aptitude tests are highly specific with regard to the job in question—for example, by measuring the degree of a particular type of manual dexterity. Others are more general, for example, those mental ability tests designed to assess a wider band of potential for learning. It is possible, of course, that both specialized knowledge and aptitude tests may be administered in a given employment situation. An applicant for a job as a file clerk might be asked to complete both a test of her spelling ability and a test of her capability for learning new filing methods.

Promotion decisions involve still another round of procedures, again open to bias and unfair discrimination. Supervisory judgment is the most frequently used method for identifying, evaluating, and selecting employees who are to be promoted, although in many cases seniority clauses in union-management contracts act to constrain the number of persons who may be considered. Judgments may be based on an individual's performance on his present job and on his job history, his apparent motivation, the likelihood of his being capable of acquiring the additional knowledge or skills required at the higher level, and other related factors. A candidate's immediate supervisor usually will discuss his recommendations and impressions with the next higher level of management before a final decision is reached, with the final choice made from among candidates nominated by several supervisors.

Aptitude tests may be used once again to help in making promotion decisions. Tests of task proficiency involving specialized knowledge, for example, are widely used by government agencies to assist in determining promotability; the use of such tests is far less common in private industry.

When substantial differences exist in requirements between lower level and higher level jobs, formal training is often provided, and successful completion of training can be a clear index of promotability— assuming, of course, that the training is, in fact, necessary for successful job performance. Such use of training as a final screen for promotion clearly suggests that promotions might well be made after training rather than before, a sequence that does not always obtain.

Some firms, recognizing the importance of promotion decisions, have developed more elaborate evaluation procedures to aid in making judgments. For example, some use a formally designated promotion committee comprised of representatives from labor and management, from the personnel or industrial relations department, and from various other functional areas. One common approach is for such a committee periodically to qualify as promotable or nonpromotable those employees who have expressed an interest in being advanced to supervisory jobs. The employees designed as promotable are placed in a manpower pool, to be drawn from as new positions become available. Information accessible to such promotion committees usually includes the employee's education and work history, his job assignments and training experience in the firm, job performance reports, and aptitude test results. Often, the candidate is brought before the committee at one of its regular meetings, and a brief interview is conducted.

Some firms—among them AT&T, SOHIO, General Electric, General Motors, IBM, and Sears—have developed comprehensive supervisory assessment programs in which a candidate's performance in group discussion and in various simulated supervisory tasks is observed and made a part of the package of information taken into account in making promotion decisions. Still another vehicle for judging promotion potential, used by several business organizations especially in the assessment of executives, involves an intensive evaluation of employees by outside consultants.

The entire range of events outlined above—from the initial simple contract between applicant and receptionist to the most complex promotion procedures—are appropriate foci of concern in considering the potential for inappropriate and unfair personnel decisions.

Hazards Inherent in Employment and Promotion Decisions

Decisions regarding the selection and promotion of personnel inevitably involve a degree of subjectivity. Objective data are, of course, typically available to the employer, including biographical data, references, interview data, and test results. But no practical statistical method exists for appropriately combining such data, in light of more general considerations, so that one could obtain a single numerical index or decision rule. Among these general considerations are present job requirements, possible changes in job design, opportunities for remedial training, job transfers in case of inadequate performance, and labor market conditions.

Subjective interpretation and integration of information takes place even when some of the individual sources of information appear to be predictive of specific aspects of job behavior—for example, when scored or "weighted" application blanks, or test information expressed in the form of expectancy tables, are available. Because of their relative objectivity, psychological tests, properly designed and used, are potentially less discriminatory than other personnel assessment techniques, but it is apparent that no single step in the sequence can properly be adjudged as *the* primary source of unfair distinction. Instead, possibilities for such discrimination exist at every stage in the employment or promotion process, particularly among the disadvantaged.

The threat to fair practices may begin even before an applicant has presented himself— that is, in the recruiting phase. For example, an employer could easily restrict the number of applicants from minority groups by failing to recruit or seek referrals from schools or neighborhoods in which such groups predominate. The same effect could occur in promotion, if, for example, nominations of candidates were not sought from groups with relatively more minority members.

Biases also may begin to operate at the very outset of the selection process. Although the interaction between applicant and receptionist may be brief and may appear superficial, nevertheless it is a point at which quick decisions are made and unfair discrimination can occur. In a survey of 39 employers in the San Francisco area, Rusmore (1967) found that many receptionists were completely uninformed of any rules or standards to apply in this first screening of an applicant. Officials of a firm may be doing their best to assure fair employment practices, but if they fail to give explicit directions to the receptionist, in practice the firm might be pursuing a pervasive policy of unfair treatment.

The use of data contained in application forms also is open to bias, although this clearly need not be the case. One procedure, for example, capitalizes on past behavior as a basis for predicting future job performance by using scored or "weighted" application forms. In effect, elements of background—among them marital history, previous employment, school activities, hobbies—studied in relation to job success, are used as predictive indexes of varying strength. Although this process has been applied successfully to a wide variety of jobs, it is still uncommon to find such approaches in actual use. It is far more usual for application information to be interpreted subjectively; for example, attendance at one school may be seen as better than another school, or participation in school activities, sports, or civic affairs may be seen as important or ignored completely. Interpretation may be a matter of intuitive or clinical judgment by someone who knows the job or jobs for which the applicant is being considered. Such subjectivity obviously is open to a variety of biasing factors, especially when the decision rules and bases of judgment are not made explicit.

Carefully weighted application blanks are themselves no guarantee of objectivity. Biographical information often shows wide differences between persons from contrasting population subgroups. Examples include data describing schools attended, extracurricular activities, father's occupation, number of books and magazines in the home, hobbies, arrests, and health status. Thus, weighted application blanks that help select candidates from middle-class applicants may be invalid for non-middle-class groups.

The use of interview impressions in selection is hazardous since they can be affected by both conscious and unconscious perceptual bias, as can later observations of an individual's job performance. Perceptual bias may also affect reports obtained during reference checking, nominations of candidates to be considered for training programs or for promotion, and reactions of higher officials as they interview promotional candidates.

The employment interviewer normally attempts to do more than simply collect data. He usually undertakes to make judgments about such characteristics as job interests, work motivation, and ability to get along with others. Because an interviewer has no formula for judging the relative importance of the various pieces of collected information, the possibility is great for unfair discrimination to occur at this stage of the employment process. All interviewers are prone toward an unconscious sifting of facts. Data are usually selected to support the early impression gained by the interviewer (Webster, 1964); applicants toward whom interviewers form favorable early impressions tend unintentionally to be overvalued, while those toward whom interviewers form unfavorable initial impressions tend to be undervalued. It is impossible to judge accurately the degree of unfairness resulting from such unconscious predisposing factors inherent in the typical interview situation, but it may be substantial.

Promotion decisions. These decisions, so important because the relative job effectiveness of supervisors and managers has broad impact on many other persons and on the success of the total organization, are often handled like selection decisions, that is, in a generally subjective and nonsystematic manner. As a result, here, too, unjust discrimination can occur in a variety of ways.

In the promotion process, problems inherent in supervisory appraisals are many and well known. First, a supervisor typically sees only a small number of the possible candidates in the organization and he rarely has an accurate notion of the total range of available talent. Second, the supervisors may hold varying standards of job performance and nurture contrasting concepts of the requirements in higher level jobs. A supervisor's perception of how well an employee is doing his present job, and his expectation for the employee if he were promoted, often may be affected by such essentially extraneous factors as the employee's racial characteristics.

An individual's entire job career in a firm may be affected by the degree of his superior's success in avoiding either conscious or unconscious distortions in observations of job performance. Here, as in selection decisions, the interpretation of objective data is often made without clear evidence of their relation to desired behaviors or to success in jobs under consideration. Often equally illogical is the use of training in the promotion process. The logical sequence is for training to precede promotion, but a frequent practice is to promote first. The use of training as a screening method requires not only that the training clearly be matched to job requirements, but also that objective and reliable measures of performance during training be available.

SPECIAL PROBLEMS IN THE USE OF TESTS

Skill and Knowledge Tests

Tests of specialized, job-relevant knowledges and skills or of samples of job performance are, in themselves, free of bias. An individual can be shown either to possess sufficient knowledge or skill to do a given job or not. Moreover, an applicant rejected for lack of such knowledge or skill—for example, an unacceptably low typing speed—can be counseled to acquire further training and to return again for reconsideration. It is possible, of course, to question whether or not doing a job actually requires the knowledge or skill being tested; a knowledge test in advanced calculus, for example, would hardly be regarded as a proper employment test for a job involving the operation of an adding machine. The crucial question is whether or not the test activities accurately reflect the job behaviors.

Aptitude Tests

The question of possible systematic bias in aptitude tests is, by far, a more subtle and complex issue. Aptitude tests, just as with skill tests, measure developed abilities, reflecting the interaction between an individual's experiences and his innate endowments. Because experiences during the early years of life are particularly important in this developmental interaction, individuals and groups with widely different childhood and youth experiences may differ in adult aptitude level partly because of their disparity in background. As a group, the disadvantaged do score substantially lower than others on nearly all aptitude tests, but it is this same group whose early environment is so often marked by cultural deprivation. A number of additional possible factors have been suggested to explain their test performance. These include anxiety induced by the testing situation, unfairness of test content, improper interpretation of test scores, and lack of content relevance. Each of these factors will be discussed briefly.[2]

Test-induced anxiety. It is likely that disadvantaged persons may score poorly on tests partly because of the anxiety occasioned by their lack of familiarity with the testing situation. Moreover, anxiety may be most readily induced when tests are administered by persons representing more advantaged backgrounds. Unfortunately, it is difficult to estimate the nature and magnitude of effects on test performance of such anxiety, and virtually no fundamental research has been accomplished in employment settings to do so.

From Rusmore's survey of San Francisco employers, it is known, however, that proper testing procedures as specified in test manuals are frequently ignored by test users. Over half the companies included in this limited sample did not provide even a separate room for administering tests; most testing was conducted in settings judged inadequate in terms of space, lighting, and frequent interruptions. Since much testing is apparently conducted in such poor surroundings, it seems likely that other prescribed procedures—for example, for allaying anxiety and assuring motivation—are also being ignored. Greatly needed is a program of research to identify influences on test performance of various test administration factors such as the directions given, the setting, and the characteristics of the administrator. Moreover, the impact of such factors must be evaluated separately for various kinds of tests—performance, paper-pencil, speed, verbal, and others. From the results of such a research program, one could specify procedures to prevent unfair discrimination against persons from disadvantaged backgrounds as a result of anxiety induced by the testing situation.

Unfairness of test content. Most tests, especially verbal ones, emphasize concepts and information to which disadvantaged persons may never have been exposed. In a speech[3] by a chairman of the Equal Employment Opportunity Commission, it was charged that the identification of subtle distinctions in word meanings demands knowledge differentially available in various ethnic subcultures. Many who feel that existing tests are too loaded with middle-class items to be fair to disadvantaged groups propose "culture-free" or "culture-fair" tests as substitutes.

In reality, however, the term "culture-free" is misleading, for no instrument that measures behavior can be free of cultural influences. More reasonable seems to be the culture-fair or culture-common tests, that is, tests based on experiences equally familiar or unfamiliar to advantaged or disadvantaged groups. Unfortunately, efforts in this direction have not been successful. It would appear that test scores will continue to reflect both innate differences and variations in experience. Instead of trying to remove cultural effects, research can turn more profitably to the questions: (a) Can we identify among the low scorers those whose test performance *may* be due to lack of experience, and (b) for such low scorers, how readily and at what ages can the lack of experience be overcome?

Improper interpretation of test scores. A logical contention is that test scores do not carry the same behavioral predictions for the disadvantaged that they do for more advantaged groups. This hypothesis, that test scores have different meanings for different subgroups, requires extensive research for confirmation or rejection; existing evidence is inadequate to determine whether aptitude tests actually discriminate unfairly because of their different validities from one subgroup to another.

On the basis of their results, some investigators have claimed that differing patterns of test validity are already demonstrable for samples of Negroes and whites.[4] However, because such studies are few in number and because many methodological inadequacies are unresolved, no firm conclusions can be drawn from them. Faced with inadequate evidence, the need is highlighted for more and better research designed specifically to pinpoint the behavioral interpretations that properly may be attached to scores on aptitudes tests, whether obtained by advantaged or disadvantaged members of the population. Lacking such research data, it is impossible to recommend how or whether predictions from test scores should be interpreted differently for different groups.

Lack of content relevance. Items contained in some aptitude tests show no obvious relevance to the requirements of job performance. When this is the case, decisions to use such tests must be based on demonstrated relationships between overall scores on the tests and behavior on the same or similar jobs. Unless evidence for such relationships can be produced, there is no basis for rejecting low-scoring disadvantaged persons, for it may be that they can learn the necessary skills and knowledges after being hired. Recognizing the importance of the training or apprenticeship period in developing skills needed for certain kinds of jobs, some maintain that many persons can be taught what they need to know *regardless* of scores achieved on aptitude tests. This claim also can be tested empirically with the collaboration of those using tests in specific job settings. If the claim is found to be true, another question arises as to who should bear the costs of this additional training.

SPECIFIC RECOMMENDATIONS

The foregoing review of current practices in employment and promotion—specifically of their potential hazards for unfair discrimination—suggests a number of recommendations. Following, then, are immediate, practical steps employers may take to reduce the potential for bias at various specific points in the employment and promotion process.

The Receptionist

Because the receptionist is usually the first personal contact an applicant has with his potential employer, she should be informed daily of the jobs available and the responses she should make to applicants. The safest approach here is to disallow any screening by the receptionist; that is, everyone but clearly inappropriate applicants—for example, the drunk and disorderly—should be allowed an application blank. Employers should give explicit directions to receptionists or other persons involved in initial employment contacts with applicants, to insure that they have no decision-making power to screen or reject on the basis of private criteria.

The Interview

Employers should be fully cognizant of the pervasiveness of opportunities for unfair discrimination inherent in the typical personnel or employment interview. It is unlikely that perceptual biases can be overcome merely through training or by informing interviewers of their existence. It may be necessary to change the purpose of the employment interview from one of evaluation and decision making to that of the mere recording of information. The interviewer, functioning in the role of recorder, could then transmit his information to others, who would combine it with all other available information about the applicant in reaching a final decision. Personnel interviewers should be trained to be more aware of the vagaries inherent in the formation of interpersonal impressions and, in particular, of the dangers of acting on unintended and unconscious bias when interviewing minority group members. The employer should recognize the possibility of bias in his interviewers in spite of measures to improve the interviewing procedures and should take such other steps as are necessary to eliminate discrimination.

Testing

Employers using psychological tests to aid in employment or promotion decisions should consider the following recommendations:

1. Good physical conditions for administering tests should be provided for *all* applicants. Matters such as clarity of instructions and strict

adherence to time limits are so essential to satisfactory test administration that they should require little discussion, yet apparently it is necessary to recommend to employers that they attend closely to the procedures specified in test manuals. Any changes in time limits, for example, require re-standardization and development of local norms for the test. Firms with limited resources for proper handling of test administration should take advantage of the recent trend toward using recorded instructions and timing in the test situation.

2. When a test has been validated against job performance in a given setting, it may be possible to specify one or more "cutting scores" on the test. Properly set, such cutting scores should identify persons who show different likelihoods of performing or learning to perform the job in question. The meaning of various test scores in terms of expected job behaviors can best be portrayed by using an expectancy table (Guion, 1965; Lawshe & Balma, 1966; Wesman, 1949); this provides a device for readily estimating the relative likelihood that an applicant at any given score level will do the job properly if he is hired. When individualized strategies are applied in reaching personnel decisions —that is, when each candidate's potential is intensively and individually examined from many points of reference—the test scores and their meaning will be taken into account along with other information to make a final decision. However, when individualized strategies are not possible—for example, when a large number of candidates are being screened to fill jobs in a new plant—it is best to use the single most valid predictor as an initial screening device. In such instances, one or more cutting scores may be set to assure an optimal overall selection rule that will maximize the ratio of correct to incorrect decisions for the mass screening of available manpower.

3. It often may be the case that no direct validity studies have been done in connection with any of the sources of information—biographical data, interviews, or tests—involved in personnel decisions. In such cases, it becomes necessary to judge critically the relative merit of various measures as possible aids in making employment or promotion decisions. There is, of course, no fully satisfactory substitute for direct validity evidence obtained in a specific situation. Pending such studies, one should turn to validity studies conducted elsewhere. However, pending the accumulation of acceptable evidence of validity, all judgments made on the basis of tests or other selection techniques must be regarded as tentative. This implies that cutting scores should be set only on an experimental basis, and at as low a level as possible, while research data continue to be obtained.[5]

ADDITIONAL SUGGESTIONS

There are a number of concrete suggestions that go beyond employment testing that employers may wish to consider in the interest of achieving maximum effectiveness of manpower resources. Equally important, these suggestions also may provide the means through which unfair practices can be avoided in structuring personnel decision-making processes, and broader usage of disadvantaged manpower can be achieved. Many of the items listed below help clarify the nature and extent of discrimination in employment and promotion procedures described earlier.

Specifically, employers might consider the following suggestions:

1. Maintain records of information assembled and actions taken in relation to all personnel decisions, particularly in selection and promotion. These records would include fairly detailed résumés of biographical, interview, job performance, test, and other data taken into account in making a decision, as well as notations of factors underlying the action taken. Records of this type would aid considerably in providing information both for research and the formulation of recommendations for constructive approaches to personnel decision making.

2. Be prepared to specify the manner in which personnel decisions are made, including the contingencies and influences operating to affect the type and sequence of decisions for each individual candidate. In effect, employers should be able to describe in detail their own approach toward individualized personnel decision making within the framework described earlier in this statement. In addition, records might show how various tests have been used—for example, their cutting scores—and how they aid in the total process of personnel actions.

3. Experiment with training programs specifically designed both to develop and upgrade employment skills of disadvantaged and other minority group members. In recent years, the Department of Labor has offered grants to support the costs of such special training efforts in many cities through the country. As knowledge from these projects accumulates, employers will have additional and firmer guidelines for undertaking such specialized training activities.

4. Devote attention to the possibilities of designing jobs to be more appropriate to existing skills and knowledges possessed by a wider range of potential employees. A great deal of emphasis has been given during the last decade to "job enlargement" for the sake of assuring higher degrees of "self-actualization" of employees in industry. Similar attention needs to be devoted to the possibility of innovative breakthroughs in structuring and designing jobs with a view toward increased man-

power usage. An entirely new structure of job families or of new service industries might be developed in the process.

5. Give increased attention to recruitment procedures from among minority groups. Several companies recently have tested the efficacy of recruiting directly in Negro ghettos and of making hiring decisions on the spot. Recruitment procedures may be designed to increase the number of applicants from minority groups, and improved approaches may be developed for conducting interviews, for checking background and references, for assessing the potential of minority group applicants, and for educating them in more effective job-seeking strategies.

6. Conduct studies designed to determine the accuracy of various types of personal information for predicting not global estimates of job "success," but various elements of behavior desired in different jobs. Such determinations should be made for individual population subgroups, the disadvantaged and advantaged, Negroes and whites.

7. Consider along with unions the impact on employment practices of strict seniority provisions for promotion. When such provisions are rigidly enforced, the employer often sets requirements at the entry level that are relevant to the very top job, with the result that many who otherwise could qualify for entry on secondary jobs are excluded. Often, too, overqualified persons, having to pass slowly through positions not using their fullest abilities, tend to terminate. Other employment strategies, therefore, should be considered. For example, it might be that a more appropriate strategy would involve a mix of ability levels, thus permitting employees to advance as a result of their demonstrated performance as well as their seniority.

8. Develop training experiences for supervisors and other members of management to give more specific understanding and skills in interacting with employees from disadvantaged groups.

9. Support fundamental research designed to illuminate and resolve the myriad problems and complex issues surrounding the full use of our nation's manpower resources. Research support can take many forms. Firms may make direct financial contributions to agencies, foundations, or individuals engaged in such research; they may provide manpower to direct research projects; they may provide research subjects and/or aid in developing and maintaining records of significant career actions and outcomes for such subjects; and, most important, they may simply extend a cooperation and support to persons, agencies, foundations, and institutes doing research by assuring an open-door policy for developing information as quickly as possible in the critical area of manpower utilization.

It is true, of course, that a high level of expertise is required for properly auditing personnel programs and for designing and mounting effective research activities. In choosing professionals to aid in such activities, employers may be guided by a number of criteria, seeking especially the following: those having advanced education in a relevant field; manpower experience in industry, government, or the armed services; a history of published research in personnel procedures such as selection, training, and performance appraisal; a diploma in Industrial Psychology awarded by the American Board of Professional Psychology; fellowship status in appropriate divisions of the American Psychological Association; or other tangible evidence of equivalent relevant training or experience.

TECHNICAL, METHODOLOGICAL, AND RESEARCH CONSIDERATIONS

Although, as already noted, a number of specific and general steps can be taken to reduce the hazards of unfair discrimination, there is a continuing need for more knowledge concerning possible differential effects of current personnel procedures on various segments of the population, a need made explicit in this section. Considered here also are technical problems involved in pursuing necessary research and strategies for initiating such efforts.

Central to the issues raised by selection and promotion procedures is the problem of defining and measuring job success, and of relating the criteria selected, either statistically or rationally, to information available at the time personnel decisions are made. Relevant to this problem are job analysis, performance appraisal, and strategies of validating employment information, considered now in turn.

Job Analysis

A major purpose of making personnel decisions is to predict job behavior. This demands a thorough understanding of jobs and the patterns of behavior that will accomplish them. To gain such an understanding is one of the most difficult challenges posed to the field of industrial psychology. Job names or titles are rarely adequate for inferring the behaviors involved in job performance. Many approaches to job analysis, therefore, have been developed; underlying all of them is the goal of providing descriptions of the actual behaviors necessary for successful job performance, and their relative frequency and importance. Only from such data may inferences be drawn about knowledges, skills, or aptitudes that are likely to be necessary for doing a job or for learning to do it.

Clearly, then, to a great extent, the relevance of biographical or test information used in making personnel decisions depends on the adequacy of prior job analyses and inferences drawn from them. Failure to perform adequate job analyses frequently leads to false inferences about necessary skills, knowledges, or aptitudes. For example, certain Air Force jobs once were said to require a knowledge of trigonometry; careful job analyses indicated, however, that such knowledge was required only for developing certain tables and nomographs, and not for interpreting them. Trigonometric knowledge, it turned out, was not actually necessary, and the removal of trigonometry requirements as a selection standard eased considerably the burden of recruiting and training qualified men.

Job Performance Measurement

Prediction of job behavior requires first that such behavior be observed and recorded. Job analysis data describe which behaviors may be important in doing a job properly, and suggest the kinds of measures and observations necessary for assessing job success. It must be recognized at the outset, however, that no simple or single measure of job success exists. Behavior on the job, job performance, and, therefore, job success are multidimensional. Moreover, behavioral requirements differ from time to time in nearly all jobs, the most usual change being due to the varying pattern of job demands even as a new employee is learning his job. For example, Ghiselli and Haire (1960) showed that the total production (amount of fares collected) by cab drivers during their first few weeks of employment involved patterns of job behavior very different from the patterns after four and one-half months on the job.

The fact of changing requirements inherent in most jobs renders the validation of personnel information unusually difficult. Even if the behaviors necessary for successful accomplishment of a job are identified and agreed upon, the problems of making these definitions operational in order to form actual measures or criteria of job effectiveness are many. One must realize that an individual's job performance may be affected significantly by such situational factors as the kind of boss he has, his co-workers, or the economic conditions of his sales territory. Often, therefore, the most appropriate criterion for evaluating tests is a direct measure of the degree of job skill developed by an employee *after* an appropriate period of time on the job—that is, a "job sample" measure of task proficiency.

If supervisor ratings are used as criteria, it must be assured that raters understand the scales and regard them as important, and that they be trained to observe systematically and accurately the job behaviors of persons they are asked to describe. Greater attention must be given to the development of systematic procedures for observing and measuring job behavior, and for using such data to learn exactly how employee job behaviors are related to other organizational measures such as over-all rankings of success, promotion rates, productivity indexes, quality measures, work sample scores, job satisfaction and morale, and the many other overall measures of performance readily available in most work settings.

Strategies of Validation

It should be noted at the outset that "validation" refers merely to the process of learning as much as possible about what a measure predicts, that is, to the behavioral meaning that may properly be attached to any item of information about an applicant, whether it be his level of educa-tion, his marital status, his prison record, or his score on an aptitude test. Two issues relevant to unfair and discriminatory test usage are implied by this definition: What methodological steps are involved in the proc-esses of validation? And, what strategies may be useful in learning whether or not particular items of information may differ in meaning for particular individuals, especially those belonging to different sub-groups such as disadvantaged and advantaged, Negroes and whites?

No attempt is made here to provide a comprehensive statement of the technical procedures involved in validation.[6] Major attention is devoted instead to the second question posed above, with a view toward and offering guidelines for accomplishing, in a systematic way, the indi-vidualized prediction strategies proposed earlier.

It should be emphasized first that no single validity exists for any item of information or test. Instead, each datum must be understood in relation to the total network of interpretations that may be reliably derived from it. At any point in time, meaning can be derived only from the total accumulation of rationally and empirically developed knowl-edge available in relation to a given predictor. When relatively more information is available about the meaning of an aptitude test, for example, relatively more "clues" can be used for judging its possible rele-vance for making particular personnel decisions.

The test user must be alert constantly to the necessity of developing new information about interpretive meanings that may be attached to scores on the test. In this sense, the process of validation never ends; this is as it should be. Publishers, authors, and users of tests should assume joint responsibility for accumulating records and research infor-mation about tests, in order to extend knowledge about their meaning, interpretability, and potential uses.

Concurrent validation of an aptitude test—that is, simultaneous testing and derivation of job performance data—yields information only about behaviors concomitantly related to scores on the test. Such studies may underestimate the true degree of relationship between test scores and job behaviors since employees studied do not include those who were rejected initially, those who have failed and terminated employment, and those who, through outstanding effectiveness, may have been promoted to more responsible positions. The extent to which such factors can lead to an underestimate of empirical validity was shown recently by Peterson and Wallace (1966), who suggested that valid predictors may often be discarded simply because they failed to show significant validities in concurrent investigations. Little actually can be assured about a test's *predictive* usefulness from concurrent investigations; whenever possible, therefore, disadvantaged persons should be employed, tested, and then followed over time in longitudinal investigations to determine the true predictive behavioral meanings of tests.

Experimental validation strategies for learning about the meaning of test scores deserve much greater attention than they have received by applied psychologists. This is particularly important in view of the severe problems noted in interpreting the results of concurrent studies, and the low probability that many firms will hire applicants solely for the purpose of conducting predictive test validation studies.

The advantages of experiments designed to identify differential meanings of test scores are many. Subjects may be chosen to be much more representative of meaningful populations; for example, they may include all Negro or all white applicants applying for employment with a particular firm, or all Negroes with a certain level of educational attainment or with a particular background, or a variety of other subgroupings. Moreover, tests can be administered under the conditions and according to the standardizations specified by the manual, and behaviors against which to validate the test scores can be specified with much greater care and measured with much greater objectivity and precision than the typical job performance criteria currently available in industry. Most important, the effects of innumerable factors on both test performance and job behaviors can be determined; examples of such factors include race of test administrator, conditions of testing, extent and type of training used for job orientation, various job designs, length of time between testing and measurement of job behaviors, and many others.

THE SPECIAL RESPONSIBILITY OF PSYCHOLOGISTS

Psychologists and other professionals experienced in the field of testing bear a heavy responsibility in serving employers who seek help in effective manpower utilization. Many of these responsibilities, summarized below, are implicit in earlier sections of this statement.

- Before making any recommendations on the probable appropriateness of tests, the psychologist should insist on an opportunity to complete a comprehensive job analysis. Reliance on simple job descriptions is a dangerous practice.
- A careful search for all relevant studies bearing upon the jobs under consideration is essential.
- Careful study should be made of the implications of recommendations as they may unfairly affect the disadvantaged and other minority groups.
- In formulating hiring suggestions, less reliance should be placed on the overall correlation between test and criterion measure, and more on analyses of patterns that show the probabilities of successful performance for those at each test score level.
- A major effort should be directed at the development of sound measures of job performance, avoiding those already available that may be based either on biased observations, or contaminated by factors not reflecting employee effectiveness.
- Psychologists should insist on test administration practices that will provide both the employee and the employer with the soundest measures possible.
- Whenever opportunities permit, separate test validity studies should be obtained and reported for the disadvantaged so that the role of disadvantaged status as an important variable in personnel procedures can be further evaluated.

CONCLUDING DISCUSSION

When a company official makes a personnel decision, he assumes that it will have beneficial effects on the overall accomplishment of his organization's goals. This is true whatever the nature of the decision—for example, to hire or reject an applicant for employment; to promote, demote, or transfer an employee; to change his level of financial compensation; to include an employee in a specialized training or educational program; to redesign certain jobs; or to remodel the organizational structure of his firm. In a more immediate way, such decisions are made with the assumption that they will relate in some favorable way to expected employee job behaviors; that the employee's behaviors on the job will contribute to rather than detract from the overall success of his firm. Thus, he hopes to reject applicants who may be the least capable of contributing productively to his firm's well-being; he withholds financial rewards from less effective employees; or he chooses training or educational programs in the hope that employees attending them will return with new skills or attitudes that may enable them to perform their jobs more effectively.

The achievement of these corporate goals, however, must be seen as congruent with the realization of the individual's personal potentialities. Employers bear a legal as well as a moral commitment to hire, train, and place persons in jobs according to their skills and abilities, and without regard to personal characteristics such as sex, race, color, religion, or national origin. Employers, of course, have always been concerned with maintaining as high a level of accuracy as possible in their personnel decisions. Traditionally, however, they have been more concerned with avoiding costs related to errors when persons placed on jobs subsequently have failed (Select errors) than with costs incurred by the erroneous rejection of persons who, if placed on the job, would have been successful (Reject errors). It is clear that employers should give greater attention than they have to errors of the second type, which include increased costs involved in locating and evaluating additonal candidates, lowered productivity caused by job vacancies during periods of tight labor market conditions, and, equally important, the less tangible costs incurred by individuals and society when manpower resources go unused or underused.[7] The employer's stance should shift gradually from pure selection strategies to vocational guidance or accommodative strategies oriented toward using all available personnel methods to assure job success for all employees to whom a job commitment has been made.

The two goals, organization and personal, are intimately related in personnel decision making. It is important that those who make such decisions should avoid static concepts of jobs, people, organizations, and their interrelationships. The process is complex and constant, including individual diagnosis, job design and redesign, specialized training, counseling and vocational guidance, and the removal of organizational constraints blocking the exercise of employees' full potentialities.

Judgments about the selection of applicants or the promotion of employees should be made with full awareness, then, of the broader process of manpower use. The ultimate wisdom of accuracy in the selection of promotion decisions needs to be judged not simply in terms of traditional validity coefficients but, instead, according to the relative contributions made by individuals in accomplishing the aims of the organization. Thus, if an individual's capabilities can be enhanced through training, if the job can be changed by design or by other circumstances, or if initial errors in job placement can be rectified rather easily through transfers, such actions will help to define the true relationship between the results of individual assessment and job behavior outcomes. Knowledge about the results of such actions should be gathered and taken into account as an integral part of selection and promotion decisions.

Industry's primary goal in making personnel decisions should be to reach as wise and as informed a judgment as possible about each candidate for employment or promotion. The objective is to assure that the right people move into the right jobs at the right times and under the right circumstances. To accomplish this goal requires the gathering of evidence systematically concerning the individual characteristics of people, the special requirements of jobs, and the fit between the two. More broadly, it means that personnel decision making should move toward *individualized* prediction strategies in which each job candidate's individual merits and shortcomings are examined separately and in the context of *all* possible personnel actions—including job analysis and the development of job requirements, job design, vocational guidance, training or personnel development, and organizational planning.

Individualized strategies may not always be feasible, particularly when a firm must hire or promote large numbers of persons in a short period of time. Nonetheless, individualized prediction should be the primary aim, and it should be approximated as closely and as often as possible. In the final analysis, such a strategy merely grows out of the obvious principle that decisions about people and the work they do are among the most important made by industry. They should be individualized in much the same way as are management decisions regarding the choice of plant sites, capital expenditures for equipment, or mergers with other companies.

The ideal of full conservation of human resources demands careful appraisal of the curent capabilities of individuals in our society. Only by learning as much as possible about each person's relevant job skills, knowledges, and aptitudes can his special individuality be used in the optimum possible way for himself and for his society. Thus, individual appraisal is crucial as a means of differentiating from among a group those persons who have attributes particularly well suited for doing certain jobs or tasks, or those for whom specialized training may be particularly suitable. Personalized information of this kind is necessary for planning and organizing all other personnel decisions about men, jobs, and their interactions. Informed use of manpower, particularly disadvantaged manpower, cannot be well served by abrogating such appraisal procedures. If there were no individual appraisal, many job seekers would undergo a series of employment experiences ending in failure and leading eventually to demoralization as well as continued economic insecurity. People want the best job they can get, but they also want a job in which they can have some assurance of being successful. They want, in other words, to profit from a *sound* and *objective* discrimination of personal strengths and weaknesses in employment and promotion—not from the unfair and prejudging discrimination often seen in job settings.

No single personnel procedure—least of all psychological tests—can automatically be implicated or cleared in relation to unfair discriminatory practices. Such practices, with members of minority or disadvantaged groups as victims, have occurred in many different ways: failing to recruit in certain residential or geographic areas; demanding an advanced education for a clerk's job; refusing proper job training or orientation to minority group members; or utilizing a job-irrelevant or unduly difficult aptitude test to screen applicants or candidates for promotion. Such unfair practices will hardly be removed by focusing only on test usage as a target for special action, quite apart from actions directed toward the total personnel decision-making system.

Unfair discrimination in the world of work is a serious social ailment. In a sense, poor showing on tests may be one of many symptoms of this ailment. It is clear, however, that careful, informed, and judicious use of tests to aid in making personnel decisions can be essentially a positive rather than a negative action toward persons with backgrounds of limited opportunity. Moreover, effective use of tests may not be assured always by requiring the mere demonstration of a significant validity coefficient. Tests may be used as one objective way of identifying certain characteristics, proficiencies, or deficiencies believed by informed people to be relevant to behavior outcomes within a particular setting. To determine whether such test usage is unfair would require knowing whether the variables in question are actually measured by the tests, or whether they are, in fact, relevant at all to the presumed behavioral outcomes.

Full and fair use of our nation's manpower resources demands care and sophistication in *all* aspects of personnel decision making. Individual assessment—aided, where appropriate, by objective test information—is, to be sure, merely the first step in the personnel decision making, but it is the crucial first step. Such assessment structures all other personnel actions, and must be designed, therefore, with the ultimate objective of using effectively the unique characteristics of each member of society in the world of work. At issue are the dignity and self-respect of each citizen, and the social and economic well-being of his society.

Notes

[1]Members of the Committee are: Brent Baxter, *Chairman,* Douglas W. Bray, Abraham Carp, Marvin Dunnette, Robert L. Ebel, Samuel J. Messick, and Alexander G. Wesman. Albert P. Maslow and Julius Segal served as consultants on this project.

Requests for reprints should be sent to Brent N. Baxter, American Institutes for Research, 135 North Bellefield Avenue, Pittsburgh, Pennsylvania 15213.

[2]A more detailed discussion of each of these areas is provided by Doppelt and Bennett (1967).

[3]Delivered before the Greater Philadelphia Chamber of Commerce on June 8, 1967.

[4]In the prediction of scholastic performance, the evidence (Boney, 1966; Cleary, 1966; Cleary & Hilton, 1966; Munday, 1965; Stanley, Biaggio, & Porter, 1966; Stanley & Porter, 1967) strongly confirms that verbal and mathematics tests predict performance equally well for Negroes and whites. In predicting job performance, studies (Gordon, 1955; Kirkpatrick, Ewen, Barrett, & Katzell, 1967; Tenopyr, 1967) have yielded no clear trends, and no firm conclusions are possible.

[5]Further information concerning test construction and the requirements for a good test may be found in a technical report, *Standards for Educational and Psychological Tests and Manuals,* published by the American Psychological Association (1966).

[6]For these technical details, the reader is referred to such texts as Thorndike, 1949; Guion, 1965; or Dunnette, 1966.

[7]Different types of costs incurred by inaccuracies in personnel decisions are discussed more fully by Dunnette (1966), pp. 2-11 and 174-184.

References

American Psychological Association. *Standards for educational and psychological tests and manuals.* Washington, D.C.: Author, 1966.

Boney, J. D. Predicting the academic achievement of secondary school Negro students. *Personnel and Guidance Journal,* 1966, *44,* 700-703.

Cleary, T. A. Test bias: Validity of the scholastic aptitude test for Negro and white students in integrated colleges. (Research Bulletin 66-31) Princeton, N.J.: Educational Testing Service, 1966.

Cleary, T. A., & Hilton, T. L. An investigation of item bias. (Research Bulletin 66-17) Princeton, N.J.: Educational Testing Service, 1966.

Dunnette, M. D. *Personnel selection and placement.* Belmont, Calif.: Wadsworth, 1966.

Doppelt, J. E., & Bennett, G. K. Testing job applicants from disadvantaged groups. *Test Service Bulletin,* No. 57. New York: Psychological Corporation, 1967.

Ghiselli, E. E., & Haire, M. The validation of selection tests in the light of the dynamic character of criteria. *Personnel Psychology,* 1960, *13,* 225-231.

Gordon, M. A. Influence of background factors upon the prediction of success in Air Force Training Schools: A review of the literature. Lackland Air Force Base, Texas. Air Force Personnel and Training Research Center, June 1955, Research Report AFPTRC-TN-55-4.

Guion, R. M. *Personnel testing.* New York: McGraw-Hill, 1965.

Guion, R. M. Synthetic validity in a small company: A demonstration. *Personnel Psychology,* 1965, *18,* 49-65.

Kirkpatrick, J. J., Ewen, R. B., Barrett, R. S., & Katzell, R. A. Differential selection among applicants from different socio-economic or ethnic backgrounds. *Final Report to Ford Foundation,* New York University, 1967.

Lawshe, C. H., & Balma, M. J. *Principles of personnel testing.* (2nd ed.) New York: McGraw-Hill, 1966.

Munday, L. Predicting college grades in predominantly Negro colleges. *Journal of Educational Measurement,* 1965, *2,* 157-160.

Peterson, D. A., & Wallace, S. R. Validation and revision of a test in use. *Journal of Applied Psychology,* 1966, *50,* 13-18.

Rusmore, J. T. *Psychological tests and fair employment: A study of employment testing in the San Francisco Bay area.* State of California Fair Employment Practice Commission, 1967.

Stanley, J. C., Biaggio, A. B., & Porter, A. C. Relative predictability of freshman grade-point averages from SAT scores in Negro and white southern colleges. Paper read at AERA and NCME, Chicago, February 1966.

Stanley, J. C., & Porter, A. C. Correlation of scholastic aptitude test score with college grades for Negroes versus whites. *Journal of Educational Measurement*, 1967, *4*, 199-229.

Tenopyr, M. L. Race and socioeconomic status as moderators in predicting machineshop training success. Paper presented at the meeting of the American Psychological Association, Washington, D.C., September 1967.

Thorndike, R. L. *Personnel selection: Test and measurement techniques.* New York: Wiley, 1949.

Webster, E. C. *Decision making in the employment interview.* Montreal, Quebec: McGill University, 1964.

Wesman, A. G. Expectancy tables—A way of interpreting test validity. *Test Service Bulletin*, No. 38. New York: Psychological Corporation, 1949.

Bibliography

Ash, P. Selection techniques and the law: Discrimination in hiring and placement. *Personnel*, Nov.-Dec., 1967, *44*, 8-17.

Ash, P. The implication of the Civil Rights Act of 1964 for psychological assessment in industry. *American Psychologist*, 1966, *21*, 797-803.

Balma, M. J. The concept of synthetic validity. *Personnel Psychology*, 1959, *12*, 395-396.

Berdie, R. F. Intra-individual variability and predictability. *Educational and Psychological Measurement*, 1961, *21*, 663-676.

Bianchini, J. C., Heath, R. W., Danielson, W. F., & Hilliard, C. A. The Berkeley project: Race and socio-economic status in the selection testing of municipal personnel. City of Berkeley, California, October 1966. (Mimeo)

Campbell, D. T., & Fiske, D. W. Convergent and discriminant validation by the multitrait-multimethod matrix. *Psychological Bulletin*, 1959, *56*, 81-105.

Dunnette, M. D. A note on *the* criterion. *Journal of Applied Psychology*, 1963, *47*, 251-255.

Dunnette, M. D., & Kirchner, W. K. Validation of psychological tests in industry. *Personnel Administration*, 1958, *21*, 20-27.

Ebel, R. L. Must all tests be valid? *American Psychologist*, 1961, *16*, 640-647.

Fair employment practices equal good employment practices—guidelines for testing and selecting minority job applicants. Prepared by the *Technical Advisory Committee on Testing* (an Advisory Committee of the Fair Employment Practice Commission), State of California, May 1966.

Flanagan, J. C. The critical incident technique. *Psychological Bulletin*, 1954, *51*, 327-358.

Frederiksen, N., & Gilbert, A. C. Replication of a study of differential predictability. *Educational and Psychological Measurement*, 1960, *20*, 759-767.

Frederiksen, N., & Melville, S. D. Differential predictability in the use of test scores. *Educational and Psychological Measurement*, 1954, *14*, 647-656.

Gardner, J. W. *Excellence.* New York: Harper, 1961.

Ghiselli, E. E. Differentiation of individuals in terms of their predictability. *Journal of Applied Psychology*, 1956, *40*, 374-377.

Ghiselli, E. E. The prediction of predictability. *Educational and Psychological Measurement*, 1960, *20*, 3-8.

Ghiselli, E. E. Differentiation of tests in terms of the accuracy with which they predict for a given individual. *Educational and Psychological Measurement*, 1960, *20*, 657-684.

Ghiselli, E. E. Moderating effects and differential reliability and validity. *Journal of Applied Psychology*, 1963, *47*, 81-86.

Grooms, R. R., & Endler, N. S. The effect of anxiety on academic achievement. *Journal of Educational Psychology*, 1960, *51*, 229-304.

Guion, R. M. Criterion measurement and personnel judgments. *Personnel Psychology*, 1961, *14*, 141-149.

Guion, R. M. Employment tests and discriminatory hiring. *Industrial Relations*, 1966, *5*, 20-37.

Klein, S. P., Rock, D. A., & Evans, F. R. *The use of multiple moderators in academic prediction.* (Research Bulletin 67-50) Princeton, N.J.: Educational Testing Service, 1967.

Lockwood, H. C. Developing fair employment programs: Guidelines for selection. *Personnel,* 1966, *43,* 50-57.

Lockwood, H. C. Testing minority applicants for employment. *Personnel Journal,* 1965, *44,* 357-360.

Lykken, D. T., & Rose, R. Psychological prediction from actuarial tables. *Journal of Clinical Psychology,* 1963, *19,* 139-151.

Parrish, J. A., Lockwood, H. C., Lopez, F. M., Jr., Dugan, R. D., Krug, R. E., & Bayroff, A. G. The industrial psychologist: Selection and equal employment opportunity (a symposium). *Personnel Psychology,* 1966, *19,* 1-39.

Rusmore, J. T. Psychological tests and fair employment: A study of employment testing in the San Francisco Bay area. *Fair Employment Practice Commission,* State of California, January 1967.

Seashore, H. G. *Women are more predictable than men.* Presidential address, Division 17, presented at the meeting of the American Psychological Association, New York, September 1961.

Sorenson, W. W. Configural scoring of biographical items for predicting scales success. Unpublished doctoral dissertation, University of Minnesota, 1964.

United States Civil Service Commission. *Job element examining: Handbook for Wage Board occupations.* Washington, D.C.: Author, October 1967.

United States Civil Service Commission. *Job element examining instruction manual.* Washington, D.C.: Author, December 1967.

Wallace, S. R. Criteria for what? *American Psychologist,* 1965, *20,* 411-417.

Wesman, A. G. What is an aptitude? *Test Service Bulletin,* No. 36. New York: Psychological Corporation, 1948.

Racial Differences in Validity of Employment Tests: Reality or Illusion?

FRANK L. SCHMIDT[1]
JOHN G. BERNER
JOHN E. HUNTER

The fit of data in the literature on single-group validity of employ-ment tests to a statistical model assuming equal true validities for blacks and whites was tested. For both subjective and objective criterion measures, observed frequencies of both kinds of single-group validity (significant for whites but not for blacks and vice versa) were not significantly different from those predicted by the null differences model. These findings cast serious doubt on the existence of single-group and differential validity as substantive phenomena. It was concluded that psychologists concerned with the applicability of employment tests to minority groups should direct their future efforts to the study and determination of test fairness rather than to the pseudoproblem of racial differences in test validity.

The possibility that employment tests and other selection devices might be unfair to, and/or inappropriate for, blacks and other minority group members has caused great concern in recent years. Although it is often not made clear, there are two different and distinct phenomena involved in this area: (a) test fairness and (b) validity differences. Although there is disagreement as to the definition of test fairness (Cleary, 1968; Dar-lington, 1971; Thorndike, 1971), no one disputes the proposition that subgroup differences in validity coefficients are a separate phenomenon.

Boehm (1972) distinguishes between two kinds of validity differ-ences: (a) differential validity, in which there is a significant difference

---

Reprinted from *Journal of Applied Psychology,* 1973, *58*(1), 5-9. Copyright © 1973 by the American Psychological Association. Reprinted by permission of the publisher and the authors.

between the validity coefficients obtained for the two ethnic groups and one or both coefficients are significantly different from zero; and (b) single-group validity, in which the obtained validity is significantly different from zero for one group only and there is no significant difference between the two coefficients. In her review, Boehm (1972) noted that the frequency of single-group validity was about five times that of differential validity.

The purpose of the present study is to determine whether a statistical model of the validation situation which assumes there are no true differences between blacks and whites in validity of employment tests can adequately account for the findings of single-group validity reported in the literature. There are a number of a priori reasons for hypothesizing that such a model may fit: (a) small sample sizes, especially for blacks, are quite common in these studies; (b) large differences between sample sizes for the two races are quite common, greatly increasing probabilities of single-group validity; and (c) failure to cross-validate (after ex post facto identification of single-group validities) is apparently a universal practice.[2]

It has been suggested (Boehm, 1972; Bray & Moses, 1972) that findings of validity differences by race are associated with the use of subjective criteria, such as ratings, rankings, grades, etc., and that validity differences seldom occur when more objective criteria are employed. A second purpose of the present study is to test this hypothesis by examining the fit of the null differences model separately for the two kinds of criteria. In essence, this hypothesis predicts that, using objective criteria, the model will fit validity data generated, but that the frequency of single-group validity with subjective criteria will be higher than can be accounted for by chance.

The model to be tested is illustrated in Figure 1. Validity coefficients are in the form of Fischer's Z, which has an approximately normal distribution for all values of r. $SD_Z = 1 \sqrt{N} - 3$, which for the white sample of 100 is .10 and for the black sample of 20 is .24. In this hypothetical, but perhaps typical, situation the true validity of both races is .34 ($Z = .35$). If both these distributions are transformed to unit normal distributions [$N(0,1)$], the probability of obtaining a nonsignificant validity coefficient in the white sample is the area a (approximately .07) and the probability of a significant coefficient is the area $1 - a$ (here approximately .93). The minimum Fischer Z validity needed for significance at the .05 level when $N = 100$ is .20. In the black sample, area b represents the probability of a nonsignificant coefficient (.69 here), and $1 - b$ or .31 is the probability of a significant coefficient. When $N = 20$, the minimum Fischer Z needed for significance at the .05 level is .47.

Figure 1
Statistical Model of Biracial Validation When
True Validity for Both Races is .34 (Fischer's $Z = .35$)

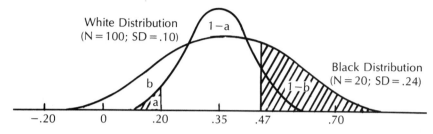

Fischer's Z Transformation of Validities

Now, since outcomes in the two distributions are independent (given the assumption of uncorrelated errors of measurement), the probability of a joint event is the product of its individual probabilities. Thus, the probability of obtaining a nonsignificant coefficient for blacks and a significant one for whites [$p(W_s, B_{ns})$] is $b(1 - a)$ or $(.69)$ $(.93)$. Similarly, the probability that the validity for both groups will reach significance [$p(W_s, B_s)$] is $(1 - a)$ $(1 - b)$ or $(.93)$ $(.31)$. Validities will be nonsignificant for both samples $p(W_{ns}, B_{ns})$ with probability $a b$ or $(.07)$ $(.69)$, and the probability that the black but not the white sample will show a significant coefficient [$p(W_{ns}, B_s)$] is $a(1 - b)$ or $(.07)$ $(.31)$. The sum of these four joint probabilities is 1.00. It should be noted that, even though true validity is the same for both races, the probability of nonsignificance for blacks and significance for whites is much greater than the reverse outcome (.64 vs. .02). This model takes into account not only the size of each sample, but the difference in size between samples and the overall level of validity.

Method

Nineteen studies reporting employment test validities separately by race were found; these studies included 86 different predictors and 74 different criterion measures. A total of 410 pairs of validity coefficients and sample sizes were reported.[3] For each of these pairs, both validities were converted to a Fischer Z and averaged to provide an estimate of the true validity. Application of the model[4] shown in Figure 1 using a computer program[5] written for this purpose yielded estimates of the probabilities of each of the four possible validation outcomes (W_{ns}, B_{ns}; W_s, B_s; W_s, B_{ns}; and B_s, W_{ns}) for each of the 410 data sets. Probabilities of each outcome were summed across data sets to provide the expected frequency of each outcome. Observed frequencies were then tested against those expected using chi-square. This analysis was then done separately for the 161 and 249 data sets involving subjective and objective criterion measures, respectively. All ratings, rankings, etc., and grades in training (when not based on performance measures) were considered as subjective criteria; performance measures such as quality and quantity of output, job sample measures of proficiency, errors, attendance, tenure, written job knowledge tests, and the like were considered objective criteria. Although they depend to some extent on subjective evaluations, salary level and promotions were considered to be closer to objective than subjective criteria and were classified as the former.

Results and Discussion

Table 1 shows the distribution of the four validation outcomes for each of the 19 studies reviewed, the observed totals for each outcome, and the expected frequency for each outcome as predicted by the null model. The chi-square of 1.39 does not even approach significance, and for each of the four validation outcomes the predicted frequency is quite close to the observed frequency.[6] The separate analyses for validities computed on objective and subjective criteria are shown in Table 2. As predicted, the model-generated predictions are not significantly different from observed frequencies for the data based on objective criteria; however, the hypothesis that observed single-group validity would be more frequent with subjective criteria than would be predicted by the null model was not borne out. The slight trend in the direction of the hypothesis is neither statistically nor practically significant.

The proportion of validity pairs showing single-group validity was significantly higher for subjective than objective criterion measures (.37 vs. .20, $p < .001$). But this difference is apparently due to differences between the two data sets in individual sample sizes, differences between black and white sample sizes, and general level of validity—factors which the model takes into account—rather than to differences intrinsic to the two kinds of criterion measures. The conclusion indicated is that when the extrinsic factors are controlled, ratings, rankings, and other subjective criteria are no more likely to generate instances of single-group validity than are more objective criterion measures, and neither kind of criterion measure is associated with frequencies of single-group validity higher than would be expected on the basis of chance alone.

A conservative interpretation of these findings is that they cast serious doubt on the existence of single-group validity as a substantive phenomenon. The close fit of the null model likewise indicates that differential validity—which is much less frequently reported in the

Table 1

Observed and Model-Predicted Validation Outcomes in
19 Studies of Racial Differences in Validity

Study	Both ns	Both s	W_s, B_{ns}	W_{ns}, B_s
Campbell, Pike, & Flaugher (1969)	0	8	0	0
Campion & Freihoff (1970)	5	0	1	4
Farr (1971)				
Study 1	1	0	4	0
Study 2	79	0	7	4
Farr, O'Leary, & Bartlett (1971)				
Study 1	17	0	2	2
Study 2	28	7	22	3
Flaugher, Campbell, & Pike (1969)	16	9	3	8
Gael & Grant (1972)	14	6	14	1
Grant & Bray (1970)	0	8	0	0
Kirkpatrick, Ewen, Barrett, & Katzell (1968)				
Study 1	23	0	1	0
Study 2	22	0	4	2
Study 3[a]	2	1	0	3
Study 5	2	8	6	0
Lopez (1966)	8	3	4	1
Mitchell, Albright, & McMurry (1968)	2	0	0	0
Ruda & Albright (1968)	0	1	1	0
Wollowick, Greenwood, & McNamara (1969)	15	3	5	1
Wood (1969)	7	2	1	0
U.S. Department of Labor (1969)[b]	3	1	0	5
Observed totals[c]	244 (59.5%)	57 (12.9%)	75 (18.3%)	34 (8.3%)
Totals predicted from model[c]	233.8 (57.0%)	63.4 (15.5%)	75.5 (18.4%)	37.3 (9.1%)

Note. Abbreviations: ns = nonsignificant, s = significant, W = white, B = black.
[a] Included Spanish Americans, which were excluded for the purposes of this analysis.
[b] Data includes one American Indian.
[c] X^2 = 1.39, ns ($p > .80$).

literature—is probably illusory in nature. Psychologists concerned with
the applicability of employment tests to minority groups should probably direct their future efforts to the study and determination of test

Table 2
Observed and Predicted Validation Outcomes for Objective and Subjective Criteria

Validation Outcome	Both ns	Both s	W_s, B_{ns}	W_{ns}, B_s	Total
		Objective criteria[a]			
Observed	162 (65.1%)	37 (14.9%)	33(13.3%)	17 (6.8%)	249
Predicted	155.0 (62.3%)	34.2 (13.7%)	36.5 (14.7%)	23.3 (9.4%)	249
		Subjective criteria[b]			
Observed	82 (50.9%)	20 (12.4%)	42 (26.1%)	17 (10.5%)	161
Predicted	78.8 (48.9%)	29.2 (18.1%)	39.0 (24.2%)	14.0 (8.7%)	161

Note. ns = nonsignificant, s = significant, W = white, B = black.
[a] $\chi^2 = 3.91$, ns ($p > .20$).
[b] $\chi^2 = 2.59$, ns ($p > .50$).

fairness rather than to the pseudoproblem of subgroup differences in validity coefficients.

Notes

[1] Frank L. Schmidt, John G. Berner, and John E. Hunter were affiliated with Michigan State University, East Lansing, Michigan, at the time of publication of this article. Requests for reprints should be sent to Frank L. Schmidt, Department of Psychology, Michigan State University, East Lansing, Michigan 48823.

[2] Of the 19 researches on validity differences reviewed for this study, none employed cross-validation. This is true despite the fact that many studies involved ex post facto examination of large numbers of pairs of coefficients. Farr, O'Leary, and Bartlett (1971), for example, reported 80 pairs of coefficients.

[3] Average sample size for blacks across the 19 studies reviewed here was 49.4; for whites it was 99.7.

[4] Alpha level used was .05; likewise, in tabulating the observed frequencies of each validation outcome in the literature, all validities significant at or beyond .05 were tabulated as significant.

[5] Copies of this program are available from the senior author.

[6] The relatively high frequency (observed and predicted) of lack of validity for both races is probably due in part to direct restriction in range on predictor scores; in several of the studies, some of the predictors had previously been employed as part of the selection procedure for the job in question (Kirkpatrick, Ewen, Barrett, & Katzell, 1968, Studies 1 and 2; Lopez, 1966; Mitchell, Albright, & McMurry, 1968; Ruda & Albright, 1968). In addition, indirect restriction in range (Thorndike, 1949, pp. 169-176) was probably a factor in these and other studies, inasmuch as incumbents serving as subjects were probably selected at least partly on tests correlated with the predictors investigated.

References

Boehm, V. R. Negro-white differences in validity of employment and training selection procedures. *Journal of Applied Psychology*, 1972, *56*, 33-39.

Bray, D. W., & Moses, J. L. Personnel selection. *Annual Review of Psychology*, 1972, *23*, 545-576.

Campbell, J. T., Pike, L. W., & Flaugher, R. L. *Prediction of job performance for Negro and White medical technicians—a regression analysis of potential test bias: Predicting job knowledge scores from an aptitude battery.* (Rep. No. PR-69-6) Princeton, N.J.: Educational Testing Service, 1969.

Campion, J. E., & Freihoff, E. C. *Unintentional bias when using racially mixed employee samples for test validation.* (Experimental Publication System, Ms. No. 285-2) Washington, D.C.: American Psychological Association, 1970.

Cleary, T. A. Test bias: Prediction of grades of Negro and white students in integrated colleges. *Journal of Educational Measurement*, 1968, *5*, 115-124.

Darlington, R. B. Another look at "cultural fairness." *Journal of Educational Measurement*, 1971, *8*, 71-82.

Farr, J. L. The use of work sample and culture-fair tests in the prediction of job success with racially mixed groups. Paper presented at the meeting of the American Psychological Association, Washington, D.C., September 1971.

Farr, J. L., O'Leary, B. S., & Bartlett, C. J. Ethnic group membership as a moderator of the prediction of job performance. *Personnel Psychology*, 1971, *24*, 609-636.

Flaugher, R. L., Campbell, J. T., & Pike, L. W. *Ethnic group membership as a moderator of supervisor's ratings.* (Research Bulletin No. PR-69-5) Princeton, N.J.: Educational Testing Service, 1969.

Gael, S., & Grant, D. L. Employment test validation for minority and nonminority telephone company service representatives. *Journal of Applied Psychology*, 1972, *56*, 135-139.

Grant, D. L., & Bray, D. W. Validation of employment tests for telephone company installation and repair occupations. *Journal of Applied Psychology*, 1970, *54*, 7-14.

Kirkpatrick, J. J., Ewen, R. B., Barrett, R. S., & Katzell, R. A. *Testing and fair employment.* New York: New York University Press, 1968.

Lopez, F. M. Current problems in test performance: I. *Personnel Psychology*, 1966, *19*, 10-18.

Mitchell, M. D., Albright, L. E., & McMurry, F. D. Biracial validation of selection procedures in a large southern plant. *Proceedings of the 76th Annual Convention of the American Psychological Association*, 1968, *3*, 575-576. (Summary)

Ruda, E., & Albright, L. E. Racial differences on selection instruments related to subsequent job performance. *Personnel Psychology*, 1968, *21*, 31-41.

Thorndike, R. L. *Personnel selection.* New York: Wiley, 1949.

Thorndike, R. L. Concepts of culture fairness. *Journal of Educational Measurement*, 1971, *8*, 63-70.

United States Department of Labor, Manpower Administration. *Development of U.S.T.E.S. Aptitude Test Battery for Welder, Production Line (Welding).* (Tech. Rep. No. S-447) Washington, D.C.: U.S. Training and Employment Service, 1969.

Wollowick, H. B., Greenwood, J. M., & McNamara, W. J. Psychological testing with a minority group population. *Proceedings of the 77th Annual Convention of the American Psychological Association*, 1969, *4*, 609-610. (Summary)

Wood, M. T. Validation of a selection test against a turnover criterion for racial and sex subgroups of employees. Paper presented at the meeting of the Midwestern Psychological Association, Chicago, May 1969.

Negro-White Differences in Validity of Employment and Training Selection Procedures: Summary of Research Evidence[1]

VIRGINIA R. BOEHM[2]

Thirteen recent research studies dealing with Negro-white differences and similarities in the validity of employment and training selection procedures are examined. One hunderd of the 160 validity coefficients computed in this research are not significant for either Negroes or whites, indicating the need for validation prior to operational use. The valid coefficients rarely differ in degree of validity for Negroes and whites with significant differences being found only in seven instances. Statistical significance of validity coefficients for one group and not the other occurs in 33 instances. These instances of single-group validity appear to be related to the use of ratings rather than more objective measures as criteria and to the use of small samples. The combination of ethnic groups yields lower validity than for either group separately on only 3 out of 120 instances. Overall, there is very little evidence of differential validity, and single-group validity appears linked to the methodology of the study.

The possibility of different validities for Negroes and whites of employment tests and other employment and training selection devices has caused great concern during recent years. If the same procedures used in a selection situation demonstrate either significantly different validities for these groups or significant validity for one group but not the other, the implications are serious both from the viewpoint of those concerned with equal employment opportunity and the users of selection

Reprinted from *Journal of Applied Psychology*, 1972, 56(1), 33-39. Copyright © 1972 by the American Psychological Association. Reprinted by permission of the publisher and the authors.

tests. This review examines the presently available empirical data on this topic, focusing on two kinds of situations—differential validity and single-group validity.

A situation where *differential validity* exists is here defined as one where: (a) There is a significant difference between the correlation coefficient of a selection device and a criterion obtained for one ethnic group and the correlation of the same device with the same criterion obtained for the other group. And (b) the validity coefficients are significantly different from zero for one or both groups.

A related but not identical situation is that where a given predictor exhibits validity significantly different from zero for one group only, and there is no significant difference between the two validity coefficients. This situation is here termed *single-group validity*.

As the area investigated is employment and job-training selection procedures, studies in conventional school settings are not considered, although industrial training situations are included. Also excluded are studies where the samples of the two groups are drawn from different sources.

Thirteen studies that cover a variety of occupations and involve widely varying numbers of Ss are discussed here. They differ greatly in techniques used and the methodological sophistication. Some of the studies used experimental tests, other studies used the actual predictors used in the selection process. In some, the criterion measures used were devised especially for the study. In others, the investigators used routine company ratings, termination indexes, or other measures. Among the 13 studies, 57 predictors and 38 criterion measures are used. Only the roughest comparison across studies is possible as they have in common only the elements for which they were selected, that is, at least one predictor and one criterion, with separate correlations for white and Negro Ss in a situation involving employment or training selection procedures.

Criterion-Related Validity

Before the questions of differential or single-group validities can be dealt with, the data from these studies should be examined to assess the extent of any criterion-related validity for either or both groups. Table 1 lists the studies, the occupations involved, the number of Negro and white Ss, the number of predictors and criteria, the number of correlation coefficients computed for each ethnic group, and the number of those that were significant at the .05 level (in either direction) for either or both groups.

It would appear that complete lack of criterion-related validity is a serious problem in these studies. The majority (100 out of 160) of the

Table 1
Criterion-Related Validity in Differential Validity Studies

Investigator	Occupation	Ss		NO. measure		Validity coefficient	
		White	Negro	Predictors	Criteria	Computed	p < .05 for either or both ethnic groups
Campbell, Pike, & Flaugher (1969); Flaugher, Campbell, & Pike, 1969; Pike, 1969	Medical technicians	297	168	8	1	8	8
Grant & Bray (1970)	Telephone craftsmen	219	211	8	1	8	8
Kirkpatrick, Ewen, Barrett, & Katzell (1968)							
Study 1	Clerical workers	100	26	5	6	30	1
Study 2	Clerical workers	39	33	7	4	28	6
Study 3a[a]	General maintenance	30	50	2	2	4	3
Study 3b[a]	Heavy vehicle operator	39	38	2	1	2	1
Lopez (1966)	Toll collectors	80	102	4	4	16	7
Mitchell, Albright, & McMurry (1968)	Semiskilled hourly workers	830	194	1	2	2	0
Ruda & Albright (1968)	Office personnel	176	67	2	1	2	2
Tenopyr (1967)[b]	Machine shop trainees	84	83	4	10	40	12
Wollowick, Greenwood, & McNamara (1969)[c]	Administrative personnel	60	60	4	2	8	5
Wood (1969)	Psychiatric aides	544	222	1	3	3	1
United States Department of Labor (1969)[d]	Welders	59	57	9	1	9	6
Total						160	60

a These studies also included Spanish Americans not discussed here. Two other studies in the book by Kirkpatrick et al. (1968) are not included because the Negro and white samples were drawn from different sources, and one also involved a school setting.
b Twelve additional criterion measures used by Tenopyr (1967) were grades earned in each quarter of the training courses. The final grades are included here and the use of the quarter grades was felt to be unnecessary.
c The white subsample, matched with the Negro sample on total test scores, was used in this analysis.
d One American Indian is grouped with the Negro sample in the data analysis.

predictor and criterion combinations used did not yield significant correlations for either ethnic group.

In several of these studies (Kirkpatrick, Ewen, Barrett, & Katzell, 1968, Studies 1 & 2; Lopez, 1966; Mitchell, Albright, & McMurry, 1968; Ruda & Albright, 1968; Tenopyr, 1967) at least some of the predictors in the studies had been used as part of the selection procedure for the occupation being investigated, with resultant restriction of range. The predictors in these studies were generally of low validity. Since only one study (Lopez, 1966) investigated restriction of range, it cannot be clearly determined to what extent low criterion-related validities can be attributed to this cause.

The use of tests or other predictors in selection prior to their validation for the occupation or training program, in addition to creating restriction of range problems of unknown severity for the investigator, tends to exclude a higher proportion of Negro than white applicants at the outset, as Negroes tend to score lower on many kinds of tests (Dreger & Miller, 1968; Moore & MacNaughton, 1966; Rosen, 1970; Wallace, Kissinger, & Reynolds, 1966). This exclusion appears to have happened in some cases (Kirkpatrick et al., 1968, Study 2; Mitchell et al., 1968; Ruda & Albright, 1968) so that methodological problems of range restriction are compounded by small Ns in the Negro group.

Other studies that did not use the experimental predictors as heavily weighted parts of the selection procedure demonstrated methodological improvements. In one study (Grant & Bray, 1970) the investigators were able to exert considerable control over the hiring process itself, assuring that substantial numbers of Negroes and whites who did not meet usual hiring standards were employed and included in the sample. They were therefore able to maximize the chances of equating the predictor means of the Negro and white samples, removing one source of variation that tends to complicate interpretation of these studies. The use of a task criterion also represented an improvement in that it removed a source of potential bias from the assessment procedure.

Wollowick, Greenwood, and McNamara (1969) attempted to control several sources of variation by matching the Negro sample with three white subsamples, one matched on total test score, one on supervisors' rating, and one on salary. While other kinds of controls, for example, tenure and education, could be investigated, this study is notable for the emphasis placed on the existence of secondary differences in S population that frequently interact with the primary difference.

The low validity obtained in many of these studies could also be viewed as a function of the criterion measures used. Campbell, Pike, & Flaugher (1969) compare both aptitude test scores and supervisors' ratings against the same criterion, a "Job Knowledge Test," so as to be able to examine not only the validity of the predictor tests but also the validity of supervisors' ratings. Their discovery that rating differences were related to both the supervisors' and the workers' ethnic group membership suggests a whole line of research that requires further exploration. In view of the fact that supervisory ratings of some form are by far the most common criteria used in validity studies (Bennett, 1969; Guion, 1965; Owens & Jewell, 1969) the potential implications of such a finding are great.

That there might be biasing factors in some of the ratings used in these studies is indicated by the fact that the obtained validities in the Campbell, Pike, and Flaugher (1969) study using the Job Knowledge Test were quite high, as were those in the research of Grant and Bray (1970) where a performance criterion was also used.

Differential and Single-Group Validities

Because the one instance where the correlations of a predictor and criterion, while insignificant for both groups were significantly different from each other, cannot properly be considered differential validity, this discussion of differential and single-group validities deals only with those 60 instances in Table 1 where the predictor concerns showed some significant criterion-related validity with one or both ethnic groups.

Table 2 divides the number of significant validity coefficients into those significant for Negroes only, whites only, and both. The last column contains the number of instances where the correlation coefficients are significantly different at the .05 level (two-tailed test) for Negroes and whites, according to the procedure outlined by Guilford (1965, pp. 189–190).

When differential validity is strictly defined as a significant difference in the Negro and white validity coefficients, there are seven occurrences out of the 60 instances where some validity was present for one or both ethnic groups. While this is a number slightly higher than would be expected if differential validity were a chance outcome, it does not indicate a widespread phenomenon, especially since three of these seven were from the Lopez (1966) study where the total group correlations were uncorrected and the subgroup ones corrected for restriction of range.

These instances and the more common event of single-group validity which occurs in 33 instances (6 of which overlap with the instances of differential validity) can be attributed to inadequate samples in many cases. None of the studies where the N of both Negro and white samples exceeded 100 (Campbell et al., 1969; Grant & Bray, 1970; Mitchell et al., 1968; Wood, 1969) contributed any instances of either differential or single-group validity.

Table 2

Differential and Single-Group Validities for Negroes and Whites

Investigator	No. Validity Coefficients Significant for:			No. Cases Significantly Different Validity
	Both Groups	White Only	Negro Only	
Campbell, Pike & Flaugher (1969); Flaugher, Campbell, & Pike, 1969; Pike, 1969	8	0	0	0
Grant & Bray (1970)	8	0	0	0
Kirkpatrick, Ewen, Barrett, & Katzell (1968)				
Study 1	0	1	0	0
Study 2	0	4	2	1
Study 3a	0	0	3	1
Study 3b	1	0	0	0
Lopez (1966)[a]	2	4	1	3
Mitchell, Albright, & McMurry (1968)	0	0	0	0
Ruda & Albright (1968)	1	1	0	1
Tenopyr (1967)	5	5	2	0
Wollowick, Greenwood, & McNamara (1969)[b]	0	5	0	0
Wood (1969)	1	0	0	0
United States Department of Labor (1969)	1	0	5	1
Total	27	20	13	7

[a] This analysis uses the actual rating sample N rather than the applicant population N from the Lopez (1966) study.

[b] Wollowick et al. (1969) report three significantly different validities. However, these are not significant when a two-tailed test is used.

There is also some indication that single-group validity, like absence of validity, may depend on the criterion involved. Table 2 indicates that of 60 instances where some validity was demonstrated, 27 involved significant validity coefficients for both groups, and 33 were cases of single-group validity (20 cases of validity for whites only, 13 cases of validity for Negroes only). Examination of the studies involved shows that in 22 of the 27 cases of overall validity, the criterion used was something other than a rating, ranking, or grade. On the other hand, 19 of the 33 instances of single-group validity involved some type of rating criteria.

It would seem that when some objective measure of job performance or a complex behavioral measure such as termination, salary, etc.
is used as a criterion, single-group validity is uncommon. It seems possible, however, that supervisors and instructors may in some instances
rate Negro and white employees differently enough so that predictors
valid for one group are not valid for the other when a rating criterion
is used.

Other theoretically possible situations that might contribute to
discrimination in selection tests (although not involving differential or
single-group validity) have been described by Bartlett and O'Leary
(1969, pp. 4–5). These situations could result when there is a mean difference between the Negroes and whites on either the predictor or the
criterion, resulting in a validity coefficient for the combined sample
smaller than that for either group.

In Table 3, those instances from Table 1 where total-group as well
as single-group correlations are available are divided into three situations: (a) those where the combined validity coefficient is numerically
less than that for either subgroup, (b) those where it is greater, and (c)
situations where the combined validity coefficient is between or the same
as the two ethnic group validities.

It is quite clear that combining the two groups is more likely to add
to the overall validity than subtract from it. There are only 3 cases out
of 120 where validity is decreased by combining the groups as opposed
to 23 cases where it is increased. In over three-fourths of the cases, the
combined validity coefficient is between that of the two groups, as would
be expected if the Negroes and whites in the same occupation were considered two samples drawn from the same population.

Discussion

The concept of differential validity has received far more attention than
the data would seem to justify. There appear to be at least five reasons
for this. In the first place, the practical significance of even occasional
incidents of differential validity can be severe. While the data would
indicate that such cases are the exception, a routine check for differential
validity should be made when the samples used in validity studies permit it.

Also, the initial published research study (Lopez, 1966) showed the
strongest indications of differential validity yet obtained. As has been
mentioned previously, however, the statistical procedures used in the
Lopez study make interpretation and evaluation of the results difficult.
But since it represented the first empirical evidence in this socially relevant area, the Lopez study received disproportionate attention.

Table 3

Comparison of Negro, White, and Total Group Validity Coefficients

Investigator	Validity Coefficient Computed[a]	Instances Where Numerical Value of the Total Group Validity Coefficient is:		
		Lower Than Either Ethnic Group	Higher Than Either Ethnic Group	Between the Ethnic Groups or Equal
Grant & Bray (1970)	8	0	2	6
Kirkpatrick, Ewen, Barrett, & Katzell (1968)				
Study 1	30	0	0	30
Study 2	28	2	2	24
Ruda & Albright (1968)	2	0	0	2
Tenopyr (1967)	40	0	15	25
Wood (1969)	3	1	0	2
United States Department of Labor (1969)	9	0	4	5
Total	120	3	23	94

Note.—The Campbell, Pike, & Flaugher (1969); Mitchell, Albright, & McMurry (1968); and Wollowick, Greenwood, & McNamara (1969) studies do not provide validity coefficients for the total group. The data from Kirkpatrick, Ewen, Barrett, & Katzell (1968), Studies 3a and 3b, includes the Spanish-American *S*s in the total group correlations. Lopez (1966) presents correlations corrected for restriction of range for the ethnic groups and uncorrected for the total group. For these reasons, data from these studies are not included in this table.
[a] Computed from Table 1.

Another reason for the popularity of the differential validity concept is the use of nonvalidated tests. Lack of relevance of selection procedures is a prime consideration of those concerned with equal employment opportunity (APA, 1969; Doppelt & Bennett, 1967; Enneis, 1969; Equal Employment Opportunity Commission, 1970). Judging from the studies reviewed here, the use of nonvalidated methods for selection is apparently not uncommon. A nonvalidated test often excludes a disproportionate number of Negroes for reasons unrelated to job performance, inviting the charge that the selection process is unfair to Negroes. Since the whites fare better, they have less reason to question the validity of the procedure. What results is that nonvalidity (or unknown validity) masquerades as differential validity.

Also, there has been a tendency not to differentiate between two situations that are statistically quite different, differential validity and single-group validity. Differential validity is very apt to involve single-group validity, but single-group validity, a much more common occurrence in the data available, usually does not involve significant group differences. Single-group validity may be related to inadequate sample size or to the use of a rating criterion. The determination as to which of these two elements is most closely linked to the phenomenon depends on further research as the studies to date which use larger samples also tend to use criteria other than ratings. Whether single-group validity is more than a methodological problem cannot be determined without further research. It is, in any case, a less serious problem than differential validity. Where differential validity is proof of unfairness, single-group validity is only lack of proof of fairness.

The fifth reason stems from the confusion of differential validity with differences in mean scores. Guion (1965) addressed himself to this point:

> A difference between group means is not competent evidence of unfair discrimination if that difference is also associated with performance on the criterion. That is, the very factors that depressed test performance may also depress trainability or speed of performance or whatever criterion is to be predicted [p. 492].

While there was very little differential validity found in the studies reviewed here, there were several cases of significant differences in both predictor and criterion, resulting in similar validities. In four studies (Campbell et al., 1969; Tenopyr, 1967; Wollowick et al., 1969; United States Department of Labor, 1969) whites scored significantly higher than Negroes both on most predictors and most criteria. Two of these studies (Tenopyr, 1967; United States Department of Labor, 1969) also demonstrated evidence of improved validity when the two groups were combined (see Table 3).

Such results reflect long-standing social practices that have disadvantaged the Negro over a period of generations. Factors such as competitiveness, time sense, adherence to instructions, conformity, etc. that could be hypothesized to aid an individual in satisfactory test performance could reasonably be expected to relate to job performance also. In these cases, both predictor and criterion reflect the norms of the prevailing culture. To the extent that the demands of the culture are consistent in the selection and work situations, the validities of selection procedures should be similar for Negroes and whites.

While nonvalidity (or unknown validity) appears to be common in the selection devices used in this research, it can be concluded that differential validity is a rare occurrence in the data currently available although there are a fairly large number of cases of single-group validity. However, more research is needed in this area as even the occasional instance of differential validity can have consequences both socially and practically undesirable. The work to date must be regarded as indicative rather than conclusive. Particularly needed is more careful attention given to criterion development. The research indicates that the existence of subtle biases in rating-type criteria is a definite possibility that needs careful investigation.

Notes

[1]The opinions and findings expressed in this article are those of the author and not necessarily those of the New York State Department of Labor, Division of Employment.

[2]Virginia R. Boehm was affiliated with the New York State Department of Labor, Division of Employment, at the time of publication of this article. Requests for reprints should be sent to Virginia Boehm, 166 West 76th Street, New York, New York 10023.

References

American Psychological Association, Task Force on Employment Testing of Minority Groups. Job testing and the disadvantaged. *American Psychologist*, 1969, *24*, 637-650.

Bartlett, C. J., & O'Leary, B. S. A differential prediction model to moderate the effects of heterogeneous groups in personnel selection and classification. *Personnel Psychology*, 1969, *22*, 1-17.

Bennett, G. K. Factors affecting the value of validation studies. *Personnel Psychology*, 1969, *22*, 265-268.

Campbell, J. T., Pike, L. W., & Flaugher, R. L. *Prediction of job performance for Negro and white medical technicians—A regression analysis of potential test bias: Predicting job knowledge scores from an aptitude battery.* (Educational Testing Service Rep. PR-69-6) Princeton, New Jersey: Educational Testing Service, 1969.

Doppelt, J. E., & Bennett, G. K. *Testing job applicants from disadvantaged groups.* (Test Service Bulletin No. 57) New York: Psychological Corporation, 1967.

Dreger, R. M., & Miller, K. S. Comparative psychological studies of Negroes and whites in the United States: 1959-1965. *Psychological Bulletin*, 1968, *70* (3, Pt. 2).

Enneis, W. H. Minority employment barriers from the EEOC viewpoint. Paper presented at the meeting of the American Psychological Association, Washington, D.C., September 1969.

Equal Employment Opportunity Commission. Guidelines on employment selection procedures. *Federal Register*, 1970, *35*, 12333-12335.

Flaugher, R. L., Campbell, J. T., & Pike, L. W. *Prediction of job performance for Negro and white medical technicians—Ethnic Group membership as a moderator of supervisor's ratings.* (Educational Testing Service Rep. PR-69-5) Princeton, New Jersey: Educational Testing Service, 1969.

Grant, D. L., & Bray, D. W. Validation of employment tests for telephone company installation and repair occupations. *Journal of Applied Psychology*, 1970, *54*, 7-14.

Guilford, J. P. *Fundamental statistics in psychology and education.* (4th ed.) New York: McGraw-Hill, 1965.

Guion, R. M. *Personnel testing.* New York: McGraw-Hill, 1965.

Kirkpatrick, J. J., Ewen, R. B., Barrett, R. S., & Katzell, R. A. *Testing and fair employment.* New York: New York University, 1968.

Lopez, F. M., Jr. Current problems in test performance of job applicants. *Personnel Psychology*, 1966, *19*, 10-18.

Mitchell, M. D., Albright, L. E., & McMurry, F. D. Biracial validation of selection procedures in a large southern plant. *Proceedings of the 76th Annual Convention of the American Psychological Association*, 1968, *3*, 575-576. (Summary)

Moore, C. L., Jr., & MacNaughton, J. F. An exploratory investigation of ethnic differences within an industrial selection battery. Paper presented at the meeting of the American Psychological Association, New York, September 1966.

Owens, W. A., & Jewell, D. O. Personnel selection. *Annual Review of Psychology*, 1969, *20*, 419-446.

Pike, L. W. *Prediction of job performance for Negro and white medical technicians—Development of the instrumentation.* (Educational Testing Service Rep. PR-69-4) Princeton, New Jersey: Educational Testing Service, 1969.

Rosen, D. B. *Employment testing and minority groups.* (New York State School of Industrial and Labor Relations Key Issues Series No. 6) Ithaca, New York: Cornell University, 1970.

Ruda, E., & Albright, L. E. Racial differences on selection instruments related to subsequent job performance. *Personnel Psychology*, 1968, *21*, 31-41.

Tenopyr, M. L. Race and socioeconomic status as moderators in predicting machine-shop training success. Paper presented at the meeting of the American Psychological Association, Washington, D.C., September 1967.

Wallace, P., Kissinger, B., & Reynolds, B. Testing of minority group applicants for employment. Washington, D.C.: Office of Research and Reports, Equal Employment Opportunity Commission, 1966.

Wollowick, H. B., Greenwood, J. M., & McNamara, W. J. Psychological testing with a minority group population. *Proceedings of the 77th Annual Convention of the American Psychological Association*, 1969, *4*, 609-610. (Summary)

Wood, M. T. Validation of a selected test against a turnover criterion for racial and sex subgroups of employees. Paper presented at the meeting of the Midwestern Psychological Association, Chicago, May 1969.

United States Department of Labor, Manpower Administration. *Development of USTES aptitude test battery for welder, production line (welding) 810.884.* (United States Training and Employment Service Tech. Rep. S-447) Washington, D.C.: United States Department of Labor, Manpower Administration, 1969.